2nd Edition

Mortgage
Loan Brokering

TM

Walt Huber
Glendale College - Professor of Real Estate

William Pivar
Professor Emeritus

Walt Zozula
Community Commerce Bank
Chief Review Editor

COPYRIGHT ©1998, 2002 2nd EDITION

Educational Textbook Company, Inc.
P.O. Box 3597
Covina, California 91722

(626) 339-7733
FAX (626) 332-4744
www. etcbooks. com

Library of Congress Cataloging-in-Publication Data

Huber, Walt
California Mortgage Brokering, Walt Huber and William Pivar

Summary: Covers all material in California Mortgage Brokering and Lending Criteria classes with special emphasis on California Real Estate Finance. Very clear and simple language, easy-to-read format with photographs, charts, and graphs. Includes glossary and index; suitable for consumers, students, and teachers wishing information regarding personal real estate transactions.

1. Real Estate Business - Finance—California 2. Real Estate Property—California Real Estate 3. Real Property—California

332.7209   [332.72]

ISBN: 0-916772-71-3
Printed in the United States of America

The intention of the authors and publisher is to provide information as to Mortgage Brokering and Lending Criteria. This book should not be used as a substitute for or in lieu of obtaining legal, accounting, or other professional services. The authors and publisher are not engaged in providing such services. Should legal advice, accounting, or other professional services be required, then the services of applicable professionals should be obtained.

Preface

MORTGAGE LOAN BROKERING has moved into the Internet age, with emphasis on Internet addresses and essential real estate financing concepts highlighted in *GRAY INK*. We've selected key topics and highlighted them so that they jump off the page and stand out in the student's mind. This unique approach makes *MORTGAGE LOAN BROKERING* not only an excellent introductory real estate finance text, but also an essential reference book.

This textbook has been written in accordance with the strict outline developed by the Department of Real Estate so salespeople, brokers, and the general public have a better understanding of California laws and regulations relating to mortgage loan brokering.

This Internet edition covers all matters related to originating, assigning, and selling loans on real property. Commonly used forms are shown and explained in detail. Each chapter includes a multiple-choice quiz to test the reader's comprehension of the material. Answers are given in the back of each chapter which enables students to work at their own pace and test themselves. Vocabulary words are in BOLDFACE followed by concise definitions in *SCRIPT*.

I want to express my appreciation to the many people who helped to make this text possible. I received advice and helpful suggestions from the California Department of Real Estate (www.dre.ca.gov.) and the California Association of Realtors® (www.car.org).

Special thanks, too, for the valuable assistance from: Rick Lee, executive editor; Philip Dockter, art director; and Melinda Winters, cover design, all of whom helped to design and produce this book.

WALT HUBER

All Internet addresses are preceded by:

"Hubie" the R E Internet Mouse

TM

Join the Internet Revolution

Lenders will gain market share if they integrate the Web into their business plans.

Loans over the Web!

Lending will never be the same

Yes! Real estate loans are now being advertised; buyers are being qualified, information is being received and a few loans are even being funded over the net.

The Internet, by its nature, lowers loan rates and gives unbiased loan information.

Large lenders have been joining or creating Web sites to keep ahead of competition. A lender wants the ability to inform, qualify, and start a borrower on the loan process at a lower cost. Lenders of all sizes can create a Web page and go online. The largest and best known lending Internet sites have comprehensive and informative programs that take the borrower step-by-step through the lending process with much more, including renting verses buying scenarios. Each day thousands of inquiries (hits) are made at those large "name brand" loan orgination Web sites, such as:

www.E-Loan.com (a group of several large lenders)
www.HomeShark.com (a group of several large lenders)
www.Quicken.com (Intuit Inc., a software company)
www.Countrywide.com (a publicly owned home lender)

The Internet has lowered financing "cost" forever!

The fact is, a person can obtain a real estate loan initiated over a sophisticated loan Internet program at a lower cost. Once a person has applied for a loan over the Internet and found out that the points charged are much lower than a loan made face-to-face, why would they pay thousands more? The financing fees and loan points charged by the large Internet lenders are about one-half the cost of a face-to-face generated loan. Once the general public realizes this fact the popularity of Internet lending will increase quickly.

It is predicted that 30% of all real estate loans will be initiated over the Internet within a decade.

Large Internet lenders have many cost savings. An Internet lender can use a program to qualify and initiate a loan without: 1) fancy locations; 2) many salespeople; and 3) costly media advertising. Of course unusual, non-residential, and difficult loans will continue to be made face-to-face.

The Web will create a more well informed borrower.

Internet business strategy is to give free information that entices, educates, and creates a more well informed borrower. Smaller lenders can start a stand-alone site or join an aggregate or mortgage site.

Smaller lenders profit if partnered with an advertiser.

Known brand advertisers like Quicken, E-Loan, or Homeshark, which enable the public to comparison shop (compare rates, companies, and services), will attract more visitors than an independent site that offers a limited selection. These lending advertisers draw many customers to their sites, which allows their partners to focus on their expertise.

Borrowers will be more educated than ever before approaching lenders.

Table of Contents

Understanding Legal Citations

A number of legal citations are found throughout the text. The following will give you a basic understanding of each citation as well as where to find it should you wish to read the complete and original court decision for a case.

Each filed case generally involves two names. The first name is the plaintiff who is bringing the legal action and the second name is the defendant against whom the action has been brought. If the first name is "People," it is an action brought by the government rather than a private individual.

The year of the case is the year in which the court decision was rendered.

A legal citation begins with a volume number, followed by the description of the series in which the volume is found, followed by a page number. Most of the cases in this text have "C.A." or "C" designations. *C.A. stands for California Appellate decisions from the California Court of Appeals. C stands for California Reports which are California Supreme Court decisions.* Because of the sheer volume of cases, many books are divided into series so that "C.A. 3rd" would mean California Appellate Third Series.

To better understand descriptions, let us dissect the decision of *Richardson v. Rose* (1961) 107 C.A. 2d 318. In this case, Richardson is the appellant and has brought action against Rose who is the respondant. The case was decided in 1961 and can be found in volume 107 of the California Appellate Decisions, 2nd Series, on Page 107.

There are series for other states, regional series as well as federal series of case books. The librarian in the law library at your County Court house will be happy to explain any citation you do not understand and will show you where it can be found.

COURSE OBJECTIVE

The objective of this course is to provide students with broad technical knowledge of the State and Federal laws which govern the practice of mortgage loan brokerage and lending in the State of California.

SUNSET BROKERS

Scott Chapin

http://www.bankhomes.com

4357

Chapter 1

Scope
of Mortgage
Loan Brokerage

KEY WORDS AND TERMS

Back-end ratio
Bankruptcy score
Brokerage
Collateral
Collaterally secured
Conforming loan
Equity loan
FICO Bureau Scores
Front-end ratio
Hard-money loan
Impound accounts
Institutional lender
Junior lien
Mortgage banker
Mortgage broker
Mortgage company
Mortgage warehousing

Nonconforming loans
Open-end loans
Partially amortized loans
Piggyback loans
Points
Portfolio loans
Primary financing
Primary mortgage market
Principals
Private lenders
Private mortgage insurance
Purchase money loans
Secondary financing
Secondary mortgage market
Unconscionable contracts
Usury

LEARNING OBJECTIVES

This chapter will provide you with an appreciation and overview of what role mortgage brokers and mortgage bankers play in meeting the needs of consumers in our marketplace. You will also gain an in-depth perception of financial qualifications. This material will serve as a foundation for the rest of this course.

Introduction

Effective January 1, 1994, a course entitled *Mortgage Loan Brokering and Lending* became one of the optional courses required by license applicants to satisfy real estate broker examination requirements. There are no prerequisites to this course although a prior course in Real Estate Finance would be helpful. This text was written to meet the needs of this course and follows an outline prepared by the California Department of Real Estate.

 www.dre.ca.gov (California Department of Real Estate)

Brokerage

DEFINITION

The term **BROKERAGE** *is defined as the business of a broker.* A broker is an agent or third party who arranges transactions between parties directly involved in the transaction. These parties are known as principals. Therefore, a broker brings people together so that a transaction is able to happen. In loan brokerage these principals are the borrower and the lender.

Therefore, **REAL ESTATE BROKERAGE** *involves arranging loans for borrowers and lenders.*

> *The real estate broker in loan brokerage is a catalyst who makes things happen.*

WHY HAVE LOAN BROKERAGE?

INSTITUTIONAL LENDERS *are financial institutions that are regulated by law.* They include banks, savings and loan associations, insurance companies and credit unions. Mortgage companies, discussed later in this chapter, make loans which they sell. The buyers of these loans are primarily institutional lenders.

> *Institutional lenders are often unable or unwilling to make loans that do not fit into their loan guidelines.*

Real estate loan brokers are able to fill a lending void by locating lenders willing to meet the borrowing needs of a great number of people, who for a variety of reasons, are unable to obtain loans from institutional lenders or mortgage companies.

WHY LOANS ARE REFUSED BY INSTITUTIONAL LENDERS

The following are reasons why lenders turn down loan applicants.

Type of Property

Most institutional lenders prefer residential-property loans as residential property is the most liquid of all types of real estate.

This means that due to demand, it is easier to dispose of real property and turn it into cash than other types of property. Most institutional lenders are reluctant to make loans on:

A. Undeveloped raw land.

B. A lot, unless it is tied in with a construction loan.

C. Commercial property that is vacant or has serious problems such as:

(1) a history of high vacancy;

(2) hazardous waste or hazardous substances on the premises;

(3) failure to meet earthquake safety codes;

(4) flood area problems;

(5) the need for extensive corrective work not being taken care of by the loan;

(6) vacant industrial property;

(7) vacant office structures; and

(8) commercial and office structures at a time when other borrowers are defaulting on loans for such property.

Down Payment

In making purchase-money loans (loans to initially finance a purchase of property), lenders like to see a significant down payment.

A buyer with a significant down payment is less likely to default on a loan than a buyer who has very little money in the property. Institutional lenders will, however, make loans with low or no down payment in cases where they are protected by government guarantees or insurance or even Private Mortgage Insurance (PMI). Private Mortgage Insurers still require a specified down payment. Applicants who fail to meet the down payment requirements of the Institutional lender, FHA or Private Mortgage Insurance carriers will be denied a loan.

Credit of Borrower

Institutional lenders want monthly payments like clockwork. They don't want problems in collections. Least of all, they don't want to end up owning the security for their loans.

> *If the borrower has had credit problems, the lender will be reluctant to make a loan, regardless of the value of the property and the borrowers ability to make payments.*

Some of the problems that would likely result in a refusal to make a loan include:

1. Judgments against the borrower;
2. A history of legal actions and judgments involving collections of debts;
3. Present loans that are delinquent in payments;
4. A history of late payments;
5. Debts which have been turned over to collection agencies;
6. A recent bankruptcy; and
7. A pattern of debt and bankruptcy.

Borrower's Capacity

An institutional lender will not approve a loan for a borrower who fails to satisfy the lender's requirements as to capacity to make the loan payments. Capacity is generally measured by two ratios both of which must be satisfied for the lender to make the loan. (Capacity is also measured by several scores.)

1. **Front-end ratio.** This ratio reflects the relationship of the monthly housing costs *(PITI - PRINCIPAL, INTEREST, TAXES AND INSURANCE PAYMENTS)* to gross monthly income. The ratio is determined by dividing the total monthly payment by the gross monthly income. Generally, lenders will want to see a front-end ratio of 28 percent or less:

$$\frac{\text{Total Monthly Payment}}{\text{Gross Monthly Income}} = 28\%$$

Assume an applicant for a loan has a monthly income of $3,800 and wishes to purchase a home where the PITI payments will amount to $1,250:

$$\frac{\$1,250}{\$3,800} = 32.8\%$$

In this instance, the applicant would likely be turned down for the loan because the front-end ratio is too high.

If the applicant found a home where the total payments (PITI) were only $1,050, then:

$$\frac{\$1,050}{\$3,800} = 27.6\%$$

In this case the applicant would meet the front-end ratio requirements.

2. **Back-end ratio.** This ratio reflects the relationship of the monthly housing costs (PITI) plus long-term debt payments to total monthly income. It is necessary to consider this second ratio as well as the first ratio (front-end ratio) in determining a buyer's capacity to make the payments. As an example, a person might have sufficient income to meet the front-end ratio but the payments on a luxury car and furniture could leave the applicant with insufficient funds to met a mortgage payment. Generally, lenders want to see a back-end ratio of 36 percent or less:

$$\frac{\text{PITI + Debt Payments}}{\text{Gross Monthly Income}} = 36\%$$

Assume the borrower we previously discussed with the PITI of $1,050 also has long-term debt payments of $530 per month. $1,050 + $530 = $1,580

$$\frac{\$1,580}{\$3,800} = 41.58\%$$

Since the back-end ratio is over 36 percent, this loan applicant would likely be refused a loan.

Although they are not cast in stone and will vary slightly as to type of loan, ratios are still the primary criteria used by institutional lenders in determining borrower capacity. However, there are two other mathematical methods of **SCORING** *to determine if a loan should be funded.* These scores have been shown to accurately reflect risk.

Not everyone who shows low risk will necessarily honor their obligations and many borrowers who show high risk will honor their obligations. These scores are based upon a number of factors and lenders using them use only one, not both, scoring methods:

3. **FICO Bureau Scores.** These scores range from 400 to 900 with the 400 score indicating likely borrower default and a 900 score indicating just a slight chance of borrower default.

4. **Bankruptcy Score.** This score ranges from 0 to 1300. With a higher number indicating a greater risk of default.

Questions About Capacity

> *Some lenders stay away from borrowers who have just recently achieved higher earnings, especially if the earnings are related to a new job.*

They are concerned as to the likelihood of continuance of such income.

Another problem is persons paid by commissions. Several months of high earnings are not likely to mean much to a lender when prior months were of much lower income.

Self-employed individuals pose another problem. Often tax returns fail to reflect actual net. In many cases a self-employed person is able to take deductions for tax purposes which distort the true income picture. Whether honest deductions or tax fraud, self-employed persons often have great difficulty in obtaining real estate financing through institutional lenders.

> *Self-employed tax returns often fail to reflect actual net.*

Private lenders are more likely to understand that tax returns are not always indicative of what a person is able to pay.

Collateral

The lender's appraisal is likely to be on the conservative side. A low appraisal, even with a substantial down payment, could result in a lender declining to make a loan. The lender might feel the collateral securing the loan is insufficient to protect them should the borrower default on the loan.

Mortgage Loan Brokers

Mortgage loan brokers fill a void in that they are able to find financing for borrowers who could not otherwise be financed.

They do this by matching return to risk. (Naturally, higher risk loans deserve a greater return to the lender to offset the greater risk.) They also match lenders who are willing to make the loans with borrowers who desire loans.

CHARACTERISTICS OF MORTGAGE BROKER LOANS

The following are general characteristics of loans arranged by mortgage loan brokers.

Hard-Money Loans

Mortgage loan brokers are involved in hard-money lending.

Hard-money loans are given for cash. Generally, hard-money loans are not regarded as purchase loans. In a *HARD-MONEY LOAN situation the owner accepts cash from a lender in exchange for a promise to pay (note) secured by the real estate owned by the borrower.* The financing instrument used will generally be a deed of trust. The term hard-money loan has come to mean loans funded by individual investors rather than lending institutions.

Purchase-money loans (loans made at the time of purchase) are not regarded as hard-money loans.

Mortgage loan brokers at times will be involved with a purchase-money loan when a prospective buyer is unable to obtain a loan from more conventional sources for reasons previously discussed.

SOFT-MONEY LOANS are loans where cash does not change hands. The usual soft-money loan occurs when a seller finances the buyer for the equity being transferred. This is commonly called "carry-back" financing. The seller gives title in exchange for a note secured by a deed of trust which is a lien against the property conveyed.

Real estate loan brokers are seldom involved in soft-money financing.

Equity Loans

EQUITY LOANS *are loans made based upon an owners equity in real property.*

Equity is the difference between fair market value and the indebtedness against the property.

An equity loan is generally secondary financing in that there is at least one prior loan against the property. *The first, or priority lien is known as* **PRIMARY FINANCING**.

At times, mortgage brokers will arrange to refinance one or more existing loans. The new loan would be considered primary financing in that it would be the senior lien against the property. The refinanced loan would likely include some cash to the borrower as well as consolidation of existing loans.

Mortgage loan brokers were once the major source for equity financing. With financial deregulations, banks and savings banks have entered the arena of home equity financing. They extensively advertise for **HOMEOWNER LINES OF CREDIT**, *which are simply open-end loans where homeowners can borrow against their home up to the limit agreed upon.*

Even though institutional lenders charge considerably higher interest for home equity loans than for purchase-money loans, total loan costs for these loans from banks, savings banks or credit unions are still likely to be considerably less than the costs involved in a loan arranged by a mortgage loan broker.

Broker-arranged mortgage loans are likely to be made where institutional lenders are unwilling to meet the needs of the borrower.

Short-Term Loans

Loans arranged by mortgage loan brokers are likely to be of a shorter term than loans made by institutional lenders.

They are likely to be **PARTIALLY AMORTIZED LOANS**: *This means that while equal payments are based on a long-term payment period, the entire balance will be due prior to the end of the payoff period.* This usually means that the borrower will have to arrange a new loan with added costs.

Interest Rates

Interest rates on mortgage-broker arranged loans are likely to be considerably higher than for loans made by institutional lenders.

Borrower Costs and Fees

Borrower costs and fees involved in funding mortgage broker arranged loans can be expected to go considerably higher than for loans funded through an institutional lender or a mortgage company. These costs and fees are covered in detail in Chapter 12.

Nonconforming Loans

CONFORMING LOANS *are loans which meet the purchase requirements of Fannie Mae (Federal National Mortgage Association) or Freddie Mac (Federal Home Loan Mortgage Corporation). A conforming loan can be readily sold. A loan which does not meet these purchase requirements is a* **NONCONFORMING LOAN**. Many institutional lenders will turn down borderline loans to avoid having to hold the loan in their portfolio. Many institutional lenders have become loan originators who sell all the loans which they make. Their profit comes from loan costs and fees received in the origination process.

Mortgage loan brokers do not really worry about a nonconforming loan. The majority of their loans are funded by individuals who are investing for interest income, not resale.

Source of Funds

Although, with full disclosure, mortgage brokers could use their own funds to make loans, they generally serve in a third-party capacity as the arranger of a loan between a lender and borrower.

However, some mortgage brokers will invest their own funds in particularly attractive loan situations. In such cases they are dealing for their own account. This is relatively rare. At other times when a prospective lender backs out, a mortgage broker might use his or her own funds for the loan if they are certain that the loan can be quickly sold. Such loans are not a violation of real estate law as long as the borrower understands that the broker is acting as a principal. The broker is acting as a mortgage banker and not in a brokerage role when funding a loan.

Generally, the loan broker will seek individual lenders.

LOAN LENDERS *are persons or firms who wish to receive a higher rate of return for their savings than would be possible from other available investments.* Many of these investors have successfully invested their funds in trust deeds arranged by mortgage brokers for over 30 years. Investors realize that they have the safety of the security.

Private investors who wish to invest in real estate loans are almost compelled to do so through a real estate broker because of the usury law.

Private individuals may not make a loan which exceeds 10 percent interest or five percent above the San Francisco Federal Reserve Bank's rate for advances to member banks, whichever is greater.

 www.frbsf.org (Federal Reserve Bank of San Francisco, 12th District)

If the San Francisco Federal Reserve Bank's rate to member banks is 6 1/2 percent interest, then individuals could charge up to 11 1/2 percent as this would be the higher rate. However, if the Federal Reserve Bank rate was 4 percent interest, then 4% + 5% = 9%. Since 10 percent is the higher rate, an individual could charge up to 10 percent interest. If an individual charges points (**ONE POINT** *is one percent of the loan*), as an origination fee, it is considered to be interest in determining if the loan is usurious.

On November 6, 1979, Proposition 2 was approved by the voters and is now law. The proposition exempts loans made or arranged by real estate brokers from the usury restrictions. Civil Code Section 1916.1 sets forth this broker exemption.

Broker Exemption from Interest Rate Limitation

1916.1. The restrictions upon rates of interest contained in Section 1 of Article XV of the California Constitution shall not apply to any loan or forbearance made or arranged by any person licensed as a real estate broker by the State of California, and secured, directly or collaterally, in whole or in part by liens on real property. For purposes of this section, a loan or forbearance is arranged by a person licensed as a real estate broker when the broker (1) acts for compensation or in expectation of compensation for soliciting, negotiating, or arranging the loan for another, (2) acts for compensation or in expectation of compensation for selling, buying, leasing, exchanging, or negotiating the sale, purchase, lease, or exchange of real property or a business for another and (A) arranges a loan to pay all or any portion of the purchase price of, or of an improvement to, that property or business or (B) arranges a forbearance, extension, or refinancing of any loan in connection with that sale, purchase, lease, exchange of, or an improvement to, real property or a business, or (3) arranges or negotiates for another a forbearance, extension, or refinancing of any loan secured by real property in connection with a past transaction in which the broker had acted for compensation or in expectation of compensation for selling, buying, leasing, exchanging, or negotiating the sale, purchase, lease, or exchange of real property or a business. The term "made or arranged" includes any loan made by a person licensed as a real estate broker as a principal or as an agent for others, and whether or not the person is acting within the course and scope of such license.

While loans made or arranged by real estate brokers are exempt from usury limitations, they are not without any limitations.

Contract law holds that an **unconscionable contract** will not be enforced by the courts. If the rate of interest was so high that the courts would determine it to be offensive and beyond good conscience, the courts would be unlikely to allow it to be enforced.

Many individuals who have agreed to loan terms will go to mortgage loan brokers to finalize their agreement. They are willing to incur some extra costs to remove the loan from the usury restriction. The lender would not fund the loan with a usury restriction.

Besides private lenders desiring a secured high-yield investment, private trusts and smaller pension plans regularly invest in mortgages and trust deeds through mortgage brokers. These loans increase their yield.

Case Example

Carboni v. Arrospide (1991) 2 CA 4th 76

A broker loaned $4,000 secured by real estate. Interest on the loan was set at 200 percent. The broker made several additional advances to the borrower even though the original loan had passed the due date until the total sum owed, with interest, exceeded $99,000. The trial court entered judgment for foreclosure but set the interest rate at 24 percent.

The Court of Appeals held that while the loan was exempt from the usury law because it was made by a licensed real estate broker, the loan was still subject to Civil Code 1670.5 which allows the court to refuse to enforce unconscionable contracts. Therefore, the judgment of the trial court was affirmed.

Case Example

Winet v. Roberts (1986) 179 CA 3d 909

The plaintiffs, in this case, borrowed from the defendants, securing the debt by a deed of trust on real property. The note specified interest at 40 percent. The plaintiffs claimed that the rate of interest was usurious. The trial court held that the loan was not usurious since one of the plaintiffs was a licensed real estate broker.

The Court of Appeals reversed the trial court holding that the usury rate exemption applies to a broker who makes or arranges a loan. In this case the broker was not a third party in arranging or making the loan.

Case Example

Direnfield v. Stabile (1988) 198 CA 3d 126

A private lender had made loans through a real estate salesperson previously employed by a licensed real estate broker. After the salesperson ended his employment, he arranged loans without disclosing that he was not employed by a real estate broker. The loans, which would not have been usurious had the salesperson been employed by a broker, were usurious. The lender settled a complaint for usury and then obtained a judgment against the salesperson for fraud. The Department of Real Estate refused to use the recovery fund to pay for the lender's judgment. The court held that the lender was an innocent member of the public who the Statue (B&PC 10471) was intended to protect and the lender could recover from the recovery fund.

Case Example

Stickel v. Harris (1987) 196 CA 3d 575

A broker was a partner in a joint venture that received a loan. The broker had solicited the loan from the lender and offered 30 percent interest. The broker told the lender that the rate did not violate the usury law. The borrowers refused to pay the interest claiming that the loan was usurious since it exceeded the statutory limit for individuals. (cont'd.)

The borrowers claimed that the broker was not acting as a broker but as a borrower so that they did not fall into the broker exemption as to usury.

The Court of Appeals upheld the trial court award of interest to the lender. The question for the court was, "Did the broker arrange the loan?" The court determined the broker did. While the court indicated that the broker must receive compensation to be exempt from usury, compensation need not be in cash. It could be in benefits. In this case, the broker expected profits from the venture.

Note: The lender could have alleged fraud and the court could have awarded punitive damages.

PRIMARY MORTGAGE MARKET

Mortgage loan brokers deal primarily as intermediaries in what is known as the primary mortgage market. In the **PRIMARY MORTGAGE MARKET**, *loans are made directly to borrowers.*

Mortgage loan brokers do not customarily get involved in the secondary mortgage market. The **SECONDARY MORTGAGE MARKET** *involves the sale of existing loans.*

Occasionally, a mortgage broker will be asked to sell a loan when the lender needs liquidity. Then the mortgage loan broker in seeking and arranging the loan transfer would be engaging in the secondary mortgage market.

Figure 1-1 illustrates the difference between mortgage loan brokers and mortgage bankers (mortgage companies).

Mortgage Bankers

Mortgage bankers are also known as mortgage companies.

A real estate broker's license allows a broker to engage in mortgage brokerage and mortgage banking activities. Even though mortgage bankers and mortgage brokers operate under the same license and have the same qualifications, they are not the same. Their activities differ significantly.

Figure 1-1

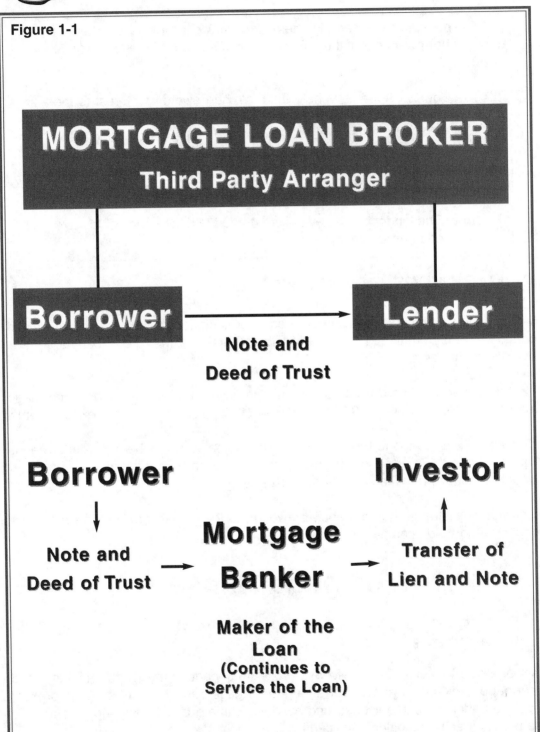

PRINCIPALS TO THE LOAN

MORTGAGE BANKERS *differ from mortgage brokers in that the former generally are not third parties to a loan.* They generally fund the loan with their own funds.

While at times a mortgage banker might act in a broker capacity, particularly if the loan is for an amount beyond the capacity of the mortgage banker to fund, this would be the exception rather than the rule.

SECONDARY MARKET ACTIVITIES

Loans made by mortgage bankers are customarily resold to other lenders and investors in the resale market known as the secondary market.

> *Mortgage loan bankers are engaged in the primary mortgage market when making the loan and in the secondary mortgage market in the sale of the loan.*

Many of the loans made by mortgage bankers are made for particular investors such as other lenders and pension plans. They will make the loans to meet the lending criteria desired by these particular investors. Much of their activities deal with out-of-state lenders and investors who desire to make long-term loans secured by California real estate. Because of the size of our real estate market, California mortgage bankers can assemble packages of trust deeds of significant value.

TYPES OF PROPERTY

Most mortgage bankers deal primarily in residential property, the majority of which is single-family dwellings. However, some mortgage bankers handle a variety of property and might specialize in large commercial or industrial loans. They work with lenders who desire the highest interest possible from this type of loan.

PORTFOLIO LOANS

PORTFOLIO LOANS *are loans held by a lender as an investment.* It is rare for a mortgage banker to tie up capital in a portfolio of loans. Lending is a capital intensive activity that requires a great deal of capital or the availability of such capital.

SERVICING LOANS

> *Mortgage bankers generally want to service the loans they make and resell.*

SERVICING LOANS *means doing the accounting necessary for a loan.* The one-quarter percent to one-half percent service fee can be a significant profit center for the mortgage banker when thousands of loans are serviced.

With today's computer-servicing programs, servicing loans is no longer the labor-intensive activity that it was just two decades ago. Errors in computations have been virtually eliminated.

An advantage of servicing the loans is the control of impound accounts for taxes and insurance when it is collected in advance with loan payments. These funds, when deposited in a bank give a mortgage banker tremendous clout when they are borrowers from banks holding such funds. They are able to borrow funds at extremely attractive interest rates.

SPECULATING

Mortgage bankers, like commercial bankers, speculate on interest rates. If a mortgage banker believes that interest rates will rise, the mortgage banker will want to resell loans in the shortest possible time. Should rates rise, the value of loans held at below-market rates of interest will fall. Such loans will have to be sold at a discount from face value unless the mortgage banker has a firm purchase commitment from an investor.

> *If a mortgage banker believes that interest rates will fall, he or she will want to hold as large a loan inventory as possible.*

The mortgage banker might not want to enter into firm agreement for the resale of such loans. If rates do fall, the higher interest mortgages will be more valuable on the secondary mortgage market and should sell at a premium to face value.

MORTGAGE WAREHOUSING

Some lenders want huge dollar packages of mortgages. One reason is that they might wish large packages in order to issue mortgage-backed securities. At other times, mortgage bankers might be speculating on falling interest rates which means the bankers will have a great deal of their own funds and borrowed funds tied up in loans.

Mortgage bankers borrow from commercial banks using their mortgage inventory to obtain additional capital for loans (*loans secured by other loans are* **COLLATERALLY SECURED**). There is a risk in mortgage warehousing in a movement of interest rates contrary to expectations. If rates fall, the mortgage banker would have a large inventory of loans which has to be sold at a price that could not only wipe out profits but be a financial loss.

Conforming Loans

Some mortgage companies make only conforming loans. They sell to savings and loans, thrifts and other lenders who want the ability to readily resell the loans should a sale be desirable.

Nonconforming Loans

Mortgage bankers will only make a nonconforming loan when they either have a buyer for such a loan or know that a resale will not create a problem. Examples of such loans would be larger residential loans which exceed Fannie Mae and Freddie Mac maximums.

MULTIPLE LENDERS

Mortgage bankers will at times put together large commercial loans as either the lender or loan arranger which is divided among several lenders. Sometimes the reason for such a loan is sheer size. Many lenders would shy away from a billion dollar commercial loan for a new mall, but they might like a piece of the action because of the desirable interest rate.

Mortgage bankers are often able to put together a consortium of lenders to handle such a loan.

Another multiple-lender loan is a **PIGGYBACK LOAN**, *where a single loan is divided into parts and the parts have varying degrees of risk*. As an example, assume a million dollar loan is sought on a project valued at $1.3 million. One lender might agree to take $700,000 of the loan as the bottom portion at 9 1/2 percent interest. A second lender might agree to take the top portion of the loan ($300,000) at 12 1/2 percent interest. It is like a first and second trust deed written as a single loan. The second lender is subordinated to the first lender.

Lender A has the bottom portion of the loan with the least amount of risk.

Lender B has greater risk, so then B would want a higher rate of interest or loan points to make the risk palatable.

To further reduce the risk, the loan might call for all principal payments to apply to Lender B until the top portion is paid off.

> **Lender B**
> **$300,000**

> **Lender A**
> **$700,000**

COLLATERAL

While mortgage brokers place their greatest emphasis on loan collateral and relatively low interest on credit and capacity, mortgage bankers place emphasis on credit, capacity and collateral because the lenders they sell to don't want to end up being property owners. In addition, mortgage bankers will have to service loans they sell and they do not want to be creating a headache for themselves.

SUMMARY

Mortgage loan brokers are intermediaries who arrange loans between borrowers and lenders.

I. Mortgage loan brokers:

    A. seldom use their own funds;

    B. seldom service the loans they arrange;

    C. fulfill a need where loans are not available from other lenders because of:

        1. type of property;

        2. credit problems of borrowers;

        3. capacity of borrower to make payments;

    D. are relatively high-cost lenders;

    E. make hard-money loans;

    F. primarily locate private investors to fund the loans that they arrange;

    G. primarily make equity loans (secondary financing) although they can make purchase loans;

H. are involved in the primary mortgage market;

I. are more concerned with collateral value than borrower's credit history or capacity;

J. are exempt from usury limitations.

II. Mortgage bankers:

A. generally use their own funds to make loans although at times they may act as a intermediary;

B. prefer to service the loans they make;

C. resell the loans they make to other lenders or large investors such as pension funds;

D. often make loans to meet the purchase criteria of specific lenders;

E. might speculate on changes in interest rates by holding a greater number of loans when the belief is that interest rates will drop;

F. borrow on their inventory of loans for operating capital. The loans they make are said to be collaterally secured since they are secured by the inventory of loans held;

G. might arrange large loans with multiple lenders;

H. are concerned with borrower's capacity, credit history and also collateral, as they may have to hold the loan if it fails to meet the lending criteria of the ultimate investor/buyer of the loan;

I. operate in both the primary and secondary mortgage markets.

> *Mortgage bankers or mortgage companies are direct lenders in that they actually make loans.*

CLASS DISCUSSION TOPICS

1. Using a local telephone book, check the category for mortgage loans. From your experience evaluate the lenders listed as mortgage brokers and mortgage bankers. Continue the evaluation as to the types of loan activities these lenders are most active in.

2. Which local lender would you approach for a prospective buyer who appears to be well qualified for a purchase loan on a single-family home?

3. Which local lender would you approach for a construction loan for a special purpose cold-storage building on an industrial site? Is there any other information you might want to know?

4. Which local lender would you approach for a second mortgage on a home where the prospective borrower has recently gone through bankruptcy?

5. Be prepared to discuss sales you were either involved in or know of which failed to close because of financing problems. In retrospect, could the sale(s) have been saved? If so, how?

6. Before investing your funds in a trust deed arranged by a mortgage broker, what would you want to know?

CHAPTER 1 QUIZ

1. Institutional lenders include all EXCEPT: (p. 2)
    A. banks
    B. insurance companies
    C. mortgage brokers
    D. savings and loans

2. Institutional lenders would prefer loans secured by: (p. 3)
    A. raw land
    B. residential property
    C. vacant commercial property
    D. vacant lots

3. Which of the following would reflect the front-end ratio? (pp. 4-5)
    A. Appraised Value
       Loan Amount
    B. Total Loan Payment
       Gross Monthly Income
    C. Gross Monthly Income
       Net Income
    D. Long-Term Debt
       Short-Term Debt

4. Hard-money loans can best be described as: (p. 7)

A. purchase-money loans
B. seller carry-back financing
C. loans where cash is exchanged for a note secured by a lien
D. loans payable only in coinage

5. Mortgage loan brokerage activities customarily involve all of the following EXCEPT: (p. 9)

A. secondary mortgage market activities
B. primary mortgage market activities
C. secondary financing
D. hard-money loans

6. Characteristics of mortgage broker arranged financing include all EXCEPT: (p. 9)

A. shorter terms than institutional lender loans
B. high loan origination costs
C. meeting the purchase requirements of Fannie Mae
D. having relatively high interest

7. Most loans arranged by mortgage loan brokers are funded by: (p. 10)

A. the mortgage loan broker
B. individual lenders
C. mortgage companies
D. institutional lenders

8. Usury laws: (p. 10)

A. exempt loans arranged by loan brokers
B. limit institutional and private lenders to nine percent interest
C. are no longer applicable to any California loans
D. limit home loans to 30 years

9. A characteristic of mortgage bankers is that they: (p. 15)

A. limit their lending to second trust deeds
B. keep the loans they make
C. use their own funds to make loans
D. must be licensed by the corporation commissioner

10. Lenders who service the loans they make are: (p. 16)

A. mortgage loan brokers
B. mortgage bankers
C. both A and B
D. neither A nor B

11. Mortgage bankers are more likely to hold on to a large inventory of loans when they believe that: (p. 16)

    A. interest rates will drop

    B. interest rates will rise

    C. the economy will become inflationary

    D. housing prices will rise

12. Mortgage warehousing refers to: (pp. 16-17)

    A. selling mortgage to intermediate lenders

    B. accumulating a stock of mortgages for long-term investment purposes

    C. giving mortgages to an independent mortgage service

    D. borrowing on an inventory of mortgages

Answers: 1. C; 2. B; 3. B; 4. C; 5. A; 6. C; 7. B; 8. A; 9. C; 10. B; 11. A; 12. D

Chapter 2

The California Department of Real Estate

 www.dre.ca.gov (California Department of Real Estate)

KEY WORDS AND TERMS

Accusation
Administrative Procedures Act
Broker
Corporate Broker
Hearing
Injunction
Judicial Review
Notice of Defense
Partnership

Pre-hearing
Real Estate Advisory Commission
Real Estate Commissioner
Receiver
Reconsideration
Restricted License
Salesperson
Statement of Issues
Statement to Respondent

LEARNING OBJECTIVE

This chapter will serve as an introduction to the purpose and function of the California Department of Real Estate. You will gain an insight into the disciplinary process as well as the licensing requirements for both real estate brokers and real estate salespersons.

California Department of Real Estate

The California Department of Real Estate is a department within the California's **Business and Transportation Agency**.

REAL ESTATE COMMISSIONER

*The principal officer of the Department of Real Estate (DRE) is the **Real Estate Commissioner**.* The Commissioner is appointed by the governor and serves at the pleasure of the governor. The position of Commissioner requires five years of active participation in the real estate business in California as a broker. As an alternative, the Commissioner must possess related experience with California real estate activity for five years within the prior ten years.

While serving as real estate Commissioner, the Commissioner cannot actively engage in broker or salesperson activities that are regulated by the Department of Real Estate. Also prohibited from such activities are full-time deputies of the Real Estate Commissioner.

REAL ESTATE ADVISORY COMMISSION

While the Real Estate Commissioner is a full-time salaried position, this is not the case as to the ten-member Real Estate Advisory Commission. Members of this advisory group are appointed by the Commissioner. Six members must be licensed real estate brokers and four members shall be public members not licensed by the Department of Real Estate.

Members of the advisory commission are paid per diem salary when called to meetings as well as actual and necessary expenses.

> *The Commissioner must call meetings of the advisory commission at least four times each year.*

The Commissioner presides over these meetings. The Commissioner consults with the commission on the functions and policies of the Department of Real Estate and determines how the DRE can best serve the needs of the people of California while recognizing the legitimate needs of the industry and the licensees the DRE regulates. Suggestions from members of the public as well as from licensees are solicited at these meetings.

While the commission may make recommendations and suggestions of policy to the Commissioner, it is the Commissioner's final decision as to policy implementation.

The records of the commission are open records and are available to the public during regular business hours.

RESPONSIBILITIES OF THE COMMISSIONER

It is the responsibility of the Real Estate Commissioner to enforce the real estate law.

The Commissioner also has the full power to regulate and control the issuance of licenses, both temporary and permanent, as well as their revocation.

The **California attorney general** *is the legal advisor to the Real Estate Commissioner and shall render opinions as to questions of law submitted by the Commissioner.* The attorney general will also represent the Commissioner in legal actions involving the Department of Real Estate.

 caag.state.ca.us (California Attorney General)

The Commissioner has the power to adopt, amend or repeal rules and regulations necessary for the enforcement of the real estate law. The adoption, amendment or repeal of regulations must be in accordance with the **Administrative Procedures Act**.

The Real Estate Advisory Commission must be given at least 30 days advance notice of the Commissioner's intent to adopt, modify or repeal regulations.

Injunction

The Commissioner may bring legal action in Superior Court in the name of the people of the State of California asking for an injunction against a person who the Commissioner believes has violated or is about to violate provisions of the real estate law. An **injunction** *is a court order which forbids a person from performing or permitting an act.* An order or judgment awarding a preliminary or final injunction may not be entered into record (recorded) unless the defendant is given at least five days notice.

Receiver

If the Commissioner can show to the court's satisfaction that the violations or threatened violations jeopardize funds and properties of others that are in the custody or under control of the defendant, the court may appoint a receiver to manage the defendant's business, including, but not limited to, funds and properties of others.

If an audit, conducted by the Commissioner, reveals commingling or conversion of more than $10,000 in trust funds, the court may prevent the licensee from performing any acts in furtherance thereof, as well as from further exercising any privileges of his or her real estate license pending a further court order.

Within five days of such an order a hearing must be held. After such a hearing, the court may appoint a receiver who may exercise all of the powers of the licensee including filing a petition for bankruptcy.

Order to Desist and Refrain

If the Commissioner determines, through an investigation, that a person is in violation of a law or regulation subject to the Commissioner's regulation, the Commissioner may issue a Desist and Refrain order. The desist and refrain order shall specify the activity as well as the factual and legal basis for the order. The respondent, upon receipt of the order shall cease the described activity.

Within 30 days after receipt of an order to desist and refrain, the respondent may request a hearing. The hearing shall be commenced within 30 days of receipt of the request. If a hearing is not commenced within 30 days, the order shall be considered rescinded.

DISCIPLINARY ACTION

The Real Estate Commissioner can deny, suspend or revoke any license issued by the Department of Real Estate.

The statute of limitations for the Commissioner bringing action against a licensee is no later than three years from the occurrence of the alleged grounds for disciplinary action unless the alleged act or omission involves fraud, misrepresentation or false promise, in which case the statute of limitations is one year after discovery of the fraud, misrepresentation or false promise or three years from occurrence, whichever is later.

There is however a 10-year cap on bringing disciplinary action.

Accusation

The first step in a disciplinary action against a licensee is known as the **ACCUSATION**. Hearings for denial, revocation or suspension of a real estate license shall be in accordance with the Administrative Procedures Act.

Administrative Procedures Act

Section 11503 of the Administrative Procedures Act sets forth the form and basis of the accusation.

Accusation

11503. A hearing to determine whether a right, authority, license or privilege should be revoked, suspended, limited or conditioned shall be initiated by filing an accusation. The accusation shall be a written statement of charges which shall set forth in ordinary and concise language the acts or omissions with which the respondent is charged, to the end that the respondent will be able to prepare his or her defense**...**

Statement of Issues

The hearing, which the accused party is entitled to, is initiated by filing a Statement of Issues. The **STATEMENT OF ISSUES**, *which is set forth in Section 11504 of the Administrative Procedures Act, sets forth statutes and rules with which the accused must show compliance.*

Statement Of Issues

11504. A hearing to determine whether a right, authority, license or privilege should be granted, issued or renewed shall be initiated by filing a statement of issues. The statement of issues shall be a written statement specifying the statutes and rules with which the respondent must show compliance by producing proof at the hearing, and in addition any particular matters which have come to the attention of the initiating party and that would authorize a denial of the agency action sought**...**

Statement to Respondent

Upon the accusation, the accused receives a **STATEMENT TO RESPONDENT**, *which sets forth the right to request a hearing.*

11505(b). The statement to respondent shall be substantially in the following form:

> Unless a written request for a hearing signed by or on behalf of the person named as respondent in the accompanying accusation is delivered or mailed to the agency within 15 days after the accusation was personally served on you or mailed to you, (here insert name of agency) may proceed upon the accusation without a hearing. The request for a hearing may be made by delivery or mailing the enclosed form entitled Notice of Defense, or by delivering or mailing a notice of defense as provide by Section 11506 of the Government Code to: (here insert name and address of agency). You may, but need not, be represented by counsel at any or all stages of these proceedings**...**

Notice of Defense

The accused has a right to request a hearing, object to the accusation, admit to the accusation, present new evidence, etc. These rights are set forth in Section 11506 (a) of the Administrative Procedures Act.

Notice of Defense

11506(a). Within 15 days after service of the accusation the respondent may file with the agency a notice of defense in which the respondent may:

> (1) Request a hearing.
> (2) Object to the accusation upon the ground that it does not state acts or omissions upon which the agency may proceed.
> (3) Object to the form of the accusation on the ground that it is so indefinite or uncertain that the respondent cannot identify the transaction or prepare a defense.
> (4) Admit the accusation in whole or in part.
> (5) Present new matter by way of defense.
> (6) Object to the accusation upon the ground that, under the circumstances, compliance with the requirements of a regulation would result in a material violation of another regulation enacted by another department affecting substantive rights**...**

Prehearing

Sections 11507 and 11511.7 of the Administrative Procedures Act set forth prehearing activities.

A prehearing conference may be called to clarify issues, obtain initial rulings, object to evidence etc., as well as to explore settlement possibilities without the necessity of a hearing. The Prehearing Conference is set forth in Section 11511.5 of the Administrative Procedures Act.

The Hearing

An administrative law judge presides over the hearing. Strict rules of evidence need not apply as hearsay evidence may be used to explain other evidence.

Reconsideration

The accused party or the Department of Real Estate can ask for reconsideration of all or part of the decision by the administrative law judge.

A person whose license has been revoked can petition the Department of Real Estate for reinstatement or reduction of penalty.

Judicial Review

A licensee may file a petition for judicial review of disciplinary action before the Superior Court. Further court appeals are possible. As a general rule, decisions by the administrative law judge would only be overruled if the decision was considered arbitrary or capricious.

Penalties

The result of disciplinary hearings can be fines, restitution, suspension or revocation of a license.

A restricted license can be issued by the Commissioner as set forth in Business and Professions Code 10156.5

Section 10156.6 of the Business and Professions Code sets forth the restrictions that are authorized.

Restricted License - Restrictions Authorized

10156.6. A restricted license issued pursuant to Section 10156.5 as the Commissioner in his or her discretion finds advisable in the public interest may be restricted:

(a). By term.

(b). To employment by a particular real estate broker, if a salesperson.

(c). By conditions to be observed in the exercise of the privileges granted.

(d). If a salesperson licensee or applicant has not complied with Section 10153.4 within 18 months after issuance of the license.

The restricted license does not give a licensee any privileges or automatic renewal rights. This is set forth in Business and Professions Code Section 10156.7.

Restricted License- Privileges - Suspension - No Renewal Rights

10156.7(a). A restricted license issued pursuant to Section 10156.5 does not confer any property right in the privileges to be exercised thereunder, and the holder of a restricted license does not have the right to the renewal of the license.

(b). Except as provided in subdivision (c), the Commissioner may, without hearing, issue an order suspending the licensee's right to further exercise any privileges granted under a restricted license pending final determination made after formal hearing.

(c). A restricted salesperson license containing a condition requiring compliance with Section 10153.4 shall be automatically suspended upon the licensee's failure to comply with the condition. The suspension shall not be lifted until the suspended licensee has submitted the required evidence of course completion and the Commissioner has given written notice to the licensee of the lifting of the suspension.

Not Retroactive

It is important that a person be licensed at the time a commission was earned.

A later revocation of a license would not disqualify a person for entitlement to a commission if the commission was earned while a person was licensed. As an example, a former licensee could be entitled to a commission for arranging a loan if the completed loan agreement was in escrow at the time of license revocation. The commission was earned while the person was licensed although payment may not have been until close of escrow.

Recovery Account

There is a separate account within the Real Estate Fund called the **Recovery Account** *to reimburse individuals who suffer losses because of wrongful actions by real estate licensees*. This fund is sustained by a fee charged every licensee when obtaining or renewing a license.

Injured persons must first obtain a judgment against the licensee and the judgment must be shown to be uncollectible. The injured party can then apply to the Real Estate Commissioner for reimbursement.

The Real Estate Fund shall be liable for no more than $20,000 for any single action and no more than $100,000 for any licensee.

The Business and Professions Code, beginning with Section 10470, sets forth the rights of both claimant and Commissioner.

Provision for Augmentation

10470. If, on June 30 of any year, the balance remaining in the Recovery Account in the Real Estate Fund is less than two hundred thousand dollars ($200,000), every licensed broker, when obtaining or renewing any broker license within four years thereafter, shall pay, in addition to the license fee, a fee of seven dollars ($7), and every licensed salesperson, when obtaining or renewing such license within four years thereafter, shall pay, in addition to the license fee, a fee of four dollars ($4). The fees from both broker and salesperson licensees shall be paid into the State Treasury and credited to the Recovery Account.

Transfer of Funds

10470.1(a). In addition to the amount paid into the Recovery Account as set forth in Section 10450.6, the Real Estate Commissioner may authorize the transfer from the Real Estate Fund to the Recovery Account of any amounts as are deemed necessary.

(b). If the balance remaining in the Recovery Account contains more than four hundred thousand dollars ($400,000), the Commissioner may authorize the transfer of all or part of the surplus amount into the Real Estate Fund.

(c). The Commissioner may authorize the return to the Recovery Account of all or any amount previously transferred to the Real Estate Fund under this section.

Application for Payment from Recovery Account

10471(a). When an aggrieved person obtains a final judgment in a court of competent jurisdiction or an arbitration award which includes findings of fact and conclusions of law rendered in accordance with the rules established by the American Arbitration Association or another recognized arbitration body, and in accordance with Sections 1281 to 1294.2, inclusive, of the Code of Civil Procedure where applicable, and where the arbitration award has been confirmed and reduced to judgment pursuant to Section 1287.4 of the Code of Civil Procedure, against a defendant based upon the defendant's fraud, misrepresentation, or deceit, made with intent to defraud, or conversion of trust funds arising directly out of any transaction not in violation of Section 10137 or 10138 in which the defendant, while licensed under this part, performed acts for which that license was required, the aggrieved person may, upon the judgment becoming final, file an application with the Department of Real Estate for payment from the Recovery Account, within the limitations specified in Section 10474, of the amount unpaid on the judgment which represents an actual and direct loss to the claimant in the transaction.

(b). The application shall be delivered in person or by certified mail to an office of the department not later than one year after the judgment has become final.

(c). The application shall be made on a form prescribed by the department, verified by the claimant, and shall include the following:

(1) The name and addresses of the claimant.
(2) If the claimant is represented by an attorney, the name, business address, and telephone number of the attorney.

(3) The identification of the judgment, the amount of the claim and an explanation of its computation.

(4) A detailed narrative statement of the facts in explanation of the allegations of the complaint upon which the underlying judgement is based.

(5) A statement by the claimant, signed under penalty of perjury, that the complaint upon which the underlying judgement is based was prosecuted conscientiously and in good faith. As used in this section, "conscientiously and in good faith" means that no party potentially liable to the claimant in the underlying transaction was intentionally and without good cause omitted from the complaint, that no party named in the complaint who otherwise reasonably appeared capable of responding in damages was dismissed from the complaint intentionally and without good cause, and that the claimant employed no other procedural tactics contrary to the diligent prosecution of the complaint in order to provide access to the Recovery Account.

(6) The name and address of the judgment debtor or, if not known, the names and addresses of persons who may know the judgment debtor's present whereabouts.

(7) The following representations and information from the claimant:

(A) That he or she is not a spouse of the judgment debtor nor a personal representative of the spouse.

(B) That he or she has complied with all of the requirements of this chapter.

(C) That the judgment underlying the claim meets the requirements of subdivision (a).

(D) A description of searches and inquiries conducted by or on behalf of the claimant with respect to the judgment debtor's assets liable to be sold or applied to satisfaction of the judgment, an itemized valuation of the assets discovered, and the results of actions by the claimant to have the assets applied to satisfaction of the judgment.

(E) That he or she has diligently pursued collection efforts against other judgment debtors and all other persons liable for the underlying judgment.

(F) That the underlying judgment and debt have not been discharged in bankruptcy, or, in the cause of a bankruptcy proceeding that is open at the time of the filing of the application, that the judgement and debt have been declared to be non-dischargeable.

(G) That the application was mailed or delivered to the department no later than one year after the underlying judgment was final.

(d). The application form shall include detailed instructions with respect to documentary evidence, pleadings, court rulings, the products of discovery in the underlying litigation, and a notice to the applicant of his or her obligation to protect the underlying judgment from discharge in bankruptcy, to be appended to the application.

Notice to Be Served on Judgment Debtor

10471.1(a). The claimant shall serve a copy of the notice prescribed in subdivision (c) upon the judgment debtor by personal service or by registered mail, together with a copy of the application.

(b). If the judgment debtor holds a current license issued by the department, service of the notice and a copy of the application may be made by registered mail addressed to the judgment debtor at the latest business or residence address on file with the department. If the judgment debtor does not hold a current license issued by the department and personal service cannot be effected through the exercise of reasonable diligence, the claimant shall serve the judgment debtor by one publication of the notice in each of two successive weeks in a newspaper of general circulation published in the county in which the judgment debtor was last known to reside.

(c). The notice served upon the judgment debtor shall include the following statement:

"NOTICE: Based upon a judgment entered against you in favor of name of claimant) _____, application for payment from the Recovery Account of the Real Estate Fund is being made to the Department of Real Estate.

> *"If payment is made from the Recovery Account, all licenses and license rights that you have under the Real Estate Law will be automatically suspended on the date of payment and cannot be reinstated until the Recovery Account has been reimbursed for the amount paid plus interest at the prevailing rate.*

"If you wish to contest payment by the Real Estate Commissioner, you must file a written response to the application addressed to the Department of Real Estate at _____ within 30 days after mailing, delivery, or publication of this notice and send a copy of that response to the claimant. If you fail to do so, you will have waived your right to present your objections to payment."

(d). If a judgment debtor fails to file a written response to the application with the department within 30 days after personal service, mailing, or final publication of the notice, the judgment debtor shall not thereafter be entitled to notice of any action taken or proposed to be taken by the Commissioner with respect to the claim.

Deficient or Substantially Complete Application

10471.2(a). If the Commissioner determines that the application as submitted by the claimant fails to comply substantially with the requirements of Section 10471 or with the requirements of a regulation adopted by the Commissioner under authority of Section 10080, the Commissioner shall, within 15 days after receipt of the application, mail an itemized list of deficiencies to the claimant**...**

Final Decision - Settlement

10471.3(a). The Commissioner shall render a final written decision on the application with 90 days after a completed application has been received unless the claimant agrees in writing to extend the time within which the commissioner may render a decision. If the Commissioner fails to render a written decision in response to the claim within 90 days after its receipt or within the extended period agreed to by the claimant, the claim shall be deemed to have been denied by the Commissioner on the final day for rendering the decision**...**

Notice of Decision

10471.5(a). The Commissioner shall give notice of a decision rendered with respect to the claim to the claimant and to a judgment debtor who has filed a timely response to the claim in accordance with Section 10471.1.

(b). If the application is denied, the notice to the claimant and judgment debtor shall include the following:

"Claimant's application has been denied. If the claimant wishes to pursue the application in court, the claimant must file the application in the court in which the underlying judgment was entered not later than six months after receipt of this notice, pursuant to Section 10472 of the Business and Professions Code.

(c). If the decision of the Commissioner is to make a payment to the claimant out of the Recovery Account, the following notice shall be given to the judgment debtor along with a copy of the decision of the Commissioner:

"The decision of the Real Estate Commissioner on the claim of _____ is to pay $_____ from the Recovery Account. A copy of that decision is enclosed. "Pursuant to Section 10475 of the Business and Professions Code, all of your licenses and license rights under the Real Estate Law will be suspended effective on the date of the payment, and you will not be eligible for reinstatement of any license issued under authority of the Real Estate Law until you have reimbursed the Recovery Account for this payment plus interest at the prevailing legal rate.

"If you desire a judicial review of the suspension of your licenses and license rights, you may petition the superior court in the county in which the judgment which is the basis of this claim was rendered, for a writ of mandamus. To be timely, the petition must be filed with the court within 30 days of receipt of this notice."

License Suspension

10475. Should the Commissioner pay from the Recovery Account any amount in settlement of a claim or toward satisfaction of a judgment against a licensed broker or salesperson, the license of the broker or salesperson shall be automatically suspended upon the date of payment from the Recovery Account. No broker or salesperson shall be granted reinstatement until he or she has repaid in full, plus interest at the prevailing legal rate applicable to a judgment rendered in any court of this state, the amount paid from the Recovery Account on his or her account. A discharge in bankruptcy shall not relieve a person from the penalties and disabilities provided in this chapter.

Insufficient Funds - Priority of Payment When Money Deposited

10476. If, at any time, the money deposited in the Recovery Account is insufficient to satisfy any duly authorized claim or portion thereof, the Commissioner shall, when sufficient money has been deposited in the Recovery Account, satisfy the unpaid claims or portions thereof, in the order that the claims or portions thereof were originally filed, plus accumulated interest at the rate of 4 percent a year.

Waiver of Rights

10480. The failure of an aggrieved person to comply with all of the provisions of this chapter shall constitute a waiver of any rights hereunder.

Disciplinary Action Against Licensee

10481. Nothing in this chapter limits the authority of the Commissioner to take disciplinary action against any licensee for a violation of the Real Estate Law, or of Chapter 1 (commencing with Section 11000) of Part 2, or of the rules and regulations of the Commissioner; nor shall the repayment in full of all obligations to the Recovery Account by any licensee nullify or modify the effect of any other disciplinary proceeding brought pursuant to the Real Estate Law.

Real Estate Brokers

The purpose of licensing is to "protect the public" by regulating those who engage in real estate activities in an agency capacity.

Section 10130 of the Business and Professions Code makes it "unlawful for any person to engage in the business, act in the capacity of advertise or assume to act as a real estate broker or a real estate salesperson within this state without first obtaining a real estate license from the department."

DEFINITION OF A REAL ESTATE BROKER

Section 10131 of the Business and Professions Code sets forth activities for which a real estate broker's license is required.

Broker Defined

No license is required if one is acting for himself or herself.

10131. A ***real estate broker*** *within the meaning of this part is a person who, for a compensation or in expectation of a compensation, regardless of the form or time of payment, does or negotiates to do one or more of the following acts for another or others*:

(a). Sells or offers to sell, buys or offers to buy, solicits prospective sellers or purchasers of, solicits or obtains listings of, or negotiates the purchase, sale or exchange of real property or a business opportunity.

(b). Leases or rents or offers to lease or rent, or places for rent, or solicits listings of places for rent, or solicits for prospective tenants, or negotiates the sale, purchase or exchanges of leases on real property, or on a business opportunity, or collects rents from real property, or improvements thereon, or from business opportunities.

(c). Assists of offers to assist in filing an application for the purchase or lease of, or in locating or entering upon, lands owned by the state or federal government.

(d). Solicits borrowers or lenders for or negotiates loans or collects payments or performs services for borrowers or lenders or note owners in connection with loans secured directly or collaterally by liens on real property or on a business opportunity.

(e). Sells or offers to sell, buys or offers to buy, or exchanges or offers to exchange a real property sales contract, or a promissory note secured directly or collaterally by a lien on real property or on a business opportunity, and performs services for the holders thereof.

ADDITIONAL ACTIVITIES REQUIRING LICENSING

In this text we will be primarily concerned with several additional activities requiring a real estate license.

> *Section 10131.1 of the Business and Professions Code deals with "loan brokerage on mortgage banker" activities while Section 10131.3 of the code deals with listing and negotiating the sale, purchase or exchange of securities.*

Broker Definition Continued - Buying/Selling Notes, etc.

10131.1. A real estate broker within the meaning of this part is also a person who engages as a principal in the business of buying from, selling to, or exchanging with the public, real property sales contracts or promissory notes secured directly or collaterally by liens on real property, or who makes agreements with the public for the collection of payments or for the performance of services in connection with real property sales contracts or promissory notes secured directly or collaterally by liens on real property.

Broker Definition Continued - Securities

10131.3. A real estate broker within the meaning of this part is also a person who, for another or others, for compensation or in expectation of compensation, issues or sells, solicits prospective sellers or purchasers of, solicits or obtains listings of, or negotiates the purchase, sale, or exchange of securities as specified in Section 25206 of the Corporations Code.

The provisions of this section do not apply to a broker-dealer or agent of a broker-dealer licensed by the Commissioner of Corporations under the provisions of the Corporate Securities Law of 1968.

EXEMPTIONS FROM LICENSING

Exemptions from licensing are set forth in Chapter 5.

INDIVIDUAL BROKERS

Licenses are issued to individuals who have met educational and experience requirements and have taken and passed the real estate brokers' examination.

All licensees are required to be fingerprinted.

REQUIREMENTS TO OBTAIN A BROKER'S LICENSE

Requirements to obtain a broker's license include the following:

Age

An applicant must be 18 years of age or older.

Residence

California residency is not a requirement of licensing.

California does not have reciprocity with any other state that allows any waiver of requirements to obtain a California broker's license.

Courses completed out of state must have been or be evaluated for California equivalency.

Honesty

License applicants must be honest and truthful. Conviction of a crime which is either a felony or involves moral turpitude may result in denial of a license.

Failure to reveal a criminal conviction on an original license application may also result in the denial of a license.

Education

Applicants for a real estate broker license examination must have successfully completed the following statutorily required college-level courses:

1. Real Estate Practice,

2. Legal Aspects of Real Estate,

3. Real Estate Finance,

4. Real Estate Appraisal,

5. Real Estate Economics or Accounting,

6. and three * courses from the following group:

    (a) Real Estate Principles

    (b) Business Law

    (c) Property Management

    (d) Escrows

    (e) Mortgage Loan Brokering and Lending

    (f) Advanced Legal Aspects of Real Estate

    (g) Advanced Real Estate Finance

    (h) Advanced Real Estate Appraisal

    (i) Real Estate Office Administration

* If applicant has completed both accounting and real estate economics, only two courses from group 6 are required.

Experience

> *A minimum of two-years, full-time experience is required as a real estate salesperson. Form RE 226 is required for verification (See Figures 2-1 and 2-2).*

Equivalent experience will be considered. See RE-227 (Figures 2-3 and 2-4).

Education in Lieu of Experience

Four-Year Degree

> *A four-year degree from an accredited college exempts the applicant from the experience requirement.*

Law Graduates

> *Graduates of accredited law schools are exempt from the experience and education requirements.*

A.A. Degree

> *Persons having an AA degree need only have one year of experience as a salesperson.*

Application

Applicants for a salesperson's license file Form 400A (Not shown). Applicants for a broker's license must file Form RE 400B (Not shown).

PARTNERSHIPS

> *There is no partnership license, although a broker can be a partner with another.*

Section 10137.1 of the Business and Professions Code provides that the partnership can perform acts for which a real estate broker's license is required providing every partner through whom the partnership so acts is a licensed real estate broker.

Figure 2-1

STATE OF CALIFORNIA

DEPARTMENT OF REAL ESTATE
LICENSING

EMPLOYMENT VERIFICATION

(FOR *LICENSED* REAL ESTATE EXPERIENCE ONLY.)

RE 226 (Rev. 1/92)

❖ ❖ *Please read instructions on page 2 before completing this form.* ❖ ❖

EMPLOYMENT VERIFICATION

1. APPLICANTS NAME — LAST, FIRST & MIDDLE

2. APPLICANT'S RESIDENCE ADDRESS — STREET ADDRESS, CITY, STATE AND ZIP CODE

3. LIST NUMBER OF TRANSACTIONS COMPLETED DURING THE TIME SPECIFIED ON ITEM #9.

PROPERTIES LISTED	SALES	TRADES	LEASES
SECURITIES SALES	MORTGAGE LOANS	SYNDICATES	RENTALS

4. APPROXIMATE EARNINGS

5. EXPLANATION OF TYPE OF LICENSED REAL ESTATE EXPERIENCE IF TRANSACTION NOT LISTED ABOVE.

6. DID APPLICANT HAVE OTHER EMPLOYMENT OR BUSINESS ACTIVITY? ☐ YES ☐ NO IF YES, EXPLAIN.

7. WORK TIME DEVOTED ☐ FULL TIME ☐ PART TIME	8. HOURS PER WEEK	9. CONTINUOUS EMPLOYMENT CERTIFICATION (MM/DD/YY) FROM	To

Certification

I hereby certify to the nature and scope of applicant's activities while employed by me as a salesperson. Realizing that a false certification is basis for suspension or revocation of my license under Sections 10177(a), 10177(f), and 10177(h) of the Real Estate Law, I certify under penalty of perjury that the foregoing is true and correct.

SIGNATURE OF CERTIFYING BROKER ➤	DATE
PRINTED NAME OF CERTIFYING BROKER	BUSINESS TELEPHONE NUMBER ( )

COMPANY OR CORPORATION NAME (IF ANY)

BUSINESS ADDRESS

The California Department of Real Estate

Figure 2-2

Instructions ...

❖ Read this form carefully before completing and signing.

❖ This form is to be submitted with the Examination Application (RE 400) and the proper broker examination fee.

❖ Items #1–9 are to be completed by the Employing Broker of the applicant.

❖ Type or print clearly in ink.

❖ Do not submit photocopies of this form.

Full Time Experience ...

Under the Real Estate Law, an applicant for broker license must have at least two years of *active full-time experience* as a licensed real estate salesperson or the equivalent. The experience must be gained during the five-year period immediately preceding the date of application. Possession of a salesperson license without actual licensed experience is not sufficient to meet the experience requirement.

Full time experience means at least 40 hours per week. If applicant worked less than 40 hours per week, credit is granted on a prorated basis. Time is not awarded if applicant devoted less than 10 hours per week. If applicant had any other employment, it must be set forth where indicated even though 40 or less hours are devoted to an employing broker.

Equivalent Experience ...

Applications for equivalent experience by an unlicensed person must be submitted on an Equivalent Experience Verification (RE 227) form. Refer to the Instructions To License Applicants brochure for more information.

Employment Certifications ...

If it is impossible to secure certifications of employment from former employing brokers, the applicant must complete the Employment Verification (RE 226) in full and indicate the reason why applicant could not obtain broker's signature in the space labeled "Signature of Certifying Broker" (i.e., deceased, litigation, etc.). The applicant must also attach *at least two* Employment Certification forms (RE 228) from persons in a position to attest to applicant's experience and activity. *Out-of-state brokers who are self-employed may also use this format, since we cannot accept an applicant's own verification.*

Figure 2-3

STATE OF CALIFORNIA   DEPARTMENT OF REAL ESTATE
            LICENSING

EQUIVALENT EXPERIENCE VERIFICATION

(FOR *UNLICENSED* REAL ESTATE EXPERIENCE ONLY.)

RE 227 (Rev. 4/89)

❖   ❖   *Please read instructions on reverse side before completing this form.*   ❖   ❖

EQUIVALENT EXPERIENCE

1. APPLICANT'S NAME — LAST, FIRST & MIDDLE

2. APPLICANT'S RESIDENCE ADDRESS — STREET ADDRESS, CITY, STATE, & ZIP CODE

3. TYPE OF EQUIVALENT EXPERIENCE CLAIM

4. APPROXIMATE VOLUME OF ACTIVITY COMPLETED WHILE PERFORMING IN THE ABOVE CAPACITY?

5. APPROXIMATE EARNINGS

6. DETAILED DESCRIPTION OF RESPONSIBILITIES (ATTACH EXTRA SHEETS IF NECESSARY.)

7. WORK TIME DEVOTED	8. APPROX. HOURS PER WEEK	9. CONTINUOUS EMPLOYMENT CERTIFICATION (MM/DD/YY)
❏ FULL TIME ❏ PART TIME		FROM TO

Certification

We, the undersigned, hereby certify to the nature and scope of the applicant's activities as indicated above.

COMPANY OR CORPORATION NAME (IF ANY)

CERTIFYING SIGNATURE DATE	CERTIFYING SIGNATURE DATE
➤	➤
PRINTED NAME OF SIGNER	PRINTED NAME OF SIGNER
TITLE	TITLE
BUSINESS ADDRESS	BUSINESS ADDRESS
BUSINESS TELEPHONE NUMBER	BUSINESS TELEPHONE NUMBER

Figure 2-4

Instructions ...

❖ Submit this form with a completed Examination Application (RE 400) and the proper fee for the broker examination.

❖ Read carefully before completing and signing this form.

❖ Type or print clearly in ink.

❖ Do not submit photocopies of this form.

Equivalent Experience ...

An applicant for the broker examination who has not been a licensed real estate salesperson may be eligible for the examination provided the applicant has equivalent experience. Regardless of the experience, the statutory real estate courses are required and do not qualify as part of the experience. Refer to the Instructions To License Applicants brochure for types of equivalent experience that are acceptable.

To make a proper evaluation of the applicant's equivalent experience, this form must be completed in full and properly signed.

- **Two signatures are required on *each* form** (i.e., employers, associates, or other person verifying applicants experience).

- Submit *one* form for *each* job performed and/or company employed by.

  Example: three forms would be required for the following experience
  - 3 years as an escrow officer for Company A
  - 2 years as an escrow officer for Company B
  - 5 years as a loan officer for Company B

CORPORATE BROKERS

A corporation can be licensed as a real estate broker.

At least one officer of the corporation must be licensed as a real estate broker. The corporate real estate broker would be the responsible designated broker/officer.

Additional Brokers

If the corporation desires any other officer to act under its license as a real estate broker, such additional officer(s) must procure broker's licenses. (Business and Professions Code 10158.)

Broker Limited to Corporation

The designated broker of a corporation can only act on behalf of the corporation he or she is licensed to under the corporate broker's license. (Business and Professions Code 10159.)

Supervision Requirements

The "designated broker for a corporate licensee is responsible for the supervision and control" of the activities conducted on behalf of the corporation by all other officers and employees so as to ensure full compliance with the law. (Business and Professions Code 10159.2)

Background of Officers and Directors

A background statement is required for each director, chief executive officer and other officers who have policy-formation responsibility. Section 2746 of the Commissioner's Regulations sets forth the type of information required.

2746. Corporate Real Estate Brokers, Officers, Directors and Shareholders(a). At the time of application for, or in the reinstatement of, an original real estate broker license, the designated officer shall file a background statement of information for each director, the chief executive officer, the president, first level vice presidents, secretary, chief financial officer, subordinate officers with responsibility for forming policy of the corporation and all natural persons owning or controlling more than ten percent of its shares, if such person has been the subject of any of the following:

(1) Received an order or judgment issued by a court or governmental agency during the preceding 10 years temporarily or permanently restraining or enjoining any business conduct, practice or employment;

(2) Has had a license to engage in or practice real estate or other regulated profession, occupation or vocation during the preceding 10 years;

(3) Engaged in acts requiring a real estate license of any state without the benefit of a valid license or permit authorizing that conduct during the preceding 10 years which have been enjoined by a court of law or administrative tribunal;

(4) Been convicted of a crime which is substantially related to the qualifications, functions or duties of a licensee of the Department as specified in Section 2910 of these Regulations (excluding drunk driving, reckless driving and speeding violations)...

Salesperson Controlled Corporation

A salesperson could conceivably own the controlling interest of a corporation if the officer or director responsible for real estate activity was a real estate broker.

Real Estate Salespersons

A real estate salesperson is licensed by the Department of Real Estate to work under the control and supervision of a licensed broker.

A **real estate salesperson** is defined by Section 10132 of the Business and Professions Code as a natural person (a salesperson cannot be licensed as a corporation) who for or in expectation of compensation is employed by a broker to perform an act for which a license is required. Supervision of salespersons is covered in Chapter 6.

LICENSING REQUIREMENTS

Employment by a broker is not a prerequisite to obtaining a real estate salesperson's license. However, real estate activity may only be performed by the licensee while in the employ of a licensed broker.

Requirements for a real estate salesperson include the following:

Age

The applicant must be at least 18 years of age.

Honesty

The applicant must be honest.

Education

The applicant must have completed a three-semester unit (or four-quarter unit) college-level course in Real Estate Principles.

Additional educational requirements must be met within 18 months after issuance of the salesperson's license.

Application

Applicant must submit an application (Form RE 400A) to take the examination.

SUMMARY

The Real Estate Commissioner, who is appointed by the governor, is the principal officer of the Department of Real Estate. The Department of Real Estate is a department within California's Business and Transportation Agency.

The Commissioner is responsible for final decisions but has a ten-member advisory committee who consult with the Commissioner on functions and policies of the Department of Real Estate.

The Real Estate Commissioner can bring action to have the courts issue an injunction, appoint a receiver or issue a desist and refrain order. The Commissioner can also initiate disciplinary action against a licensee.

In order to discipline a licensee, action must be taken within three years of the offense or, in cases of fraud or misrepresentation, within one year of discovery or three years from occurrence, whichever is later.

The first step in a disciplinary action is known as an Accusation. A Statement of Issues sets forth the offenses. The Statement to Respondent sets forth the rights of the accused. The accused has a right to a hearing. Hearings are before an Administrative Law Judge. Penalties possible include fines, restitution requirements, license suspension as well as license revocation.

A restricted license may be issued. Restrictions may be to term, employment by a particular broker, as well as to other conditions set by the Commissioner.

Applicants for the brokers examination must complete specified courses of study and have two-year, full-time experience as a salesperson (or equivalent). A four-year degree can be substituted for the two-year experience requirement.

Applicants for the salesperson's examination must have completed a course in Real Estate Principles.

CLASS DISCUSSION TOPICS

1. Several past real estate commissioners have gone to work for real estate brokerage and loan firms after their service as real estate commissioner. Are there any problems that you see with regulators taking positions with firms they once regulated?

2. The Department of Real Estate issues a quarterly bulletin containing the names of licensees who have been subject to disciplinary action, the action taken and the applicable code offense. Several dozen brokers and salespeople are usually listed each quarter. Why do you suppose that discipline is such a problem for real estate licensees?

3. What are advantages of a brokerage firm being organized as a corporation?

4. Are there any other forms of business organizations that could provide the same advantages offered by a corporation?

5. When could a broker be a partner with a person who is not licensed as a broker or real estate salesperson?

6. How would it be possible for a non-licensee to directly benefit from real estate activities requiring a broker's license?

CHAPTER 2 QUIZ

1. The Real Estate Commissioner can: (p. 27)
    - A. be active as a real estate broker while serving as commissioner
    - B. be overruled by a majority vote of the advisory commission
    - C. adopt regulations to enforce the real estate law
    - D. bring action against a licensee within ten years of any wrongful action

2. The first step in a disciplinary action against a licensee is known as the: (p. 29)
    - A. statement of issues
    - B. accusation
    - C. judgment
    - D. judicial review

3. A restricted license gives the licensee: (p. 32)
    - A. a right to a permanent license if no further complaints are made within one year
    - B. a right to a renewal if no further complaints are made in the 90 days prior to renewal
    - C. both A and B
    - D. neither A nor B

4. To earn a commission a broker must: (p. 33)
    - A. have been licensed at close of escrow
    - B. have been licensed when the commission was earned
    - C. both A and B
    - D. neither A nor B

5. The purpose of real estate licensing is to: (p. 39)
    - A. protect the public
    - B. control the number of licensees
    - C. earn revenue for the state
    - D. protect the industry against uncontrolled competition

6. Which of the following acts for compensation does NOT require a license? (p. 39)
    - A. An owner selling four homes in one year for a profit
    - B. Offering to exchange a business opportunity for another
    - C. Soliciting lenders for loans
    - D. Offering to exchange a promissory note secured by real property

7. The following acts for compensation require a real estate license. (p. 40)

    A. Soliciting listings of places to rent

    B. Offering to assist others in applying for leases to government owned land

    C. Soliciting borrowers for real estate secured loans

    D. All of the above

8. A real estate license would be issued to all EXCEPT: (p. 41)

    A. a person who has been accused of a crime

    B. a person who is not a resident of California

    C. a person who does not have a college degree

    D. a person under the age of 18

9. In order to take the real estate broker examination, a person must take all the following courses EXCEPT: (p. 42)

    A. Mortgage Loan Brokering and Lending

    B. Real Estate Finance

    C. Legal Aspects of Real Estate

    D. Real Estate Appraisal

10. An applicant for a real estate broker's examination never finished high school. How much experience must that person have as a salesperson in order to take the broker's examination? (p. 43)

    A. None

    B. One year

    C. Two years

    D. Four years

11. Licenses will be issued to all EXCEPT: (p. 43)

    A. nonresidents

    B. partnerships

    C. corporations

    D. unmarried women

12. Who is responsible for the real estate activities of a corporation? (p. 53)

    A. The CEO

    B. The principal stockholder

    C. The designated broker-officer

    D. The chief financial officer

Answers: 1. C; 2. B; 3. D; 4. B; 5. A; 6. A; 7. D; 8. D; 9. A; 10. A; 11. C; 12. C

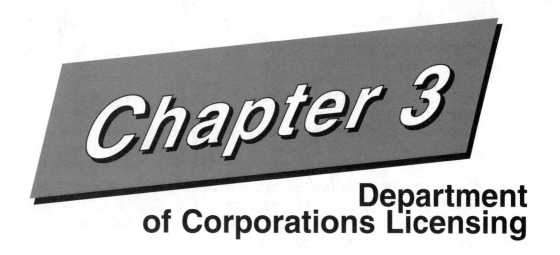

Chapter 3

Department of Corporations Licensing

www.leginfo.ca.gov/.html/corp_table_of_contents.html
(California Corporations Code)

KEY WORDS AND TERMS

California Finance Lenders Law
California Residential Mortgage Lending Act
Commercial Finance Lender
Personal Property Broker
Residential Mortgage Loan Report

LEARNING OBJECTIVE

While this course is primarily concerned with activities requiring licensing by the Department of Real Estate, you will learn that much of what we regard as real estate broker activities can be accomplished without a real estate broker's license. Licensing is nevertheless required, but another agency is involved.

> *The Department of Corporations issues licenses which duplicate many of the functions authorized by real estate broker licensing.*

The **CALIFORNIA DEPARTMENT OF CORPORATIONS** *licenses lenders for both personal property and real property loans.* You will see that there is an area of overlap where lenders can engage in real estate lending with licensing by either the Department of Real Estate or the Department of Corporations.

Personal Property Brokers

Section 22000 et seq. of the Financial Code was formerly known as the *Personal Property Broker's Law.*

PERSONAL PROPERTY BROKERS *included all persons engaged in lending money and taking as security any contract or obligation that could result in the forfeiture of rights in or to personal property.* In other words, liens secured by personal property. Examples would be vehicle and furniture loans.

DEFINITION

The Financial Code, Section 2209, defines Personal Property Broker as "all those who are engaged in the business of lending money and taking in the name of the lender, or in any other name, in whole or in part, are security for such loan, any contract or obligation involving the forfeiture of rights in or to personal property, the use and possession of which property is retained by other than the mortgagee or lender, or any lien on, assignment of, a power of attorney relative to wages, salary, earnings, income or commission."

REPEAL

The licensing requirements for Personal Property Brokers set forth in the Financial Code was repealed by Stats 1985 C. 552 Sec. 3.

REPLACEMENT

> *The Consumer Finance Lenders Law has effectively replaced the Personal Property Brokers Law.*

You will see that the Consumer Finance Lenders Law has far greater scope than the Personal Property Brokers Law.

Personal Property Brokers were:

1. restricted to making loans secured in whole or in part by personal property;
2. restricted in brokering loans in that they could only broker them to Personal Property Brokers.

California Finance Lenders Law

The Department of Corporations licenses lending activities under the California Finance Lenders Law.

Section 22100 of the Financial Code requires all persons engaged in the business of finance lender or broker to be licensed by the Commissioner.

CONSUMER FINANCE LENDERS LICENSE

A **CALIFORNIA FINANCE LENDER (CFL)** *is any person licensed under this law (Sec. 24008.1 Financial Code)*. Loans made or brokered under this license may be secured by personal property, or a combination of real and personal property. Real property secured loans must be for over $5,000.

LICENSING

A California Finance Lender can be licensed as a lender, a broker or both lender and broker.

BROKERING CFL LOANS

A CFL broker is restricted to the type of lender they can broker their loans to.

A CFL broker may only broker loans to a direct lender licensed under the California Finance Lenders Law by the Department of Corporations.

The brokering of a loan secured by real property to any other lender such as a bank, savings bank or thrift and loan is not authorized under the authority of the license. (Such a loan would be under the jurisdiction of the Department of Real Estate or under a different corporation commission license.)

LOAN REQUIREMENTS

In order for a loan to be made by a CFL licensee, all of the following criteria must be met.

1. **Approval.** The licensee approves the loan but can use lending criteria established by an institutional lender.

2. **Licensee is Beneficiary.** The licensee must be the beneficiary on the promissory note.

3. **Licensee Funding.** The licensee must provide funding for the loan from sources exclusive of any funding advances received from an institutional investor committed to purchasing the loan. (The licensee must use his or her own funds to make the loan. In many cases lenders will acquire necessary funds through a document loan or line of credit.)

FORM OF LICENSE

A CFL licensee may be an individual, partnership, corporation, joint venture, association, joint stock company, trust, government entity or political subdivision of a government (any person or group would seem likely to qualify for licensing).

NO EXAMINATION

No examination is required for licensing although an application and proper fees must be submitted.

An affidavit must be signed that the applicant has read and is familiar with the applicable laws and rules.

NET WORTH

Applicants must have a net worth of $25,000 at the time of license application and this amount of net worth must be maintained while licensed. The application fee for each license is $200 and the investigation fee is $100. Both of these fees are non-refundable.

SCOPE OF ACTIVITY

The CFL broker's license allows the brokering of consumer as well as commercial loans secured by real estate, personal property, a combination of real and personal property as well as unsecured loans.

These loans can only be brokered to a CFL lender. It is not a mortgage broker's license, it is a consumer loan-broker's license. While some licensees hold both CFL and real estate licenses, a real estate license is not necessary for these CFL loans.

MULTIPLE PLACES OF BUSINESS

Every location at which a CFL broker wishes to conduct business must be licensed.

This requires an application and associated fees for each location. This is set forth in the following sections of the Financial Code:

Section 22101 Application form; master license

An application for a license under this division shall be in the form and contain the information that the commissioner may by rule require and shall be filed upon payment of the fee specified in Section 22103. *A license issued pursuant to an application filed under this section shall be designated a MASTER LICENSE.* (Added by Stats. 1994, c. 1115 (A.B.2885), 2, operative July 1, 1995.)

Section 22102 Subsidiary license; locations of business

(a). A person licensed pursuant to an application filed under Section 22101 may conduct business under this division, either directly or through one or more subsidiary corporations, at the locations that are authorized by the commissioner pursuant to this section. An application to establish a location pursuant to this section shall be in the form and contain the information that the commissioner may by rule require, and shall be filed upon payment of the fee specified in Section 22103. *A license issued pursuant to an application filed under this section shall be designated a SUBSIDIARY LICENSE.*

(b). On approval of an application filed pursuant to this section, the commissioner shall issue an original license endorsed to authorize the conduct of business at the location specified in the application.

(c). For the purpose of this section, "subsidiary corporation" means a corporation that is wholly owned by a licensee.

(d). This section does not apply to changes in the address or location of a location previously authorized or licensed under this section.

(Added by Stats. 1994, c. 1115 (A.B.2885), 2, operative July 1, 1995.)

EMPLOYEES

Employees of licensees can only work at licensed locations. Employees are not permitted to solicit loans from the public or to perform any act of brokering. (The employees work is restricted to their office.)

REPORTS

The California Finance Lenders Law sets forth report requirements.

Annual Report

> *By the 15th of March, every licensee must file an annual financial and statistical report for the prior calendar year. Failure to file the report will result in license revocation.*

The financial statement submitted must reflect that the licensee is in compliance with the minimum net worth requirements ($25,000).

Residential Mortgage Loan Report

Sections 35814 through 25816 of the California Health and Safety Code require all licensed lenders in specified transactions to report activities related to applications and loans made to the public for home purchase and/home-improvement purposes.

> *This report (State of California Residential Mortgage Loan Report) must be submitted by March 31 of each year for the prior calendar year.*

The form must be filed by lenders who:

1. make regularly qualifying loans on one-to-four unit residential real property which totals at least 10 percent of the loans made during the preceding calendar year. (**REGULARLY** *means at least 12 transactions during the year prior to reporting that total more than $500,000 in value*);

2. have total assets of 10 million or less and do not report to a federal or state regulatory agency as provided by the Home Mortgage Disclosure Act of 1975 (12 CFR 103); or

3. have total assets of more than 10 million dollars and claim an exemptions from the reporting requirements of the Home Mortgage Disclosure Act. (See Chapter 10 for information on the Home Mortgage Disclosure Act.)

ANNUAL ASSESSMENT

Failure to pay assessments will result in revocation of license.

Every licensee is responsible for a pro rata share of all costs and expenses incurred in the administration of the CFL law. The **PRO RATA SHARE** *is the proportion which a licensee's gross income (as reported on the annual report) bears to the aggregate gross income of all licensees.* The minimum annual assessment is $250 per location.

Commercial Finance Lenders

Commercial Finance Lenders are licensed by the Department of Corporations and are covered by Financial Code 26000 et. seq.

A **COMMERCIAL LOAN** *means a loan of $5,000 or more or a loan under an open-end credit program for commercial purposes.*

Section 24055 of the Financial Code exempts real estate brokers from corporation commission licensing for commercial loans that are secured by real estate.

The Department of Corporations also issues additional lender licenses including one for industrial loans.

California Residential Mortgage Lending Act

The **CALIFORNIA RESIDENTIAL MORTGAGE LENDING ACT** *, administered by the Commissioner of Corporations, provides for a Residential Mortgage Lending License.* Persons, partnerships and corporations so licensed may make and service residential loans.

Choice of License

A real estate license is not a requirement for this license. In fact, a real estate broker who operates as a mortgage-loan broker under his or her real estate license cannot also operate under a Commissioner of Corporations mortgage lending license. A person must decide under which license he or she will operate under. It is one or the other.

Application and Exemptions

The Residential Mortgage Loan license applies to one-to-four California residential units only.

Business lenders (including agricultural lenders) as well as commercial lenders are exempt from the California Residential Mortgage Lending Act (CRMLA). Also exempt are banks, savings banks, insurance companies, credit unions as well as private individual investors who make residential loans using their own funds.

If the individual investor intends to sell eight or more loans in one calendar year, he or she must be licensed.

Employees or persons working for a licensee need not be separately licensed.

It takes 60 to 90 days from receipt of CRMLA license application to receipt of license.

ASSESSMENTS

The commissioner of Corporations is authorized to assess licensees a proportionate share of costs incurred in administering the California Residential Mortgage Lending Act.

This assessment is allowed to be up to $5,000 annually.

Because of the high costs and requirements of this act, it is doubtful that many loan brokers presently operating under their real estate broker's licenses would wish to set their broker's licenses aside to operate under a Commissioner of Corporations License which also restricts residential loans to one-to-four dwelling units.

However, the new license is likely to appeal to persons who have been unable to pass the California Real Estate Brokers Examination and wish to engage in residential lending activities.

CHOICE OF LICENSES

A licensee under the California Residential Mortgage Lending Act may hold a license as a lender, a servicer or both. The CRMLA authorizes the licensee to make or service federally related mortgage loans as defined by the Real Estate Settlement Procedures Act of 1974 (RESPA).

CRMLA Lender

A **CRMLA LENDER** *directly makes a residential mortgage loan and makes the credit decision in the loan transaction.* Making a loan includes processing, underwriting, or, as a lender, using or advancing one's own funds to a loan applicant for a residential mortgage loan.

In order to be licensed as a CRMLA, the applicant must first be an approved lender for the Federal Housing Administration, Department of Veteran's Affairs, Rural Economic and Community Development Administration (formerly the Farm Home Administration), Government National Mortgage Association or the Federal Home Loan Mortgage Corporation.

In addition to making loans, a lender with a CRMLA license may:

1. buy and sell residential mortgage loans to or from institutional lenders;
2. enter into an agency contract with an institutional lender and provide solicitation of loans, application processing and use of underwriting criteria for mortgage loans to be funded by the lender; or
3. provide brokerage services on behalf of a borrower for loans made. To conduct this activity the lender must have a written brokerage agreement with the borrower.

The number of loans brokered is limited to five percent of the number of loans made by the licensee.

After the first year this limit increases to 10 percent.

Servicing Loans

A **CRMLA LOAN SERVICER** *is one who receives more than three (3) installment payments of principal, interest, or other amounts placed in escrow pursuant to the terms of a mortgage loan and performs services relating to the receipt and enforcement of the receipt of such funds on behalf of the holder of the note.*

In order to obtain a license as a servicer, the applicant must first be approved as a loan servicer for the Federal Housing Administration, Department of Veteran's Affairs, Rural Economic and Community Development Administration or Federal Home Loan Mortgage Corporation.

WHO CAN BE LICENSED?

Any form of organization not prohibited from this activity may obtain a CRMLA license.

This includes natural persons, sole proprietorships, corporations, partnerships, limited liability companies, associations, trusts, joint ventures, unincorporated organizations, joint stock companies, government or political subdivision of governments and any other entity.

WHO MUST BE FINGERPRINTED?

All individuals named in the application are required to file fingerprint cards which must be cleared through the California Department of Justice.

For public companies, the Commissioner may waive fingerprint requirements for persons named on the application.

SPECIFIC LICENSING REQUIREMENTS

Net Worth

A tangible net worth of at least $250,000 is required at the time of application. The tangible net worth must be maintained at all times.

Bond

The applicant must provide and maintain a surety bond of $50,000.

The bond shall be used for recovery of expenses, fines and fees levied by the Commissioner or for losses or damages incurred by borrowers or consumers (if not paid by licensee) as a result of a licensees noncompliance with the requirements of the act.

Fees

Applicants for the Residential Mortgage Lending License must pay a $100 investigation fee and a $100 filing fee.

SCOPE OF LICENSE

One license covers all the lending and servicing business conducted by the licensee.

Branches operate under the one license but are issued certificates of authorization to operate under the license. If an out-of-state location conducts any California business, then authorization is required for that location. The Department of Corporations must be notified when a licensee moves.

EDUCATIONAL REQUIREMENTS

No testing or examination is required for a CRMLA license.

There is, however, an educational requirement for employees who will be conducting brokerage services. Prior to providing brokerage services and thereafter once every four years, such employees must complete a three-hour course in ethics, professional conduct and legal aspects of real estate plus a three-hour course in agency relationships and duties in a real estate brokerage practice.

USE OF INDEPENDENT CONTRACTORS FORBIDDEN

CRMLA licensees cannot use independent contractors to handle lending services.

The CRMLA licensees must be responsible for acts of persons acting for the licensee, therefore such persons must be employees.

RECORDS

Licensees need not have a California place of business.

However, records of the licensee must be available for examination in California within 10 calendar days of request or the licensee must pay the expense for Department of Corporations personnel to check the records at the out-of-state location.

A licensee is subject to an examination of books and records anytime, but such an examination shall be at least once every 24 months.

Affiliates of a licensee are subject to examination by the Commissioner when reports from an examination of a licensee provides documented evidence of unlawful activity between a licensee and affiliate benefiting, affecting or arising from the activity regulated. Annual assessments cover routine examinations. The licensee is required to pay the costs of non-routine examinations.

REPORTS

On or before March 1st, each licensee must file an annual report for the prior calendar year whether or not any business was conducted.

Failure to file the report within 10 days of the due date will result in a penalty of $100 per day up to 10 days, thereafter penalty shall constitute grounds for suspension.

Audits

Each licensee is responsible for having its books and accounts audited at the end of each fiscal year by an independent, certified public accountant.

The audited report must be filed with the Commissioner within 105 days of the end of the licensee's fiscal year.

Residential Mortgage Loan Report

The State of California Residential Mortgage Loan Report must be submitted to the Department of Corporation by March 31 of each year. The form must be filed by lenders that:

1. regularly make qualifying loans on one-to-four unit residential real property which total at least 10 percent of the loans made during the preceding calendar year. Regularly means at least 12 or more transactions annually during the immediately preceding calendar year that in aggregate total more than $500,000 in value;

2. have total assets of $10 million or less and do not report to a federal or state regulating agency as provided by the Home Mortgage Disclosure Act of 1975; or

3. have total assets of more than $10 million and claim an exemption from the reporting requirements of the Home Mortgage Disclosure Act of 1975. (See Chapter 10.)

Additional Reports

The Housing Finance Discrimination Act of 1977 (The Holden Act) requires certain reporting for loans made in California.

(These reports are separate from the annual report of CRMLA licensees). The reports are mailed to licensees in January of each year and record transactions through December 31 of the prior year.

 www.leginfo.ca.gov/cgi-bin/calawquery? codesection=hsc&codebody=&hits=20 (California Health & Safety Code)

Sections 35814 through 35816 of the California Health and Safety Code require all licensed lenders in certain types of transactions to report all activity related to applications and loans made to the public for home purchases. (See Chapter 10.)

35814. The secretary shall issue such rules, regulations, guidelines, and orders as are necessary to interpret and enforce the provisions of this part and to affirmatively further the provisions of this part...

35815(a). The secretary or the secretary's designee shall monitor and investigate the lending patterns and practices of financial institutions for compliance with this part, including the lending patterns and practices for housing accommodations which are not occupied by the owner. If a finding is made that such patterns or practices violate the provisions of this part, the secretary or the secretary's designee shall take such action as will effectuate the purposes of this part...

(b). The secretary shall annually report to the Legislature on the activities of the appropriate regulatory agencies and departments in complying with this part...

35816. The secretary shall adopt regulations applicable to all persons who are in the business of originating residential mortgage loans in this state, including, but not limited to, insurers, mortgage bankers, investment bankers and credit unions and who are not depository institutions within the meaning of subsection (2) of Section 2802 of Title 12 of the United States Code. The regulations for residential mortgage loans shall impose substantially the same reporting requirements by geographic area and loan product as are imposed by the federal Home Mortgage Disclosure Act of 1975, as amended (12 U.S.C. Sec. 2801 et seq.).

This section does not apply to subsidiaries of depository institutions or subsidiaries of depository institution holding companies which are currently reporting to a federal or state regulatory agency as provided by the Home Mortgage Disclosure Act of 1975, as amended (12 U.S.C. Sec. 2081 et seq.) or are subject to substantially the same reporting requirements by geographic area and loan product pursuant to an act of a federal or state regulatory agency.

CODE AUTHORIZATION

The following section of the Financial Code gives authorization to residential mortgage brokers.

4:35.1. Residential Mortgage Brokers (New)

A person in the business of making, arranging, selling, or servicing federally regulated residential mortgage loans is required to hold a license issued by the Commissioner of Corporations. (Fin C 50002, 50003[d], 50003[o].) A residential loan is a loan secured by residential property containing four units or less. (Fin C 50003[t].) However, most of the persons or entities in the business of residential mortgage brokerage are excepted from, or exempt from, the regulations and the requirement of licensure. A person claiming an exemption has the burden of proof. (Fin C 50313.) The exemptions include the following (Fin C 50003[g]):

1. Any federally or any state chartered or licensed bank, trust company, insurance company, or industrial loan company authorized to transact business within the state.
2. A federally chartered or any state savings bank association or credit union, authorized to transact business within the state, or any wholly owned service corporation thereof.
3. A person engaged solely in business, commercial or agricultural mortgage lending.
4. A person making loans with his or her own funds for his or her own investment without the intent to sell more than eight loans in any calendar year.

5. An federal, state or municipal instrumentality or agency.

6. A pension plan that makes loans only to participants.

7. Any person who only makes loans to its employees or the employees of a holding company, or to a person who controls the lender or to a subsidiary or affiliate of the lender.

8. A fiduciary acting under court authority.

9. A licensed real estate broker.

10. A trustee under a deed of trust who collects delinquencies or other amounts in a foreclosure proceeding.

11. A trustee under a deed of trust who collects delinquencies or other amounts in a foreclosure proceeding.

In order to obtain a license, an application must be filed with the Commissioner of Corporations. (Fin C 50120-50129.) The issued license may authorize the licensee to make and arrange loans, or to service loans, or both. (Fin C 50122, 50130.) A licensee must submit an annual audited financial statement with a net worth of a minimum of $250,000 (Fin C 50200, 50201), maintain a $50,000 bond (Fin C 50122[b][6], 50205), and comply with trust fund regulations (Fin C 50202). The licensee also must make an annual report to the Commissioner. (Fin C 50307.)

A person licensed by the Commissioner of Corporations may not make or service a residential mortgage loan pursuant to a license or exemption from licensure under the Real Estate Law. (Fin C 50120[c], 50130[c].) However, the licensee can buy from or sell loans to institutional investors by using or advancing his or her own funds (Fin C 50129[a][1]), or he or she can solicit and process applications pursuant to a contract with an institutional lender, but not engage in brokerage services for the lender, if no fees are earned except from funds received by the lender and there is written disclosure that the licensee is not the lender. (Fin C 50129[a][2].) The performance of brokerage services, which includes solicitation of more than one institutional lender, requires an agreement with the borrower. (Fin C 50129[b].)

No fees can be collected, except for actual costs and, in certain cases, an application fee, commitment fee, or rate-lock fee, prior to the escrow closing for the loan. (Fin C 50203.) All costs and application fees must be returned to the borrower if a commitment is not obtained, or the loan escrow does not close, unless the failure to obtain the commitment or to close the loan is the fault of the borrower. (Fin C 50203[b].)

Financial Code Section 50204 declares that the following acts are violations of the code:

1. Disbursing loan proceeds other than to the borrower's account.
2. Failing to disburse funds according to a commitment.
3. Accepting undisclosed fees.
4. Violating CC 2941 (requiring a certificate of discharge or reconveyance upon payment of a loan.)
5. Obtaining any instrument with blanks to be completed after execution.
6. Delaying the close of a loan escrow in order to increase interest, costs or charges.
7. Engaging in fraudulent underwriting practices or acts in violation of B & P C 17200 and 17500 (unfair business practices.)
8. Paying fees to influence an appraisal.
9. Knowingly misrepresenting or concealing material information regarding a transaction involving the licensee.
10. Committing fraud or dishonest dealing or any act in violation of CC1695.13 taking unconscionable advantage of a person in foreclosure).
11. Making or servicing a loan that is not a residential mortgage loan.

SUMMARY

Personal Property Broker's licenses have been replaced by licensing under the California Finance Lenders Law (CFL).

Persons operating under a CFL license may make loans secured by real estate, secured by personal property or by both. Real property secured loans must be for over $5,000. Licensing is for a lender, broker or both lender and broker.

Loans brokered by a CFL broker can only be brokered to a CFL lender (not to institutional lenders).

The CFL lender must use his or her own funds in making loans.

While no examination is required for a CFL license, the applicant must have a minimum net worth of $25,000.

If a CFL broker wishes to maintain multiple places of business, an application and associated fees must be paid for each location.

A CFL broker can hold a real estate broker's license but dual licensing is not necessary.

Employees of CFL brokers are restricted to work at licensed locations (no field work).

Employees may not solicit loans from the public or perform any act of brokering. Licensees are responsible for a pro rata share of costs incurred in administering the CFL loan. The minimum assessment is $250 per location.

The Department of Corporations also licenses commercial finance lending. Real estate brokers who make commercial loans secured by real property are exempt from licensing.

The California Residential Mortgage Lending Act (CRMLA) provides for a Department of Corporations license to engage in residential lending (one-to-four units). A person cannot operate under both a CRMLA license and a real estate broker's license. It is one or the other.

No examination is required for a CRMLA license. Assessments for administering the act can be up to $5,000 annually for each licensee.

A CRMLA licensee is authorized to make and service federally related loans. Besides making loans, a CRMLA licensee can buy and sell residential mortgage loans to or from institutional lenders. They can also make loans as an agent for institutional lenders, and serve as borrowers' brokers in arranging loans.

The CRMLA licensee is limited in brokerage activities to five percent of the loans made by the licensee during the first year. (This amount increases to 10 percent after one year.)

Every individual named in the license application for a CRMLA license must be fingerprinted. (It can be waived for public companies.)

Licensing requirements include:

   Net worth of $250,000.

   $50,000 surety bond.

   $100 investigation fee and $100 filing fee.

One license covers all the lending and servicing business conducted by a licensee. All branches operate under the one license but receive certificates of authorization to do so.

While there is no examination required for a CRMLA license there is a minimal educational requirement for employees who will be conducting brokerage activities.

These are:

> A three-hour course in ethics, professional conduct and legal aspects of real estate.

> A three-hour course in agency relationship and duties in a real estate brokerage practice.

Licensees are subject to examination of books and records (at least once every 24 months) affiliates of licensees are subject to an examination if an examination of a licensee's records documents evidence of unlawful activity between the licensee and the affiliate.

Annual reports are required as well as an independent audit.

Like other lenders, the CRMLA requires a Residential Mortgage Loan Report (reports evidence of redlining).

CLASS DISCUSSION TOPICS

1. Why would it be difficult to conduct mortgage-banker activities under the California Finance Lenders Law?

2. Why couldn't a mortgage lender operate as a third party arranger of loans under a CFL license?

3. Who can hold a CFL license?

4. Why would a mortgage lender prefer to be licensed under the California Residential Mortgage Lending Act then as a real estate broker?

5. Why would a loan officer prefer to be employed by a CRMLA licensee rather than a real estate broker?

6. What, if any, are the problems with two agencies providing licensing for mortgage lending?

CHAPTER 3 QUIZ

1. Personal Property Broker licenses: (p. 56)
    A. will only be issued to real estate brokers
    B. have replaced California finance lender licenses
    C. are the licenses preferred by mortgage brokers
    D. have been replaced by the Consumer Finance Lender Law

2. A California Finance Lender may make all of the following types of loans EXCEPT: (p. 57)
    A. a loan secured by personal property
    B. a loan secured by both real and personal property
    C. a personal property secured loan under $5,000
    D. a real property secured loan under $5,000

3. A California Finance Lender can be licensed as: (p. 57)
    A. a lender
    B. a broker
    C. neither A nor B
    D. both A and B

4. A California Finance Lender can only broker loans to: (p. 58)
    A. banks
    B. savings banks
    C. thrift and loan associations
    D. a lender licensed under the California Finance Lenders Law

5. As to loans made by a California Finance Lender, which of the following is a true statement? (p. 58)
    A. The licensee can use lending criteria established by an institutional lender
    B. The licensee must be the beneficiary on the promissory note
    C. The licensee must use his or her own funds to make the loan
    D. All of the above

6. As to examinations for a California Finance Lender's license: (p. 58)
    A. the examination fee is $1,000
    B. less than 25 percent of applicants pass the examination
    C. there is no examination
    D. four years experience may be substituted for the examination

7. A person operating under a California Residential Mortgage Lending License CANNOT: (p. 62)

A. make real estate loans that do not involve personal property

B. also operate as a mortgage loan broker under a real estate broker's license

C. service residential loans

D. have unlicensed employees

8. Which of the following are exempt from licensing under the California Residential Mortgage Lending Act (CRMLA)? (p. 62)

A. Individual investors handling fewer than eight loan sales per year

B. Employees of persons licensed under the act

C. Banks

D. All of the above

9. An advantage a CRMLA license has over a license issued by the Department of Real Estate would be: (p. 65)

A. no examination requirement

B. no net worth requirement

C. ability to service loans

D. lower license fees

10. An applicant for a CRMLA license must: (pp. 64-65)

A. have a tangible net worth of at least $250,000

B. provide a surety bond of $50,000

C. pay an investigation fee

D. all of the above

11. Educational requirements for employees of a CRMLA licensee who will be conducting brokerage activities include: (p. 65)

A. any four-year degree

B. a four-year degree in finance

C. the identical educational requirements as for a real estate broker

D. a three-hour course in ethics, professional conduct and legal aspects as well as a three-hour course in agency relationships and duties

12. Persons working for CRMLA licensees in arranging loans: (p. 65)

A. can be independent contractors

B. can be either independent contractors or employees

C. must be separately licensed

D. must be employees of the CRMLA licensee

Answers: 1. D; 2. D; 3. D; 4. D; 5. D; 6. C; 7. B; 8. D; 9. A; 10. D; 11. D; 12. D

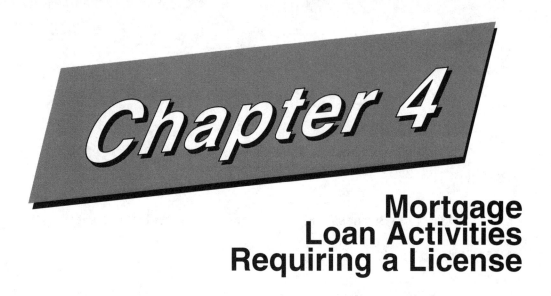

Chapter 4

Mortgage Loan Activities Requiring a License

KEY WORDS AND TERMS

Advance Fee
In the Business
Loan Correspondent

LEARNING OBJECTIVE

In this chapter you will learn about mortgage loan activities that require a real estate broker's examination. You will see that these activities go beyond soliciting lenders and borrowers.

Broker Defined

www.leginfo.ca.gov/.html/bpc_table_of_contents.html
(California Business and Professions Code)

Section 10131 of the Business and Professions Code provides a definition of broker.

COMPENSATION

The **BROKER** *is a person who for a compensation or in expectation of a compensation, regardless of the form or time of payment, performs one of the acts designated by 10131.*

> *It is not necessary that payment be received or that it be in money.*

As an example, if a commercial tenant agreed to lease a vacant unit for a landlord and the landlord agreed to give the tenant free rent for the last month of the lease, it would be compensation.

Assume the landlord denied the verbal agreement after the tenant arranged the lease for the vacant space. Even though the tenant received no compensation, the action was accomplished in the expectation of compensation.

ACTING AS AN AGENT FOR ANOTHER OR OTHERS

Business and Professions Code 10131 in the definition of broker states "...does or negotiates to do one or more of the following acts for another or others."

It is not necessary for the person to be successful to fall into the definition of broker. Attempting to perform an act requiring licensing by negotiation is enough to require a real estate license. Success is not a prerequisite.

> *"For another or others" is, however, essential as to the definition of 10131. While a person could perform listed acts as a principal (for themselves), acting for others falls within the definition of "broker".*

Specific Activities Requiring a Real Estate License

The Business and Professions Code lists activities requiring a real estate license. Section 10131, 10131.1, 10131.2, 10131.3 and 10131.4 list these activities.

A. Sell, offer to sell, buy or offer to buy, solicit sellers or purchasers of, solicit or obtain listings of, or negotiates the purchase, sale or exchange of real property or a business opportunity while acting for another and for compensation.

B. Lease or rent or offer to lease or rent, place for rent, or solicit listings of places for rent, or solicit for prospective tenants, or negotiates the sale, purchase or exchange of leases on real property, or on a business opportunity for another and for compensation.

C. Assists or offers to assist another in filing an application for the purchase or lease of, or in locating or entering upon, lands owned by the state or federal government for compensation.

D. Solicits borrowers or lenders for or negotiates loans or collects payments or performs services for borrowers or lenders or note owners in connection with loans secured directly or collaterally by liens on real property or a business opportunity acting for another for compensation.

Case Example

Vinci v. Kennedy (1986) 185 C.A. 3d 1251

Kennedy, a real estate salesperson claiming to be a real estate broker, induced Vinci to invest in short-term trust deeds. Kennedy never invested the money but used it for personal expenses. Vinci obtained a judgment against the real estate salesperson for fraud, but the judgment was uncollectible as the salesperson did not have any assets. Vinci asked the Real Estate Commissioner to reimburse his losses from the recovery fund. The Commissioner refused because the loan transactions involved required a real estate broker's license. Since the salesperson was not licensed as a broker, the salesperson was precluded from engaging in the loan activity.

The recovery fund is to reimburse members of the public for wrongful acts of licensees for acts where a license was required. Even though Kennedy lacked the license, the purpose of the statute was to protect persons such as Vinci. The Commissioner was ordered to pay.

Case Example

Harvey v. Davis (1968) 69 C 21 362

Defendants purchased real property through an exchange agreement in which they gave 24 promissory notes secured by second trust deeds on real property for the property received.

The defendants purchased the trust deeds for the purpose of using them for this trade. They had a total face value of $80,000. The defendants were able to buy the trust deeds at a discount. They paid $52,000. The property they traded for was valued at $80,000.

The question before the court was whether the defendants were in violation of the real estate licensing law.

The Business and Professions Code requires persons who act as a principal in the business of buying and selling more than eight loans secured by real estate in one calendar year be licensed.

E. Sells or offers to sell, buys or offers to buy, or exchanges or offers to buy, or exchanges or offers to exchange a real property sales contract, or a promissory note secured directly or collaterally by a lien on real property or on a business opportunity, and performs services for the holder thereof for compensation.

F. Engaging as a principal **in the business** of buying from, selling to, or exchanging with the public, real property sales contracts or promissory notes secured directly or collaterally by liens on real property, or who makes agreements with the public for the collection of payments or for the performance of services in connection with real property sales contracts or promissory notes secured directly or collaterally by liens on real property.

IN THE BUSINESS refers to acquiring loans for resale, not to keep as an investment. To be in the business means acquiring eight or more real estate loans in one calendar year.

Note: This section allows real estate brokers to act as principals (not just as agents as in E.). What it really says is that anyone buying eight or more real estate secured loans for resale must be licensed as a real estate broker.

G. A person who, for another or others, for compensation, issues or sells, solicits prospective sellers or purchaser of, solicits or obtains listings of or negotiates the purchase, sale or exchange of securities as specified in Section 25206 of the Corporation Code.

> **Note:** Business and Professions Code 10131.3 authorizes real estate brokers to sell securities (See Chapter 13.)

H. A real estate broker is also a person who acts for another for compensation in a transaction for the sale, lease, exchange of mineral oil and gas property. Soliciting borrowers or lenders or collecting payments on loans requires licensing as well as renting or collecting royalties. Also subject to licensing are persons who assist others for fees in the lease or purchase of mineral oil and gas property owned by the state or federal government.

> **Note:** A number of licensees advertise that for a fee such as $50 they will enter a person's name in a lottery for federal oil and gas lease rights. They indicate millions are possible. As a matter of fact, even if the person is lucky at the draw, the properties going to lottery are usually of little if any value.

"In The Business" Defined

As used in this section, "in the business" means any of the following:

(a). The acquisition for resale to the public, and not as an investment, of eight or more real property sales contracts or promissory notes secured directly or collaterally by liens on real property during a calendar year.

(b). The sale to or exchange with the public of **eight or more** real property sales contracts or promissory notes secured directly or collaterally by liens on real property during a calendar year. However, no transaction negotiated through a real estate licensee shall be considered in determining whether a person is a real estate broker within the meaning of this section.

As used in this section, "sale," "resale," and "exchange" include every disposition of any interest in a real property sales contract or promissory note secured directly or collaterally by a lien on real property, except the original issuance of a promissory note by a borrower or a real property sales contract by a vendor, either of which is to be secured directly by a lien on real property owned by the borrower or vendor.

Broker Definition Continued - Advance Fees

10131.2. A real estate broker within the meaning of this part is also a person who engages in the business of claiming, demanding, charging, receiving, collecting or contracting for the collection of an advance fee in connection with any employment undertaken to promote the sale or lease of real property or of a business opportunity by advance fee listing, advertisement or other offering to sell, lease, exchange or rent property or a business opportunity, or to obtain a loan or loans thereon.

Broker Definition Continued - Securities

10131.3. A real estate broker within the meaning of this part is also a person who, for another or others, for compensation or in expectation of compensation, issues or sells, solicits prospective sellers or purchasers of, solicits or obtains listings of or negotiates the purchase, sale or exchange of securities as specified in Section 25206 of the Corporations Code.

The provisions of this section do not apply to a broker-dealer or agent of a broker-dealer licensed by the Commissioner of Corporations under the provisions of the Corporate Securities Law of 1968.

Broker Definition Continued - Mineral, Oil, or Gas Property

10131.4 A real estate broker within the meaning of this part is also a person who acts for another or others for compensation or in expectation of compensation, to do one or more of the following acts:

(a). To sell or offer for sale, buy or offer to buy, solicit prospective sellers or purchasers, solicit or obtain listings or negotiate the purchase, sale or exchange of mineral, oil or gas property.

(b). To solicit borrowers or lenders for or negotiate loans on mineral, oil, or gas property, or collect payments for lender in connection with these loans.

(c). To lease or offer to lease or negotiate the sale, purchase or exchange of leases on mineral, oil or gas property.

(d). To rent or place for rent, mineral, oil or gas property or to collect rent or royalties from mineral, oil or gas property or improvements thereon.

(e). Other than as an officer or employee of the state or federal government, to assist or offer to assist another or others in filing an application for the purchase or lease of, or to locate or enter upon mineral, oil or gas property owned by the state or federal government.

Advance Fee

Business and Professions Code 10131.2. describes a real estate broker as a person who engages in the business of claiming, demanding, charging, collecting or contracting for the collection of an advance fee to promote the sale or lease of real property or of a business opportunity.

ADVANCE FEE DEFINED

An ***ADVANCE FEE***, *as defined by Business and Professions Code Section 10026, is a fee for advertising, other than in a newspaper of general circulation, for the purpose of promoting a sale or to solicit borrowers or lenders or to negotiate loans on real property or business opportunities.*

> *There are agents who accept fees to find loans for prospective borrowers. These agents are customarily referred to as "advance fee brokers."*

Advance Fee

10026. The term "advance fee" as used in this part is a fee claimed, demanded, charged, received, collected or contracted from a principal for a listing, advertisement or offer to sell or lease property, other than in a newspaper of general circulation, issued primarily for the purpose of promoting the sale or lease of business opportunities or real estate or for referral to real estate brokers or salesmen or soliciting borrowers or lenders for, or to negotiate loans on, business opportunities or real estate. As used in this section, "advance fee" does not include "security" as that term is used in Section 1950.5 of the Civil Code, or a "screening fee" as that term is used in Section 1950.6 of the Civil Code. This section does not exempt from regulation the charging or collecting of a fee under Section 1950.5 or 1950.6 of the Civil Code, but instead regulates fees that are not subject to those sections.

APPROVAL REQUIREMENTS

The real estate commissioner requires that solicitation material used by advance fee brokers be submitted to the commissioner at least "ten days" prior to use.

The commissioner can order that material not be used if it is deemed to be misleading. The use of such material would be a misdemeanor punishable by a fine up to $1,000 and/or up to six months in county jail.

Advance Fee Agreements and Materials

10085. The commissioner may require that any or all materials used in obtaining advance fee agreements, including but not limited to the contract forms, letters or cards used to solicit prospective sellers, and radio and television advertising, be submitted to him or her at least **10 calendar days** before they are used. Should the commissioner determine that any such matter, when used alone or with any other matter, would tend to mislead, he or she may, within 10 calendar days of the date he or she receives same, order that it not be used, disseminated nor published. Any person using, disseminating or publishing any matter which the commissioner has ordered, pursuant to this section, not to be used, published or disseminated shall be guilty of a misdemeanor punishable by a fine not exceeding one thousand dollars ($1,000) or by imprisonment in the county jail not exceeding six months, or both, for each such use, dissemination, or publication.

The commissioner may determine the form of the advance fee agreements, and all material used in soliciting prospective owners and sellers shall be used in the form and manner which he or she determines is necessary to carry out the purposes and intent of this part.

Any violation of any of the provisions of this part or of the rules, regulations, order or requirements of the commissioner thereunder shall constitute grounds for disciplinary action against a licensee, or for proceedings under Section 10081 of this code, or both. These sanctions are in addition to the criminal proceedings hereinbefore provided.

ADVANCE FEES FOR REAL PROPERTY LOANS

Business and Professions Code Section 10085.5. provides that the only person who can collect an advance fee for securing loans that are secured by real property is a real estate broker. There are several exceptions to this requirement which include banks, savings banks, credit unions and lenders licensed by the Department of Corporations. Violations of 10085.5 can result in a fine up to $10,000 and/or up to six months imprisonment. For a corporation the fine can be up to $50,000.

Payment of Advance Fee - Loan Secured by Lien on Real Property

10085.5(a). It shall be unlawful for any person to claim, demand, charge, receive, collect or contract for an advance fee (1) for soliciting lenders on behalf of borrowers or performing services for borrowers in connection with loans to be secured directly or collaterally by a lien on real property, before the borrower becomes obligated to complete the loan; or (2) for performing any other activities for which a license is required, unless the person is a licensed real estate broker and has complied with the provisions of this part.

> *It shall be unlawful for any person to claim, demand, charge, receive, collect or contract for an advance fee for soliciting lenders on behalf of borrowers.*

(b). This section shall not prohibit the acceptance or receipt of an advance fee by any bank, savings bank association, credit union, industrial loan company or person acting within the scope of a license issued to that person pursuant to Division 9 (commencing with Section 22000), Division 10 (commencing with Section 24000), or Division 11 (commencing with Section 26000), of the Financial Code, in connection with loans to be secured directly or collaterally by a lien on real property. This section shall not apply to charges made by title insurers and controlled escrow companies pursuant to Chapter 1 (commencing with Section 12340) of Part 6 of Division 2 of the Insurance Code.

(c). A violation of this section is a public offense punishable by a fine not exceeding ten thousand dollars ($10,000), or by imprisonment in the county jail for a term not to exceed six months, or by both fine and imprisonment, or if by a corporation, punishable by a fine not exceeding fifty thousand dollars ($50,000).

ADVANCE FEE AGREEMENTS

> *In addition to the Business and Professions Code, Section 2970 sets forth the size type required for advance fee agreements as well as approval process and other restrictions.*

2970. Advance Fee Materials

(a). A person who proposes to collect an advance fee as defined in Section 10026 in the Code shall submit to the Commissioner not less than **ten calendar days** before publication or other use, all materials to be used in advertising, promoting, soliciting and negotiating an agreement calling for the payment of an advance fee including the form of advance fee agreement proposed for use.

(b). Material used in advertising, promoting, soliciting and negotiating an advance fee agreement shall not be approved if it:

(1) Includes any representation which is false, misleading or deceptive.

(2) Does not set forth a specific, complete description of the services to be rendered for the advance fee.

(3) Does not set forth the total amount of the advance fee along with the date on which the fee shall become due and payable.

(4) Contains any provision which purports to relieve or exempt the person collecting the advance fee from an obligation to fulfill verbal commitments and representations made by employees and agents of the person contracting for the advance fee.

(5) Contains any provision which purports to give a guarantee that the real property or business opportunity in question will be purchased, leased or exchanged or that a loan secured by real property will be obtained as a result of the services rendered by the person collecting the advance fee.

(6) Does not set forth a definite date for full performance of the services promised under the advance fee agreement.

Loan Correspondents

A "loan correspondent" is a person or firm that acts for a lender in arranging loans or the sale of existing loans for compensation.

SAVINGS BANKS (SAVINGS AND LOAN ASSOCIATIONS)

Business and Professions Code 10133.1(a)(8) provides an exemption from broker licensing. The section reads as follows:

"Any person authorized in writing by a savings institution to act as an agent of that institution, as authorized by 6520 of the Financial Code or comparable authority of the Federal Home Loan Bank Board by its regulations when acting under the authority of such written authorization."

Mortgage Loan Activities Requiring a License

The above exemption from licensing only applies to a loan correspondent when that correspondent is acting under a written agreement with one savings bank.

Licensing would be required if a loan correspondent acted under written agreements with more than one savings bank.

This exemption of mortgage loan correspondent only applies to savings bank associations which are licensed to do business within the State of California. Agents of savings bank associations (either state or federally chartered) that are not authorized to do business in California are not exempt from obtaining a real estate license.

Scope of Exemption

The exemption for an authorized agent of a savings bank only applies to Article 5 (Transactions in Trust Deeds and Real Property Sale Contracts) and Article 6 (Real Property Securities Dealers) of the Real Estate Law.

Federal Housing Administration and Department of Veterans Affairs

The exemption from licensing requirements for loan correspondents do not apply to FHA or DVA loans.

 www.hud.gov/history.html (Housing and Urban Development)

 www.va.gov (Veterans Administration Loans)

SUMMARY

A broker is a person who, in the expectation of compensation, performs or attempts to perform designated acts for another. These acts include:

1. Selling or attempting to buy, sell or negotiate the purchase, sale or exchange of real property or of a business opportunity.

2. Lease or attempt to lease or solicit tenants or landlords for the purpose of leasing or attempting to purchase or exchange leases on real property or on a business opportunity.

3. Offering or assisting another in filing an application for purchase or lease of government owned land.

4. Soliciting borrowers or lenders or negotiating or servicing loans secured by real property or a business opportunity.

5. Offering to sell or buy or exchange real property sales contracts or promissory notes secured by real property or by a business opportunity.

6. As a principal, buying from, selling to or exchanging with the public eight or more real estate secured loans within one year.

7. Offering to sell, purchase or exchange securities or list securities for sale or exchange.

8. Offering to sell, lease or exchange mineral oil and gas property.

9. Collecting an advance fee for advertising a property.

A loan correspondent is a person who acts for a lender in arranging loans or the sale of existing loans.

Savings Banks are exempt from licensing.

CLASS DISCUSSION TOPICS

1. During a time of high interest rates a party advertised that they had access to money to lend on well secured commercial property. The rates they quoted were below market rates. They agreed to process loans at a nominal charge of $100 paid in advance. When funding was approved and placed with a named escrow (a foreign

bank) the borrower was to pay the agent a fee of from 5 percent to 10 percent of the loan. Borrowers were given the impression that this was either Arab oil money or money being laundered. The prospective borrowers were informed by a letter from a Cayman Island bank that their loans were approved and funds had been deposited in the bank. Papers were sent for final signature. After the agent was paid the commission, the loans failed to close because of claimed technical and currency delays. Apparently, although legally chartered, the bank was controlled by the agent and never had any money to loan. Discuss the violations of the law in this case.

2. Why should attempting to do an act that was never done be a violation of the real estate law?

3. Give examples of when a person would charge a fee for helping another apply for purchase or lease of government land.

4. Give examples of present advance fee brokers.

5. Why would persons pay an advance fee to list property when other brokers will promote a property without an advance fee?

CHAPTER 4 QUIZ

1. The definition of a broker requires: (p. 78)
    A. compensation actually received
    B. compensation be in money
    C. success in completion of the act requiring licensing
    D. none of the above

2. When acting for another for compensation, which of the following actions would require a real estate broker's license? (p. 79)
    A. Soliciting purchasers for real property
    B. Soliciting an exchange of a business opportunity
    C. Soliciting sellers of real property
    D. All of the above

3. Albert accepted $100 for helping a friend in applying for a lease of government land. As to this payment: (p. 79)
    A. it clearly violates the law
    B. it is alright if the work was worth the $100
    C. Albert is a real estate broker, he has done nothing wrong
    D. it would be regarded as an advance fee

4. A broker may properly: (pp. 79-81)

    A. collect payments on loans secured by real property

    B. solicit lenders for loans to be secured by real property

    C. negotiate loans to be secured by real property

    D. do any of the above

5. A person is "in the business" and requires a real estate brokers license if that person acquires how many real estate loans for resale in one year? (p. 81)

    A. 8 or more

    B. 10 or more

    C. 12 or more

    D. More than 20

6. A person need not have a real estate license if he or she: (p. 81)

    A. buys real estate for personal use

    B. sells a parcel of real estate and handles the financing himself or herself

    C. buys and sells securities as his or her own investments

    D. do any of the above

7. Advance fees are: (p. 84)

    A. commission payments received before a sale

    B. prepaid advertising costs

    C. escrow costs paid before closing

    D. any of the above

8. Advance fees collected by a broker are: (pp. 84-85)

    A. illegal

    B. void

    C. proper

    D. grounds for license revocation

9. The real estate commissioner requires that advance fee solicitation material be submitted to the commissioner: (p. 86)

    A. 24 hours prior to use

    B. 3 days prior to use

    C. 10 days prior to use

    D. 30 days prior to use

10. Who can properly receive an advance fee for soliciting a loan secured by real property? (pp. 84-85)

    A. A real estate broker

    B. A newspaper of general circulation

    C. A private investor

    D. None of the above

11. A loan correspondent is: (p. 86)

    A. a person who solicits loans by direct mail

    B. a person acting for a lender in arranging loans

    C. a foreign lender

    D. an unlicensed lender

12. Loan correspondents need not be licensed as brokers if they are authorized in writing to act as an agent of: (p. 86)

    A. a savings bank association

    B. a private trust

    C. a relative

    D. any of the above

Answers: 1. D; 2. D; 3. C; 4. D; 5. A; 6. D; 7. B; 8. C; 9. C; 10. C; 11. B; 12. A

Chapter 5

Exemptions
From Licensing Requirements

KEY WORDS AND TERMS

Agricultural Cooperative
Agricultural Credit Corporation
Attorney at Law
Cemetery Authority
Clerical Exemption
Escrow Agent
Film Location Representative

Finders Fee
Marketing Cooperative
Mineral Oil and Gas Transaction
Power of Attorney
Securities Broker
Trustee's Sale

LEARNING OBJECTIVE

In this chapter you will learn that there are a significant number of groups who are exempt from real estate licensing. Generally, these exemptions apply to particular activities and have limitations. You will see that these activities are generally removed from normal real estate brokerage activities when Department of Real Estate licensing is not required.

Broker Defined

As previously covered, Section 10131.1. of the Business and Professions Code expands and modifies Section 10131. Section 10131 defines a real estate broker as a person who performs any of the listed acts for a compensation or the expectation of a compensation "for another or others."

Section 10131.1 expands the definition to persons who engage as a principal "in the business" of buying from, selling to or exchanging with the public, real property sales contracts or promissory notes secured by real property.

This section defines "in the business" to mean any of the following:

ACQUISITION FOR RESALE

In the business includes acquiring, for the purpose of resale to the public, eight or more real property sales contracts or promissory notes secured directly or collaterally by liens on real estate during a calendar year.

SALE OR EXCHANGE

"In the business" includes the sale or exchange of **eight or more** real property sales contracts or promissory notes secured directly or collaterally by liens on real property during a calendar year.

Principal

While licensing requirements are generally based on doing acts for others, a principal deals for him or herself.

A principal generally does not require a real estate license. There are several exceptions to non-licensing of principals.

BUYING AND SELLING MORTGAGES AND TRUST DEEDS

As previously pointed out, Business and Professions 10131.1 requires persons engaged as principals "in the business" of buying from, selling to or exchanging with the public, real property sales contracts or promissory notes secured directly or collaterally by liens on real property must be licensed as real estate brokers if the transactions number eight or more in a calendar year.

The statute exempts seven or fewer transactions from licensing requirements.

MINERAL, OIL AND GAS TRANSACTIONS

A person who buys, leases or takes an option on mineral oil or gas property for the purpose of sale, exchange, lease or sublease must be licensed as a real estate broker.

There is no threshold number of MOG transactions allowed prior to the real estate broker licensing requirement.

Without Compensation

The California Attorney General (32 Ops Atty Gen. 210) has stated that "for a compensation" is critical to require licensing. According to the Attorney General, unless buying and selling of promissory notes secured by a deed of trust is done "for a compensation" the person buying and selling such notes is not a real estate broker within the requirements of the real estate law.

Doing acts without compensation may exempt a person from licensing requirements.

Case Example

In Re Porterfield (1946) 28 C 2d 91

The California Supreme Court determined that a person has the right to speak privately or in public as to social and economic advantages of home ownership. Even though this person might convince others to make purchase offers, that person cannot be subject to sanction under Business and Professions Code Sections 10130 and 10134 (now 10131).

Real estate law requires that the engagement in listed activities be for compensation.

Without compensation, licensing is not required. In this case the court held that the defendant was merely exercising a right of free speech that is guaranteed by the Constitution.

Business and Professions Code 10133

This act provides for the following exemptions from licensing:

OFFICERS OF CORPORATIONS/PARTNERS

A regular officer of a corporation or a general partner of a partnership can lease or sell real property owned by the corporation or partnership as well as buy or lease real property for the corporations or partnership.

However, the acts of such officer or partner cannot be for or in the expectation of special compensation relating to the acts. What this means is that the corporate officer or general partner can be compensated for working for the corporation or partnership but cannot receive a specific fee or commission (personally, that is) directly related to their real estate activities.

POWER OF ATTORNEY

Persons holding an executed power of attorney from the owner of real property can sell or lease the property under the power of attorney. This is based on the legal concept that if a person can deal with their own property then they can transfer that right to another.

AN ATTORNEY AT LAW

An attorney at law, while rendering legal services to a client, can buy, sell or lease real property for compensation without being licensed by the Department of Real Estate.

Examples of when an attorney at law would render legal services include the following.

Dissolution of Partnership

The attorney would arrange the disposition of property to divide the assets.

Probate

The attorney would arrange for the sale of property to pay the debts of the estate and distribute the assets.

Dissolution of Marriage

The attorney could handle the sale to allow division of the community property.

Dissolution of Joint Ownership such as Tenancy in Common

The attorney could handle a sale of the whole property (sale of the whole normally would yield significantly more than sales of undivided interests).

An attorney at law could not take sale listings or otherwise engage in licensed activities when not directly related to acting in a legal capacity.

RECEIVERS/TRUSTEES/COURT ORDERS

A receiver or trustee in bankruptcy or any person acting under orders of a court of competent jurisdiction can sell or lease property.

TRUSTEE'S SALE

A trustee for the beneficiary of a deed of trust when selling under authority of that deed of trust (trustee sale or trustee foreclosure under the power of sale in the deed of trust).

Note: Exemptions set forth above are not applicable to a person who uses or attempts to use the exemption for the purpose of evading the licensing provisions of the real estate law.

Case Example

Sheetz v. Edmonds (1988) 201 C.A. 3d 1432

Sheetz managed 23 separate properties for compensation. All of the properties were owned by a friend. Sheetz was not licensed although engaged full time in property management. Sheetz was operating under a power of attorney and he claimed Business and Professions Code 10133(a) (2) exempted him from Department of Real Estate licensing.

The real estate commissioner issued a cease and desist order for Sheetz to stop managing these properties. Sheetz was the plaintiff in this action against Edmonds (The Real Estate Commissioner). (cont'd.)

The Court of Appeals upheld the action of the real estate commissioner. The court determined that the exemption for a power of attorney applied to particular transactions or very limited periods. The exemption cannot be used as a substitute for obtaining a broker's license.

In this case, it was clear that the power of attorney was given for the purpose of evading licensing requirements.

Exemptions from License Requirements

10133(a). The acts described in Section 10131 are not acts for which a real estate license is required if performed by:

(1) A regular officer of a corporation or a general partner of a partnership with respect to real property owned or leased by the corporation or partnership, respectively, or in connection with the proposed purchase or leasing of real property by the corporation or partnership, respectively, if the acts are not performed by the officer or partner in expectation of special compensation.
(2) A person holding a duly executed power of attorney from the owner of the real property with respect to which the acts are performed.
(3) An attorney at law in rendering legal services to a client.
(4) A receiver, trustee in bankruptcy or other person acting under order of a court of competent jurisdiction.
(5) A trustee for the beneficiary of a deed of trust when selling under authority of that deed of trust.

(b). The exemptions in subdivision (a) are not applicable to a person who uses or attempts to use them for the purpose of evading the provisions of this part.

Mortgage Brokers and Lenders

Section 10133.1 of the Business and Professions Code provides for lender exemptions from licensing as real estate brokers.

This is a limited exemption, from broker licensing in that it applies to servicing loans secured by real property, soliciting borrowers or lenders for loans, offering to sell, buy or exchange notes secured by real estate (trust deeds and mortgages), negotiation of loans and handling real property security transactions. Section 10133.1 would not allow any of the exempt groups or individuals to list property for lease or resale or perform any acts not specifically covered by the exemption. Exemptions of Section 10133.1 include the following.

Licensed and Chartered Lenders

Persons and employees doing business under the law of any state or of the United States relating to banks, trust companies, savings bank associations, industrial loan companies pension trusts, credit unions or insurance companies.

> *These financial-type institutions, acting under a state or federal license or charter, can handle loan transactions and securities secured by real estate even though they are not licensed as real estate brokers.*

AGRICULTURAL COOPERATIVES

Nonprofit cooperative associations organized under the Food and Agricultural Code (agricultural cooperatives) are exempt in loaning and advancing money.

MARKETING COOPERATIVES

Corporations, associations, syndicates, joint stock companies and partnerships engaged exclusively in the business of marketing agricultural, horticultural, viticultural, dairy, livestock, poultry or bee products on a nonprofit basis are exempt in loaning and advancing money to members in connection with such business.

AGRICULTURAL CREDIT CORPORATIONS

Corporations securing money or credit from any federal intermediate credit bank organized under the Agricultural Credit Act are exempt in loaning or advancing money or credit.

ATTORNEYS AT LAW

This exemption applies to negotiations of loans in connection with providing legal services. The exemption cannot be used to evade licensing.

The attorney may not share fees or disbursement directly or indirectly with other persons who negotiated the loan or with the lender.

CORPORATION CODE LICENSEES

Exempt from licensing are personal property brokers (see Chapter 3), consumer finance lenders or a commercial finance lender while acting under the authority of their license.

CEMETERY AUTHORITY

Exempt from broker licensing are Cemetery authorities or their agents who are authorized to do business in California.

AGENTS OF SAVINGS BANK INSTITUTIONS

Any person acting under written authorization of a state or federally chartered savings bank is exempt while acting under their written authorization.

A loan correspondent can only act on behalf of one savings bank institution (Section 6520 of the California Financial Code).

SECURITIES BROKERS/DEALERS

Persons licensed as securities brokers or securities dealers under California or federal law or agent/employee of that person acting within the scope of their authority as to the sale, purchase or exchange of a security that represents an ownership in a pool of promissory notes secured directly or indirectly by liens on real estate when the transaction is subject to the laws of California or federal law governing the sale of securities (see Chapter 13).

RESIDENTIAL MORTGAGE LENDERS

Persons licensed under the Corporation Commissioner as residential mortgage lenders or servicers are exempt while acting within the scope of such license (See Chapter 3).

SERVICING LOANS

The following persons are exempt as to collection of payments or performing services for lenders in connection with loans secured directly or collaterally by real estate.

Exemptions From Licensing Requirements

Ten or Fewer Loans

Persons making collections on 10 or fewer of these loans or in the amount of forty thousand dollars ($40,000) or less in any calendar year.

This exemption applies to low volume loan servicers.

Escrow Agents

A corporation licensed as an escrow agent in accordance with the financial code when all payments are deposited and maintained in the escrow agent's trust account.

Employees of Real Estate Brokers

Employees of real estate brokers who are agents of:

a. a governmental entity or federal agency;

b. banks or other lending institutions chartered or licensed to do business in any state;

c. trustees of pension, profit sharing or welfare funds with a net worth of $15 million or more;

d. any corporation having securities registered under Section 12 of the Security Exchange Act of 1934 (a public company); or

e. any syndication or combination of the above organized to purchase promissory notes.

Brokers - Lenders - Exemptions from License

10133.1(a). Subdivisions (d) and (e) of Section 10131, Section 10131.1, Article 5 (commencing with Section 10230), Article 6 (commencing with Section 10237) and Article 7 (commencing with Section 10240) and Section 1695.13 of the Civil Code do not apply to any of the following:

(1) Any person or employee thereof doing business under any law of this state, any other state, or of the United States relating to banks, trust companies, savings bank associations, industrial loan companies, pension trusts, credit unions or insurance companies.

(2) Any nonprofit cooperative association organized under Chapter 1 (commencing with Section 54001) of Division 20 of the Food and Agricultural Code, in loaning or advancing money in connection with any activity mentioned therein.

(3) Any corporation, association, syndicate, joint stock company or partnership engaged exclusively in the business of marketing agricultural, horticultural, viticultural, dairy, livestock, poultry or bee products on a cooperative nonprofit basis, in loaning or advancing money to the members thereof or in connection with any such business.

(4) Any corporation securing money or credit from any federal intermediate credit bank organized and existing pursuant to the provisions of an act of Congress entitled the "Agricultural Credits Act of 1923," in loaning or advancing money or credit so secured.

(5) Any person licensed to practice law in this state, not actively and principally engaged in the business of negotiating loans secured by real property, when that person renders services in the course of his or her practice as an attorney at law, and the disbursements of that person, whether paid by the borrower or other person, are not charges or costs and expenses regulated by or subject to the limitations of Article 7 (commencing with Section 10240), provided the fees and disbursements shall not be shared, directly or indirectly, with the person negotiating the loan or the lender.

(6) Any person licensed as a personal property broker, a consumer finance lender or a commercial finance lender when acting under the authority of that license.

(7) Any cemetery authority as defined by Section 7018 of the Health and Safety Code which is authorized to do business in this state or its authorized agent.

(8) Any person authorized in writing by a savings institution to act as an agent of that institution, as authorized by Section 6520 of the Financial Code or comparable authority of the Federal Home Loan Bank Board by its regulations, when acting under the authority of such written authorization.

(9) Any person who is licensed as a securities broker or securities dealer under any law of this state, or of the United States, or any employee, officer or agent of that person, if that person, employee, officer or agent is acting within the scope of authority granted by that license in connection with a transaction involving the offer, sale, purchase or exchange of a security representing an ownership interest in a pool of promissory notes secured directly or indirectly by liens on real property, which transaction is subject to any law of this state or the Untied States regulating the offer or sale of securities.

(10) Any person licensed as a residential mortgage lender or servicer when acting under the authority of that license.

(b). Persons described in paragraph (1), (2) or (3) are exempt from the provisions of subdivisions (d) and (e) of Section 10131 or Section 10131.1 with respect to the collection of payments or performance of services for lenders or on notes of owners in connection with loans secured directly or collaterally by liens on real property:

(1) The person makes collections on 10 or less of those loans, or in amounts of forty thousand dollars ($40,000) or less in any calendar year.

(2) The person is a corporation licensed as an escrow agent under Division 6 (commencing with Section 17000) of the Financial Code and the payments are deposited and maintained in the escrow agent's trust account.

(3) An employee of a real estate broker who is acting as the agent of a person described in paragraph (4) of subdivision (b) of Section 10232.4.

For purposes of this subdivision, performance of services does not include soliciting borrowers, lenders or purchasers for, or negotiating, loans secured directly or collaterally by a lien on real property.

Other Exemptions - Business and Professions Code 10133.15

These exemptions only apply to Article 5 (B&PC 10230 et seq.) and Article 7 (B&PC 10248 et seq. (mortgage loan broker activities).

Exempt from licensing as real estate brokers are persons whose business is that of acting as an authorized representative, agent or loan correspondent (or any person or employee thereof) doing business under any state or federal law relating to banks, trust companies, savings bank associations, industrial loan companies, pensions trusts, credit unions or insurance companies. The exemption also applies when making loans qualified for sale to any of the above.

Other Exemptions

10133.15. The provisions of Articles 5 (commencing with Section 10230), 6 (commencing with Section 10237) and 7 (commencing with Section 10240) of this chapter do not apply to any person whose business is that of acting as an authorized representative, agent or loan correspondent of any person or employee thereof doing business under any law of this state, any other state or of the United States relating to banks, trust companies, savings bank associations, industrial loan companies, pension trusts, credit unions or insurance companies or when making loans qualified for sale to any of the foregoing insofar as such business is concerned.

Clerical Exemption

Persons performing clerical work, such as stenographers, bookkeepers, receptionists, telephone operators and other clerical personnel are exempt while carrying on their clerical function.

Managers and Employees - Business and Professions Code 10131.01

The licensing for leasing activity as set forth in Business and Professions 10131 (a) and (b) do not apply to the following.

MANAGER

A manager of a hotel, motel or auto and trailer park, resident manager of an apartment building, apartment complex or court or to an employee of any such manager.

TRANSIENT OCCUPANCY

Any person or entity (including an employee of a broker) who solicits or arranges and accepts reservations and/or money for transient occupancies in a single-family dwelling or apartment building or complex.

EMPLOYEES OF PROPERTY MANAGEMENT FIRMS

Nonresident employees of property management firms under the control or supervision of a broker need not be licensed to handle management. Activities allowed by such an employee include the following.

Showing

Showing rental units and common areas to prospective tenants.

Rental Applications

Providing or accepting preprinted rental applications, or responding to inquiries from prospective tenants concerning the completion of the application.

Deposits

Accepting deposits or fees for credit checks or administrative costs and accepting security deposits and rents.

Information

Providing information about rental rates and other terms and provisions of a lease or rental agreement as set out in a schedule provided by an employer.

Lease Acceptance

Accepting signed leases and rental agreements from prospective tenants.

FCC Regulated Enterprises

The licensing provisions of Business and Professions Code 10131 and 10131.2 relating to business opportunities do not apply to persons acting for others, who offer, sell, offer to sell, solicits prospective sellers or purchasers of, solicits or obtains listings of, advertises for sale, buys or offers to buy or negotiates the purchase, sale or exchange of radio, television or cable enterprises which are licensed and regulated by the Federal Communications Commission.

The purchase, sale or exchange of radio, television or cable business opportunities are not regarded as a transfer of real property but are nevertheless exempted from Business Opportunity Sales requirement of licensing.

Mineral, Oil and Gas Exemptions

Business and Professions Code 10133.35 exempts the following limited "mineral, oil and gas activities" from licensing as a real estate broker.

DEPOSITORY

Acting as a depository under an oil lease, gas lease or oil and gas lease for purposes other than a sale.

COURT ORDER

Engaging in any transaction by order of a court of competent jurisdiction.

PRODUCTION

Engaging in the business of drilling for or producing oil or gas or mining for or producing minerals.

NEGOTIATING LEASES

Negotiating lease agreement between an owner of mineral oil or gas lands, lease or mineral rights and a person organized for or engaging in oil or gas or mineral or metal production, or entering leases or agreements with an owner of oil or gas lands, leases or mineral rights on behalf of a disclosed or undisclosed person organized for and engaging in oil, gas and mineral or metal production.

Film Location Representative

A person acting in the capacity of a "film location representative in connection with a transaction" is exempt from real estate licensing.

Exemption - Film Location Representative

1033.4(a). The provisions of subdivision (b) of Section 10131 do not apply to persons acting in the capacity of a film location representative in connection with a transaction which complies with the requirements of subdivision (c).

(b). As used in this section:

(1) "Film location representative" means an employee of a principal arranging for the use of real property for photographic purposes.
(2) "Principal" means the person who will use the real property for photographic purposes.

(c). In every transaction arranged by a film location representative, the principal shall maintain liability insurance insuring both that principal and the real property owner against death, bodily injury and property damage arising out of or in connection with the use, ownership or maintenance of the real property which is the subject of the transaction. The amount of the insurance coverage shall not be less than five hundred thousand dollars ($500,000) per person or one million dollars ($1,000,000) per occurrence for personal injury and five hundred thousand dollars ($500,000) for property damage. It must be issued by an insurance carrier authorized to sell such insurance in California.

Exemptions from Articles 5 and 6

The licensing requirements for loan brokers and persons engaged in real property security transactions need not be complied with for any person who is an approved lender, mortgagee, seller or servicer for the Federal Housing Administration, Department of Veterans Affairs, Rural Economic and Community Development Administration, Government National Mortgage Association, Federal National Mortgage Association or Federal Home Loan Mortgage Corporation as to making loans to be sold to or when servicing loans on behalf of and subject to audit by any of the above with respect to those loans. (**Business and Professions Code 10133.5**)

No Negotiations

Finders fees are legal in California providing the finder is "simply paid for introducing the parties and takes no part in the negotiations."

This distinction is set forth in *Spielberg v. Granz* (1966) 185 C.A. 2d 283.

In *Tyrone v. Kelley* (1973), 9 C 3d 1, the California Supreme Court indicated that the licensing statutes inclusion of the word "solicits" as to borrowers and lenders was not intended that a finders exception to licensing be made inapplicable. Finders can be compensated.

SUMMARY

Section 10131.1 of the Business and Professions Code requires persons "in the business" of buying, selling to or exchanging with the public, real estate sales contracts or notes secured by real property to be licensed as real estate brokers. The section describes eight or more transactions as being in the business, so seven or fewer transactions in a single year would be an exemption from licensing.

Principals, acting for themselves, are generally exempt from licensing with the exceptions of handling eight or more of the transactions described in the prior paragraph or buying, leasing or taking options on mineral oil and gas property for the purpose of sale, lease or exchange. [There is no threshold exemption for mineral, oil and gas (MOG) transactions.]

Generally, performing acts without compensation or the expectation of compensation exempts a person from broker licensing.

Business and Professions Code Section 10133 exempts the following from licensing (with some limitations):

1. Officers of corporations and general partners.
2. Persons operating under a power of attorney.
3. An attorney at law while acting as an attorney at law.
4. Receivers, trustees and others acting under a court order.
5. Trustees selling under a power of sale in a trust deed.

Section 10133.1 of the Business and Professions Code exempts the following from broker licensing as related to the mortgage loan activities of servicing loans, soliciting borrowers or lenders, offering to sell, buy or exchange real estate secured loans, negotiating loans and handling real property security transactions:

1. Licensed and chartered lenders.
2. Agricultural cooperatives.
3. Agricultural marketing cooperatives.
4. Agricultural credit corporations.
5. Attorney at law.
6. Corporation code licensees.
7. Cemetery authority agents.

8. Agents of savings institutions.

9. Securities brokers/dealers.

10. Residential mortgage lenders (corporation code).

11. Certain loan servicers:

    a. Ten or fewer loans in the amount of $40,000 or less in any year.

    b. Escrow agents.

    c. Employees of real estate brokers who are agents of certain designated principals.

Also exempt from broker licensing are representatives of persons doing business under any law relating to banks, trust companies, savings bank associations, industrial loan companies, pension trusts or insurance companies. (Applies to Article 5 and Article 7 mortgage-loan broker activities).

Persons performing clerical duties such as bookkeepers, receptionists, telephone operators and other clerical duties are exempt from licensing while performing such duties.

There are a number of exemptions from licensing for persons involved in property management. They include:

1. Managers of hotels, motels, auto and trailer parks.

2. Resident managers of apartment structures or complexes.

3. Handling transient occupancy in single-family dwellings or apartments.

4. Employees of property management firms working under the supervision of a broker.

There is a special business opportunity exemption for transactions involving FCC regulated enterprises (radio, television and cable enterprises).

Some mineral oil and gas activities are exempt from licensing. These include:

1. Acting as a depository for funds from other than a sale.

2. Acting under a court order.

3. Engaging in production activities relating to mineral, oil and gas.

4. Negotiating MOG leases for an entity engaged in MOG production.

5. Dealing with mineral rights or other land rights as a principal. (Not buying for resale.)

Film location representatives are exempt from licensing for their leasing or purchase activities.

A number of approved lenders are exempt from licensing activities dealing with Article 5 and Article 6 of the real estate law.

Finders who do not negotiate but merely introduce parties may receive compensation for their activities even though they are not licensed.

CLASS DISCUSSION TOPICS

1. Finders fees are illegal in some states. What are the dangers associated with allowing brokers and others to pay finders fees to unlicensed individuals?

2. Why should a principal be limited in the number of trust deeds he or she can buy and sell when there are no limits on the number of properties that some persons can buy and sell without having a real estate license?

3. Why should a person without a license be able to buy and sell real property but is restricted from buying mineral, oil and gas leases or rights for the purpose of resale?

4. Could a nonprofit organization list and sell real estate without a a license if they did not receive any compensation?

5. An official of a pension fund saw an advertisement in the Wall Street Journal where a firm agreed to pay a fee of 10 percent to anyone who could locate a $4,000,000 first mortgage for them on raw land appraised at $6,500,000. The official called about the ad and obtained a written finders fee agreement. The pension fund official had the prospective borrower submit the loan application to the pension fund. The pension fund official voted for the loan and convinced others to do the same.

Discuss the issues raised by this actual case example.

CHAPTER 5 QUIZ

1. A real estate license is required if a person buys, for the purpose of resale, real estate sales contracts or promissory notes secured by real estate when during a calendar year the number of such transactions is: (p. 94)

    A. 3 or more
    B. 7 or more
    C. 8 or more
    D. 12 or more

2. A person who buys mineral, oil and gas leases for the purpose of resale is exempt from broker licensing if he engages in: (p. 95)

    A. only one transaction per year

    B. no more than seven transactions in any year

    C. eight or more transactions in any year

    D. none of the above would exempt a person from licensing

3. A former broker, whose license had expired, handled a sale of real property for a friend. The former broker would have done nothing wrong if: (p. 95)

    A. the license was brought current within two years of expiration

    B. the work was performed without compensation

    C. the friend agreed in writing to the representation with the knowledge that the former broker was no longer license

    D. the broker donated the commission to charity

4. An officer of a corporation would NOT be exempt from licensing if she sold corporate property: (p. 96)

    A. as part of her normal corporate duties

    B. received additional compensation for making the sale

    C. if the corporation were publicly owned

    D. was paid on a salary basis

5. A person whose license was revoked could act as a broker in listing and selling property if he: (p. 96)

    A. had each owner give him a power of attorney

    B. obtained a license to practice law

    C. either A or B

    D. neither A nor B

6. A person opened an office for the purpose of making loans, selling loans and brokering loans. While the person was not licensed as a real estate broker, it was alright since she: (pp. 98-99)

    A. was licensed as a securities dealer

    B. was acting under a power of attorney from a lender

    C. did not service the loans she arranged

    D. was licensed by the corporation commissioner as a residential mortgage lender

7. Activities that are exempt from state licensing would include: (pp. 104-105)

   A. typing loan applications
   B. preparing loan applications for broker approval
   C. handling the books of a mortgage broker
   D. all of the above

8. Which of the following would be exempt from real estate licensing? (p. 104)

   A. The manager of a hotel
   B. The resident manager of an apartment building
   C. The manager of a trailer park
   D. All of the above

9. An employee of a broker who does not have a real estate license can properly: (p. 105)

   A. show rental units to prospective renters
   B. accept preprinted rental applications from prospective tenants
   C. accept deposits for credit checks
   D. all of the above

10. A person engaged in the sale of business opportunities did not have a California real estate brokers license. This was alright because the person specialized in: (p. 105)

   A. financing sales with her own funds
   B. mobile home parks
   C. radio stations
   D. businesses having fewer than six employees

11. Mineral, oil and gas activities that are exempt from broker licensing include: (p. 106)

   A. acting under court order
   B. selling mineral rights as the owner of the land
   C. engaging in drilling for oil
   D. all of the above

12. A person received $10,000 for introducing a prospective buyer of a California apartment complex to the owner of the property. The person was not licensed by the Department of Real Estate. Receiving the fee would be proper if the person receiving the fee was: (p. 107)

   A. licensed by the Department of Corporations
   B. paid for the introduction only and played no part in the negotiations
   C. licensed as a securities dealer
   D. also the person who convinced the buyer to place the offer and the seller to accept it

Answers: 1. C; 2. D; 3. B; 4. B; 5. C; 6. D; 7. D; 8. D; 9. D; 10. C; 11. D; 12. B

Exemptions From Licensing Requirements

Chapter 6

Supervision and Licensing Compliance

KEY WORDS AND TERMS

Blockbusting
Branch Office
Cold Calling (Telemarketing)
Commingling
Comparative Market Analysis
Fictitious Name
Fictitious Name Statement
Fraud

Misrepresentation
Mortgage Loan Consultants
Open House
Secret Profit
Send-out Slip
Service Providers
Unlicensed Assistants

LEARNING OBJECTIVES

In this chapter you will learn:

1. responsibilities of a real estate broker or designated officer to supervise salespersons and brokers working under their direction;
2. actions and activities that are violations of the law which subject a licensee to disciplinary action by the Department of Real Estate;
3. broker's duty to notify the Department of Real Estate as to changes in employment as well as license violations of salespersons;
4. the requirement for branch offices;
5. the use of and requirements for the use of fictitious names;
6. the commissioner's guidelines for use of unlicensed assistants covering telemarketing (cold calling), loan processing, documentation preparation and compliance;
7. additional problems in telemarketing involving senior citizens; and
8. abuses by mortgage loan consultants.

Responsibility of Broker or Designated Officer to Supervise

A broker has both a "need and legal duty to supervise" his or her salespeople.

NEED TO SUPERVISE

A broker is liable for wrongful acts of his or her salespeople within the scope of employment. This means that a broker could be held financially liable for acts of others who seemingly could be beyond the control of the broker.

The need to supervise should really begin at the time of hiring. Because a salesperson has met state licensing requirements does not mean that the salesperson will act properly.

> *For their own protection, brokers should know as much about the character of their salespersons as reasonably possible.*

In a multi-salesperson office, salespersons generally spend a great deal of time out of the office dealing with buyers, sellers, lessors, lessees, lenders and/or borrowers. It is impossible for a broker to monitor every aspect of a salesperson's activities. Even when in the office, much of the salesperson's activities are private, such as telephone conversations. Monitoring salespersons telephone calls is considered unprofessional by many, and even if it were done with the knowledge of the salesperson, such monitoring raises ethical questions. In this type of environment, salespersons tend to be evaluated in the following two ways.

Results

If a salesperson is producing completed transactions, the salesperson is generally considered a good salesperson.

Complaints

Often the first inclination a broker receives about a problem with a salesperson is a complaint from another salesperson or from the public.

> *Correction of a problem after the fact can be expensive and it might also place the broker's license in jeopardy.*

Case Situation

A large California brokerage firm realized that the firm had very few sales involving Mexican-American buyers and sellers. The firm did not employ any Spanish-speaking agents. To gain a part of this market, the firm was successful in hiring a Mexican-American agent fluent in Spanish.

The agent was very successful and became one of the top producers in the office. Her sales almost exclusively involved Spanish-speaking buyers, many of whom had extremely limited skills in speaking English.

The first inclination of a problem occurred when an English-speaking relative of one of the agent's prospective buyers contacted the broker. The firm's agent had refused to give the relatives back their $1,000 good-faith deposit despite the fact that she (the agent) had been unable to find the prospective buyers a home which met their needs.

Investigation by the broker revealed that the agent demanded a fee which she called a good-faith deposit of $1,000. After receipt of this fee, she would find the prospective buyers a home. The fee was for the agent's efforts and did not apply to the purchase price of the property. Apparently over 20 such fees were received.

Only through a complaint did the broker learn of these unauthorized advance fees which violated a number of statutes.

Case Example

Barry v. Raskov (1991) 232 C. A. 3d 447

This case involved a mortgage broker who hired an independent appraiser to appraise a home. There was an existing $100,000 loan on the home and the owner was seeking an additional $175,000 at 23 percent interest. The loan documentation indicated that after the loan, there would still be an owner-equity cushion of $125,000 based on the $400,000 appraisal.

A loan was made and the borrower defaulted on the first payment. Raskov, the broker, hired another appraiser who concluded that the property was only worth $98,000. One comparable for the first appraisal did not exist and another was a nursery school sold as a business. A third appraisal was only half the size shown and sold for $175,000 and not the $375,00 claimed. (cont'd.)

Broker Raskov claimed that the first appraiser was an independent contractor who worked for the defendant on a fee basis.

While not allowing punitive damages, the trial court awarded the plaintiff investor his investment plus 23 percent interest. The appeals court agreed that there was no clear evidence of broker fraud so punitive damages were not allowed.

The court held that it was proper to hold the employer liable since the relationship was such as to impose an employer/employee relationship (the broker used the appraiser on a regular basis). The court noted that the broker could exert considerable leverage over the workmanship of the appraiser through the incentive for future business.

LEGAL DUTY TO SUPERVISE

Business and Professions Code 10177(h) provides that brokers are subject to disciplinary action if they fail to "exercise reasonable supervision and control over the activities of their salespersons."

This section also provides that this duty extends to the designated officer of a corporate licensee as to the control of activities of the corporation for which a real estate license is required.

Section 10159 of the Business and Professions Code provides that any licensed officer of a corporation licensed to act as a real estate broker is licensed only for and on behalf of the corporation as an officer of that corporation (the license cannot be used for non-corporate activities).

Further Grounds for Disciplinary Action

10177. The commissioner may suspend or revoke the license of any real estate licensee, or may deny the issuance of a license to an applicant, who has done, or may suspend or revoke the license of, or deny the issuance of a license to, a corporate applicant if an officer, director or person owning or controlling 10 percent or more of the corporation's stock has done, any of the following:

(a). Procure, or attempted to procure, a real estate license or license renewal, for himself or herself or any salesperson, by fraud, misrepresentation or deceit or by making any material misstatement of fact in an application for a real estate license, license renewal or reinstatement.

(b). Entered a plea of guilty or *nolo contendere* to, or been found guilty of, or been convicted of, a felony or a crime involving moral turpitude**...**

(c). Knowingly authorized, directed, connived at or aided in, the publication, advertisement, distribution or circulation of any material false statement or representation concerning his or her business, or any business opportunity or any land or subdivision (as defined in Chapter 1 (commencing with Section 11000) of Part 2) offered for sale.

(d). Willfully disregarded or violated the Real Estate Law Part 1 (commencing with Section 10000) or Chapter 1 (commencing with Section 11000) of Part 2 or the rules and regulations of the commissioner for the administration and enforcement of the Real Estate Law and Chapter 1 (commencing with Section 11000) of Part 2.

(e). Willfully used the term "realtor" or any trade name or insignia of membership in any real estate organization of which the licensee is not a member.

(f). Acted or conducted himself or herself in a manner which would have warranted the denial of his or her application for a real estate license**...**

(g). Demonstrated negligence or incompetence in performing any act for which he or she is required to hold a license.

(h). As a broker licensee, failed to exercise reasonable supervision over the activities of his or her salespersons, or, as the officer designated by a corporate broker licensee, failed to exercise reasonable supervision and control of the activities of the corporation for which a real estate license is required.

(i). Has used his or her employment by a governmental agency in a capacity giving access to records, other than public records, in such manner as to violate the confidential nature of the records.

(j). Engaged in any other conduct, whether of the same or a different character than specified in this section, which constitutes fraud or dishonest dealing.

(k). Violated any of the terms, conditions, restrictions and limitations contained in any order granting a restricted license.

(l). Solicited or induced the sale, lease or the listing for sale or lease, of residential property on the ground, wholly or in part, of loss of value, increase in crime or decline of the quality of the schools, due to the present or prospective entry into the neighborhood of a person or persons of another race, color, religion, ancestry or national origin.

(m). Violated the Franchise Investment Law Division 5 (commencing with Section 31000) of Title 4 of the Corporations Code or regulations of the Commissioner of Corporations pertaining thereto.

(n). Violated the Corporations Code or the regulations of the Commissioner of Corporations relating to securities as specified in Section 25206 of the Corporations Code.

(o). Failed to disclose to the buyer of real property in a transaction in which the licensee is an agent for the buyer, the nature and extent of a licensee's direct or indirect ownership interest in that real property**...**

The commissioner may not deny or suspend the license of a corporate real estate broker if the offending officer, director or stockholder has been completely disassociated from any affiliation or ownership in the corporation.

Corporations - Authority of Licensed Officer

10159. Each officer of a corporation through whom it is licensed to act as a real estate broker is, while so employed under such license, a licensed real estate broker, but licensed only to act as such for and on behalf of the corporation as an officer.

Notification Duties of Real Estate Brokers

EMPLOYMENT AND TERMINATION

Section 10161.8 of the Business and Professions Code requires that a broker "notify the commissioner immediately and in writing whenever employment of a real estate salesperson is terminated."

The commissioner must also be notified of the following.

Address of Licensee Changes

The broker should also mark out the former address on the face of the license and type or write the new address on the reverse side and initial it.

New Employees

When a real estate salesperson changes brokers, the name of the former broker on the face of the license shall also be marked off and the new broker's name shall be written on the reverse side and initialed.

DISCHARGE FOR VIOLATIONS

Business and Professions Code Section 10178 provides that when a salesperson is discharged for a violation of the real estate law that could subject the salesperson to disciplinary action by the commissioner, a certified written statement of the facts must be immediately provided the commissioner.

The broker's failure to notify the commissioner could result in suspension or revocation of the broker's license.

Effect of Salesperson Violation on Broker

While a broker could be civilly liable for a wrongful act of a salesperson, even though the broker had no guilty knowledge of such violation, Section 10179 of the Business and Professions Code provides that a violation by the salesperson shall not cause the revocation or suspension of the broker's license unless it appears that the employer had guilty knowledge of such violation. **GUILTY KNOWLEDGE** *could include knowing an action was to be taken which would be in violation of the law and failing to take proper steps to prevent it.*

Business and Professions Code Section 10180 provides that the commissioner can deny, suspend or revoke a real estate license of a corporate officer or agent acting under its license without revoking the license of the corporation.

Additional Violations Leading to Disciplinary Action

There are other statutes in addition to Business and Professions Code Section 10177 set forth earlier in this chapter.

BUSINESS AND PROFESSIONS CODE 10171

Code 10171 provides that in addition to paragraph (h) which is the duty to supervise, a license may be subject to disciplinary action when:

1. The licensee procured or attempted to procure a real estate license or license renewal by fraud or by making a material misstatement of fact or license application or renewal. As an example, some license applicants have tried to have others take the license examination for them.

2. The licensee has entered a guilty or no contest plea or has been found guilty of a felony or a crime involving moral turpitude.

3. Knowingly engaged in the use of false statements or misrepresentations concerning the agents business, a business opportunity or any land or subdivision.

4. The licensee willfully disregarded or violated the real estate law or rules and regulations of the commissioner for the administration and enforcement of the real estate law.

5. The licensee used the term "Realtor" or any trade name or insignia of any real estate organization of which the licensee is not a member.

6. The licensee's conduct would have warranted denial of a license or has had a license denied, revoked or suspended by another agency or another state if that action would have been grounds for disciplinary action by the Department of Real Estate.

7. The licensee has demonstrated negligence or incompetence in performing any licensed act.

8. The licensee has used his or her government employment giving access to records so as to violate the confidentiality of the records. As an example, a licensee on a planning commission might inform a favored client of a proposed zoning change that was not yet made public which might have a significant effect on property value.

9. The licensee has engaged in conduct other than specified that constitutes fraud or dishonest dealings.

10. The licensee has violated the conditions of a restricted license.

11. The licensee has engaged in blockbusting by soliciting the sale or lease of residential property due to a claimed increase in crime or loss of value because of entry into the neighborhood of persons of another race, color, religion, ancestry or national origin.

12. The licensee has violated provisions of the Franchise Investment Law.

13. The licensee has violated the regulations of the Corporation Commissioner relating to securities.

14. The licensee failed to reveal an agents interest in property to a buyer or a close relationship of the licensee to the owner.

Note: For the above violations, the commissioner may not deny or suspend the license of a corporate real estate broker if the offending officer, director or stockholder has been completely disassociated from any affiliation or ownership in the corporation.

BUSINESS AND PROFESSIONS CODE 10176

Business and Professions Code 10176 also contains violations that can result in disciplinary action against a licensee. These violations include:

1. Making any substantial misrepresentation.

2. Making a false promise of a character likely to influence or persuade others to act.

3. Engaging in a continued and flagrant course of misrepresentation.

4. Acting for more than one party to a transaction without the knowledge or consent of all parties thereto.

5. Commingling personal or business funds with funds of others.

6. Claiming a compensation under an exclusive listing that does not include a definite termination date.

7. Making a secret profit.

8. Exercising an option taken with a listing without disclosing the amount of the licensees profit and obtaining the owner's consent to such profit.

9. Any other conduct which constitutes fraud or dishonest dealing.

10. Use of a "send out slip" where person agrees only to deal for a property through the named agent without the written authorization of the owner.

BUSINESS AND PROFESSIONS CODE 10176.5

This section provides for disciplinary action for violation of the Civil Code Section 1102 et seq. which deals with required disclosures upon transfer of residential real estate.

Real Estate Transfer Disclosure Statement Violations

10176.5(a). The commissioner may, upon his or her own motion, and shall upon receiving a verified complaint in writing from any person, investigate an alleged violation of Article 1.5 (commencing with Section 1102) of Chapter 2 of Title 4 of Part 4 of Division 2 of the Civil Code by any real estate licensee within this state. The commissioner may suspend or revoke a licensee's license if the licensee acting under the license has willfully or repeatedly violated any of the provisions of Article 1.5 (commencing with Section 1102) of Chapter 2 of Title 4 of Part 4 of Division 2 of the Civil Code.

(b). Notwithstanding any other provision of Article 1.5 (commencing with Section 1102) of Chapter 2 of Title 4 of Part 4 of Division 2 of the Civil Code, and in lieu of any other civil remedy, subdivision (a) of this section is the only remedy available for violations of Section 1102.6b of the Civil Code by any real estate licensee within this state.

BUSINESS AND PROFESSIONS CODE 10177.1

This section provides for suspension without a hearing in cases where a license was obtained by fraud, misrepresentation or deceit, or by the making of a material misstatement of fact in the application for the license.

Suspension Without Hearing for Fraud, etc., in Obtaining a License

10177.1. The commissioner may, without a hearing, suspend the license of any person who procured the issuance of the license to himself by fraud, misrepresentation, deceit or by the making of any material misstatement of fact in his application for such license.

The power of the commissioner under this section to order a suspension of a license shall expire 90 days after the date of issuance of said license and the suspension itself shall remain in effect only until the effective date of a decision of the commissioner after a hearing conducted pursuant to Section 10100 and the provisions of this section.

A statement of issues as defined in Section 11504 of the Government Code shall be filed and served upon the respondent with the order of suspension. Service by certified or registered mail directed to the respondent's current address of record on file with the commissioner shall be effective service.

The respondent shall have 30 days after service of the order of suspension and statement of issues in which to file with the commissioner a written request for hearing on the statement of issues filed against him or her. The commissioner shall hold a hearing within 30 days after receipt of the request therefore unless the respondent shall request or agree to a continuance thereof...

A hearing conducted under this section shall in all respects, except as otherwise expressly provided herein, conform to the substantive and procedural provisions of Chapter 5 (commencing with Section 11500) of Part 1 of Division 3 of Title 2 of the Government Code applicable to a hearing on a statement of issues.

BUSINESS AND PROFESSIONS CODE 10177.2

This section deals with mobile home sale violations. Violations include:

1. Using a false or fictitious name or knowingly concealing any material fact in the application for registration of a mobile home.
2. Failing to provide for the delivery of a properly endorsed certificate of ownership or title to a mobile home from the seller to the buyer.
3. Knowingly participating in the purchase, sale or disposal of a stolen mobile home.
4. Submitting a check to the Department of Housing and Community Development for an obligation or fee due the state that is dishonored.

BUSINESS AND PROFESSIONS CODE 10177.4

Section 10177.4 provides for disciplinary action against a licensee who claims, demands or receives compensation or referral of customers to an escrow agent, structural pest control firm, home protection company, title insurer, controlled escrow company or underwritten title company.

Figure 6-1

Fraudulent Loan Applications

From the March 7, 1997 issue of the Los Angeles Times:

Twenty-seven indictments were issued against Southern California mortgage brokers as a result of FBI stings known as "Phony Funds" and "Broker Bust". Posing as persons wanting home loans, agents targeted brokers who were believed to have submitted fraudulent loan documentation to federally insured lenders in order for borrowers, who would otherwise fail to qualify for loans, to qualify for loans.

In some instances, brokers fabricated a source of income for loan applicants and even provided false tax returns and supporting employment dates.

Five-hundred million in fraudulent loan applications are reported annually in the Los Angeles and Orange County area. Jean Kawahara, an assistant U.S. Attorney in Santa Ana, stated that one of the reasons for this sting was to target the professionals.

Defrauding a federally insured lender or agency is a federal crime punishable by up to 30 years imprisonment and up to one million in fines.

Referral of Customers for Compensation

10177.4. Notwithstanding any other provision of law, the commissioner may, after hearing in accordance with the provisions of this part relating to hearings, suspend or revoke the license of a real estate licensee who claims, demands or receives a commission, fee or other consideration, as compensation or inducement, for referral of customers to any escrow agent, structural pest control firm, home protection company, title insurer, controlled escrow company or underwritten title company.

The term "other consideration" as used in this section does not include:

(1) Bona fide payments for goods or facilities actually furnished by a licensee or for services actually performed by a licensee, provided such

payments are reasonably related to the value of the goods, facilities or services furnished;

(2) Furnishing of documents, services, information, advertising, educational materials or items of a like nature which are customary in the real estate business and which relate to the product or services of the furnisher and which are available on a similar and essentially equal basis to all customers or the agents of such customers of the furnisher;

(3) Moderate expenses for food, meals, beverages and similar items furnished to individual licensees or groups or associations of licensees within a context of customary business, educational or promotional practices pertaining to the business of the furnisher; or

(4) Items of a character and magnitude similar to those in subsections (2) and (3) which are promotional of the furnisher's business customary in the real estate business, and available on a similar and essentially equal basis to all customers, or the agents of such customers, of the furnisher.

Nothing in this section shall relieve any licensee of the obligation of disclosure otherwise required by this part.

BUSINESS AND PROFESSIONS CODE 10177.5

Section 10177.5 provides that a licensee is subject to disciplinary action if a judgment is obtained in a civil action based upon fraud, misrepresentation or deceit with reference to a transaction for which a license is required.

Fraud in a Civil Action

10177.5. When a final judgment is obtained in a civil action against any real estate licensee upon grounds of fraud, misrepresentation or deceit with reference to any transaction for which a license is required under this division, the commissioner may, after hearing in accordance with the provisions of this part relating to hearings, suspend or revoke the license of such real estate licensee.

BUSINESS AND PROFESSIONS CODE 10185

Section 10185 provides that violations listed in prior sections shall be considered misdemeanors punishable by a fine not to exceed $10,000 and/or up to six months imprisonment.

Violations are Misdemeanors

10185. Any person, including officers, directors, agents or employees of corporations, who willfully violates or knowingly participates in the violation of this division shall be guilty of a misdemeanor punishable by a fine not exceeding ten thousand dollars ($10,000), or by imprisonment in the county jail not exceeding six months, or by a fine and imprisonment.

BUSINESS AND PROFESSIONS CODE 10175.2

Section 10175.2 provides that the commissioner has the authority to permit a licensee to pay a mandatory penalty for a violation in lieu of license suspension.

Monetary Penalty in Lieu of Suspension

(Editor's Note: Text of section operative July 1, 1997.)

10175.2(a). If the Real Estate Commissioner determines that the public interest and public welfare will be adequately served by permitting a real estate licensee to pay a monetary penalty to the department in lieu of an actual license suspension, the commissioner may, on the petition of the licensee, stay the execution of all or some part of the suspension on the condition that the licensee pay a monetary penalty and the further condition that the licensee incur no other cause for disciplinary action with a period of time specified by the commissioner**...**

(d). The amount of the monetary penalty payable under this section shall not exceed two hundred fifty dollars ($250) for each day of suspension stayed nor a total of ten thousand dollars ($10,000) per decision regardless of the number of days of suspension stayed under the decision.

(e). Any monetary penalty received by the department pursuant to this section shall be credited to the Recovery Account of the Real Estate Fund.

Responsibility to Review Documents

The Commissioner's Regulation 2725 formerly required broker review, initialing and dating of all transaction documents of his or her salespeople within 5 days after preparation or signing, or before close of escrow whichever comes first.

This 5-day review has been changed by a rewritten Section 2725 of the Commissioner's Regulations. The broker is charged with reasonable supervision of the activities of his or her salespeople. *REASONABLE SUPERVISION includes the establishment of policies, rules, procedures and systems as well as a system to monitor compliance of a salesperson's activities set forth in the regulations.*

The broker is allowed to use the services of salespersons and other brokers to assist in administering salesperson supervision.

2725. Broker Supervision

A broker shall exercise reasonable supervision over the activities of his or her salespersons. Reasonable supervision includes, as appropriate, the establishment of policies, rules, procedures and systems to review, oversee, inspect and manage:

(a) Transactions requiring a real estate license.

(b) Documents which may have a material effect upon the rights or obligations of a party to the transaction.

(c) Filing, storage and maintenance of such documents.

(d) The handling of trust funds.

(e) Advertising of any service for which a license is required.

(f) Familiarizing salespersons with the requirements of federal and state laws relating to the prohibition of discrimination.

(g) Regular and consistent reports of licensed activities of salespersons.

The form and event of such policies, rules, procedures and systems shall take into consideration the number of salespersons employed and the number and location of branch officers.

A broker shall establish a system for monitoring compliance with such policies, rules, procedures and systems. A broker may use the services of brokers and salespersons to assist in administering the provision of this section so long as the broker does not relinquish overall responsibility for supervision of the acts of salespersons licensed to the broker.

Written Employment Contract

A broker must have a written employment contract with his or her salespeople. This requirement is set forth in the commissioner's regulation 2726.

2726. Broker-Salesperson Relationship Agreements

Every real estate broker shall have a written agreement with each of his or her salespersons, whether licensed as a salesperson or as a broker under a broker-salesperson arrangement. The agreement shall be dated and signed by the parties and shall cover material aspects of the relationship between the parties, including supervision of licensed activities, duties and compensation.

Branch Offices

A broker must maintain a definite place of business in California.

This is the place where his or her license is to be displayed. The broker is not authorized to do business except at the location specified on his or her license. (Business and Professions Code 10162.)

Business and Professions Code 10163 provides for an additional license for each branch office maintained by the broker.

The Commissioner's Regulation 2728 provides that a real estate broker who is a member of a partnership operating as a real estate brokerage (under a written agreement) may operate from a branch office without acquiring a branch office license if another member of the partnership has a branch office license at the location in question.

If a real estate broker is acting as a salesperson to another broker under a written contract, that broker may perform services on behalf of the employing broker at any location for which the employing broker is licensed. (Regulation 2728.5)

Fictitious Business Names

A "fictitious name" is a name other than the surname of the principal(s). It is also known as an "assumed name."

If a person operates and contracts under a fictitious name but has failed to comply with the fictitious-name statues, that person could not sue to enforce a contract entered into under the fictitious name.

To comply with the fictitious-name statute, a fictitious name must be filed within 40 days of starting business. The statement filed must identify the principal(s), the business and the name being used. Within 30 days of filing, the fictitious-name statement must be published once a week for four weeks in a newspaper of general circulation.

Fictitious-name statements are good for five years (from December 31 of the year filed) and can be renewed.

Section 10159.5 of the Business and Professions Code provides that licensees who wish to do business under a fictitious name shall file, with their application, a certified copy of the fictitious-name statement filed with the county clerk.

The Commissioner's Regulation Section 2731 provides that only persons whose license bears a fictitious name can use a fictitious name.

The commissioner may refuse to issue a license with a fictitious name if the name is:

1. **Misleading.** A misleading name would be false advertising.

2. **Implies a non-existent partnership or corporation.** As an example, a person operating alone could not call himself or herself Henderson, Jacobs, Nixon, Reagan, Goldwater and Associates.

3. **Includes the name of a real estate salesperson.**

4. **Violates provisions of the law.**

5. **A name that was formerly used by a licensee whose license has been revoked.**

Telemarketing, Loan Processing, Documentation Preparation and Compliance

On November 10, 1995, the commissioner issued guidelines for unlicensed assistants. These guidelines are set forth below.

GUIDELINES FOR UNLICENSED ASSISTANTS

Preamble

The designated officer of a corporation is explicitly responsible for the supervision and control of the activities conducted on behalf of a corporate broker by its officers and employees as necessary to secure full compliance with the Real Estate Law, including but not limited to the supervision of salespersons licensed to the corporation in the performance of acts for which a real estate license is required. It is inherent with respect to individuals engaging in business as a real estate broker that they are also similarly charged with the responsibility to supervise and control all activities performed by their employees and agents in their name during the course of a transaction for which a real estate license is required, whether or not the activities performed require a real estate license.

To assist brokers and designated broker/officers to properly carry out their duty to supervise and control activities conducted on their behalf during the course of a licensed transaction, it is important for the broker to know and identify those activities which do and do not require a real estate license. This knowledge assists the broker to use licensed persons when required, and to extend and provide the necessary quantum of supervision and control over licensed and non-licensed activities as required by law and good business practices.

Identifying licensed activities has become difficult for many brokers as brokerage practices have changed and evolved in response to new laws, the need for new efficiencies in response to consumer demands, and new technology. The following is a guideline, and nothing more, of defined activities which generally do not come within the term "real estate broker," when performed with the broker's knowledge and consent.

Broker knowledge and consent is a prerequisite to the performance of these unlicensed activities, since without these elements there can be no reasonable assurance that the activities performed will be limited as set forth below.

Cold Calling

COLD CALLING *involves making telephone calls to canvass for interest in using the services of a real estate broker.* Should the person answering the call indicate an interest in using the services of a broker, or if there is an interest in ascertaining the kind of services a broker can provide, the person answering shall be referred to a licensee, or an appointment may be scheduled to enable him or her to meet with a broker or an associate licensee. (See definition on page 135.) At no time may the caller attempt to induce the person being called to use a broker's services. The canvassing may only be used to develop general information about the interest of the person answering and may not be used, designed or structured for solicitation purposes with respect to a specific property, transaction or product. (The term "solicitation" as used herein should be given its broadest interpretation.)

Open House

With the principal's consent, assisting licensees at an open house intended for the public by placing signs, greeting the public, providing factual information from or handing out preprinted materials prepared by or reviewed and approved for use by the licensee or arranging appointments with the licensee. During the holding of an open house, only a licensee may engage in the following: Show or exhibit the property, discuss terms and conditions of a possible sale, discuss other features of the property, such as its location, neighborhood or schools, or engage in any other conduct which is used, designed or structured for solicitation purposes with respect to the property.

Comparative Market Analysis

Making, conducting or preparing a comparative market analysis subject to the approval of and for use by the licensee.

Communicating With the Public

Providing factual information to others from writings prepared by the licensee. A non-licensee may not communicate with the public in a manner which is used, designed or structured for solicitation purposes with respect to a specific property, transaction or product.

Arranging Appointments

Making or scheduling appointments for licensees to meet with a principal or party to the transaction. As directed by the licensee to whom the broker has delegated such authority, arranging for and ordering reports and services from a third party in connection with the transaction, or for the provision of services in connection with the transaction, such as a pest control inspection and report, a roof inspection and report, a title inspection and/or a preliminary report, an appraisal and report, a credit check and report or repair or other work to be performed to the property as a part of the sale.

Access to Property

With the principal's consent, being present to let into the property a person who is either to inspect a portion or all of the property for the purpose of preparing a report of issuing a clearance, or who is to perform repair work or other work to the property in connection with the transaction. Information about the real property which is needed by the person making the inspection for the purpose of completing his or her report must be provided by the broker or associate licensee, unless it comes from a data sheet prepared by the broker, associate licensee or principal, and that fact is made clear to the person requesting the information.

Advertising

Preparing and designing advertising relating to the transaction for which the broker was employed, if the advertising is reviewed and approved by the broker or associate licensee prior to its publication.

Preparation of Documents

Preparing and completing documents and instruments under the supervision and direction of the licensee if the final documents or instruments will be or have been reviewed or approved by the licensee prior to the documents or instruments being presented, given or delivered to a principal or party to the transaction.

Delivery and Signing Documents

Mailing, delivering, pickup up or arranging the mailing, delivery or picking up of documents or instruments related to the transaction, including obtaining signatures to the documents or instruments from principals, parties or service providers in connection with the transaction. Such activity shall not include a discussion of the content, relevance, importance or significance of the document, or instrument or any portion thereof, with a principal or party to the transaction.

Trust Funds

Accepting, accounting for or providing a receipt for trust funds received from a principal or a party to the transaction.

Communicating With Principals, etc.

Communicating with a principal, party or service provider in connection with a transaction about when reports or other information needed concerning any aspect of the transaction will be delivered, or when certain services will be performed or completed, or if the services have been completed.

Document Review

Reviewing, as instructed by the licensee, transaction documentation for completeness or compliance, providing the final determination as to completeness or compliance is made by the broker or associate licensee.

Reviewing transaction documentation for the purpose of making recommendations to the broker on a course of action with respect to the transaction.

These "Guidelines," when strictly followed, will assist licensees and their employees in complying with the license requirements of the Real Estate Law. They present specific scenarios which allow brokers to organize their business practices in a manner that will contribute to compliance with the Real Estate Law. As such, they were drafted to serve the interests of both licensees and the public they serve. Nothing in them is intended to limit, add to or supersede any provision of law relating to the duties and obligations of real estate licensees, the consequences of violations of law or licensing requirements.

Licensees should take heed that because of the limiting nature of guidelines, as opposed to a statute or regulation, that they will not bind or obligate, nor are they intended to bind and obligate courts or others to follow or adhere to their provisions in civil proceedings or litigation involving conduct for which a real estate license may or may not be required.

Brokers and others who may refer to these "Guidelines" from time to time should be aware that it does not take very much to go from unlicensed to licensed activity. For example, it is a commonly held belief and understanding among licensees and others that participation in "negotiations" is somehow limited to the actual bargaining over terms and conditions of a sale or loan, when in fact the courts in this state have given much broader application to this terms to include activity which may directly assist or aid in the negotiations or closing of a transaction.

The term *ASSOCIATE LICENSEE means and refers to either a salesperson employed by the listing or selling broker in the transaction, or a broker who has entered into a written contract with a broker to act as the broker's agent in transactions requiring a real estate license.*

Hereafter, the term "licensee" means "broker" or "associate licensee."

Problems in Telemarketing Loans

There are a great many telemarketing firms seeking applicants for mortgages. The firms are normally selling consumers higher rate and cost products such as home equity loans and reverse mortgages.

> *These firms do not generally serve the best interest of consumers in that they sell "debt."*

Some of the "service providers" who do the telemarketing claim they only sell information and not loans. They do not represent lenders. They simply explain the products that are available and direct the borrower to mortgage lenders. They do not get kickbacks from the lenders. What the "service providers" do get is a contract with consumers who agree to pay the provider a percentage of the consumers' loans for the information they received.

Some of the "service providers," as they call themselves, feel that they are operating outside the real estate law and therefore need not be licensed.

Section 10131(d) of the Business and Professions Code seems to prohibit unlicensed telemarketing in the definition of "broker."

> *(d) solicits borrower or lenders for or negotiates loans or collects payments or performs services for borrowers or lenders or note owners in connection with loans secured directly or collaterally by liens on real property or on a business opportunity.*

Figure 6-2 provides details on one type of telemarketing scheme.

Mortgage Loan Consultants

The legislature found that homeowners, whose residences are in foreclosure, are subject to fraud, deception, harassment and unfair dealings by foreclosure consultants from the time a Notice of Default is recorded until the foreclosure sale.

Figure 6-2

A Telemarketing Scheme

Information taken from an article by Kenneth Harney in the April 6, 1997, issue of the Los Angeles Times:

Consumer advocates are distressed by telemarketing schemes involving reverse mortgages. A typical telephone pitch beings with:

"May I send you, at absolutely no obligation, information on how you can turn your home equity into monthly income at no cost to you?"

This "free" offer is made by service providers who charge seniors significant fees for simply referring applicants to a mortgage lender. These unregulated marketers pocket between eight-to-ten percent of loans they have referred. The "service provider" does little but end up with more money than anyone.

On March 17, 1997, HUD directed lenders to stop dealing with "service providers." According to HUD, there are about 100 companies nationwide operating referral services at high consumer costs.

HUD informed lenders that they will be disqualified from FHA programs if they knowingly make loans to people who are obligated to pay these fees.

"Service Providers" are also referring seniors to insurance companies who persuade seniors to obtain a large lump-sum reverse mortgage and use the proceeds to buy an annuity sold by the insurance company.

Seniors who want information on the advantages and pitfalls of reverse mortgages were instructed to call the National Center for Home Equity Conversion (612) 953-4474.

Foreclosure consultants claim to be able to assist owners in default. They generally charge a high fee secured by a deed of trust on the residence to be saved. The legislature considers their service to be worthless. In addition, homeowners' efforts are diverted from taking beneficial steps and often lose their homes, many times to the "consultants" who purchase the homes prior to foreclosure at a fraction of their value.

Civil Code Section 2945 et. seq. sets forth the Mortgage Loan Consultants Law.

The purpose of the law is:

1. To require mortgage law consultants' contracts to be in writing;

2. To safeguard the public against deceit and financial hardship; and

3. To permit rescission of foreclosure consultation contracts to encourage fair dealings in the rendition of foreclosure services.

Section 2945.1 of the Civil Code sets forth activities that are subject to the law.

2945.1. Definitions

The following definitions apply to this chapter:

(a). *FORECLOSURE CONSULTANT* *means any person who makes any solicitation, representation or offer to any owner to perform for compensation or who, for compensation, performs any service which the person in any manner represents will in any manner do any of the following:*

(1) Stop or postpone the foreclosure sale.

(2) Obtain any forbearance from any beneficiary or mortgagee.

(3) Assist the owner to exercise the right of reinstatement provided in Section 2924c.

(4) Obtain any extension of the period within which the owner may reinstate his or her obligation.

(5) Obtain any waiver of an acceleration clause contained in any promissory note or contract secured by a deed of trust or mortgage on a residence in foreclosure or contained in any such deed of trust or mortgage.

(6) Assist the owner to obtain a loan or advance of funds.

(7) Avoid or ameliorate the impairment of the owner's credit resulting from the recording of a notice of default or the conduct of a foreclosure sale.

(8) Save the owner's residence from foreclosure.

NOTICE REQUIREMENTS

2945.3. Written contract; contents; language, date and signature; notice of cancellation; form

(a). Every contract shall be in writing and shall fully disclose the exact nature of the foreclosure consultant's services and the total amount and terms of compensation.

(b). The following notice, printed in at least **14-point boldface type** and completed with the name of the foreclosure consultant, shall be printed immediately above the statement required by subdivision (c):

NOTICE REQUIRED BY CALIFORNIA LAW

_____ or anyone working for him or her CANNOT:
(Name)

(1) Take any money from you or ask you for money until _____
                                                                                    (Name)
completely finished doing everything he or she said he or she would do; and

(2) Ask you to sign or have you sign any lien, deed of trust or deed.

(c) The contract shall be written in the same language as principally used by the foreclosure consultant to describe his services or to negotiate the contract; shall be dated and signed by the owner; and shall contain in immediate proximity to the space reserved for the owner's signature a conspicuous statement in a size equal to at least **10-point bold type**, as follows: "You, the owner, may cancel this transaction at any time prior to midnight of the third business day after the date of this transaction. See the attached notice of cancellation form for an explanation of this right."

(d) The contract shall contain on the first page, in a type size no smaller than that generally used in the body of the document, each of the following:

   (1) The name and address of the foreclosure consultant to which the notice or cancellation is to be mailed.

   (2) The date the owner signed the contract.

(e) The contract shall be accompanied by a completed form in duplicate, captioned "notice of cancellation," which shall be attached to the contract, shall be easily detachable, and shall contain in type of at least 10-point the following statement written in the same language as used in the contract:

NOTICE OF CANCELLATION

_____
(Enter date of transaction) (Date)

You may cancel this transaction, without any penalty or obligation, within three business days from the above date.

To cancel this transaction, mail or deliver a signed and dated copy of this cancellation notice, or any other written notice, or send a telegram to

_____
(Name of foreclosure consultant)

at _____
(Address of foreclosure consultant's place of business)

NOT LATER THAN MIDNIGHT OF _____
(Date)

I hereby cancel this transaction _____
(Date)

_____
(Owner's signature)

(f) The foreclosure consultant shall provide the owner with a copy of the contract and the attached notice of cancellation.

PROHIBITED ACTIVITIES

2945.4. Prohibited Practices

It shall be a violation for a foreclosure consultant to:

(a). Claim, demand, charge, collect or receive any compensation until after the foreclosure consultant has fully performed each and every service the foreclosure consultant contracted to perform or represented he or she would perform.

(b). Claim, demand, charge, collect or receive any fee, interest or any other compensation for any reason which exceeds 10 percent per annum of the amount of any loan which the foreclosure consultant may make to the owner.

(c). Take any wage assignment, any lien of any type on real or personal property, or other security to secure the payment of compensation. Any such security shall be void and unenforceable.

(d). Receive any consideration from any third party in connection with services rendered to an owner unless such consideration is fully disclosed to the owner.

(e). Acquire any interest in a residence in foreclosure from an owner with whom the foreclosure consultant has contracted. Any interest acquired in violation of this subdivision shall be voidable, provided that nothing herein shall affect or defeat the title of a bona fide purchaser or encumbrancer for value and without notice of a violation of this article. Knowledge that the property was "residential real property in foreclosure," shall not constitute notice of a violation of this article.

This subdivision shall not be deemed to abrogate any duty of inquiry which exists as to rights or interests of persons in possession of residential real property in foreclosure.

(f). Take any power of attorney from an owner for any purpose, except to inspect documents as provided by law.

(g). Induce or attempt to induce any owner to enter a contract which does not comply in all respects with Sections 2945.2 and 2945.3.

PROHIBITED WAIVER

2945.5. Waiver

Any waiver by an owner of the provisions of this article shall be deemed void and unenforceable as contrary to public policy.

Any attempt by a foreclosure consultant to induce an owner to waive his rights shall be deemed a violation of this article.

SUMMARY

This chapter covers a broad and important area of supervision. Areas of particular importance include:

1. Failure to reasonably supervise salespersons is grounds for disciplinary action against a broker.

2. The broker must notify the Department of Real Estate when there is:

   a. An address change.

   b. Employment of an agent is terminated.

   c. New licensed employees are hired.

   d. An employee is discharged for a violation of the real estate law (requires a certified statement of facts).

3. Broker can be civilly liable for wrongful acts of salespersons. But unless the broker had guilty knowledge of the wrongful action, it would not be the basis of disciplinary action against the broker.

4. The license of a corporate officer can be revoked or suspended without revoking the license of the corporation.

5. Additional basis for disciplinary action include:

   a. fraud in procurement of a license.

   b. licensee is found guilty of a felony involving moral turpitude.

   c. making false statements and misrepresentations.

d. willfully disregarding real estate law or rules and regulations of the commissioner.

e. use of the term "realtor" or other trade name by a person not entitled to do so.

f. any conduct that would have warranted denial of license or the revocation, suspension or denial of a license by another agency or state.

g. demonstrated negligence or incompetence.

h. using or providing confidential information received while working in a governmental capacity to the detriment of other persons.

i. engaging in conduct which constitutes fraud or dishonest dealings.

j. violating any conditions of a restricted license.

k. engaging in "blockbusting."

l. violating any provision of the franchise investment law.

m. violations of corporation commissioner regulations concerning securities.

n. failure to reveal an interest in a property or a close relationship with the owner.

o. making any substantial misrepresentation.

p. making a false promise to induce an action.

q. engaging in a continued and flagrant course of misrepresentation.

r. acting for more than one party to a transaction without the knowledge or consent of all parties.

s. commingling funds.

t. claiming compensation under an exclusive listing that does not have a definite termination date.

u. making a secret profit.

v. exercising an option obtained with a listing without owners approval as to profit

w. any other conduct constituting fraud or dishonest dealings.

x. use of a "send-out slip" without the owner's permission.

y. violations of transfer disclosure requirements.

z. using a false or fictitious name or concealing material facts in the registration of a mobile home.

aa. failing to provide for the delivery of a certificate of ownership or title to a buyer of a mobile home.

bb. knowingly participating in the purchase or sale of a stolen mobile home.

cc. submitting a check that fails to clear for a mobile home registration.

dd. receiving or demanding kickbacks from service providers.

ee. being found liable in a civil action based on fraud, misrepresentation or deceit.

6. A license can be suspended without a hearing where it was obtained by fraud, misrepresentation or deceit.

7. The commissioner can impose a monetary fine in lieu of suspension or revocation of a license.

8. A broker has review responsibilities and must establish policies, rules, procedures and systems to monitor compliance of salespersons' activities.

9. A broker must have a written contract with each licensee salesperson.

10. A broker must maintain a definite place of business.

11. An additional branch-office license must be obtained for each additional office maintained.

12. A broker may use a fictitious name if the broker complies with the fictitious name statute and his or her license contains the fictitious name.

13. Unlicensed assistants have created a number of problems. They must be supervised by their employing licensees. The commissioner's guidelines for unlicensed assistants is important and should be understood.

14. "Service Providers" have been a problem in that consumers are paying substantial fees for a simple referral.

15. Mortgage loan consultants are regulated and their contracts must provide for a cancellation right within three business days.

CLASS DISCUSSION TOPICS

1. Which violations of statute that are grounds for disciplinary action against a licensee would be applicable to mortgage-loan brokering and lending? Give examples of each.

2. Why do you suppose mortgage loan brokers would falsify income of prospective borrowers?

3. What can be done to stop or reduce fraud directed at borrowers as well as lenders?

4. Which violations of the real estate law do you feel could be made by a basically honest licensee?

5. Do you know agents who use unlicensed assistants? If so, what are their duties? What is the level of supervision?

CHAPTER 6 QUIZ

1. A real estate broker must notify the real estate commissioner in all of the following situations EXCEPT when: (p. 121)
    A. the broker changes his or her business address
    B. a salesperson leaves the broker's employment
    C. a salesperson buys an office-listed property
    D. a salesperson from another firm comes to work for the broker

2. A broker discovers that one of her salespersons has been guilty of of an action which would justify revocation of the salesperson's license. The broker should: (p. 121)
    A. tear up the salesperson's license
    B. impose a fine on the salesperson
    C. send the commissioner a certified written statement of the facts
    D. wait to see if a complaint will be filed

3. In order for a broker's license to be revoked based on a violation of a salesperson, the broker must have: (p. 121)
    A. profited by the act
    B. failed to run a background check when hiring the salesperson
    C. been held civilly liable for the action
    D. had guilty knowledge of the wrongful act

4. Grounds for disciplinary action include all EXCEPT: (p. 123)

    A. acting for more than one party in a transaction with the knowledge and consent of all parties
    B. procuring a license by fraud
    C. entering a guilty plea to a crime involving moral turpitude
    D. using the term "Realtor" when the person is not a member of NAR

5. Which of the following would be the basis for disciplinary action against a licensee? (p. 123)
    A. Making a secret profit
    B. Commingling personal and client funds
    C. Claiming a commission under an exclusive listing that has no termination date
    D. All of the above

6. A broker has how many days to review documents prepared by his or her salesperson? (pp. 128-129)

    A. 1 day

    B. 2 days

    C. 3 days

    D. No specific number of days are stated

7. As to a broker's branch office: (p. 130)

    A. it must have a separate branch office license

    B. it cannot be larger than the main office

    C. it must be under a fictitious name

    D. none of the above

8. Which of the following is MOST LIKELY a fictitious name? (p. 131)

    A. ACME Realty

    B. Jones Realty

    C. Jones, Smith and Jacobs Realty

    D. Jackson and Jackson Realty

9. A broker operating a one-person office wanted to operate under a fictitious name. Which name would the commissioner MOST LIKELY REFUSE to allow the broker to use? (p. 131)

    A. All Property Realty

    B. Bill and Hillary Clinton Realty

    C. Professional Realty Company

    D. International Realty

10. Telephone canvassing by an unlicensed person is proper when: (p. 132)

    A. canvassing for interest in real estate services

    B. selling a particular property

    C. inducing a person to use a broker's services

    D. obtaining listings

11. At an open house, only a licensee can: (p. 133)

    A. discuss terms and conditions of a possible sale

    B. show the property

    C. discuss features of the property

    D. all of the above

12. An unlicensed assistant can: (p. 133)

    A. prepare a comparative market analysis

    B. arrange appointments for a licensee

    C. greet the public at an open house

    D. do any of the above

Answers: 1. C; 2. C; 3. D; 4. A; 5. D; 6. D; 7. A; 8. A; 9. B; 10. A; 11. A; 12. D

Agency

KEY WORDS AND TERMS

Agency
Agency by Estoppel
Agency by Implication
Agency by Ratification
Agency Disclosure
Agent
Attorney-In-Fact
Borrower's Agent
Confidentiality
Customary Authority
Diligence
Dual Agency
Employee
Equal Dignities Rule
Escrow
Express Agency
Express Authority

Fiduciary Duty
Frivolous Offer
Full Disclosure
General Agent
Honesty
Implied Authority
Independent Contractor
Lender's Agent
Loyalty
Obedience
Ostensible Agency
Power of Attorney
Principal
Respondeat Superior
Secret Profit
Special Agent
Undisclosed Agency

LEARNING OBJECTIVES

In this chapter you will learn about the general law of agency, as well as agency relationships and duties. You will also understand the agency relationships possible in real estate loan brokerage and lending situations and the importance of meeting agency duty requirements as well as making certain that the parties fully understand the agency of the broker and what it means.

Introduction

AGENCY DEFINED

California Civil Code Section 2295 defines an agent as follows:

"An **AGENT** *is one who acts for or represents another called the principal in dealing with third parties."*

> *In real estate transactions, the agent is the "broker" and the salespersons of the broker are "subagents" of the principal.*

A broker who works in the capacity of a salesperson as an associate broker under another broker would also be a subagent of the broker's principal.

PRINCIPAL DEFINED

In real estate related transactions the **PRINCIPAL** *is the person who employs an agent to represent him or her in the transaction.*

> *Any person who has the capacity to contract can be a principal and appoint an agent to represent him or her.*

Minors and persons who lack mental capacity are unable to contract for themselves so they cannot appoint an agent to deal for them. Civil Code Section 2296 makes this point very clear:

"Any person having the capacity to contract can appoint an agent, any person may be an agent."

While contractual capacity is required of the principal, it is not required of the agent. Therefore a minor could be an agent.

BROKER DEFINED

Section 10131 of the Business and Professions Code defines a broker.

10131. A *REAL ESTATE BROKER* *within the meaning of this part is a person who, for a compensation or in expectation of a compensation, regardless of the form or time of payment, does or negotiates to do one or more of the following acts for another or others:*

(a). Sells or offers to sell, buys or offers to buy, solicits prospective sellers or purchasers of, solicits or obtains listings of or negotiates the purchase, sale or exchange of real property or a business opportunity.

(b). Leases or rents or offers to lease or rent, or places for rent, or solicits listings of places for rent, or solicits for prospective tenants, or negotiates the sale, purchase or exchanges of leases on real property, or on a business opportunity, or collects rents from real property, or improvements thereon, or from business opportunities.

(c). Assists or offers to assist in filing an application for the purchase or lease of, or in locating or entering upon, lands owned by the state or federal government.

(d). Solicits borrowers or lenders for or negotiates loans or collects payments or performs services for borrowers or lenders or note owners in connection with loans secured directly or collaterally by liens on real property or on a business opportunity.

(e). Sells or offers to sell, buys or offers to buy, or exchanges or offers to exchange a real property sales contract, or a promissory note secured directly or collaterally by a lien on real property or on a business opportunity, and performs services for the holders thereof.

Agent - Employee - Independent Contractor

AGENT

By definition an agent has the power to represent a principal (as spelled out in the agency agreement).

A principal is liable for acts of the agent acting within the scope of the agency.

An agency relationship carries with it duties and obligations of the agent. These are discussed later in detail.

Compensation to the agent is not a factor in determining if an agency exists.

The fact that an agent is not asking for compensation does not lessen the agent's duties.

As an example, assume a broker agreed to find a mortgage lending opportunity for a family member. Assume the broker did not charge the relative for the services rendered. Assume, because of the broker's negligence, the broker represented the loan as a first mortgage when in fact there were two existing mortgages against the property. The broker had a duty to use reasonable care in representing the relative. This would include ascertaining the condition of the title and any existing encumbrances. If the broker's failure to use reasonable care resulted in a loss to the relative then the agent, even though serving in a gratuitous capacity, could be held liable for the loss.

EMPLOYEE

An **EMPLOYEE** *is a person who works under the direction and control of another.* An employee does not necessarily have the power to represent the principal, but it is possible for the employer to give the employee agency status.

> *An agent generally has more discretion than an employee, who must follow the directions of an employer in the accomplishment of a task.*

The English doctrine of *Respondeat Superior* is that a master is liable for the wrongs of the servant. This doctrine continues in California in that an employer is liable for the actions of the employee within the scope of employment and a principal is liable for acts of his or her agent within the scope of the agency.

> *Because a broker has a supervisory duty as to his or her salespeople, the Department of Real Estate considers real estate salespersons to be employees of their broker (as well as a subagent of the principal).*

A problem that frequently arises is a situation where a salesperson has an automobile accident in the course of his or her employment. The employer might be held liable in such a situation. Because of this potential liability, many real estate brokers require their salespersons to carry high-limit liability coverage on their automobile insurance.

Some brokers have tried to avoid liability by written contracts which specify the salesperson is an independent contractor and not an employee. The courts have refused to go along with these agreements as far as public liability is concerned. In *Resnick v. Anderson and Miles*, 109. C.A. 3rd 569, the court held "A salesperson, insofar as his relationship with his broker is concerned, cannot be classified as an independent contractor. Any contract which purports to change that relationship is invalid as being contrary to the law."

Similarly, brokers have relied on independent contractor agreements to avoid paying workers' compensation insurance. Courts, in many cases, have held the broker responsible for this coverage.

Unemployment insurance was also a problem area for brokers until the law was modified to exclude brokers and salespersons who are paid by commission from the definition of employee.

INDEPENDENT CONTRACTOR

An **INDEPENDENT CONTRACTOR** *is a person hired to perform a task.* Unlike an agent or employee, the independent contractor is not subject to the direction of an employer or principal. The independent contractor is hired for the results contracted for.

The independent contractor does not have the duties of an agent to the person hiring the independent contractor, nor is that person generally liable for the wrongful acts of the independent contractor.

An exception is that a person hiring an independent contractor to perform a dangerous task could be held liable for all damages caused in the performance of the task. As an example, assume a party hired an independent contractor to remove a large tree between two structures. If a structure is damaged in the process, a court could hold the person contracting for the dangerous task to be liable for resulting damages. Similarly, a principal would be liable if the principal directed an agent to commit a civil or criminal wrong. If such a situation arose, the agent would also be liable for the wrongful act. "He told me to do it", is not a defense for a tort or a crime.

An independent contractor is responsible for his or her own social security and income taxes while an employer must withhold taxes and employee contributions to social security as well as pay the employer social security contribution.

Even though California regards real estate salespersons as employees, the IRS will treat real estate salespersons as independent contractors as to withholding income tax and social security, providing three requisites are met:

1. The real estate salesperson must be licensed.

2. There must be a written contract specifying that the salesperson is an independent contractor.

3. The salesperson's compensation must be based on success in real estate transactions not on hours worked.

Most real estate broker/salesperson and associate-broker contracts specify that the salesperson or associate-broker is an independent contractor to avoid withholding and social security contributions by the broker.

In California, the broker must have a written relationship contract with salespersons.

The contract must be signed and dated and cover aspects of the relationship including supervision of licensee activities, duties of the parties and compensation. A Broker-Associate License Contract prepared by the California Association of Realtors is shown in Figures 7-1 and 7-2.

Commissioner's Regulations
2726. Broker-Salesperson Relationship Agreements

Every real estate broker shall have a written agreement with each of his or her salespersons, whether licensed as a salesperson or as a broker under a broker-salesperson arrangement. The agreement shall be dated and signed by the parties and shall cover material aspects of the relationship between the parties, including supervision of licensed activities, duties and compensation.

FACILITATOR

Currently, there is a movement in several states to avoid agency responsibilities by changing the role of the broker and making the broker an intermediary or middle person rather than an agent. Under this concept the **FACILITATOR** *acts more as a mediator between the parties*. A number of state departments of real estate have been cold to this concept.

By law in California, the real estate broker is an agent and agency-type duties are mandated.

Without a statutory change, use of an agreement calling the broker a facilitator would not relieve the broker of agency responsibilities.

Figure 7-1

CALIFORNIA
ASSOCIATION
OF REALTORS®

BROKER-ASSOCIATE LICENSEE CONTRACT
(Independent-Contractor)

THIS AGREEMENT, made this _____ day of _____, 19_____ by and between

_____
_____ (hereinafter "Broker") and
_____ (hereinafter "Associate Licensee").
IN CONSIDERATION of the respective representations and covenants herein, Broker and Associate Licensee agree and contract as follows:

1. **BROKER:** Broker represents that he/she/it is duly licensed as a real estate broker by the State of California, ☐ doing business as _____
_____ (Firm name), ☐ a sole proprietorship, ☐ a partnership, ☐ a corporation.
Broker is a member of the _____ Board(s)/Association(s) of REALTORS7, and a Participant in the
multiple listing service(s).

2. **ASSOCIATE LICENSEE:** Associate Licensee represents that, (a) he/she is duly licensed by the State of California as a ☐ real estate broker,
☐ real estate salesperson, and (b) he/she has not used any other names within the past five years except _____
_____. Broker shall keep his/her/its license current during the term of
this agreement. Associate Licensee shall keep his/her license current during the term of this agreement, including satisfying all applicable continuing
education and provisional license requirements.

3. **LISTING AND SALES ACTIVITIES:** Broker shall make available to Associate Licensee, equally with other licensees associated with Broker, all
current listings in Broker's office, except any listing which Broker may choose to place in the exclusive servicing of Associate Licensee or one or more
other specific licensees associated with Broker. Associate Licensee shall not be required to accept or service any particular listing or prospective listing
offered by Broker, or to see or service particular parties. Broker shall not restrict Associate Licensee's activities to particular geographical areas. Broker
shall not, except to the extent required by law, direct or limit Associate Licensee's activities as to hours, leads, open houses, opportunity or floor time,
production, prospects, sales meetings, schedule, inventory, time off, vacation, or similar activities. In compliance with Commissioner's Regulation 2780,
et seq. (Title 10, California Code of Regulations, §2780, et seq.), Broker and Associate Licensee shall at all times be familiar with, all applicable federal,
California and local anti-discrimination laws.

4. **BROKER SUPERVISION:**
   (a) Associate Licensee shall submit for Broker's review:
   i. All documents which may have a material effect upon the rights and duties of principals in a transaction, within 24 hours after preparing, signing,
   or receiving same. Broker may exercise this review responsibility through another licensee provided the Broker and the designated licensee have
   complied with Commissioner's Regulation 2725 (Title 10, California Code of Regulations, §2725).
   ii. Any documents or other items connected with a transaction pursuant to this agreement, in the possession of or available to Associate Licensee,
   (I) immediately upon request by Broker or Broker's designated licensee, and/or (ii) as provided in Broker's Office Policy Manual, if any.
   iii. All documents associated with any real estate transaction in which Associate Licensee is a principal.
   (b) In addition, without affecting Associate Licensee's status, Broker shall have the right to direct Associate Licensee's actions to the extent required
   by law, and Associate Licensee shall comply with such directions. All trust funds shall be handled in compliance with Business and Professions
   Code §10145, and other applicable laws.

5. **OFFICE FACILITIES:** Broker shall make available for Associate Licensee's use, along with other licensees associated with Broker, the facilities of the
real estate office operated by Broker at _____
and the facilities of any other office locations made available by Broker pursuant to this agreement.

6. **ASSOCIATE LICENSEE'S REPORT:** Associate Licensee shall work diligently and with his/her best efforts, (a) To sell, exchange, lease, or rent
properties listed with Broker or other cooperating Brokers, (b) To solicit additional listings, clients, and customers, and (c) To otherwise promote the
business of serving the public in real estate transactions to the end that Broker and Associate Licensee may derive the greatest benefit possible, in
accordance with law.

7. **UNLAWFUL ACTS:** Associate Licensee shall not commit any act for which the Real Estate Commissioner of the State of California is authorized to
restrict, suspend, or revoke Associates Licensee's license or impose other discipline, under California Business and Professions Code Sections 10176
or 10177 or other provisions of law.

8. **LISTING COMMISSIONS:** Commissions shall be charged to parties who desire to enter into listing agreements and other contracts for services
requiring a real estate license, with Broker.
   ☐ as shown in "Exhibit A" attached which is incorporated as a part of this agreement by reference, or
   ☐ as follows: _____
   _____
   Any proposed deviation from that schedule must be reviewed and approved in advance by Broker. Any permanent change in commission schedule
   shall be disseminated by Broker to Associate Licensee.

9. **COMPENSATION TO ASSOCIATE LICENSEE:** Associate Licensee shall receive a share of commissions which are actually collected by Broker, on
listings and other contracts for services requiring a real estate license which are solicited and obtained by Associate Licensee, and on transactions of
which Associate Licensee's activities are the procuring cause.
   ☐ as shown in "Exhibit B" attached which is incorporated as a part of this agreement by reference, or
   ☐ as follows: _____
   _____
   _____
   The above commissions may be varied by written agreement between Broker and Associate Licensee before completion of any particular transaction.
   Expenses which must be paid from commissions, or are incurred in the attempt to collect commissions, shall be paid by Broker and Associate Licensee
   in the same proportion as set forth for the division of commissions.

10. **DIVIDING COMPENSATION WITH OTHER LICENSEES IN OFFICE:** If Associate Licensee and one or more other licensees associated with Broker
both participate on the same side (either listing or selling) of a transaction, the commission allocated to their combined efforts shall be divided by
Broker and paid to them according to the written agreement between them which shall be furnished in advance to Broker.

11. **COMMISSIONS PAID TO BROKER:** All commission will be received by Broker. Associate Licensee's share of commissions shall be paid to him/her,
after deduction of offsets, immediately upon collection by Broker or as soon thereafter as practicable, except as otherwise provided in (a) Paragraph
9, above, (b) Broker's Office Policy Manual, or (c) A separate written agreement between Broker and Associate Licensee. Broker may impound in
Broker's account Associate Licensee's share of commissions on transactions in which there is a known or pending claim against Broker and/or
Associate Licensee, until such claim is resolved.

12. **UNCOLLECTED COMMISSIONS:** Neither Broker nor Associate Licensee shall be liable to the other for any portion of commissions not collected.
Associate Licensee shall not be entitled to any advance payment from Broker upon future commissions.

OFFICE USE ONLY
Reviewed by Broker
or Designee _____
Date _____

EQUAL HOUSING
OPPORTUNITY

FORM I-14 REVISED 1990

Figure 7-2

13. **ASSOCIATE LICENSEE EXPENSES; OFFSETS:** Associate Licensee shall provide and pay for all professional licenses, supplies, services, and other items required in connection with Associate Licensee's activities under this agreement, or any listing or transaction, without reimbursement from Broker except as required by law. If Broker elects to advance funds to pay expenses or liabilities of Associate Licensee shall pay to Broker the full amount advanced on demand, or Broker may deduct the full amount advanced from commissions payable to Associate Licensee on any transaction without notice.

14. **INDEPENDENT CONTRACTOR RELATIONSHIP:** Broker and Associate Licensee intend that, to the maximum extent permissible by law, **(a)** This agreement does not constitute a hiring or employment agreement by either party, **(b)** Broker and Associate Licensee are independent contracting parties with respect to all services rendered under this agreement or in any resulting transactions, **(c)** Associate Licensee's only remuneration shall be his.her proportional share, if any, of commissions collected by Broker, **(d)** Associate Licensee retains sole and absolute discretion and judgment in the methods, techniques, and procedures to be used in soliciting and obtaining listings, sales, exchanges, leases, rentals, or other transactions, and in carrying out Associate Licensee's selling and soliciting activities, except as required by law or in Broker's Office Policy Manual, **(e)** Associate Licensee is under the control of Broker as to the results of Associate Licensee's work only, and not as to the means by which those results are accomplished except as required by law, or in Broker's Office Policy Manual, if any, **(f)** This Agreement shall not be construed as a partnership, **(g)** Associate Licensee has no authority to bind Broker by any promise or representation unless specifically authorized by Broker in writing, **(h)** Broker shall not be liable for any obligation or liability incurred by Associate Licensee, **(i)** Associate Licensee shall not be treated as an employee with respects to services performed as a real estate agent, for state and federal tax purposes, and **(j)** The fact the Broker may carry worker compensation insurance for his/her/its own benefit and for the mutual benefit of Broker and licensees associated with Broker, including Associate Licensee, shall not create or inference of employment.

15. **LISTING AND OTHER AGREEMENTS PROPERTY OF BROKER:** All listings of property, and all agreements for performance of licensed acts, and all acts or actions required a real estate license which are taken or performed in connection with this agreement, shall be taken and performed in the name of Broker. All listings shall be submitted to Broker within 24 hours after receipt by Associate Licensee. Associate Licensee agrees to and does hereby contribute all right and title to such listings to Broker for the benefit and use of Broker, Associate Licensee, and other licensees associated with Broker.

16. **TERMINATION OF RELATIONSHIP:** Broker or Associate Licensee may terminate their relationship under this agreement at any time, on 24 hours written notice, with or without cause. Even after termination, this agreement shall govern all disputes and claims between Broker and Associate Licensee connected with their relationship under this agreement, including obligations and liabilities arising from existing and completed listings, transactions, and services.

17. **COMMISSIONS AFTER TERMINATION AND OFFSET:** If this agreement is terminated while Associate Licensee has listings or pending transactions that require further work normally rendered by Associate Licensee, Broker shall make arrangements with another licensee associated with Broker to perform the required work, or shall perform the work him/herself. The licensee performing the work shall be reasonably compensated for completing work on those listings or transactions, and such reasonable compensation shall be deducted from Associate Licensee's share of commissions. Except for such offset, Associate Licensee shall receive his/her regular share of commissions on such sales or other transactions, if actually collected by Broker, after deduction of any other amounts or offsets provided in this agreement.

18. **ARBITRATION OF DISPUTES:** All disputes or claims between Associate Licensee and other licensee(s) associated with Broker, or between Associate Licensee and Broker, arising from or connected in any way with this agreement, which cannot be adjusted between the parties involved, shall be submitted to the Board of REALTORS® of which all such disputing parties are members for arbitration pursuant to the provisions of its Bylaws, as may be amended from time to time, which are incorporated as a part of this agreement by reference. If the Bylaws of the Board do not cover arbitration of the dispute, or if the Board declines jurisdiction over the dispute, then arbitration shall be pursuant to the rules of the American Arbitration Association, as may be amended from time to time, which are incorporated as a part of this agreement by reference. The Federal Arbitration Act, Title 9, U.S. Code, Section 1, et seq., shall govern this agreement.

19. **PROPRIETARY INFORMATION AND FILES:** Associate Licensee shall not use to his/her own advantage, or the advantage of any other person, business, or entity, except as specified provided in this agreement, either during Associate Licensee;s association with Broker or thereafter, any information gained for or from the business or files of Broker. All files and documents pertaining to listings and transactions are the property of Broker and shall be delivered to Broker by Associate Licensee immediately upon request or upon termination of their relationship under this agreement.

20. **INDEMNITY AND HOLD HARMLESS:** All claims, demands, liabilities, judgments, and arbitration awards, including costs and attorney's fees, to which Broker is subjected by reason of any action taken or omitted by Associate Licensee in connection with services rendered or to be rendered pursuant to this agreement, shall be:

☐ Paid in full by Associate Licensee, who hereby agrees to indemnify and hold harmless Broker for all such sums, or

☐ Other: _____
_____

Associate Licensee shall pay to Broker the full amount due by him/her demand, or Broker may deduct the full amount due by Associate Licensee from commissions due on any transaction without notice.

21. **ADDITIONAL PROVISIONS:** _____
_____
_____

22. **DEFINITIONS:** As used in this agreement, the following terms have the meanings indicated:

   (a) "Listing" means an agreement with a property owner or other party to locate a buyer, exchange party, lessee, or other party to a transaction involving real property, a mobile home, or other property or transaction which may be brokered by a real estate licensee, or an agreement with a party to locate or negotiate for any such property or transaction.

   (b) "Commission means compensation for acts requiring a real estate license, regardless of whether calculated as a percentage of transaction price, flat fee, hourly rate, or in any other manner.

   (c) "Transaction" means a sale, exchange, lease, or rental of real property, a business opportunity, or a mobile home which may lawfully be brokered by a real estate licensee, or a loan secured by any property of those types.

   (d) "Associate Licensee" means the real estate broker or real estate salesperson licensed by the State of California and rendering the services set forth herein for Associate Licensee.

23. **NOTICES:** All notices under this agreement shall be in writing. Notices may be delivered personally, or by certified U.S. mail, postage prepaid, or by facsimile, to the parties at the addresses noted below. Either party may designate a new address for purposes of this agreement by giving notice to the other party. Notices mailed shall be deemed received as of 5:00 P.M. on the second business day following the date of mailing.

24. **ATTORNEY FEES:** In any action, proceeding, or arbitration between Broker and Associate Licensee arising from or related to this agreement, the prevailing party shall, in the discretion of the court or arbitrator, be entitled to reasonable attorney fees in addition to other appropriate relief.

25. **ENTIRE AGREEMENT; MODIFICATION:** All prior agreements between the parties concerning their relationship as Broker and Associate Licensee are incorporated in this agreement, which constitutes the entire contract. Its terms are intended by the parties as a final and complete expression of their agreement with respect to its subject matter, and may not be contradicted by evidence of any prior agreement or contemporaneous oral agreement. This agreement may not be amended, modified, altered, or changed in any respect whatsoever except by a further agreement in writing duly executed by Broker and Associate Licensee.

BROKER: **ASSOCIATE LICENSEE:**

_____   _____
(Signature)   (Signature)

_____   _____
(Name Printed)   (Name Printed)

_____   _____
(Address)   (Address)

_____   _____
(City, State, Zip)   (City, State, Zip)

_____   _____
(Telephone)   (Fax)   (Telephone)   (Fax)

NOTE: (1) Broker and Associate Licensee should each receive an executed copy of this agreement.

            (2) Attach commission schedules Exhibits A and B if applicable.

Types of Agents

There are 2 basic types of agents—Special Agents and General Agents.

SPECIAL AGENT

A **SPECIAL AGENT** *has the limited authority set forth in the agency agreement.*

> *A real estate agent is usually a special agent employed by a principal to perform a specific task.*

A real estate agent might be a special agent of a prospective borrower to locate a lender for a loan or a special agent of a lender to locate lending opportunities.

GENERAL AGENT

A **GENERAL AGENT** *has broad authority to perform the tasks necessary to carry out an endeavor.* A chief executive officer (CEO) of a corporation would likely be a general agent as would a manager of a mortgage brokerage firm (in this case the manager could be a general agent of the broker but not of the firm's principals).

POWER OF ATTORNEY

A **POWER OF ATTORNEY** *is a written instrument authorizing the agent known as the* **ATTORNEY-IN-FACT** *to act for the principal as set forth in the instrument.* Since the attorney-in-fact acts in the shoes of the principal, an attorney-in-fact, with the proper authority of the principal, could buy and sell property, place loans against property and make loans secured by property.

> *Most powers of attorney are special or limited powers authorizing specific acts. An all-inclusive power of attorney would allow the attorney-in-fact to do any act the principal could do.*

A power of attorney might give an agent the power to place a trust deed against real property. If the attorney-in-fact signs the trust deed and that trust deed is recorded, it could be a **WILD DOCUMENT** (*outside the chain of title*).

> *Recording the trust deed would not give constructive notice of the attorney-in-fact's rights as to the property unless the power of attorney, granting this right to the attorney-in-fact, was also recorded.*

Creation of Agencies

Agencies can be created in several ways.

EXPRESS AGENCY

An **EXPRESS AGENCY** is created by a stated (verbal or written) agreement. Generally, real estate loan-brokerage agreements are written.

> *The "equal-dignities rule" is that if an act must be in writing because of the statute of frauds, then an agency agreement to enter such a contract must also be in writing.*

Under the negotiable-instrument law, a promissory note must be in writing. Therefore, the agency agreement authorizing other than the owner to sign a note would also have to be in writing.

AGENCY BY IMPLICATION

An **AGENCY BY IMPLICATION** is one created by the actions of the parties. While not specifically stated by the parties, it is understood.

An **OSTENSIBLE AGENCY** is an agency by implication where no agency was actually intended by the parties, but a third party can rely on the agency.

As an example, assume you were working on finding a lender to make a home equity loan. Assume also that you were not doing so as the agent of the property owner who had specifically told you that she would not pay for your services. If you ordered an appraisal and the owner allowed the appraiser to enter the property, knowing the purpose of the appraisal, the appraiser could reasonably assume that you were acting as the agent of the owner in ordering the appraisal. If you were unable to pay the appraisal fee, a court might hold the owner liable for the fee since the owner allowed the appearance of an agency.

AGENCY BY ESTOPPEL

A person can be prohibited from denying the existence of an agency (estopped) if his or her words or actions led another to believe that an agency existed. As an example, assume you told Rogers that Clyde had authority to approve the loans that you would fund. Assume you made this statement in jest, but Rogers was reasonable in assuming that Clyde represented you. If Rogers acted to his detriment based on your assertion, you could be estopped (prohibited) from denying the existence of the agency. As an example, Rogers could have entered into a binding contract based on Clyde's approval of funding the purchase loan.

AGENCY BY RATIFICATION

An agency by ratification is formed when a principal accepts the benefits of an unauthorized person, not authorized to act as an agent, or an act by an agent beyond the agent's authority.

> *By accepting the benefits of an agreement, the principal ratified the contract.*

Assume a real estate licensee working for you signed a broker-associate contract with another licensee as your agent, even though you had never given that person the authority to engage salespersons in your office. Assume after knowing of the agreement, the new salesperson brings in a loan which you arrange to fund. You could not refuse to pay the commission stated in the broker-associate contract based on the fact that the person signing had no authority to do so. You accepted the benefits of the agreement so you must also accept the obligations.

> *Section 2314 of the Civil Code allows a person to rescind or void his or her ratification if the ratification was made with false or imperfect knowledge as to the facts.*

As an example, if the owner took the "agents" word for the terms of the agreement and, upon receiving a copy of the agreement, discovered that the facts were far less favorable than claimed, the ratification could be rescinded.

Authority of Agents

EXPRESS AUTHORITY

*Authority that has been stated (verbally or in writing) is known as **EXPRESS AUTHORITY**.*

IMPLIED AUTHORITY

Agents have **IMPLIED AUTHORITY** (*understood but not stated*) to perform acts necessary to properly perform their express authority. A loan officer who obtains a loan application would likely have the implied authority to prepare a loan package for submission to a lender or for internal approval.

CUSTOMARY AUTHORITY

CUSTOMARY AUTHORITY *is based on the agent's position.* What authority would a person in that position customarily have?

> *A general manager of a real estate office would have the customary authority to contract for office supplies.*

Sometimes principals put limitations on an agent's authority. If these limitations are secret (not known to the parties with whom the agent is dealing) then the third parties may not be bound to these secret limitations if the agent had customary authority.

If an agent claims to have greater than customary authority, the principal is not liable if the agent had in fact exceeded his or her authority. A third person should not take an agent's word for the extent of the agent's authority when the agent claims greater authority than is customary. The third person should check with the principal. As an example, assume that a mortgage broker in arranging a loan on an apartment complex entered into a separate agreement in which the lender was to receive a rent-free apartment until the loan was paid off. While the mortgage broker may have been an agent of the apartment owner, this agreement would exceed the customary authority of the loan broker. The owner would not be obligated to this agreement unless the authority to give the rent free apartment had actually been given to the mortgage broker, or the owner, after knowing of the agreement, approved it.

Undisclosed Agency

A **SECRET AGENT** *is one who appears to third persons to be acting as a principal.* If a secret agent performs a wrongful act, a third party can sue the agent. If the third party discovers the existence of the agency after the wrongful act, then the third party has the option of suing the principal or the agent (but not both).

> *A third party dealing with a secret agent may use personal set-offs against monies due the agent.*

As an example, assume an agent personally owed a third party the sum of $1,000. If, in dealing with the third party the third party became obligated in the amount of $2,000, the third party could fulfill the obligation by paying $1,000 and use the $1,000 claim as a setoff. If the third party had known that the agent was acting in an agency capacity, then a setoff could not be taken since the $2,000 was owed to the principal and the $1,000 was personally owed by the agent.

A person might want to claim an agency existed in order to go after "deeper pockets" (sue a person with greater financial resources).

> *The person who would benefit by the existence of the agency has the duty of proof as to the existence of that agency.*

In other words, if you want to hold a supposed principal liable for the actions of an undisclosed agent, you must prove that the person you had dealings with was in fact an agent.

Duties of the Agent to Principal

> *An agent has a "fiduciary duty" to his or her principal.*

A **FIDUCIARY DUTY** *includes loyalty, obedience, confidentiality, full disclosure, the duty to use diligence, the financial duty to account for all funds of the principal that come under agent control and complete honesty.* This fiduciary duty distinguishes an agent from an independent contractor and an employee who does not also have agency responsibilities.

> *A mortgage broker owes a fiduciary duty of the highest good faith toward the principal.*

The fiduciary duty may not be delegated. Otherwise a mortgage broker could escape liability for breach of fiduciary duty by simply delegating responsibility among independent contractors.

LOYALTY

> *The agent must be loyal to his or her principal.*

The principal's interests must be paramount. As an example, a mortgage broker representing a borrower could not indicate to a prospective lender that the borrower was desperate or would pay a higher rate of interest than a lender was accustomed to receiving. Statements such as this would undermine the bargaining position of the principal.

OBEDIENCE

The agent must obey the principal as to legal directions and limits as to the agency.

However, in an emergency an agent could properly disobey his or her principal. As an example, assume a mortgage company is servicing a loan for an out-of-state lender when the mortgagee suddenly vacates the property leaving it open. Assume also the mortgage company has authority to spend reasonable sums to protect property "in the event of foreclosure." If the owner could not be contacted, the mortgage company could, because of the emergency, make reasonable expenditures to protect the property even though the property was not in foreclosure.

Should an agent's unexcused failure to obey the lawful instructions of the principal cause the principal to suffer a loss, the agent could be liable for that loss.

CONFIDENTIALITY

The agent might learn confidential information while acting in an agency capacity. The agent may not disclose the confidential information to another or use it to his or her own advantage.

Case Example

Chadur v. Edmonds (1985) 174 C.A. 3d 565

A broker sold real estate owned by the broker to a purchaser. To finance the sale, the broker used a wrap-around mortgage where the purchaser paid on an all-inclusive promissory note to the broker. The broker, while obligated to make payments on the underlying note, failed to do so. The broker used the money received from the buyer for his own purposes. The broker was found guilty of dishonest dealings. (Business and Professions Code 10177[j]).

"Engaged in any other conduct, whether of the same or a different character than specified in this section, which constitutes fraud or dishonest dealing."

After a hearing the commissioner revoked the broker's licenses. The Court of Appeals affirmed the commissioner's action stating that the broker had breached fiduciary duties. When the broker agreed to accept payments on the underlying note, an agency agreement was formed between the broker and the purchaser.

This duty of confidentiality continues beyond the life of the agency.

FULL DISCLOSURE

An agent has a duty to inform the principal as to any information the agent possesses that is of interest to the principal. This duty continues up to the close of escrow.

Should an agent discover that better loan terms were possible through a different lender, the agent would have a duty to so inform the principal (borrower) even though a binding agreement had already been entered into.

Frivolous Offer

The agent must inform the borrower of all offers made to fund a desired loan even though the agent feels that the offer is unreasonable.

An offer would have to be clearly frivolous before an agent could be excused from presenting it. The offer should be presented if the agent has any doubt. Even unreasonable offers may be accepted.

Understanding Terms

If a lender offers a borrower unusual terms which could have an onerous effect if the borrower defaults, the terms and possible repercussions should be explained.

If an agent has any questions about a proposed agreement, the agent should strongly recommend legal advise to the principal.

Before a principal signs any agreement, the agent must be certain that the principal understands.

Confidential Information

An exception to full disclosure would be information received in confidence from another party. Disclosure of the information to the principal would breach this confidence. This problem is less likely to occur if the agent clearly discloses his or her agency when dealing with third parties.

Case Example

Wyatt v. Union Mortgage Co. (1979) 24 C. 3d 773

Union Mortgage Company was sued by Wyatt who alleged a breach of fiduciary duty owed by a mortgage broker to those who engage its mortgage services. The plaintiff alleged misleading television ads (Television ads showed that a $1,000 loan could be repaid completely with principal and interest payments of $18 per month while in fact no such loan was available and the ad was to lure borrowers). Also alleged were misrepresentation of loan terms, including interest rate, amount of loan payments, the policy on late charges and the failure to call plaintiff's attention to unfavorable provisions buried in the loan papers. The lender extracted late charges on the secured loan despite the timely payment of all installments. The jury in the trial court assessed actual damages of $25,000 and punitive damages for each defendant of $200,000.

The California Supreme Court pointed out that a real estate licensee has the duty of fullest disclosure of all material facts that might affect the principal's decision and that fiduciary duty extends beyond mere written disclosure. The court determined that the defendant was involved in a civil conspiracy. By considering all payments late if one payment was late, the defendants were able to raise their late charge income from $152,000 in 1971 to over $1,000,000 in 1974. The court affirmed the judgment of the trial court.

Note: In this case the plaintiff did not read the written agreement but instead asked the broker what was stated in the agreement.

Case Example

UMET Trust v. Santa Monica Medical Investment Co. (1983)

Clients wished a loan. Rather than a conventional loan, a broker arranged a sale-leaseback arrangement which would fulfill the clients' needs. The broker neglected to inform the clients that the clients' interests could be terminated by a short notice in the event of default and that the statutory right of redemption existing in loan agreements do not exist in sale leaseback agreements.

The antideficiency judgment protection that exists in conventional loans does not apply to sale leaseback transactions. The court held in this case that the broker's fiduciary duty of disclosure of all facts that a client would reasonably want to know extended to the date of closing. While the client was represented by legal counsel, the court held that retention of separate counsel did not relieve this broker from his fiduciary duties.

Disclosure as to Protected Groups

> *Information regarding race, national origin, religion, sex, familial status or handicapped status of a borrower should not be revealed as it is not material information.*

Even if a lender requests such information it should not be provided as it could make the agent an accomplice to illegal discrimination.

Agent as a Principal/Secret Profit

> *The agent must disclose to the owner that he or she is the borrower or lender or has any interest in a loan transaction other than the agency.*

This disclosure would extend to relatives of the agent and even to close friends or associates. In doubt? The rule is disclose! If the agent is acting for more than one party to the transaction or if the agent will receive a secret profit or benefit from the transaction, the agent must make full disclosure. As an example of a benefit, if the prospective lenders had indicated that they will lend money to the broker at an attractive rate of interest if this loan is funded then the agent must reveal this fact.

Duties Without an Actual Agency

A court could hold a broker-to-fiduciary disclosure responsibilities even when an agency was never actually entered into. As an example, assume a party contacted a broker about a loan secured by an industrial property. Assume also the broker directed the prospective borrower to a lender because the broker did not want to get involved with the lender and the broker knew of no one else who would fund the loan. If the broker knew that the lender had a reputation of charging large fees for funding loans and because of fine print in the contracts used many of the loans were never funded, then failure to warn the prospective borrower could be determined to be a breach of duty even though no agency ever existed.

DILIGENCE

The agent is obligated to provide his or her knowledge and due care to his or principal.

> *An agent in representing a lender or borrower should not suggest an interest rate unless the agent has determined that the rate is fair.*

If the agent is in doubt as to a fact, the agent should find out or recommend professional assistance. The agent is expected to exercise the knowledge required for licensing. The agent is not required to be perfect, just that he or she exercises reasonable skill and care. If the agent acts negligently, the agent could be liable for damages.

Often agents will claim greater expertise than other agents. As an example, an agent might claim to be an expert in financing industrial property.

> *An agent who claims greater than usual expertise could be held by the court to a higher level of knowledge and experience.*

An agent should not undertake tasks beyond his or her ability. The agent could be at financial risk if his or her actions work to the detriment of the principal. For example, if an agent prepared a complicated commercial loan agreement secured by numerous properties by cutting and pasting clauses from other agreements into what the agent thought was applicable, the agent could be liable if an error or omission worked to the detriment of the principal.

> *In the above example, preparing other than a simple agreement might be viewed by the courts as the unauthorized practice of law.*

FINANCIAL DUTIES

> *The agent has a duty to properly account for all trust funds and to make certain that the funds are properly protected.*

The agent is accountable to his or her principal for all funds received and disbursements made. The agent cannot make any undisclosed profit from his or her dealings.

HONESTY

> *The agent must be absolutely honest with his or her principal and avoid exaggeration.*

The distinction between convictions and facts must be made so that the principal can fully understand situations. The agent must understand that agency dealings require the highest good faith.

Even the appearance of impropriety must be avoided as it reflects negatively on the real estate profession.

Figure 7-3 will help you understand agency duties.

Case Example

Whippel v. Haberle (1963) 223 C.A. 2d 477

A purchase agreement was contingent upon FHA financing. The defendant loan broker was certain that there would be loan approval so he informed the plaintiffs and the defendant-owners that the loan application had been approved. The plaintiffs moved in and expended a great deal of time and money making permanent improvements to the property. The loan was not approved and the plaintiffs received notice to vacate the premises. The plaintiffs refused to leave. The owners refused to reimburse the plaintiffs for expenditures for improvements.

The court held that while the loan broker was liable to the purchasers for the amount of their expenditures, which were induced by the false representation of the broker, the broker was not liable for treble damages assessed against the plaintiffs for their wrongful refusal to vacate after proper notice.

Delegation of Duties

Unless provided in the agency agreement, an agent cannot delegate agency duties to another. An agent cannot unilaterally decide to use subagents.

Most listing agreements authorize the agent to "cooperate" with other agents in meeting the purpose of the agency.

Just as an owner could be liable for acts of his or her agent, an owner could also be liable for acts of cooperating brokers who elect to be subagents of the seller or who elect dual agency.

Figure 7-3

Agent Duties

Obedience

Confidentialty

Full Disclosure

Diligence

Financial Duty

Honesty

Duties to Third Parties

When a broker represents a lender, the agent has a duty of fair and honest disclosure to the other party. If the broker knows of any problem with the loan or property or that the loan will not meet the lender's or borrower's needs for some reason, then the broker has a duty to disclose this fact.

> *If the broker has a personal interest in the loan or if it involves a relative, close associate or friend, this relationship should be made known to the parties.*

Termination of Agency

In some cases a principal can be held liable for actions of an agent even after the agency has been terminated. If a third party knew of an agency, but had no knowledge of the agency termination, and gave a deposit to the former agent who still claimed agency status, the former principal might still be liable for the deposit. Of course, the former agent would also be liable to the third party.

The following are ways agencies can be terminated.

RENUNCIATION

> *Because an agency is a consensual relationship, either principal or agent can unilaterally terminate an agency at any time.*

Courts will not force a person to act as an agent or to accept another as his or her agent when they don't wish the relationship to continue. However, if the renunciation is not for just cause, the party renouncing the agency could be liable for damages. As an example, a broker who terminates an agreement to service a loan prior to the expiration date without just cause could be liable for damages (in this case damages would be the lender's additional cost involved in having the loan serviced).

While a principal has the power to revoke the agency at any time, the principal doesn't have the right to do so unless the agent has breached an agency duty. This power means the principal can terminate, but without the right, the termination would be a wrongful act and could subject the principal to damages.

If an agency has been recorded and gives the agent the power to mortgage the property, a renunciation by the owner would not terminate the owner's liability as to a subsequent lender unless the agency renunciation was also recorded.

An owner cannot terminate an agency coupled with an interest.

As an example, in order to obtain a mortgage loan agreement the broker advanced funds to an owner to avoid foreclosure on an existing loan. The home owner could not now repudiate the agreement because the broker's agency is now coupled with an interest in the property.

EXPIRATION OF AGENCY

An agency for a particular period of time ends with the expiration of the agency period.

DEATH

Because an agency is a personal relationship of trust, the death of either the principal or agent automatically terminates the agency.

If, however, a principal or an agent were a corporation, death of a principal officer would not terminate the agency since a corporation has a separate life that theoretically could last forever.

If a real estate broker dies, then his or her agency agreements would be terminated unless the broker were a corporation. This is one of the reasons why many large mortgage brokers are often corporations rather than sole proprietorships.

INCAPACITY

If the agent becomes incapacitated (physical or mental) so the agent can no longer perform agency duties, then the agency would terminate.

If an owner no longer remains mentally competent, then the agency would also be terminated.

IMPOSSIBILITY OF PERFORMANCE

If the purpose of the agency becomes impossible, then the agency would terminate.

As an example, if a building were condemned by the city, an agency agreement between the owner and a broker to arrange a loan on the building would be terminated.

BANKRUPTCY

If the principal becomes bankrupt, the property, unless exempt, would transfer to a receiver which would terminate the agency.

COMPLETION OF AGENCY PERFORMANCE

Completion of the purpose of the agency ends the agency. As an example, an agreement to arrange a loan would terminate with the closing of the loan.

Types of Agency Relationships

In the past, many lenders were led to believe that agents who were concerned with their needs were working for them rather than as agents of the borrower or visa versa. This lack of understanding as to typical agency relationships led to numerous lawsuits. In some cases courts held that parties were reasonable in believing that the agent was working for them. Thus, we have dual agencies with duties to both buyers and sellers. To avoid misunderstandings and to clarify roles, the nature of the real estate agency should be made to both borrower and lender as soon as practical.

A real estate broker can be a borrower's agent, lender's agent or a dual agent of both borrower and lender.

BORROWER'S AGENT

As a borrower's agent the agent would not have any agency relationship with the lender. The lender would customarily be represented by another agent. The lender could be an institutional lender to whom a loan package was submitted by the borrower's agent.

The borrower's agency would likely be expressly set forth in the broker's agreement with the borrower to place a loan.

The fact that the lender may be paying part or all of the broker's commission does not of itself change the status of a borrower's agent. However, the broker would have a duty to fully disclose any such lender payment. Otherwise it could be regarded as a secret profit.

> *Civil Code Section 2079.19 makes it clear that payment of compensation is not determinative of the agency.*

Payment of Compensation Not Determinative of Agency

2079.19. The payment of compensation or the obligation to pay compensation to an agent by the seller or buyer is not necessarily determinative of a particular agency relationship between an agent and the seller or buyer. A listing agent and a selling agent may agree to share any compensation or commission paid, or any right to any compensation or commission for which an obligation arises as the result of a real estate transaction, and the terms of any such agreement shall not necessarily be determinative of a particular relationship.

It should be set forth in a written agency disclosure who is paying compensation, what the agency relationship is and that payment of compensation by other than the agent's principal does not alter the agency relationship that has been declared.

> *A mortgage company that is funding the loan would not be the agent of the borrower.*

The mortgage company would be a principal to the transaction rather than an agent. However, based on the relationship with the lender who will be buying the loan from the mortgage company, the mortgage company could be an agent of such a lender.

A borrower's agent must be careful when dealing with a lender so that his or her words or actions do not lead the lender or any other party to believe an agency exists between the broker and the lender. (This would be an implied or ostensible agency.)

LENDER'S AGENT

An agent can represent a lender. The agent must make certain that the borrower fully understands this agency relationship. Again compensation paid by the borrower would not by itself make the broker an agent of the borrower. However, the agent would have to disclose any borrower-paid compensation to the lender or it would be a secret profit.

> **Case Example**
>
> **Price v. Eisan (1961) 194 C.A. 2d 363**
>
> In this case, the court held that the fact that a person enters a broker's office to make an inquiry does not in itself create an agency relationship.
>
> The court held that while consideration is not a requirement to create an agency (2 Cal. Jur. 2d 658), the lack of consideration is evidence against the existence of an agency.

A lender's agent must be careful or the lender's words or acts could lead to the borrower or another party believing that a borrower's agency exists. It could be an ostensible or implied agency.

DUAL AGENCY

Agency relations can be with both borrower and lender.

To have an express dual agency, both borrower and lender must agree to the agency and both must be fully informed as to the source of all broker compensations.

Confidentiality

Information received in confidence from one principal cannot be conveyed to the other principal.

a. A broker under a dual agency cannot inform the borrower that the lender will give better terms than offered.

b. A broker in a dual agency cannot inform a lender that a borrower is prepared to pay more for a loan than the lender has asked for.

After Closing

After a loan is closed the dual agency would end. If the broker is to service the loan, then the broker would continue as the agent of the lender.

Case Example

Montoya v. McLeod (1985) 176 C.A. 3d 57

A licensed salesperson solicited plaintiffs' money for lending on behalf of the salesperson's employer, an investment broker.

The plaintiffs believed that their life savings were adequately protected by a deed of trust. However, the company to whom the money had been loaned went into receivership which reduced the value of the loan by 75 percent. The plaintiffs discovered that the note they held was unsecured. They also discovered that the borrower was actually the salesperson's broker.

In an action against the salesperson, the salesperson claimed that she was only a middle person. The court held that her actions made her a dual agent of both the lender and the broker-borrower.

The defendant was held to have breached her fiduciary duty through ignorance and was therefore liable on a constructive fraud theory. (The salesperson claimed that she did not know the broker was the borrower.)

The court made it clear that even if the defendant did not know her employer was the borrower, she had a duty to make reasonable inquiry.

The trial court verdict was reversed and the defendant was held liable for the plaintiffs' loss.

Agency Disclosure Form

The disclosure and confirmation of agency relationships required by Civil Code 2079.14 does not apply to real estate brokers solely engaged in arranging or funding loans. Civil Code 2079.14 makes clear that it applies only to listing agents and selling agents.

If the loan broker served as a buyer, seller or dual agent in the course of the sale, then the disclosure would be required.

However, it is strongly recommended that a disclosure form similar to the one set forth in 2079.16 of the Civil Code be used in loan-brokerage situations. While it is applicable as written to buyers and sellers, it could readily be modified for lenders and borrowers.

Required Form of Disclosure

2079.16. The disclosure form required by Section 2079.14 shall have this article, excluding this section, printed on the back, and on the front of the disclosure form the following shall appear:

DISCLOSURE REGARDING REAL ESTATE AGENCY RELATIONSHIP
(As required by the Civil Code)

When you enter into a discussion with a real estate agent regarding a real estate transaction, you should from the outset understand what type of agency relationship or representation you wish to have with the agent in the transaction.

SELLER'S AGENT

A Seller's agent under a listing agreement with the Seller acts as the agent for the Seller only. A seller's agent or a subagent of that agent has the following affirmative obligations:

To the Seller:

(a) A fiduciary duty of utmost care, integrity, honesty and loyalty in dealings with the Seller.

To the Buyer and the Seller:

(a) Diligent exercise of reasonable skill and care in performance of the agent's duties.

(b) A duty of honest and fair dealing and good faith.

(c) A duty to disclose all facts known to the agent materially affecting the value or desirability of the property that are not known to, or within the diligent attention and observation of, the parties.

An agent is not obligated to reveal to either party any confidential information obtained from the other party which does not involve the affirmative duties set forth above.

BUYER'S AGENT

A selling agent can, with a Buyer's consent, agree to act as agent for the Buyer only. In these situations, the agent is not the Seller's agent, even if by agreement the agent may receive compensation for services rendered, either in full or in part from the Seller. An agent acting only for a Buyer has the following affirmative obligations:

To the Buyer:

(a) A fiduciary duty of utmost care, integrity, honesty and loyalty in dealings with the Buyer.

To the Buyer and the Seller:

(a) Diligent exercise of reasonable skill and care in performance of the agent's duties.

(b) A duty of honest and fair dealing and good faith.

(c) A duty to disclose all facts known to the agent materially affecting the value or desirability of the property that are not known to, or within the diligent attention and observation of, the parties. An agent is not obligated to reveal to either party any confidential information obtained from the other party which does not involve the affirmative duties set forth above.

AGENT REPRESENTING BOTH SELLER AND BUYER

A real estate agent, either acting directly or through one or more associate licensees, can legally be the agent of both the Seller and the Buyer in a transaction, but only with the knowledge and consent of both the Seller and the Buyer.

In a dual agency situation, the agent has the following affirmative obligations to both the Seller and the Buyer:

(a) A fiduciary duty of utmost care, integrity, honesty and loyalty in the dealings with either Seller or the Buyer.

(b) Other duties to the Seller and the Buyer as stated above in their respective sections.

In representing both Seller and Buyer, the agent may not, without the express permission of the respective party, disclose to the other party that the Seller will accept a price less than the listing price or that the Buyer will pay a price greater than the price offered.

The above duties of the agent in a real estate transaction do not relieve a Seller or Buyer from the responsibility to protect their own interests. You should carefully read all agreements to assure that they adequately express your understanding of the transaction. A real estate agent is a person qualified to advise about real estate. If legal or tax advice is desired, consult a competent professional.

Throughout your real property transaction you may receive more than one disclosure form, depending upon the number of agents assisting in the transaction. The law requires each agent with whom you have more than a casual relationship to present you with this disclosure form. You should read its contents each time it is presented to you, considering the relationship between you and the real estate agent in your specific transaction.

This disclosure form includes the provisions of Sections 2079.13 to 2079.24, inclusive, of the Civil Code set forth on the reverse hereof. Read it carefully.

_____	_____
Agent	Buyer/Seller (date)
	(Signature)
_____	_____
Associate Licensee (date)	Buyer/Seller (date)
(Signature)	(Signature)

Before closing the loan, an agency confirmation similar to the one set forth in Civil Code 2079.17 should be used.

Selling Agent's/Listing Agent's Disclosures

2079.17(a). As soon as practicable, the selling agent shall disclose to the buyer and seller whether the selling agent is acting in the real property transaction exclusively as the buyer's agent, exclusively as the seller's agent, or as a dual agent representing both the buyer and the seller. This relationship shall be confirmed in the contract to purchase and sell real property or in a separate writing executed or acknowledged by the seller, the buyer, and the selling agent prior to or coincident with execution of that contract by the buyer and the seller, respectively.

(b). As soon as practicable, the listing agent shall disclose to the seller whether the listing agent is acting in the real property transaction exclusively as the seller's agent, or as a dual agent representing both the buyer and seller. This relationship shall be confirmed in the contract to purchase and sell real property or in a separate writing executed or acknowledged by the seller and the listing agent prior to or coincident with the execution of that contract by the seller.

(c). The confirmation required by subdivisions (a) and (b) shall be in the following form:

_____ is the agent of (check one):
(Name of Listing Agent)

[ ] the seller exclusively: or
[ ] both the buyer and seller.

_____ is the agent of (check one):
(Name of Selling Agent
if not the same as the Listing Agent)

[ ]   the buyer exclusively; or
[ ]   the seller exclusively; or
[ ]   both the buyer and seller.

(d). The disclosures and confirmation required by this section shall be in addition to the disclosure required by Section 2079.14.

Escrow Duties

A real estate broker can be an escrow on transactions where the agent represented the borrower, the lender, both borrower and lender or was a principal to the transaction.

If a broker suggested to his or her principal that the broker be the escrow, this could be a breach of the agent's fiduciary duty, unless the agent had the ability to perform the escrow functions in a proper manner and, acting as an escrow, the agent would in no way jeopardize the principal.

While an escrow is a neutral party to a transaction, the broker who is an escrow is also an agent which means that the broker has special duties to his or her principal as well as advocacy duties. This could result in a conflict of interest.

Because of possible agency problems, some brokers decline to handle escrows on their transactions because of possible real or perceived conflicts of interests.

Other brokers own separate corporate escrow companies. Of course, the broker's relationship with an escrow would have to be fully disclosed to both borrower and lender.

SUMMARY

An agent is one who acts for and represents another who is known as the principal. (An employee does not necessarily have the authority to represent the employer.)

A principal is liable for the wrongful acts of the agent within the scope of the agency much as an employer is liable for the wrongful acts of an employee during the scope of the employment.

An independent contractor differs from an employee or agent in that the independent contractor is hired for results only and is not under the direct control of the principal. A principal is not ordinarily liable for the wrongful acts of an independent contractor.

Types of agents include:

Special Agent. Specified agency authority.
General Agent. Broad authority to carry on an enterprise.
Power of Attorney. A written agency making the agent an attorney-in-fact who represent the principal.

Agencies are created in a number of ways.

Express Agency. Created by written or verbal agreement.
Implied Agency. An agency understood by the actions of the parties but not specifically stated.
Agency by Estoppel. An agency created when a person's words or actions led other parties to reasonably believe the agency existed and causes the parties to act to their detriment based on this belief.

Agency by Ratification. An agency formed when a principal accepts the benefits of an agreement made by one who was not the principal's agent or who was exceeding the authority of the agency.

Authority of agents is classified as:

Express Authority. That authority set forth verbally or in writing.

Implied Authority. Authority understood but not stated which is required to perform expressly authorized acts.

Customary Authority. The authority that a person in the position held would be reasonably expected by others to have.

A secret agency is undisclosed. The person dealing with a secret agent has the option of holding either the agent or principal liable for the actions of the secret agent.

The fiduciary duty of an agent includes:

1. Confidentiality
2. Diligence
3. Financial Duties
4. Full Disclosure
5. Honesty
6. Loyalty
7. Obedience

The agent has a duty of fair and honest dealing with a third party. When a broker is an agent of either a borrower or lender, the broker has a duty to inform the other party of any detrimental facts known to the broker as well as any personal interest the broker has or will have in the property or the loan.

Agencies may be terminated by:

1. Renunciation
2. Expiration of Agency
3. Death of Principal or Agent
4. Incapacity of Principal or Agent
5. Impossibility of Performance
6. Bankruptcy
7. Completion of Agency Performance

The broker should make certain that all parties understand the agency chosen by the agent and what the agency means.

CLASS DISCUSSION TOPICS

1. When should you first discuss agency relationships with a prospective borrower or investor?

2. How can you be certain that parties understand agency in a loan brokerage situation?

3. Why are agency problems more likely to arise in a loan-brokerage situation than where the broker is acting as a mortgage company?

4. Give an example of how a party could be led to believe that the broker is his or her agent.

5. Is agency disclosure less important in loan brokerage than in broker listing and sale situations?

6. Why do you suppose the law has not mandated agency disclosure in loan-broker situations?

CHAPTER 7 QUIZ

1. Which of the following is NOT essential to the creation of an agency agreement? (p. 152)

    A. Compensation
    B. An express agreement
    C. Both A and B
    D. Neither A nor B

2. An independent contractor differs from an agent in that: (p. 152)

    A. the principal is not generally liable for wrongful acts of the independent contractor
    B. the agent may not be a corporation
    C. the independent contractor is not under the direction of the principal as to how a task shall be performed
    D. both A and C

3. For IRS purposes, a real estate salesperson is treated as an independent contractor if three requirements are met. Which of the following is NOT one of the requirements? (p. 154)

    A. The salesperson must be licensed

    B. Compensation must be based on success

    C. There must be a written contract specifying that the salesperson is an independent contractor.

    D. The federal minimum wage and overtime pay requirements must be met

4. An agent hired in writing by a property owner to locate a $10,000 loan for a particular property would be a: (p. 157)

    A. general agent

    B. special agent

    C. implied agent

    D. ostensible agent

5. A person said another was his agent when no agency existed. The reason the person who said the agency existed can no longer deny the agency is: (pp. 158-159)

    A. ratification

    B. estoppel

    C. implication

    D. the equal dignities rule

6. An agency was formed when a person accepted the benefits of an agreement entered into on her behalf by a person who was not her agent. The agency was created by: (p. 159)

    A. express agreement

    B. ratification

    C. implication

    D. estoppel

7. A person assumed that the general manager of a broker loan office could hire a courier to deliver documents because of: (p. 160)

    A. express authority

    B. customary authority

    C. the rule against perpetuities

    D. estoppel

8. A person did not reveal that she was acting in an agency capacity. The secret agent breached her agreement. Who could the third party hold liable? (p. 160)

    A. The principal only

    B. The agent only

    C. Both the principal and the agent

    D. Either the principal or the agent

9. Fiduciary duties include all EXCEPT: (p. 161)

    A. loyalty

    B. compensation

    C. diligence

    D. confidentiality

10. Which of the fiduciary duties of an agent would continue after the agency has expired? (p. 162)

    A. Confidentiality

    B. Full disclosure

    C. Obedience

    D. Loyalty

11. Which of the following are true of a borrower's agent? (p. 171)

    A. Has no agency relationship with lender

    B. The agency is expressly set forth in the broker's agreement with the borrower to place a loan

    C. The agent has a duty to fully disclose any lender payment

    D. All of the above

12. A loan broker could serve as the agent of the: (p. 171)

    A. borrower

    B. lender

    C. lender and borrower

    D. any of the above

Answers: 1. C; 2. D; 3. D; 4. B; 5. B; 6. B; 7. B; 8. D; 9. B; 10. A; 11. D; 12. D

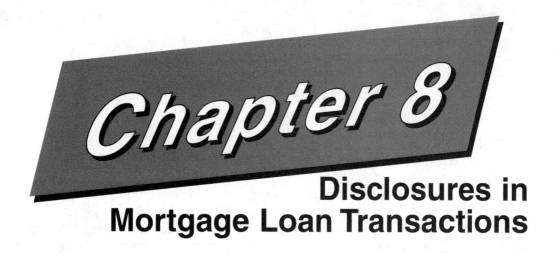

Chapter 8

Disclosures in Mortgage Loan Transactions

KEY WORDS AND TERMS

Advertising Consumer Credit
Annual Percentage Rate
Bait-and-Switch Advertising
Balloon Payment
Business Loans
Buy-Down Rate
Collateral Loan
Consumer Protection Act of 1968
Creditor
Demand Feature
Federal Block

Federal Trade Commission
Finance Charge
Lender/Purchaser Disclosure Statement
Mortgage Loan Disclosure Statement
Refinancing
Regulation Z
Rescission Rights
Trigger Terms
Truth In Lending
Variable Rate

LEARNING OBJECTIVES

This chapter is the first part of two chapters devoted to required disclosures in mortgage loan transactions.

The disclosures covered in this chapter are:

1. Truth In Lending
2. Mortgage Loan Disclosure Statement
3. Lender/Purchaser Disclosure Statement

You will learn about the requirements and exemptions of these disclosures as well as the form the disclosures must take.

Truth in Lending

www.law.cornell.edu/uscode (United States Code)

TRUTH IN LENDING is a federal act (15 U.S.C. 1601) which was enacted to promote the informed use of consumer credit by requiring lenders/creditors to disclose various terms and conditions of credit.

> *The purpose of the disclosure was to enable consumers to make credit comparisons between various credit sources so that informed decisions would be possible.*

The act, which was effective as of July 1, 1968, is part of the Consumer Protection Act of 1968 and is also known as REGULATION Z.

THE HISTORY OF TRUTH IN LENDING

Prior to the Truth in Lending Act, deception as to rates of interest charged was practically the rule rather than the exception. Various methods were used to justify an advertised rate of interest that bore no resemblance to what the creditor would actually be paying.

A number of banking bills had been introduced to require disclosure. They were vigorously opposed by the financial lobbies and were defeated. Proponents of the bill came up with an idea that insured its passage. Rather than labeling their bill with the names of those in the Congress and Senate who introduced the bill or give it a generic banking title, proponents came up with the "Consumer Protection" label as well as "Truth In Lending."

Even politicians who were heavily financed by banks found it difficult to oppose these titles because of fear of negative voter reaction against a politician who voted against "Truth." While previous acts had failed, the new titles resulted in passage of the bill.

As examples of the abuse prior to the act, lenders would advertise a rate of interest such as 6 percent. For a loan of $1,000, they would take out the interest in advance, giving the borrower $940. This is not 6 percent interest. The borrower is paying $60 interest to borrow $940, for one year, making the interest rate almost 6.4 percent.

$$\frac{\$\,60}{\$940} = .0638$$

The abuse was minor compared to other ruses lenders used. However, this charging interest for the full amount and then taking it out in advance so the borrower did not receive the principal bargained for was often combined with other methods which offered greater distortion between the interest rate advertised and the rate actually charged.

Lenders often advertised a rate which appeared accurate but was actually about one-half of the actual interest rate. A 6 percent interest rate for $1,000 for one year would be $60 in interest. However, when the loan is being repaid in 12 monthly installments, the period the borrower has use of the $1,000 is not one year (see Figure 8-1). As you can see, if the principal is repaid in 12 equal installments, the borrower only has the equivalent use of the total amount borrowed for about six months. This claimed rate of six percent was used in conjunction with the prepaid interest-rate method previously described. So, a supposed $1,000 loan at a claimed rate of six percent was actually the payment of $60 to borrow $940 for six months or to borrow $470 for one year.

$$\frac{\$\,60}{\$470} = 12.76\%$$

This is far different than the rate of six percent claimed.

Other lenders would advertise extremely low monthly costs per $1,000 of a loan. They failed to point out that the charge was not enough to pay off the loan and there would be a large balloon payment. In some cases, low payments resulted in **NEGATIVE AMORTIZATION** *so that the balloon payment would be greater than the amount borrowed.*

It has often been said that "the big print giveth and that the small print taketh away". The lending rule prior to truth in lending was that partial truths were alright in advertising as long as the loan documents dotted all the "i"s of the loan terms.

Creditors claimed that the Truth in Lending Act placed too great a burden on them and resulted in too much litigation.

The act was amended by the Truth in Lending Simplification and Reform Act in 1980.

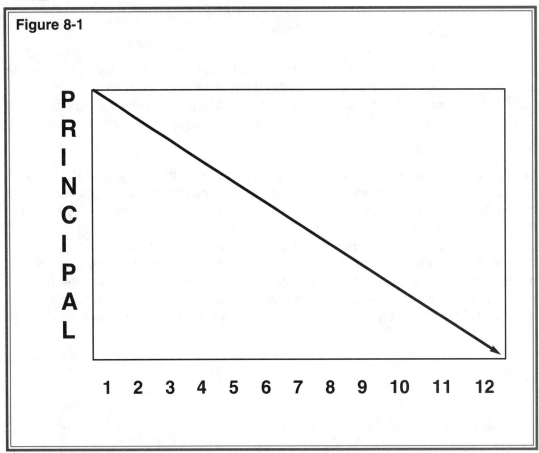

Figure 8-1

THE CREDITOR

Under Truth In Lending, the creditor (party giving the loan) is responsible for compliance with the act.

CREDITORS *include persons who extend credit more than 25 times in a year (more than five times in a year if transactions are secured by real estate).* If a mortgage banker extended credit (funded loans) four or less times in one year, the mortgage banker would be exempt from compliance.

The 1980 amended act included. "Arranger of Credit" to creditors. The Garn - St. Germain Depository Institutions Act later removed arranger of credit from the creditor definition. Loan brokers who arrange credit are not responsible for compliance with the disclosure requirements of the act. Unless the broker uses his or her own funds to fund the loan and otherwise meets the creditor requirements of the act. Some lenders have sought ways to avoid truth in lending disclosures.

Disclosures in Mortgage Loan Transactions

To be subject to the act, the credit extended must:

1. be subject to a finance charge;
2. be payable in more than four installments. A note requiring three or less installments would not be subject to the act;
3. be a written agreement payable on its face to the person extending credit.

Case Example

Clark v. Rent-It Corp. (1982) 685 F 2d 245

This case involves a consumer who rented a television set for a particular period of time. The lease included a purchase option at the end of the lease period. The purchase option was for a relatively low dollar amount. Therefore, most lessees exercised the purchase option. The court held that labeling the transaction as a lease does not make it a lease. In this case it was clearly a credit sale requiring the disclosures required by truth in lending.

Note: Rent-to-own sales that can be terminated at any time by the renter have been held not to be credit sales.

EXEMPT TRANSACTIONS

The following transactions are exempt from the disclosure requirements of the Truth In Lending Act:

Business Loans

Transactions where credit is extended primarily for a business, commercial or agricultural purpose would be exempt from truth in lending disclosures.

A transaction where the borrower intends to use property for rental purposes would make it a business purpose. The law was intended to protect consumers, not investors and business people who are generally considered more sophisticated and therefore better able to understand credit arrangements.

Loans to improve residential property are considered to be business loans if the loan is for more than four units. Improvement or maintenance loans for four or fewer dwelling units might require disclosure depending upon the circumstances of the transaction. As an example, if a property owner who owns hundreds of units borrows on a duplex to make an improvement, it would likely be regarded as a business loan.

Credit Over $25,000

Such credit is exempt from truth in lending disclosure.

> *This dollar limitation does not apply to loans secured by real estate, or by personal property used or expected to be used as the consumer's principal residence.*

A transaction secured by a boat or motor home intended to be used as a principal residence would therefore require the truth in lending disclosure even if it is over the $25,000 exemption.

FORM OF DISCLOSURE

Truth in lending disclosures regarding a credit sale or loan must be grouped together. As an example, you will often see credit information together in one block in advertisements. The credit information may not include information not related to the truth in lending disclosure requirements. Extraneous material could otherwise make comprehension more difficult.

> *The amount financed must be separately set forth. The terms "finance charge" and "annual percentage rate" must be in larger or bold-face type to stand out from other disclosures.*

Ways to segregate the required disclosures include:

1. outlining them in a box,
2. use of a different type style,
3. use of a different color or background,
4. use of a separate disclosure sheet.

*This separation is customarily referred to as the **FEDERAL BLOCK**.*

DISCLOSURES

There are 18 disclosures required by the Truth in Lending Act (not every disclosure is applicable for every loan).

Identity of Creditor

The creditor making the disclosures must be specifically identified.

Disclosures in Mortgage Loan Transactions

Amount Financed

The term "amount financed" must be used and explained. As an example:

"Amount Financed. The amount of credit provided to you on your behalf is $. . . .".

Itemization of Amount Financed

The creditor must provide the consumer with either a written itemization of the amount financed or provide a statement that the consumer is entitled to receive an itemization. In the latter instance, a space must be provided for the consumer to indicate if such an itemization is requested (if included, the itemization must be separate from the Federal Box).

> *Exempt from the itemization of the "Amount Financed" requirement are transactions subject to the Real Estate Settlement Procedures Act.*

The Real Estate Settlement Procedures Act requires the use of a **UNIFORM SETTLEMENT STATEMENT** *which effectively itemizes all charges and costs of the credit transaction included in the loan or paid by the consumer.* (See Chapter 9.)

Finance Charge

The term "Finance Charge" must be used. It must be identified so that the consumer knows it refers to his or her costs of obtaining credit. Only the total finance charge can be given.

All charges paid directly or indirectly by the consumer that are imposed by the creditor (directly or indirectly) must be included.

Finance charges include:

1. interest,
2. loan fees (assumption fees, finder's fees and buyer points),
3. mortgage guaranty premiums. (Such as MGIC or another private mortgage insurance provider).

The following is not considered to be a finance charge:

1. points paid by the seller,

The following are not finance charges providing that their amounts are reasonable and actual:

1. title fees (examination, survey, title insurance, etc.,
2. preparation of documents (deeds, mortgages, etc. required for the transaction),
3. notary fees,
4. appraisal costs,
5. credit report costs.

Fees cannot be charged for required disclosures.

Annual Percentage Rate

The term "annual percentage rate" must be used. It must be explained that the **ANNUAL PERCENTAGE RATE (APR)** *is the cost of credit expressed as a yearly rate.* Accuracy of the APR must be within one-eighth of one percent of the actual annual rate for a normal transaction. In irregular transactions, such as where there are multiple advances of funds or irregular payment periods or amounts, accuracy must be within one-fourth of one percent of the rate determined to be the actual annual rate.

Variable Rate

For loans secured by the consumer's principal residence and the loan being subject to a rate increase, the following must be included:

1. factors which would cause the interest rate to increase,
2. any limit on the increase,
3. the effect of any increase (length of loan and/or amount of payments),
4. inclusion of an example of the payment terms as the result of a rate increase,
5. when such a loan provides for increases within a period greater than one year there must be disclosure of:
   a. the variable rate feature,
   b. the fact that variable rate disclosure has been made.

Payment Schedule

There must be set forth the number, amount and timing of payments scheduled for the repayment of the credit given. When payments may be graduated, the creditor need only indicate the largest and smallest payments and that payments may vary.

Total of Payments

The total amount of payments required in order to make all payments required must be disclosed.

Disclosures in Mortgage Loan Transactions

Demand Feature

If the loan has a demand feature, such as a balloon payoff in a stated number of years, this fact must be set forth. This would not include a demand feature in the event of consumer default or a due-on-sale clause.

Total Sale Price

The total sale price must be set forth when the creditor is the seller.

Total sale price includes the amount of the down payment.

Prepayment Penalties and Rebates

A prepayment penalty must be set forth if there is any. If there isn't any prepayment penalty this fact must be disclosed. If the finance charge is not based on the principal balance, a statement must be made as to whether or not the consumer is entitled to a rebate in the event of prepayment. (This is usually in cases where total interest is added to the amount financed.) The method of rebate, such as the "rule of 78" used by most lenders, need not be disclosed.

Late Payment Charge

If there are to be charges due to late payments, this fact must be disclosed. The disclosure should indicate the amount of the charge or how it would be arrived at.

Security Interest

For loans secured by real or personal property, the security interest of the creditor must be set forth.

Insurance

If credit life, disability, accident, health or loss of income insurance premiums are excluded from the finance charges, the premium must be disclosed as well as a statement, requiring consumer signature, that the insurance is not a requirement of credit.

Security Charges

Taxes and fees paid to a public official may be excluded from the finance charges if they are disclosed.

Reference to Contract Terms

The creditor must include a disclosure statement that refers consumers to appropriate documents in the event of nonpayment default, acceleration of maturity, prepayment penalties or rebates.

Assumption Policy

For residential loan transactions, the consumer must be informed if the creditor will allow a subsequent purchaser to assume the obligation remaining under a loan (loan assumption).

Required Deposit

If a deposit, such as a savings account, is required as a condition of a loan, the creditor must state that the annual percentage rate does not reflect the effect of a required down payment.

Some lenders require a borrower to maintain a compensating balance in a low interest or no-interest account. The net effect is that the creditor does not make the full amount of the loan available to the borrower and the effective rate of interest (for the funds actually available) is greater than the rate stated in the loan. For example, assume a borrower were required to keep 25 percent of the loan proceeds in a non-interest bearing account. If the stated interest were 10 percent, the actual interest would be 13 1/3 percent.

TIME OF DISCLOSURE

Required disclosures under the Truth In Lending Act must be made prior to the consumer being "obligated" (prior to signing the note).

For loans subject to the Real Estate Settlement Procedure Act see RESPA disclosures in Chapter 9.

Variable Rate Transactions

Transactions where interest rates may be increased and the loan is secured by a lien on the borrower's residence and having a term greater than one year at the time of the loan application, (but before payment of any non-refundable fee) the consumer must be given a Federal reserve prepared booklet entitled *Handbook On Adjustable Rate Mortgages.*

Disclosures in Mortgage Loan Transactions

Disclosures must also be provided for any adjustable rate programs that the consumer has indicated an interest in.

Redisclosures

If because of an event disclosures became inaccurate, redisclosure of the correct facts are required if the APR changes more than one-eighth of one percent in a regular transaction or more than one-fourth of one percent in an irregular transaction.

For redisclosures, the creditor can simply issue corrections or a complete new set of disclosures.

Subsequent Disclosures

After consummation of a loan, there are three events which require the creditor to make disclosure:

Refinancing

Refinancing is a new transaction and requires a new set of disclosures.

Refinancing does not include:

1) an extension of a single payment obligation where other terms remain the same;
2) a reduction in the interest rate with an adjustment in the payment schedule;
3) a change in the payment schedule on collateral requirements resulting from consumer delinquency or default.

Assumption

An assumption is considered a new transaction. The creditor must make new disclosures to the new obligor based on the loan balance. (The addition of a guarantor to a loan does not change the primary responsibility of the obligor so no new disclosure is required.)

Adjustable Rate Adjustments

For adjustable rate loans secured by the consumer's principal residence, the following must be disclosed at least once every year in which a rate adjustment occurs without an accompanying payment change or between 25 and 120 days before an adjustment where the payments are to change.

1) New and prior interest rates.

2) Index on which new and prior rate were based.

3) The extent, if any, that the creditor has foregone any interest rate increase.

4) The effect of the adjustment such as new payments, term of loan and loan balance.

5) The payment required to fully amortize the loan at the new interest rate (if different than the new payment).

RIGHT OF RESCISSION

Truth in lending provides for a right of rescission in consumer credit transactions which place a lien against the principal residence of the consumer (a person only has one principal residence at a time). A dwelling could include a boat, motor home or mobile home. A dwelling could therefore be personal property.

The right of rescission is for three (3) days.

The consumer has until midnight of the third business day (includes Saturdays) following the completion of the loan transaction and delivery of the notice of right to rescission and all disclosures. If the consumer is not notified of his or her right to rescind, then the right continues until three days after the notification of the right is given. Therefore, the rescission right should be spelled out in loan documents signed by the consumer in order to prove notification of this important right.

The reasons for this rescission right were high-pressure sales of persons selling furniture, carpet, roofing, siding, furnaces, etc., where the loan papers placed a lien on the consumers' home, often without their realizing what they were doing. The rescission period allows the consumer second thoughts. However, it is possible for consumers to waive rescission rights providing the loans are for bona fide emergencies. Primarily, the persons taken advantage of that prompted rescission rights were the elderly.

EXEMPTIONS TO RESCISSION

Exemptions to rescission rights include:

Purchase Money Loans

The right to rescind does not apply to purchase money mortgages (loans made to finance the purchase of a principal residence). This exemption from rescission would apply to first and second mortgages.

Refinancing

> *When a creditor refinances an existing loan (where no new money is advanced), the consumer does not have any rescission rights.*

An example of such a refinance would be where a balloon payment becomes due and the creditor agrees to a new loan covering the amount due at the same or different terms.

Other Than the Principal Residence

Loans for any property other than the consumer's principal residence have no rescission rights.

ADVERTISING CONSUMER CREDIT

> *In advertising consumer credit, terms cannot be advertised unless the advertiser will actually make those terms available.*

Bait-and-Switch advertising is prohibited by the Truth In Lending Act. **BAIT-AND-SWITCH** *advertising involves advertising a product (loan) that is not or will not be available to the consumer.* The intent of such advertising is to bring in consumers expecting the "bargain" advertised. The consumers are then switched to other products. However, a creditor is allowed to advertise terms which will only be available for a limited time, as well as terms that will be available in the future.

The Rate

If the cost of finance is expressed in an advertisement as an interest rate, the rate must be expressed as the Annual Percentage Rate. The abbreviation APR may be used.

The **ANNUAL PERCENTAGE RATE** *is the effective rate of interest rather than the nominal rate which is the contract rate set forth in the note.* As an example, a note may be for 7 1/2 percent interest but loan origination costs and fees could result in an APR of 8.2 percent interest.

> *While the nominal rate of interest can be set forth in an advertisement, it cannot be more conspicuous than the APR.*

Adjustable Rate

When the APR listed is for an adjustable rate loan, the advertisement must indicate that the APR is subject to change.

Buydown Rates

Sellers and developers will often pay points to lenders to obtain a lower rate of interest—a buydown. If the buydown is for a specific period of time, then the advertisement must show the period the rate applies to as well as the rate that will apply at the end of that period.

Trigger Terms

The use of some (trigger) terms in advertising requires that additional disclosures be included in the advertisement. These trigger terms include:

1. The down payment either expressed as a dollar amount or a percentage of price. If an ad stated 90 percent financing, it would be said to state "10 percent down payment".
2. The loan period such as "30-year financing" or the number of payments.
3. The dollar amount of a monthly payment.
4. Finance charges (**FINANCE CHARGE** *is the total of costs paid directly or indirectly paid by the consumer to obtain the loan.* In addition to interest, it includes finders fees, points, service fees, etc.).

When Trigger Terms are Used

If any triggering term is used in an ad then the ad must include:

1. The down payment (as a dollar amount or percentage).
2. The terms of repayment (monthly payments and for how long).
3. The APR (if it can be increased, this fact must also be stated).

Disclosures in Mortgage Loan Transactions

The use of the Annual Percentage Rate (APR) by itself is not considered to be a triggering term requiring further disclosure.

ENFORCEMENT

The Federal Trade Commission can issue a cease and desist order prohibiting an activity after finding that an advertiser is in violation of truth in lending. If the advertiser continues after the cease and desist order, the advertiser would be subject to a civil penalty of $10,000 each day that the violation continues.

The Federal Trade Commission (FTC) is charged with the enforcement of the Truth In Lending Act.

If a creditor knows a practice has been determined by the FTC to be in violation of the Truth in Lending Act and nevertheless engages in such a practice, the FTC could ask the federal district court to impose a penalty of $10,000 for each violation.

When a creditor discloses an incorrect APR, the FTC can in some cases require that finance charges be adjusted to reflect the rate disclosed.

A civil penalty of twice the finance charges with a minimum of $100 and a maximum of $1,000 may be granted a consumer against a creditor for one of the following violations:

1. Failure to or improper disclosure of the rescission rights;
2. Improper disclosure of the amount financed;
3. Improper disclosure of finance charges;
4. Improper disclosure of annual percentage rate;
5. Improper disclosure of total of payments;
6. Improper disclosure of payment schedule;
7. Improper disclosure of the security interest taken by the creditor.

The above mentioned civil penalties are in addition to actual damages suffered by the consumer. If the creditor is found to have acted improperly, the consumer is also entitled to attorney fees and costs. Prior to a lawsuit or notification by the consumer, a creditor can escape liability by notifying the consumer within 60 days of discovery of an inaccuracy in disclosure and adjusts the account to reflect the true amounts.

Creditors are not considered to have violated truth in lending because of a bona fide error such as the transposition of numbers.

A creditor may be criminally liable for a willful violation of the Truth In Lending Act. Criminal penalties include fines up to $5,000 and/or imprisonment up to one year.

UNCONSCIONABLE ADVANTAGE

Full disclosure is not enough if the creditor takes unconscionable advantage of the borrower or if fraud is involved.

The following is taken from the April 23, 1997, issue of *The Wall Street Journal*:

> Mr. Bernie Roberts stopped at a roadside meat stand in 1989 and purchased $1,250 worth of meat with a $20 down payment. A meat loan was arranged by Donald McCauley from Associates First Capital Corporation which is the nation's largest finance company (80 percent owned by Ford Motor Company).
>
> Mr. Roberts, who was a retired quarry worker, owned his home free and clear. He signed his loan contract with an "X."
>
> Four months after issuing the meat loan, Mr. McCauley contacted Mr. Roberts and urged him to consolidate his debts, get cash and refinance his loan. Mr. Roberts agreed. Less than three weeks later, Mr. McCauley again recommended refinancing and again Mr. Roberts agreed. The debt was refinanced 10 times in less than four years. The refinancing generated $19,000 in loan fees for the Associates First Capital Corporation. Mr. Robert's loan proceeds were $23,000. Mr. Roberts, who lives on a total monthly income of $841 in Social Security and retirement benefits ended up with a 15-year loan with monthly payments of $633.28. This process is known as "flipping." Motivated salespersons use it to take advantage of homeowners with more equity than sense. Kathleen Keest, a lawyer with the National Consumer Law Center called the Roberts case the most rapid-fire flipping she had ever experienced.
>
> Mr. Roberts alleged in his lawsuit that the multiple refinancing was a fraud, "calculated to lead to the loss of (his) home," and that Mr. McCauley exercised undue influence over an unsophisticated customer. Associates First Capital Corporation settled the lawsuit by "forgiving" the debt so Mr. Roberts again had free and clear title to his home.
>
> Associates First Capital Corporation denied any wrongdoing and claim the loans were not abusive. They claim that refinancing was initiated by the request of Mr. Roberts and not Mr. McCauley. However, Associates does say

that since the beginning of the year they have forbidden branches from refinancing loans which provide less than 10 percent new money to the borrower. (The last seven refinancings did not meet this new criteria for Mr. Roberts.)

Mr. McCauley, a branch manager for Associates, was not penalized but a spokesperson for Associates indicated that Associate's loss would come out of Mr. McCauley's bonus.

> **Note:** Each refinancing, Mr. Roberts was charged 10 percent of the total loan in points—the maximum allowed. The fees were added to the loan.

A widely used Truth In Lending Disclosure Form is shown in Figures 8-2 and 8-3.

Mortgage Loan Disclosure Statement Borrower Disclosure

The MLDS is NOT required on federally related loans.

Article 7 of the Real Estate Law (Section 10240 of the Business and Professions Code) requires that real estate brokers who negotiate loans secured by real property provide the borrower with a written statement containing the following information (contained in Business and Professions Code 10241):

ESTIMATED MAXIMUM COSTS AND EXPENSES

Total to be paid by the borrower, including but not limited to:

1. appraisal fees;
2. escrow fees;
3. title changes;
4. notary fees;
5. recording fees; and
6. credit investigation fees.

Note: The real estate broker may be entitled to several of these fees if the broker performed the services.

TOTAL BROKER COMMISSION

The **TOTAL BROKER COMMISSION** *is a commission for the services contracted for in brokerage situations or the total of origination fees, points and other charges where the broker is to be the actual lender rather than an agent.*

Figure 8-2

TRUTH IN LENDING DISCLOSURE
(loan or carryback sale secured by real estate)

NOTE: This form only to be used for fixed rate financing.

Date:_____, 19____, at _____, California

FACTS: Items left blank or unchecked are not applicable.

Creditor: _____ Address: _____
Borrower: _____ Address: _____
Broker: _____ Address: _____

ANNUAL PERCENTAGE RATE	FINANCE CHARGE (see 3.3)	AMOUNT FINANCED (see 2.7)	TOTAL OF PAYMENTS (see 5.1)
The annual percentage rate of the charges on this financing is:	The total dollar amount of the financing charges over the life of this financing is:	The amount of funds OR credit disbursed to you or on your behalf is:	The amount you will have paid if you make all payments as scheduled is:
_____ %	$ _____	$ _____	$ _____

1. This transaction is a:
1.1 ☐ LOAN in the amount of $ _____
1.2 ☐ CARRYBACK SALE:
    a. TOTAL SALE PRICE: $ _____
    Your Total Purchase Price
    is comprised of the following:
    b. Cash downpayment: $ _____
    c. Debt assumed: $ _____
    d. Carryback note: $ _____

2. AMOUNT FINANCED:
2.1 Amounts paid to others on Borrower's behalf:
    a. Amount paid to Seller: $ _____
    b. Amount paid to lienholders: $ _____
    c. Amount paid to: _____ $ _____
2.2 TOTAL AMOUNTS PAID TO OTHERS: $ _____
2.3 AMOUNT PAID ON YOUR ACCOUNT WITH CREDITOR: $ _____
2.4 AMOUNT OF NET PROCEEDS RECEIVED BY BORROWER: $ _____
2.5 Prepaid finance charges:
    a. Loan Origination Fee $ _____
    b. Loan Discount Fee $ _____
    c. Lender Inspection/Photo Fee $ _____
    d. Underwriting Fee $ _____
    e. Tax Research Service Fee $ _____
    f. Processing/Application Fee $ _____
    g. Loan Broker Fee $ _____
    h. Assignment Fee $ _____
    i. Prepaid Interest to End of Month: $ _____
     (___ days at $_____ per day)
    j. Mortgage Insurance Premium $ _____
    k. Mortgage Insurance Reserve $ _____
    l. Property Insurance $ _____
    m. Other Prepaid Fee: $ _____
2.6 TOTAL PREPAID FINANCE CHARGES: $ _____
2.7 TOTAL AMOUNT FINANCED: $ _____

3. FINANCE CHARGES:
3.1 Interest payments scheduled: $ _____
3.2 Prepaid finance charges: (line 2.6) $ _____
3.3 TOTAL FINANCE CHARGE: $ _____

4. CLOSING COSTS:
4.1 Additional Closing Costs
    a. Appraisal Report $ _____
    b. Credit Report $ _____
    c. Appraiser Inspection Fee $ _____
    d. Flood Certification Fee $ _____

    e. Escrow Fee $ _____
    f. Document Preparation Fee $ _____
    g. Notary Fee $ _____
    h. Title Insurance Premium $ _____
    i. Recording Fees $ _____
    j. State Tax/Stamps/Certificates $ _____
    k. Pest Report Fee $ _____
    l. Other Closing Costs $ _____
4.2 SUBTOTAL: $ _____
4.3 ADDITIONAL FUNDS REQUIRED TO CLOSE ESCROW: $ _____

5. PAYMENTS:
5.1 Total of scheduled payments $ _____
5.2 Principal and interest is payable in ____ installments of $_____, on the _____ day of each _____ month, beginning on the ____ day of _____, 19____, and continuing until the ____ day of _____, 19____, when the principal is due and payable.
5.3 A final/balloon payment of $_____ is due on _____, 19____.
5.4 A late charge of $_____, or ____%, will be charged after a _____ day grace period.
5.5 If you pay off this financing early, you
    ☐ may have to pay a penalty.
    ☐ will not have to pay a penalty.
5.6 See the financing documents and contracts for any additional information about nonpayment, default, and prepayment penalties.

6. REAL ESTATE: Financing to be secured by a trust deed in favor of creditor on Borrower's
    a. ☐ principal residence, OR ☐ other real estate,
    b. ☐ owned, OR ☐ to be purchased by Borrower,
    c. located at _____.

7. ADDITIONAL PROVISIONS:
7.1 Assumption: If this financing is used to purchase the real estate described in §6, a subsequent buyer of the real estate:
    ☐ may assume the credit financing subject to a credit check and assumption fee.
    ☐ may not assume the credit financing.
7.2 Property damage and liability insurance to be purchased by Borrower. If purchased through Broker or Creditor, cost appears at §2.5(l). Borrower may choose the insurer.
7.3 Mortgage insurance premium appears at §2.5(j). Credit life and disability insurance are not required to obtain this financing.

Borrower acknowledges receipt of a copy of this disclosure statement.

_____ _____
Borrower's Signature   Date

_____ _____
Borrower's Signature   Date

Broker's Approval_____ ____/____/____

— — — — — — — — — — *PAGE ONE OF A TWO-PAGE DISCLOSURE* — — — — — — — — —

Figure 8-3

NOTICE OF RIGHT TO CANCEL
Borrower's Right to Cancel

NOTE: This page to be completed only when the debt is to be secured by a lien on the borrower's principal residence.

You are entering into a transaction which will result in a lien on your home. You have a legal right under federal law to cancel this transaction, without cost, within three business days from whichever of the following events occurs last:

- the date of this transaction: _____, 19____;
- the date you received your Truth in Lending Disclosure; or
- the date you received this notice of your right to cancel.

If you cancel the transaction, the lien is also cancelled. Within 20 days after we receive your notice, we must take steps necessary to reflect the fact that the lien on your home has been cancelled, and we must return to you any money or property you have given to us or anyone else in connection with this transaction.

You may keep any money or property we have given you until we have done the things mentioned above, but you must then offer to return the money or property. If it is impractical or unfair for you to return the property, you must offer its reasonable value. You may offer to return the property at your home or at the location of the property. Money must be returned to the address below. If we do not take possession of your money or property within 20 calendar days of your offer, you may keep it without further obligation.

How to Cancel

If you decide to cancel this transaction, you may do so by notifying us in writing, at (creditor's name and business address): _____

_____

_____ .

You may use any written statement that is signed and dated by you and states your intention to cancel, or you may use this notice by dating and signing below. Keep one copy of this notice because it contains important information about your rights.

If you cancel by mail or telegram, you must send this notice no later than midnight of _____,19___ (or midnight of the third business day following the latest of the three events listed above). If you send or deliver your written notice to cancel some other way, it must be delivered to the above address no later than that time.

I hereby cancel this transaction.

Date:_____, 19___

Borrower's Name:_____

Address: _____

_____ Phone: (___)_____

Signature: _____

Signature: _____

FORM 327   09-95   ℗1995 first tuesday, P.O. BOX 20068, RIVERSIDE, CA 92516 (909) 781-7300

LIENS AGAINST THE REAL PROPERTY

Liens disclosed by the borrower.

If the borrower fails to disclose liens or inaccurately provides balances due so a loan cannot be funded, the borrower may be liable for the broker's commission as well as costs incurred.

AMOUNT TO BE PAID

Estimation of amounts to be paid out on order of the borrower, not limited to the following:

1. fire insurance premiums;
2. payoffs on existing liens;
3. payoffs to other creditors; and
4. fees for assumption, transfer, forwarding beneficiary statements, etc.

BALANCE OF LOAN FUNDS

An estimate of balance of loan funds (if any) to be paid to the borrower.

PRINCIPAL AMOUNT OF THE LOAN

INTEREST RATE OF THE LOAN

LOAN TERMS

BALLOON PAYMENT NOTICE

A notice to the borrower (10-point bold face type) that a balloon payment could result in having to obtain a new loan which will again result in costs and commission. If a new loan is not possible then the consumer could be foreclosed.

In some cases, when the balloon payment is due, the costs of the new loan can bring the consumer's debt to an amount greater than the original loan amount. In such cases, the consumer has lifetime debt unless they can otherwise pay off the loan.

Disclosures in Mortgage Loan Transactions

NAME OF BROKER

Identification of the real estate broker negotiating the loan by name, license number and address.

BROKER FUNDS

If the loan may be made with broker funds or funds controlled by the broker, a statement to that effect must be included.

TERMS OF PREPAYMENT

The terms of prepayment and any penalties must be disclosed.

INSURANCE NOT REQUIRED

A statement must be included that the purchase of credit or credit disability insurance is not required to obtain the loan.

Because **CREDIT LIFE**, *which is a declining term insurance policy,* and disability coverage is extremely profitable for the agent, brokers formerly either required it or simply added it to the loan without notifying the consumer.

BALLOON PAYMENT TERMS

A statement for loans with a time limit of 6 years or less will be in accordance with the statutes. (Business and Professions Code 10244.1 prohibits a balloon payment for loans of 6 years or less when the loan is secured by an owner-occupied dwelling.)

COMPLIANCE WITH ARTICLE 7

A statement that the loan is in compliance with the commission and cost limitations placed on applicable loans by Article 7 (See Chapter 12).

Certified Written Statement

10240(a). Every real estate broker, upon acting within the meaning of subdivision (d) of Section 10131, who negotiates a loan to be secured directly or collaterally by a lien on real property shall, within three business days after receipt of a completed written loan application or before the borrower becomes obligated on the note, whichever is earlier, cause to be delivered to the borrower a statement in writing, containing all the information required by Section 10241. It shall be personally signed by the borrower and by the real estate broker negotiating the loan or by a real estate licensee acting for the broker in negotiating the loan. When so executed, an exact copy thereof shall be delivered to the borrower at the time of its execution. The real estate broker negotiating the loan shall retain on file for a period of three years a true and correct copy of such statement as signed by the borrower.

MORTGAGE LOAN DISCLOSURE STATEMENT (BORROWER)

_____
(Name of Broker)

_____
(Business Address)

I. SUMMARY OF LOAN TERMS

A. PRINCIPAL AMOUNT$ _____

B. ESTIMATED DEDUCTIONS FROM PRINCIPAL AMOUNT
    1. Costs and Expenses (See Paragraph III-A) $ _____
    2. Broker Commission/Origination Fee (See Paragraph III-B)* $ _____
    3. Lender Origination Fee/Discounts (See Paragraph III-B) $ _____
    4. Additional compensation will/may be received from lender
       not deducted from loan proceeds. __ YES $___(if known) __ NO
    5. Amount to be Paid on Authorization of Borrower
       (See Paragraph III-C) $ _____

C. ESTIMATED CASH PAYABLE TO BORROWER (A LESS B) $ _____

II. GENERAL INFORMATION ABOUT LOAN

A. If this loan is made, borrower will be required to pay the principal and interest at % per year, payable as follows: ____ (*number of payments*) ___ (*monthly, quarterly, annual*) payments of $ _____ and a FINAL/BALLOON payment of $ _____ to pay off the loan in full.

NOTICE TO BORROWER: IF YOU DO NOT HAVE THE FUNDS TO PAY THE BALLOON PAYMENT WHEN IT COMES DUE, YOU MAY HAVE TO OBTAIN A NEW LOAN AGAINST YOUR PROPERTY TO MAKE THE BALLOON PAYMENT. IN THAT CASE, YOU MAY AGAIN HAVE TO PAY COMMISSIONS, FEES AND EXPENSES FOR THE ARRANGING OF THE

Disclosures in Mortgage Loan Transactions

NEW LOAN. IN ADDITION, IF YOU ARE UNABLE TO MAKE THE MONTHLY PAYMENTS OR THE BALLOON PAYMENTS, YOU MAY LOSE THE PROPERTY AND ALL OF YOUR EQUITY THROUGH FORECLOSURE. KEEP THIS IN MIND IN DECIDING UPON THE AMOUNT AND TERMS OF THIS LOAN.

B. This loan will be evidenced by a promissory note and secured by a deed of trust on property identified as (street address or legal description):

_____

_____

C. Liens

1.Liens presently against this property (do not include loan being applied for):

Nature of Lien	Priority	Lienholder's Name	Amount Owing

2. Liens that will remain against this property after the loan being applied for is made or arranged (include loan being applied for):

Nature of Lien	Priority	Lienholder's Name	Amount Owing

NOTICE TO BORROWER: Be sure that you state the amount of all liens as accurately as possible. If you contract with the broker to arrange this loan, but it cannot be arranged because you did not state these liens correctly, you may be liable to pay commissions, fees and expenses even though you do not obtain the loan.

D. If borrower pays all or part of the loan principal before it is due, a PREPAYMENT PENALTY computed as follows may be charged:

_____

_____

_____

E. Late Charges: ____ YES, see loan documents. ____ NO

F. The purchase of credit life and/or credit disability insurance by a borrower is not required as a condition of making this loan.

REGULATIONS

III. <u>DEDUCTIONS FROM LOAN PROCEEDS</u>

A. Estimated Maximum Costs and Expenses of Arranging the Loan to be Paid Out of Loan Principal

PAYABLE TO

	Broker	Others
1. Appraisal fee	_____	_____
2. Escrow fee	_____	_____
3. Title insurance policy	_____	_____
4. Notary fees	_____	_____
5. Recording fees	_____	_____
6. Credit investigation fees	_____	_____
7. Other costs and expenses:		
_____	_____	_____
_____	_____	_____
Total Costs and Expenses	$ _____	

B. Compensation*
1. Brokerage Commission/Origination Fee $ _____
2. Lender Origination Fee/Discounts $ _____

C. Estimated Payment to be Made out of Loan Principal on Authorization of Borrower

PAYABLE TO

	Broker	Others
1. Fire or other hazard insurance premiums	_____	_____
2. Credit life or disability insurance premiums		
(See Paragraph II-E)	_____	_____
3. Beneficiary statement fees	_____	_____
4. Reconveyance and similar fees	_____	_____

Disclosures in Mortgage Loan Transactions

5. Discharge of existing liens against property _____ _____

_____ _____ _____

_____ _____ _____

6. Other:

_____ _____ _____

Total to Be Paid on Authorization of Borrower $ _____

If this loan is secured by a first deed of trust on dwellings in a principal amount of less than $30,000 or secured by a junior lien on dwellings in a principal amount of less than $20,000, the undersigned licensee certifies that the loan will be made in compliance with Article 7 of Chapter 3 of the Real Estate Law.

*This loan may/will/will not (delete two) be made wholly or in part from broker-controlled funds as defined in Section 10241(j) of the Business and Professions Code.

* **NOTICE TO BORROWER:** This disclosure statement may be used if the broker is acting as an agent in arranging the loan by a third person or if the loan will be made with funds owned or controlled by the broker. If the broker indicates in the above statement that the loan "may" be made out of broker-controlled funds, the broker must notify the borrower prior to the close of escrow if the funds to be received by the borrower are in fact broker-controlled funds.

_____ _____
(Name of Broker)   *(Broker Representative)*

_____ _____
(License Number)   *(License Number)*

_____ _____
(Signature of Broker)   *(Signature)*

NOTICE TO BORROWER

DO NOT SIGN THIS STATEMENT UNTIL YOU HAVE READ AND UNDERSTAND ALL OF THE INFORMATION IN IT. ALL PARTS OF THE FORM MUST BE COMPLETED BEFORE YOU SIGN.

Borrower hereby acknowledges the receipt of a copy of this statement.

DATED: _____ _____

(Borrower)

_____

(Borrower)

Lender/Purchaser
Disclosure Statement

Soliciting a person to make a loan that is secured by real property or solicitation to buy a real property sales contract or a note secured by real property requires that the real estate broker deliver a completed disclosure statement to the person solicited.

The statement shall be delivered as soon as practical but always before that person becomes obligated to make the loan or purchase.

The statement must be signed by the prospective lender (or purchaser) and the real estate broker or by a salesperson in behalf of the broker. The broker must retain a copy of this disclosure statement for **four years**.

EXEMPTIONS

Delivery of a disclosure statement does not apply to the following:

1. Securities issued pursuant to Article 6 for which a permit has been issued and qualifying under the Corporate Law of 1968. (The Corporation Code requires a purchaser be given a prospectus or other approved form of disclosure.)

2. Sellers of property who are carrying back financing.

3. Securities exempt from the Securities Law of 1968 but where the Commissioner of Corporations requires a disclosure statement prior to a prospective purchaser becoming obligated.

4. Lenders who are government entities or agencies as well as government related entities such as the Federal National Mortgage Association.

5. Banks and other lending institutions as evidenced by a license, certificate or charter issued by federal, state, district or territorial governments.

6. Trustees of profit sharing pension funds or welfare funds when these funds have a net worth of $15,000,000 or more (sophisticated lenders).

7. Corporations having outstanding securities registered under Section 12 of the Securities and Exchange Act of 1934 (these are likely to be major corporations).

8. A syndication or combination of the lenders or entities specified in a, b, c and d above.

9. A licensed real estate broker engaged in the business of selling all or part of the loan, note or contract to a lender or purchaser who is exempt from disclosure.

10. A licensed residential mortgage lender or servicer who is acting under the authority of that license.

Disclosure Statement - Delivery - Exception - Funds Handling

10232.4(a). In making a solicitation to a particular person and in negotiating with that person to make a loan secured by real property or to purchase a real property sales contract or a note secured by a deed of trust, a real estate broker shall deliver to the person solicited the applicable completed statement described in Section 10232.5 as early as practicable before he or she becomes obligated to make the loan or purchase and, except as provided in subdivision (c), before the receipt by or on behalf of the broker of any funds from that person. The statement shall be signed by the prospective lender or purchaser and by the real estate broker, or by a real estate salesperson licensed to the broker, on the broker's behalf. When so executed, an exact copy shall be given to the prospective lender or purchaser, and the broker shall retain a true copy of the executed statement for a period of three years**...**

CONTENTS OF DISCLOSURE STATEMENT

The disclosure statement shall include but is not necessarily limited to the following information:

1. Address or other identification of the property that is security for the borrower's obligation.

2. Estimated fair market value of the security. If the broker is relying on an appraisal then it shall include the appraisal date and name and affiliation of the appraiser.

3. The age, size, type of construction and description of the property improvements.

4. Identity of borrower including income, occupation, employment and credit data as represented by the borrower to the broker.

5. Terms of the promissory note.

6. Information as to property liens and other loans the borrower expects will result in liens against the security (based on actual knowledge of broker).

7. Provisions for servicing the loan, if any, including late changes and prepayment penalties.

8. Information concerning any broker arrangement where lender will be a joint beneficiary under the loan.

9. Any benefits that the broker will receive other than those dealing with costs and commissions.

FORMAT OF DISCLOSURE

Section 2846 of the Commissioner's Regulations require the commissioner to prepare and publish Lender Purchase Disclosure Statements.

2846. Approved Lender/Purchaser Disclosure Statement.

(a). The commissioner shall publish and make available to interested persons as an official form of the Department of Real Estate, an approved format and content for the disclosure statements referred to in subdivisions (a) and (b) Section 10232.5 of the Code...

The commissioner has prepared three separate disclosure statements:

1. Lender/Purchaser Disclosure Statement for loan origination (Figures 8-4 through 8-7).
2. Lender/Purchaser Disclosure Statement for Sale of an existing note (Not shown).
3. Lender/Purchaser Disclosure Statement for a collateral loan (Not shown).

SUMMARY

The purpose of the Truth In Lending Act is to provide disclosures to borrowers so that they may make informed choices as to borrowing.

Creditors who must comply with the truth-in-lending disclosures include those who extend credit 25 times per year. But for loans secured by real estate, it is five times per year. Arrangers of credit are exempt; it is the lenders who must comply. Loans subject to the act are loans which:

1. have a finance charge;
2. are payable in more than four installments; and
3. involve a written agreement payable to the person who extends the credit.

Disclosures in Mortgage Loan Transactions

Figure 8-4

LENDER/PURCHASER DISCLOSURE STATEMENT
(Loan Origination)

RE 851A (New 2/90)

DISCLOSURE STATEMENT SUMMARY

AMOUNT OF THIS LOAN (see Part 3)	MARKET VALUE OF PROPERTY (see Part 6)	TOTAL AMOUNT OF ENCUMBRANCES SENIOR TO THIS LOAN (see Part 7)	TOTAL AMOUNT OF ENCUMBRANCES ANTICIPATED OR EXPECTED TO BE JUNIOR TO THIS LOAN (see Part 7)	PROTECTIVE EQUITY (MARKET VALUE–THIS LOAN AND TOTAL SENIOR ENCUMBRANCES)
$	$	$	$	$

PART 1   **BROKER INFORMATION**

NAME OF BROKER	REAL ESTATE ID#
BUSINESS ADDRESS	TELEPHONE NUMBER

NAME OF BROKERS REPRESENTATIVE

PART 2   **BROKER CAPACITY IN TRANSACTION**

THE BROKER IDENTIFIED IN PART 1 OF THIS STATEMENT IS ACTING IN THE FOLLOWING CAPACITY IN THIS TRANSACTION: (CHECK AS APPLIES)

❑   A.   AGENT IN ARRANGING A LOAN ON BEHALF OF ANOTHER

❑   B.   PRINCIPAL AS A BORROWER OF FUNDS FROM WHICH BROKER WILL DIRECTLY OR INDIRECTLY BENEFIT OTHER THAN THROUGH THE RECEIPT OF COMMISSIONS, FEES AND COSTS AND EXPENSES AS PROVIDED BY LAW FOR SERVICES AS AN AGENT.

❑   C.   FUNDING A PORTION OF THIS LOAN. *(Multi-lender transactions are subject to Department of Corporation rules.)*

IF MORE THAN ONE CAPACITY HAS BEEN CHECKED PROVIDE EXPLANATION HERE.

IF "B" HAS BEEN CHECKED, THE BROKER INTENDS TO USE FUNDS FROM THE LENDER/PURCHASER IN THIS TRANSACTION FOR:

PART 3   **TRANSACTION INFORMATION**

THIS IS A MULTI-LENDER TRANSACTION. .... ❑ YES   ❑ NO

IF YES, YOU WILL BE A JOINT BENEFICIARY WITH OTHERS ON THIS NOTE AND YOU SHOULD CONSIDER REQUESTING A LIST OF NAMES AND ADDRESSES OF THE OTHER BENEFICIARIES AS OF THE CLOSE OF ESCROW. MULTI-LENDER TRANSACTIONS ARE SUBJECT TO DEPARTMENT OF CORPORATION RULES.

TERM OF LOAN	PRIORITY OF THIS LOAN (1ST, 2ND, ETC.)	PRINCIPAL AMOUNT $	YOUR SHARE IF MULTI-LENDER TRANS. $
INTEREST RATE __% ❑ VARIABLE ❑ FIXED	(CHECK ONE) ❑ AMORTIZED ❑ PARTIALLY AMORTIZED	❑ INTEREST ONLY ❑	**THE TRUST DEED WILL BE RECORDED.**
PAYMENT FREQUENCY ❑ MONTHLY ❑ ❑ WEEKLY	APPROXIMATE PAYMENT DUE DATE	AMOUNT OF PAYMENT $	YOUR SHARE IF MULTI-LENDER TRANS. $
BALLOON PAYMENT ❑ YES ❑ NO	APPROX. BALLOON PAYMENT DUE DATE	AMOUNT OF BALLOON PAYMENT $	YOUR SHARE IF MULTI-LENDER TRANS. $

Balloon Payment — A balloon payment is any installment payment (usually the payment due at maturity) which is greater than twice the amount of the smallest installment payment under the terms of the promissory note or sales contract.

The borrower/vendee may have to obtain a new loan or sell the property to make the balloon payment. If the effort is not successful it may be necessary for the holder of the note/contract to foreclose on the property as a means of collecting the amount owed.

THERE ARE SUBORDINATION PROVISIONS. .... ❑ YES   ❑ NO

IF YES, EXPLAIN HERE OR ON AN ATTACHMENT.

Figure 8-5

PART 4   **SERVICE ARRANGEMENTS**

If the loan is to be serviced by a real estate broker you must be notified with ten (10) days if the broker makes any advances on senior encumbrances to protect the security of your note. Depending on the terms and conditions of the servicing contract, you may be obligated to repay any advances made by the broker. The broker may not guarantee or imply to guarantee, or advance any payments to you unless a real property securities permit is obtained from the Department of Real Estate and you have received a copy.

CHECK APPROPRIATE STATEMENTS

☐ THERE ARE NO SERVICING ARRANGEMENTS   ☐ BROKER IS THE SERVICING AGENT
☐ ANOTHER PERSON WILL SERVICE THE LOAN   ☐ COPY OF THE SERVICING CONTRACT IS ATTACHED

IF BROKER IS NOT SERVICING AGENT, WHAT IS THE RELATIONSHIP BETWEEN THE BROKER AND SERVICER?

COST TO LENDER FOR SERVICING ARRANGEMENTS *(EXPRESS AS DOLLAR AMOUNT OR PERCENTAGE)*

PER   ☐ MONTH   ☐ YEAR   ☐   PAYABLE   ☐ MONTHLY   ☐ ANNUALLY   ☐

NAME OF AUTHORIZED SERVICER, IF ANY

BUSINESS ADDRESS   TELEPHONE NUMBER

PART 5   **BORROWER INFORMATION**

SOURCE OF INFORMATION

☐ BORROWER   ☐ BROKER INQUIRY   ☐ OTHER (DESCRIBE)

NAME	CO-BORROWER'S NAME
RESIDENCE ADDRESS	CO-BORROWER'S RESIDENCE ADDRESS
OCCUPATION OR PROFESSION	CO-BORROWER'S OCCUPATION OR PROFESSION
CURRENT EMPLOYER	CO-BORROWER'S CURRENT EMPLOYER
HOW LONG EMPLOYED? AGE	HOW LONG EMPLOYED? CO-BORROWER'S AGE

SOURCES OF GROSS INCOME *(LIST AND IDENTIFY EACH SOURCE SEPARATELY.)*	MONTHLY AMOUNT	CO-BORROWER SOURCES OF GROSS INCOME *(LIST AND IDENTIFY EACH SOURCE SEPARATELY.)*	MONTHLY AMOUNT
GROSS SALARY	$	GROSS SALARY	$
OTHER INCOME INCLUDING:		OTHER INCOME INCLUDING:	
INTEREST	$	INTEREST	$
DIVIDENDS	$	DIVIDENDS	$
GROSS RENTAL INCOME	$	GROSS RENTAL INCOME	$
MISCELLANEOUS INCOME	$	MISCELLANEOUS INCOME	$

TOTAL EXPENSES OF ALL BORROWERS *(DO NOT COMPLETE IF BORROWER IS A CORPORATION)*

PAYMENT OF LOAN BEING OBTAINED	$	SPOUSAL/CHILD SUPPORT	$
RENT	$	INSURANCE	$
CHARGE ACCOUNT/CREDIT CARDS	$	VEHICLE LOAN(S)	$
MORTGAGE PAYMENTS (INCLUDE TAXES AND PROPERTY INSURANCE)	$	OTHER *(FEDERAL & STATE INCOME TAXES, ETC.)*	$
TOTAL GROSS MONTHLY INCOME OF BORROWER(S) $		TOTAL MONTHLY EXPENSES OF BORROWER(S) $	

Disclosures in Mortgage Loan Transactions

Figure 8-6

THE BORROWER HAS FILED FOR BANKRUPTCY IN THE PAST 12 MONTHS. .... ❑ YES ❑ NO

IF YES, THE BANKRUPTCY HAS BEEN DISCHARGED OR DISMISSED. .... ❑ YES ❑ NO

❖ **THE FOLLOWING STATEMENTS ONLY APPLY IF THE BORROWER IS A CORPORATION, PARTNERSHIP OR SOME OTHER FORM OF OPERATING BUSINESS ENTITY.**

COPIES OF A BALANCE SHEET OF THE ENTITY AND INCOME STATEMENT COVERING THE INDICATED PERIOD
HAVE BEEN SUPPLIED BY THE BORROWER/OBLIGOR AND ARE ATTACHED. IF NO, EXPLAIN ON ADDENDUM. ❑ YES ❑ NO

IF YES, DATE OF BALANCE SHEET .... _____

INCOME STATEMENT PERIOD *(FROM-TO)* .... _____

FINANCIAL STATEMENTS HAVE BEEN AUDITED BY CPA OR PA. .... ❑ YES ❑ NO

ADDITIONAL INFORMATION IS INCLUDED ON AN ATTACHED ADDENDUM. .... ❑ YES ❑ NO

PART 6	APPRAISAL/PROPERTY INFORMATION

IDENTIFICATION OF PROPERTY WHICH IS SECURITY FOR NOTE. (IF NO STREET ADDRESS, THE ASSESSOR'S PARCEL NUMBER OR LEGAL DESCRIPTION AND A MEANS FOR LOCATING THE PROPERTY IS ATTACHED.)

STREET ADDRESS

OWNER OCCUPIED
❑ NO ❑ YES

ANNUAL PROPERTY TAXES
$ _____ ❑ ACTUAL ❑ ESTIMATED

ARE TAXES DELINQUENT?
❑ NO ❑ YES

IF YES, AMT. REQUIRED TO BRING CURRENT
$

SOURCE OF TAX INFORMATION

BROKER'S ESTIMATE OF FAIR MARKET VALUE
$

If the broker is basing his estimate of fair market value on an appraisal, the appraisal information is shown below.

FAIR MARKET VALUE (ACCORDING TO APPRAISER) *(Place this figure or brokers estimate of fair market value on line "F" of Part 8.)*
$

DATE OF APPRAISAL

NAME OF APPRAISER (IF KNOWN TO BROKER)

PAST AND/OR CURRENT RELATIONSHIP OF APPRAISER TO BROKER (EMPLOYEE, AGENT, INDEPENDENT CONTRACTOR, ETC.)

ADDRESS OF APPRAISER

DESCRIPTION OF PROPERTY/IMPROVEMENT

IS THERE ADDITIONAL SECURING PROPERTY?
❑ YES IF YES, SEE ADDENDUM.
❑ NO

AGE | SQUARE FEET | TYPE OF CONSTRUCTION

IF THE PROPERTY IS CURRENTLY GENERATING INCOME FOR THE BORROWER/OBLIGOR:

ESTIMATED GROSS ANNUAL INCOME
$

ESTIMATED NET ANNUAL INCOME
$

PART 7	ENCUMBRANCE INFORMATION

SOURCE OF INFORMATION
❑ BROKER INQUIRY ❑ BORROWER ❑ OTHER *(explain)*

ARE THERE ANY ENCUMBRANCES OF RECORD AGAINST THE SECURING PROPERTY AT THIS TIME?. .... ❑ YES ❑ NO

A. OVER THE LAST 12 MONTHS WERE ANY PAYMENTS MORE THAN 60 DAYS LATE? .... ❑ YES ❑ NO

B. IF YES, HOW MANY? .... _____

C. DO ANY OF THESE PAYMENTS REMAIN UNPAID? .... ❑ YES ❑ NO

D. IF YES, WILL THE PROCEEDS OF SUBJECT LOAN BE USED TO CURE THE DELINQUENCY? .... ❑ YES ❑ NO

E. IF NO, SOURCE OF FUNDS TO BRING THE LOAN CURRENT. .... _____

Figure 8-7

ENCUMBRANCES REMAINING AND/OR EXPECTED OR ANTICIPATED TO BE PLACED AGAINST THE PROPERTY BY THE BORROWER/OBLIGOR AFTER THE CLOSE OF ESCROW (EXCLUDING THE NOTE DESCRIBED ON PAGE 1).

ENCUMBRANCE(S) REMAINING _(AS REPRESENTED BY THE BORROWER)_

PRIORITY (1ST, 2ND, ETC)	INTEREST RATE %	PRIORITY (1ST, 2ND, ETC)	INTEREST RATE %
BENEFICIARY		BENEFICIARY	
ORIGINAL AMOUNT $	APPROXIMATE PRINCIPAL BALANCE $	ORIGINAL AMOUNT $	APPROXIMATE PRINCIPAL BALANCE $
MONTHLY PAYMENT $	MATURITY DATE	MONTHLY PAYMENT $	MATURITY DATE
BALLOON PAYMENT ☐ YES ☐ NO ☐ UNKNOWN	IF YES, AMOUNT $	BALLOON PAYMENT ☐ YES ☐ NO ☐ UNKNOWN	IF YES, AMOUNT $

ENCUMBRANCES EXPECTED OR ANTICIPATED _(AS REPRESENTED BY THE BORROWER)_

PRIORITY (1ST, 2ND, ETC)	INTEREST RATE %	PRIORITY (1ST, 2ND, ETC)	INTEREST RATE %
BENEFICIARY		BENEFICIARY	
ORIGINAL AMOUNT $	MATURITY DATE	ORIGINAL AMOUNT $	MATURITY DATE
MONTHLY PAYMENT $		MONTHLY PAYMENT $	
BALLOON PAYMENT ☐ YES ☐ NO ☐ UNKNOWN	IF YES, AMOUNT. $	BALLOON PAYMENT ☐ YES ☐ NO ☐ UNKNOWN	IF YES, AMOUNT. $

ADDITIONAL REMAINING, EXPECTED OR ANTICIPATED ENCUMBRANCES ARE SET FORTH IN AN ATTACHMENT TO THIS STATEMENT. .... ☐ YES ☐ NO

PART 8   **LOAN TO VALUE RATIO**

A. REMAINING ENCUMBRANCES SENIOR TO THIS LOAN _(FROM PART 7)_ .... $ _____

B. ENCUMBRANCES EXPECTED OR ANTICIPATED SENIOR TO THIS LOAN

   (FROM PART 7) .... + $ _____

C. TOTAL REMAINING AND EXPECTED OR ANTICIPATED ENCUMBRANCES SENIOR TO THIS LOAN .... = $ _____

D. PRINCIPAL AMOUNT OF THIS LOAN FROM PAGE 1 PART 3 .... + $ _____

E. TOTAL ALL SENIOR ENCUMBRANCES AND THIS LOAN .... = $ _____

F. FAIR MARKET VALUE FROM PAGE 3 PART 6 .... + $ _____

G. LOAN TO VALUE RATIO .... = _____ %

BROKER VERIFICATION	**ACKNOWLEDGMENT OF RECEIPT**
The information in this statement and in the attachments hereto is true and correct to the best of my knowledge and belief.	_The prospective lender/purchaser acknowledges receipt of a copy of this statement signed by or on behalf of the broker._
SIGNATURE OF BROKER OR DESIGNATED REPRESENTATIVE DATE	SIGNATURE OF PROSPECTIVE LENDER/PURCHASER DATE
➤	➤

Disclosures in Mortgage Loan Transactions

Transactions exempt from truth-in lending disclosures include:

1. business loans.
2. credit over $25,000 not secured by real property.

The disclosures required by truth in lending must be grouped together (the Federal Block) and separated from other material. The disclosures mandated by truth in lending include (as applicable) the following:

1. identity of creditor.
2. amount financed.
3. itemization of amount financed.
4. finance charges.
5. annual percentage rate.
6. variable rates (loan specifics).
7. payment schedule.
8. total of payments.
9. demand feature.
10. total sale price.
11. prepayment penalties and rebates.
12. late payment charge.
13. security interest.
14. disability and life insurance (the fact that they are not required).
15. security charges (taxes and fees paid to public officials respecting security charges are exempt from the finance charges).
16. reference to contract terms.
17. assumption policy.
18. required deposit.

The above disclosures must be made prior to the consumer being obligated to the loan.

Additional disclosures involve:

1. Variable Rate Transactions. A federal reserve booklet entitled *Handbook On Adjustable Rate Mortgages* must be given to the consumer for variable rate transactions.
2. Redisclosure. If the disclosure that was made becomes inaccurate, redisclosure is required if the APR changes by more than one-eighth percent (one-fourth percent for adjustable rate loans).

3. Subsequent Disclosure. After the loan has been made there are three events requiring new disclosure.

    A. Refinancing.
    B. Loan assumption.
    C. Adjustable rate adjustments.

Truth in lending provides for a right of rescission when the loan places a lien against the borrower's principal residence. The cancellation right is until midnight of the third business day following completion of the loan. Exemptions to the rescission rights include:

1. purchase money loans.
2. refinancing where no additional money is advanced.
3. loans secured by other than the borrower's principal residence.

In advertising consumer credit, bait-and-switch tactics are prohibited. If the rate is advertised it must include all costs of financing and be expressed as the Annual Percentage Rate (APR). If the APR is given for an adjustable rate loan it must indicate that the rate is subject to change. If a buy-down rate is used and it is for a specified period of time, the advertisement must show the period the rate applies to and the rate that will apply at the end of that period.

Trigger terms in advertising are terms used which require additional advertising disclosure. Trigger terms include:

1. the down payment.
2. the period of the loan (or number of payments).
3. monthly loan payments.
4. total finance charge.

When any trigger term is used, the advertisement must include:

1. down payment.
2. terms of repayment.
3. The APR.

Truth in lending is enforced by the Federal Trade Commission.

A Mortgage Loan Disclosure Statement must be provided to borrowers for loans arranged by real estate brokers (Article 7 of the Real Estate Law). The Mortgage Loan Statement must include:

1. estimated maximum costs and expenses.
2. total broker commissions.
3. liens against the real property.
4. amount to be paid on order of borrower and to whom.
5. balance of loan funds to be paid to borrower.
6. principal amount of the loan.
7. loan terms.
8. notice as to balloon payment (could result in having to place a new loan on property or foreclosure).
9. the name of the broker.
10. if any broker funds will be used to fund the loan.
11. prepayment terms.
12. the fact that credit life and disability insurance is not a loan requirement.
13. balloon payment specifics.
14. the fact that the loan complies with cost and commission limitations of Article 7.

A Lender/Purchaser Disclosure Statement is required to be provided to the lender on most broker arranged loans. The disclosure statement must include:

1. address or other identification of the property securing the loan.
2. estimated fair market value of the security.
3. the age, size, type of construction and description of property
4. improvements.
5. identity of borrower.
6. terms of the promissory note.
7. information as to property liens.
8. provision for servicing the loan (if any).
9. any arrangement where the broker will be a joint beneficiary of the loan.
10. any additional benefits that the broker will receive other than those dealing with loan costs and commission.

CLASS DISCUSSION TOPICS

1. Do you agree with the exemptions allowed for truth in lending disclosures?

2. Are all business owners sophisticated enough to understand loan terms?

3. Do you think the over $25,000 exemption from truth in lending should be raised? Why?

4. Do you agree with the truth in lending rescission policy? Should it be changed? How?

5. From the real estate section of your local paper and/or home finder type publications, identify ads which are in violation of the truth in lending advertising disclosure requirements because of use of trigger terms.

6. Do you agree with the necessity of the disclosure requirements mandated for borrower and lenders/purchasers?

7. What do you feel were the causes of the Associates' refinancing of Mr. Roberts' meat loan?

CHAPTER 8 QUIZ

1. The purpose of the Truth In Lending Law was to: (p. 186)
   - A. set maximum interest rates and loan costs
   - B. allow consumers to make credit comparisons
   - C. prohibit secondary financing on federally related loans
   - D. set penalties for false borrower disclosures

2. Who is responsible for compliance with the Truth In Lending Act? (p. 188)
   - A. The arranger of credit
   - B. The Department of Real Estate
   - C. The creditor
   - D. The borrower

3. Which of the following loans would be subject to the disclosures required under the Truth In Lending Act? (p. 189)
   - A. A credit sale where no finance charges are to be paid
   - B. A credit sale payable in three installments
   - C. Both A and B
   - D. Neither A nor B

4. Transactions exempt from the disclosure requirements of truth In lending include all EXCEPT: (p. 190)
   - A. agricultural loans
   - B. business loans
   - C. loans on property held for rental purposes
   - D. a $25,000 loan secured by the borrower's residence

Disclosures in Mortgage Loan Transactions

5. Which of the following is not one of the disclosures required under truth in lending? (pp. 190-194)

    A. The identity of the creditor

    B. The amount financed

    C. The amount of any prepayment penalty

    D. If the lender intends to sell the loan

6. Which of the following would not be a disclosure under truth in lending for residential loans? (p. 193)

    A. The fact that credit life insurance is a requirement of granting credit

    B. Any late payment charges

    C. The security interest of the creditor

    D. If the loan may be assumed

7. Under truth in lending, when must a new disclosure be made? (pp. 195-196)

    A. When a borrower is assessed a late charge

    B. When a guarantor is added to a loan

    C. When the interest rate and payment changes in an adjustable rate loan

    D. When the borrower is in default

8. The right of rescission when a consumer places a lien against his or her principal residence extends: (p. 196)

    A. for 24 hours after the loan has been completed

    B. until midnight of the third business day following completion of the loan

    C. for seven days after filing an application for a loan

    D. until the loan has actually been funded

9. The rescission rights under truth in lending apply to: (p. 197)

    A. purchase money loans

    B. refinancing where the creditor does not receive any new funds

    C. properties not used as a principal residence of the borrower

    D. none of the above

10. Trigger terms under truth in lending advertising include all EXCEPT advertising the: (p. 198)

    A. APR

    B. down payment

    C. monthly payment

    D. total finance charges

11. The Mortgage Loan Disclosure Statement received by the borrower would include: (pp. 201-205)

    A. an estimate of total costs and expenses
    B. the broker commission to be paid
    C. the name of the broker
    D. all of the above

12. The Lender/Purchaser Disclosure Statement required for loans arranged by real estate brokers would include: (pp. 211-212)

    A. an identification of the property securing the loan
    B. estimated fair market value of the security
    C. identity of the borrower
    D. all of the above

Answers: 1. B; 2. C; 3. D; 4. D; 5. D; 6. A; 7. C; 8. B; 9. D; 10. A; 11. D; 12. D

Disclosures in Mortgage Loan Transactions

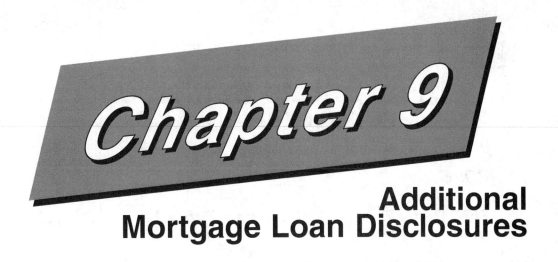

Additional
Mortgage Loan Disclosures

KEY WORDS AND TERMS

Advertising Rate Mortgage Disclosure
Computerized Loan Origination
Controlled Business Arrangement
Credit Card Disclosure
Fannie Mae
Federally Related Loans
Freddie Mac
Ginnie Mae
Good Faith Estimate
Home Mortgage Disclosure Act
Impound Account
Kickbacks
Lead Paint Disclosure

Loan Prospector Program
One-stop Shopping
Open-end Line of Credit
Ownership Counseling
Real Estate Settlement
Procedures Act
Referral Fees
Section 8
Servicing Disclosure
Settlement
Settlement Costs
Settlement Statement
Table Funding

LEARNING OBJECTIVES

In this chapter you will learn about required disclosures in addition to those covered in Chapter 8.

You will gain in-depth knowledge as to the requirements of the Real Estate Settlement Procedures Act from its purpose to the multitude of requirements and disclosures.

Other disclosures covered will include adjustable rate mortgages, seller carryback financing, lead paint disclosure, credit card disclosure, and the Home Mortgage Disclosure Act. You will also be introduced to the home ownership counseling of the Housing and Community Development Act.

Real Estate Settlement Procedures Act

PURPOSE

The Real Estate Settlement Procedures Act (12 U.S.C. 2601 et seq.) is a disclosure act.

The **REAL ESTATE SETTLEMENT PROCEDURES ACT** *provides consumers with a fair understanding of settlement costs so that residential purchasers can shop for settlement services and make informed decisions.* In passing this legislation, Congress found that significant reforms were needed in the real estate settlement process to provide greater and more timely information to the consumer on the nature and costs of the settlement process. They also found that in some cases consumers paid unnecessarily high settlement charges caused by abusive practices.

The four stated purposes of the Real Estate Settlement Procedures Act were to effect changes in the settlement process for residential real estate that will result in:

Advance Disclosure

An effective advance disclosure to home buyers and sellers of the settlement costs.

Eliminate Kickbacks

The elimination of referral fees or kickbacks which tend to unnecessarily increase the cost of certain settlement services.

Reduce Impound Accounts

The reduction of the amount homeowners were required to place in escrow accounts established to pay real estate taxes and insurance.

Requiring title insurance from a named provider is prohibited by RESPA.

Reform Title Record Keeping

The significant reform and modernization of local record keeping of land title information.

Additional Mortgage Loan Disclosures

APPLICABILITY

The Real Estate Settlement Procedures Act applies to federally related first trust deeds (and mortgages) to purchase residential property (**1-to 4-units**).

Federally Related

A loan is considered to be "federally related" if the lender has deposits that are insured by an agency of the federal government (FDIC).

A loan is also considered to be federally related if it is regulated by any agency of the federal government (such as the Federal Home Loan Bank Board), the loan has a federal guarantee (such as DVA loans), federal insurance (such as FHA loans), loans involved in any federal housing or urban development programs or for loans where the intention is that they will be sold by the originator (or through an intermediary) to Fannie Mae (FNMA), Ginnie Mae (GNMA) or Freddie Mac (FHLMC), or any non-exempt lender who invests over $1,000,000 per year in residential loans.

Residential Units

The loan proceeds must be for the purpose of the purchase of an interest in land (can be a long-term lease) upon which is a 1-to 4-unit dwelling or:

1. a mobile home,
2. upon which a 1-to 4-family dwelling is to be constructed with the loan proceeds,
3. a mobile home will be purchased with loan proceeds and placed on the property,
4. a cooperative or condominium.

RESPA provisions would also apply to permanent financing for 1-to-4 residential units to pay off a construction loan.

Purchase Loans

The RESPA act does not apply to sales of loans in the secondary mortgage market.

The requirements of disclosures apply to the original borrower for the purchase loan which must be the first lien on the property.

EXEMPTIONS FROM RESPA

The Real Estate Settlement Procedures Act need not be complied with for:

25 or More Acres

Purchase loans of parcels containing 25 or more acres.

Home Improvement Loans

Loans for home improvement where title does not transfer.

Refinancing

Loans to refinance other loans with no change in title.

Vacant Property

Loans for vacant property unless part of the loan proceeds will cover construction costs for 1-to 4-residential units.

Assumption

A sale or loan assumption where the property is subject to an existing loan.

RESPA only applies to first trust deeds and mortgages.

Construction Financing

Unless there is an agreement to be converted to permanent financing by the borrower.

Nonresidential Property

RESPA only applies to residential property.

Five or More Units

RESPA only applies to 1-to 4-residential units.

Land Owned by Borrower

Financing for construction purposes where the borrower already owns the land.

Investment for Resale

Loans where the purchase is being made with the intention of resale.

Land Contract Purchases

RESPA only applies to transactions where title transfers to a purchaser.

SETTLEMENT COSTS

The U.S. Department of Housing and Urban Development, which is responsible for administering RESPA, has prepared a booklet on Settlement Costs to meet the requirement of RESPA.

SETTLEMENT *is the formal process by which ownership of real property passes from the seller to the buyer.* RESPA does not set the prices for settlement services. Instead, it provides information in order to enable the purchaser to shop for settlement services and make informed decisions.

Under RESPA, the lender is required to provide a "Good Faith Estimate" of loan costs, as well as a Settlement Costs booklet to the borrower, within three days of the loan application.

If a lender denies credit within three days of the loan application, then the creditor need not supply the consumer with the settlement cost booklet.

The booklet is divided into two parts.

Part one describes the settlement process and the nature of settlement charges. It suggests questions which a purchaser should ask of lenders, attorneys and other providers to clarify services provided and charges quoted. Also set forth in Part One are the rights and remedies available to purchasers under RESPA. The purchaser is alerted to unfair and illegal practices.

Part Two of the booklet is an item-by-item explanation of settlement services and costs. It also provides information on comparing lender costs, calculating the transaction and other related material.

The HUD Settlement Statement is included as Figures 9-1and 9-2.

Inspection of Settlement Statement

The borrower has the right to see the Uniform Settlement Statement "on the business day prior to the day of settlement."

Figure 9-1

A. U.S. DEPARTMENT OF HOUSING AND URBAN DEVELOPMENT	B. TYPE OF LOAN		OMB No. 2502-0265
SETTLEMENT STATEMENT	1. ☐ FHA 2. ☐ FMHA 3. ☐ CONV. UNINS.		
	4. ☐ VA 5. ☐ CONV. INS.		
	6. FILE NUMBER	7. LOAN NUMBER	
	8. MORTGAGE INSURANCE CASE NO.		

C. NOTE: This form is furnished to give you a statement of actual settlement costs. Amounts paid to and by the settlement agent are shown. Items marked "(p.o.c)" were paid outside the closing; they are shown here for informational purposes and are not included in the totals.

D. NAME OF BORROWER:
   ADDRESS OF BORROWER:

E. NAME OF SELLER:
   ADDRESS OF SELLER:

F. NAME OF LENDER:
   ADDRESS OF LENDER:

G. PROPERTY LOCATION:

H. SETTLEMENT AGENT:
   PLACE OF SETTLEMENT:

I. SETTLEMENT DATE:

J. SUMMARY OF BORROWER'S TRANSACTION	K. SUMMARY OF SELLER'S TRANSACTION
100. GROSS AMOUNT DUE FROM BORROWER	**400. GROSS AMOUNT DUE TO SELLER**
101. Contract sales price	401. Contract sales price
102. Personal property	402. Personal property
103. Settlement charges to borrower (from line 1400)	403.
104.	404.
105.	405.
ADJUSTMENTS FOR ITEMS PAID BY SELLER IN ADVANCE:	**ADJUSTMENTS FOR ITEMS PAID BY SELLER IN ADVANCE:**
106. City/town taxes to	406. City/town taxes to
107. County taxes to	407. County taxes to
108. Assessments to	408. Assessments to
109.	409.
110.	410.
111.	411.
112.	412.
120. GROSS AMOUNT DUE FROM BORROWER:	**420. GROSS AMOUNT DUE TO SELLER:**
200. AMOUNTS PAID BY OR IN BEHALF OF BORROWER:	**500. REDUCTION IN AMOUNT DUE TO SELLER:**
201. Deposit or earnest money	501. Excess deposit (see instructions)
202. Principal amount of new loan(s)	502. Settlement charges to seller (line 1400)
203. Existing loan(s) taken subject to	503. Existing loan(s) taken subject to
204.	504. Payoff of first mortgage loan
205.	505. Payoff of second mortgage loan
206. Deposit with lender	506.
207.	507.
208.	508.
209.	509.
ADJUSTMENTS FOR ITEMS UNPAID BY SELLER:	**ADJUSTMENTS FOR ITEMS UNPAID BY SELLER:**
210. City/town taxes to	510. City/town taxes to
211. County taxes to	511. County taxes to
212. Assessments to	512. Assessments to
213.	513.
214.	514.
215.	515.
216.	516.
217.	517.
218.	518.
219.	519.
220. TOTAL PAID BY/FOR BORROWER	**520. TOTAL REDUCTIONS IN AMOUNT DUE SELLER**
300. CASH AT SETTLEMENT FROM/TO BORROWER:	**600. CASH AT SETTLEMENT TO/FROM SELLER:**
301. Gross amount due from borrower (line 120)	601. Gross amount due to seller (line 420)
302. Less amount paid by/for borrower (line 1400)	602. Less total reductions in amount due seller (line 520)
303. CASH (☑ from) (☐ to) BORROWER:	603. CASH (☑ to) (☐ from) SELLER:

SUBSTITUTE 1099-S: This form may be used as the written statement to the Transferor. This is important tax information and is being furnished to the Internal Revenue Service. If you are required to file a return, a negligence penalty will be imposed on you if this item is required to be reported and the IRS determines that it has not been reported. See Substitute 1099-S Information Sheet.

Previous Edition is Obsolete
ITEM 1581 (9407)

HUD-1 (3-86)
RESPA.HB 4305.2

Figure 9-2

L. SETTLEMENT CHARGES

		PAID FROM BORROWER'S FUNDS AT SETTLEMENT	PAID FROM SELLER'S FUNDS AT SETTLEMENT
700. TOTAL SALES/BROKER'S COMMISSION: at = BASED ON PRICE:			
DIVISION OF COMMISSION (LINE 700) AS FOLLOWS:			
701. to			
702. to			
703. Commission paid at settlement			
704.			
800. ITEMS PAYABLE IN CONNECTION WITH LOAN:			
801. Loan origination fee			
802. Loan discount			
803. Appraisal fee to:			
804. Credit report to:			
805. Lender's inspection fee			
806. Mortgage insurance application fee to:			
807. Assumption fee			
808.			
809.			
810.			
811.			
812.			
813.			
814.			
815.			
900. ITEMS REQUIRED BY LENDER TO BE PAID IN ADVANCE:			
901. Interest from to (days) at per day			
902. Mortgage insurance premium for months to			
903. Hazard insurance premium for years to			
904.			
905.			
1000. RESERVES DEPOSITED WITH LENDER:			
1001. Hazard insurance months at per month			
1002. Mortgage insurance months at per month			
1003. City property taxes months at per month			
1004. County property taxes months at per month			
1005. Annual assessments months at per month			
1006. months at per month			
1007. months at per month			
1008. months at per month			
1009. Aggregate Adjustment			
1100. TITLE CHARGES:			
1101. Settlement or closing fee to			
1102. Abstract or title search to			
1103. Title examination to			
1104. Title insurance binder to			
1105. Document preparation to			
1106. Notary fees to			
1107. Attorney's fees to (includes above item numbers:)			
1108. Title insurance to (includes above item numbers:)			
1109. Lender's coverage			
1110. Owner's coverage			
1111.			
1112.			
1113.			
1200. GOVERNMENT RECORDING AND TRANSFER CHARGES:			
1201. Recording fees: Deed Mortgage Releases			
1202. City/county tax/stamps: Deed Mortgage			
1203. State tax/stamps: Deed Mortgage			
1204.			
1205.			
1300. ADDITIONAL SETTLEMENT CHARGES:			
1301. Survey to			
1302. Pest inspection to			
1303.			
1304.			
1305.			
1306.			
1307.			
1400. TOTAL SETTLEMENT CHARGES (Enter on line 103, Section J, and line 502, Section K)			

I have carefully reviewed the HUD-1 Settlement Statement and to the best of my knowledge and belief, it is a true and accurate statement of all receipts and disbursements made on my account or by me in this transaction. I further certify that I have received a copy of the HUD-1 Settlement Statement.

Borrowers _____   Sellers _____

The HUD-1 Settlement Statement which I have prepared is a true and accurate account of this transaction. I have caused or will cause the funds to be disbursed in accordance with this statement.

Settlement Agent _____   Date _____

WARNING: It is a crime to knowingly make false statements to the United States on this or any other similar form. Penalties upon conviction can include a fine or imprisonment. For details see: Title 18 U.S. Code Section 1001 and Section 1010.

ITEM 1582 (9407)   PAGE 2

Record Keeping

Lenders must retain copies of settlement statements for a period of two years following the settlement date.

GOOD FAITH ESTIMATE

The lenders Good Faith Estimate must be reasonably based on what the borrower can expect to be charged at settlement.

> *The estimate is to be based on the lender's past experience in the area.*

A copy of the Good Faith Estimate of loan costs is included as Figure 9-3.

REQUIRED PROVIDER

If the lender requires a particular service provider (such as a title company) and the borrower is required to pay or share in the costs relating to the service provider, a statement must be provided setting forth:

1. names, addresses and telephone numbers of such providers;
2. services to be rendered by such providers;
3. that the estimate is based on the charges of the provider;
4. a statement setting forth the relationship, if any, between the lender and the service provider.

Figure 9-4 is a Required Provider of Settlement Services Addendum.

SERVICING DISCLOSURE

> *The lender shall disclose to the borrower whether the loan can be assigned and the fact that the right to service the loan may be transferred.*

A copy of the Servicing Disclosure Statement, as set forth in 12 U.S.C. 2603, is shown in Figures 9-5 through 9-8.

TABLE FUNDING *is a loan-closing process where the lender, brokers and principals are present at a formal closing process.* (Used in some states instead of escrow closings). Deeds are signed and checks are given during this closing process.

Additional Mortgage Loan Disclosures

Figure 9-3

[NAME OF LENDER]

The information provided below reflects estimates of the charges which you are likely to incur at the settlement of your loan. The fees listed are estimates — the actual charges may be more or less. Your transaction may not involve a fee for every item listed. The numbers listed beside the estimates generally correspond to the numbered lines contained in the HUD-1 or HUD-1A settlement statement that you will be receiving at settlement. The HUD-1 or HUD-1A settlement statement will show you the actual cost for items paid at settlement.

ITEM 2	HUD-1 or HUD-1A	Amount or Range
Loan Origination Fee	801	$_____
Loan Discount Fee	802	$_____
Appraisal Fee	803	$_____
Credit Report	804	$_____
Inspection Fee	805	$_____
Mortgage Broker Fee	[Use blank line in 800 Section]	$_____
CLO Access Fee	[Use blank line in 800 Section]	$_____
Tax Related Service Fee		$_____
Interest for [X] days at $_____ per day	901	$_____
Mortgage Insurance Premium	902	$_____
Hazard Insurance Premiums	903	$_____
Reserves	1000-1005	$_____
Settlement Fee	1101	$_____
Abstract or Title Search	1102	$_____
Title Examination	1103	$_____
Document Preparation Fee	1105	$_____
Attorney's Fee	1107	$_____
Title Insurance	1108	$_____
Recording Fees	1201	$_____
City/County Tax Stamps	1202	$_____
State Tax	1203	$_____
Survey	1301	$_____
Pest Inspection	1302	$_____
[Other fees—list here]		
_____		$_____

_____
Applicant
Date

Authorized Official _____

These estimates are provided pursuant to the Real Estate Settlement Procedures Act of 1974, as amended (RESPA). Additional information can be found in the HUD Special Information Booklet, which is to be provided to you by your mortgage broker or lender, if your application is to purchase residential real property and the Lender will take a first lien on the property.

Figure 9-4

<table>
<tr><td colspan="3">REQUIRED PROVIDER OF SETTLEMENT SERVICE ADDENDUM
TO GOOD FAITH ESTIMATE OF SETTLEMENT CHARGES</td></tr>
</table>

Date:	Loan Number:

Lender Name:

Lender Address:

Borrower(s) Name:

Property Address:

    The Lender requires that you use a particular provider for certain settlement services and/or the Lender will select particular provider from a lender-controlled list. The estimate of the charge for this settlement service contained on the Good Faith Estimate is based on the charges of the particular provider required or, if the Lender will select from among a lender-controlled list, the Good Faith Estimate contains a range of costs for the required providers on the list. The name and exact cost of the provider selected by the Lender will be specified on the HUD-1 or HUD-1A settlement statement.

The following are settlement service provides required by the Lender.

Settlement Service	Name, Address and Telephone Number of Provider	Nature of Lender Relationship with Service Provider

    For each of the following settlement services, the Lender will select the provider from among a lender-controlled list of five (5) or more providers.

Settlement Service

Borrower	Date	Borrower	Date

Borrower	Date	Borrower	Date

VMP-118 (9409)　　　　9/94
VMP MORTGAGE FORMS - (800)521-7291

Figure 9-5

SERVICING DISCLOSURE STATEMENT

NOTICE TO FIRST LIEN MORTGAGE LOAN APPLICANTS: THE RIGHT TO COLLECT YOUR MORTGAGE LOAN PAYMENTS MAY BE TRANSFERRED. FEDERAL LAW GIVES YOU CERTAIN RELATED RIGHTS IF YOUR LOAN IS MADE. SAVE THIS STATEMENT WITH YOUR LOAN DOCUMENTS. SIGN THE ACKNOWLEDGMENT AT THE END OF THIS STATEMENT ONLY IF YOU UNDERSTAND ITS CONTENTS.

Because you are applying for a mortgage loan covered by the Real Estate Settlement Procedures Act (RESPA) (12 U.S.C. 2601 et. seq.) you have certain rights under that Federal law.

This statement tells you about those rights. It also tells you what the chances are that the servicing for this loan may be transferred to a different loan servicer. "Servicing" refers to collecting your principal interest and escrow account payments, if any. If your loan servicer changes, there are certain procedures that must be followed. This statement generally explains those procedures.

Transfer practices and requirements

If the servicing of your loan is assigned, sold, or transferred to a new servicer, you must be given written notice of that transfer. The present loan servicer must send you notice in writing of the assignment, sale or transfer of the servicing not less than 15 days before the effective date of the transfer. The new loan servicer must also send you notice within 15 days after the effective date of the transfer. The present servicer and the new servicer may combine this information in one notice, so long as the notice is sent to you 15 days before the effective date of transfer. The 15 day period is not applicable if a notice of prospective transfer is provided to you at settlement. The law allows a delay in the time (not more than 30 days after a transfer) for servicers to notify you, upon the occurrence of certain business emergencies.

Notices must contain certain information. They must contain the effective date of the transfer of the servicing of your loan to the new servicer, and the name, address, and toll-free or collect call telephone number of the new servicer, and toll-free or collect call telephone numbers of a person or department for both your present servicer and your new servicer to answer your questions. During the 60 day period following the effective date of the transfer of the loan servicing, a loan payment received by your old servicer before its due date may not be treated by the new loan servicer as late, and a late fee may not be imposed on you.

Complaint Resolution

Section 6 of RESPA (12 U.S.C. 2605) gives you certain consumer rights, *whether or not your loan servicing is transferred.* If you send a "qualified written request" to your servicer, your servicer must provide you with a written acknowledgment within 20 Business Days of receipt of your request.

Figure 9-6

A "qualified written request" is a written correspondence, other than notice on a payment coupon or other payment medium supplied by the servicer, which includes your name and account number, and the information regarding your request. Not later than 60 Business Days after receiving your request, your servicer must make any appropriate corrections to your account, or must provide you with a written clarification regarding any dispute. During this 60 Business Day period, your servicer may not provide information to a consumer reporting agency concerning any overdue payment related to such period or qualified written request.

A Business Day is any day in which the offices of the business entity are open to the public for carrying on substantially all of its business functions.

Damages and Costs

Section 6 of RESPA also provides for damages and costs for individuals or classes of individuals in circumstances where servicers are shown to have violated the requirements of that Section.

Servicing Transfer Estimates

1. The following is the best estimate of what will happen to the servicing of your mortgage loan:

A. We may assign, sell or transfer the servicing of your loan while the loan is outstanding.

We are able to service your loan[ ]. We [will] [will not] [haven't decided whether to] service your loan.

[or]

B. We do not service mortgage loans [ ], and we have not serviced mortgage loans in the past three years [ ]. We presently intend to assign, sell or transfer the servicing of your mortgage loan. You will be informed about your servicer.

INSTRUCTIONS TO PREPARER: The model format may be annotated with further information that clarifies or enhances the model language. The following model language may be used where appropriate:

We assign, sell or transfer the servicing of some of our loans while the loan is outstanding depending on the type of loan and other factors. For the program you have applied for, we expect to [sell all of the mortgage servicing] [retain all of the mortgage servicing] [assign, sell or transfer ____% of the mortgage servicing].

Figure 9-7

2. For all the first lien mortgage loans that we make in the 12-month period after your mortgage loan is funded, we estimate that the percentage of such loans for which we will transfer servicing is between:

_____ [0 to 25%] or [NONE]
_____ 26 to 50%
_____ 51 to 75%
_____ [76 to 100%] or [ALL]

(This estimate *[does] [does not]* include assignments, sales or transfers to affiliates or subsidiaries.) This is only our best estimate and it is not binding. Business conditions or other circumstances may affect our future transferring decisions.

3(A). We have previously assigned, sold, or transferred the servicing of first lien mortgage loans.

[or]

3(B). This is our record of transferring the servicing of the first lien mortgage we have made in the past:

Year   Percentage of Loans Transferred
               (Rounded to nearest quartile—0%, 25%, 50%, 75% or 100%)

19___   _____ %
19___   _____ %
20___   _____ %

(this information [does] [does not] include assignments, sales or transfers to affiliates or subsidiaries.)

_____
[Signature Not Mandatory]:

_____
DATE

INSTRUCTIONS TO PREPARER: Select either Item 3(A) or Item 3(B), except if you chose the provision in 1(B) stating: "We do not service mortgage loans, and we have not serviced mortgage loans in the past three years," all of Item 3 should be omitted.

Figure 9-8

The information in Item 3(B) is for the previous three calendar years. The information does not have to include the previous calendar year if the statement is prepared before March 31 of the next calendar year. If the percentage of servicing transferred is less than 12.5% the word "nominal" or the actual percentage amount of servicing transfers may be used. If no servicing was transferred, "none" may be placed on the percentage line; if all servicing was transferred, "all" may be placed on the percentage line.

ACKNOWLEDGMENT OF MORTGAGE LOAN APPLICANT

I've have read this disclosure form, and understand its contents, as evidence by my/our signature(s) below. I understand that this acknowledgement is a required part of the mortgage loan application.

_____
APPLICANT'S SIGNATURE

_____
CO-APPLICANT'S SIGNATURE

_____

_____

_____

_____
DATE

[As amended Dec. 19, 1994, 59 F.R. 65448, eff June 19, 1995; 60 F.R. 2642, January 10, 1995, eff June 19, 1995; January 31, 1995, 60 F.R. 5962, eff June 19, 1995]

Additional Mortgage Loan Disclosures

When a loan is assigned, sold or the servicing rights are otherwise transferred, the borrower must be given written notice of the transfer within 15 days of the transfer. Figures 9-9 and 9-10 represent the form set forth in the U.S. Code for this notice.

If there is no change in the payee, then no notice is required since the servicer would remain the same. This applies to change of name, consolidations, mergers, etc.

REFERRAL FEES

The purpose of 12 U.S.C. 2607 is to eliminate unearned fees in connection with settlement charges.

Acceptance of any charge for rendering a real estate settlement service is prohibited unless that service has actually been performed.

> *Persons who give or receive kickback or referral fees can be held both civilly and criminally liable. Penalties are up to $10,000 in fines as well as up to one year imprisonment.*

Attempts to charge significant fees based on minimal effort are likely to be viewed by the federal court as a violation of RESPA.

> *The Section in RESPA concerning kickbacks is commonly known as Section 8.*

 www.law.cornell.edu/uscode (United States Code)

While RESPA allows cooperative agreements between real estate brokers that provide for a division of labor and shared compensation and that do not violate RESPA, it is unclear if real estate brokers who are also mortgage brokers can enter into such cooperative agreements. Loan brokers should be aware of Business and Professions Code Section 10177.4 that provides for possible suspension or revocation of a real estate license for referrals for compensation.

Referral of Customers for Compensation

10177.4. Notwithstanding any other provision of law, the commissioner may, after hearing, in accordance with the provisions of this part relating to

Figure 9-9

NOTICE ASSIGNMENT, SALE, OR TRANSFER OF SERVICING RIGHTS

You are hereby notified that the servicing of your mortgage loan, that is, the right to collect payments from you, is being assigned, sold or transferred from _____ to _____ effective _____.

The assignment, sale or transfer of the servicing of the mortgage loan does not affect any term or condition of the mortgage instruments, other than terms directly related to the servicing of your loan.

Except in limited circumstances, the law requires that your present servicer send you this notice at least 15 days before the effective date or transfer, or at closing. Your new servicer must also send you this notice not later than 15 days after this effective date or at closing. [In this case, all necessary information is combined in this one notice].

Your present servicer is _____. If you have any questions relating to the transfer of servicing, call between _____ a.m. and _____ p.m. on the following days _____. This is a [toll-free] [collect-call] number.

Your new servicer will be _____.

The business address for your new servicer is:

_____

_____

The [toll-free] [collect-call] telephone number of your new servicer is _____. If you have any questions relating to the transfer of servicing to your new servicer, call [toll free or collect call telephone number] between _____ a.m. and _____ p.m. on the following days

_____.

The date that your present servicer will stop accepting payments from you is _____.

The date that your new servicer will start accepting payments from you is _____. Send all payments due on or after that date to your new servicer.

[Use this paragraph if appropriate; otherwise omit]. The Transfer of sentencing rights may affect the terms of or the continued availability of mortgage life or disability insurance or any other type of optional insurance in the following manner:

_____

_____

_____

_____

and you should take the following action to maintain coverage:

_____

_____

Figure 9-10

You should also be aware of the following information, which is set out in more detail in Section 6 of the Real Estate Settlement Procedures Act (RESPA) (12 U.S.C. 2605):

During the 60-day period following the effective date of the transfer of the loan servicing, a loan payment received by your old servicer before its due date may not be treated by the new loan servicer as late, and a late fee may not be imposed on you.

Section 6 of RESPA (12 U.S.C. 2605) gives you certain consumer rights. If you send a "qualified written request" to your loan servicer concerning the servicing of your loan, your servicer must provide you with a written acknowledgment within 20 Business Days of receipt of your request. A "qualified written request" is a written correspondence, other than notice on a payment coupon or other payment medium supplied by the servicer, which includes your name and account number, and your reasons for the request. [If you want to send a "qualified written request" regarding the servicing of your loan, it must be sent to this address:]

—————————————

—————————————

Not later than 60 Business Days after receiving your request, your servicer must make any appropriate corrections to your account, and must provide you with a written clarification regarding any dispute.

During this 60 Business Day period, your servicer may not provide information to a consumer reporting agency concerning any overdue payment related to such period or qualified written request. However, this does not prevent the servicer from initiating foreclosure if proper grounds exist under the mortgage documents.

A Business Day is a day on which the offices of the business entity are open to the public for carrying on substantially all of its business functions.

Section 6 of RESPA also provides for damages and costs for individuals or classes of individuals in circumstances where servicers are shown to have violated the requirements of that Section. You should seek legal advice if you believe your rights have been violated.

[INSTRUCTIONS TO PREPARER: Delivery means placing the notice in the mail, first class postage prepaid, prior to 15 days before the effective date of transfer (transferor) or prior to 15 days after the effective date of transfer (transferee). However, this notice may be sent not more than 30 days after the effective date of the transfer of servicing rights if certain emergency business situations occur. See 24 CFR 3500.21(e)(1)(ii). "Lender" may be substituted for "present servicer" where appropriate. These instructions should not appear on the format.]

—————————————————   ——————————————
PRESENT SERVICER   Date
[Signature not required]

                                                [and][or]

—————————————————   ——————————————
FUTURE SERVICER   Date
[Signature not required]

hearings, suspend or revoke the license of a real estate licensee who claims, demands or receives a commission, fee or other consideration, as compensation or inducement, for referral of customers to any escrow agent, structural pest control firm, home protection company, title insurer, controlled escrow company or underwritten title company...

Case Example

Eisenberg v. Cornfed Mortgage Co. (1986) 629 F. Supp 1157

This case involved the anti-kickback provision of the Real Estate Settlement Procedures Act. The court rules that it does not apply to that portion of the mortgage origination fee imposed by a mortgage company for commission to a mortgage originator, commission to a branch manager and company overhead. The court ruled that this was not a referral fee as no business was referred to the bank owner and making of a mortgage loan is not a settlement service under 12 U.S.C. S. 2602.

HUD has not been enforcing anti-kickback regulations because of confusion in the industry, much of which was generated by HUD.

HUD has now released new RESPA Regulations which you will see are in opposition to California law. RESPA now allows an employee to be paid for generating business for an employer or affiliate of the employer. However, the referral fee allowed cannot be related to the dollar volume or profit from the referral. (See Controlled Business Arrangements later in this Chapter.)

ESCROW KICKBACKS WHERE THE BROKER IS THE ESCROW

The question has arisen whether real estate brokers, who are exempt from licensure as escrow agents, may compensate their salespeople for referring clients to the broker's escrow services.

While the legislature has not specifically addressed this issue, on January 6, 1993, the Attorney General of California, in Opinion No. 92-517, concluded that such compensation may not be given.

The Attorney General pointed out that he was aware that the federal government has issued new regulations to implement RESPA and it reverses the prior position as to fees and now allows the payment of fees based on the belief that increased competition may lower consumer costs.

On the other hand, the California Department of Real Estate ("Department") has taken the position, although not in a formal regulation, that the payment of fees for self-referrals by real estate brokers is prohibited by section 10177.4. In its Real Estate Bulletin (Fall 1987), the Department stated:

"A violation of Section 10177.4 is not limited to those situations in which the licensee receives the consideration from the business to which the buyer or seller was referred. The source of the consideration is irrelevant to a violation. What is relevant is the claiming, demanding or receiving of any consideration as compensation or inducement for a referral...

Therefore, the broker and salesperson may be subject to disciplinary action if the broker increases or decreases the amount of the salesperson's compensation in a transaction based on a referral...

Section 10177.4 is not simply a disclosure statute. It prohibits the receipt of consideration for referrals... "

We cannot say that the Department's position is unreasonable or clearly contrary to the language or purpose of section 10177.4. Until the Legislature acts to resolve the ambiguities of the statute, we adopt the Department's position. [*See Dix v. Superior Court* (1991) 53 Cal. 3d 442, 460 ("construction of a statute by an agency charged with responsibility for its implementation is entitled to great deference")].

> *It is concluded that real estate brokers who are exempt from licensure as escrow agents may not compensate their salespersons for referring clients to the brokers' escrow services.*

The Attorney General of California has taken the position that despite what RESPA says, do not pay salespersons for referrals for broker (or broker-affiliated) services.

RESPA provides that where state law is more restrictive, state law prevails. It appears clear that California brokers should avoid referral fees or, at the very least, obtain legal advise before entering into any cooperative agreement.

Chapter 9

The advise of the authors is "don't pay salespersons referral fees until or unless California law has been changed to coincide with federal law."

CONTROLLED BUSINESS ARRANGEMENT

CONTROLLED BUSINESS ARRANGEMENTS (CBA) *allow "one-stop shopping," where purchase, loans and service providers may all be obtained from the same source through affiliations.*

RESPA now allows controlled business arrangements where an individual or entity making a loan referral has an ownership interest (greater than one percent) in the loan company receiving the referral. The person making the referral can now receive compensation based on a profit-sharing arrangement based on the percentage of ownership. Persons making referrals are still prohibited from receiving a fee based on the fact that a referral was made or based on the fee charged the consumer.

Managerial employees of controlled business arrangements may be paid a fee from its percentage of profits based on performance. The employees must be W-2 wage earners and not independent contractors. Such an amount may not be calculated on the number or dollar value of the referral.

An employer can also allow payments to an employee for referrals to an affiliate providing the person being referred is given a written disclosure in a format set forth in the new regulations.

In order for an organization to be considered a bona fide CBA:

1. The venture must be realistically capitalized;
2. It must have its own employees;
3. It must manage its own affairs;
4. It must have an office and pay fair market rent;
5. It must provide the functions of a business of its type;
6. It must bear similar risks as would similar businesses;
7. It must not subcontract services it should do itself;
8. It sends business exclusively to one venturer;
9. It competes for business from other than a venturer.

12 U.S.C.S. 2602 defines a controlled business arrangement as follows:

3500.15 Controlled business arrangements.

(a). General. A controlled business arrangement is an arrangement in which:

(1) A person who is in a position to refer business incident to or a part of a real estate settlement service involving a federally-related mortgage loan, or an associate of such person, has either an affiliate relationship with or a direct or beneficial ownership interest of more than 1 percent in a provider of settlement services; and

(2) Such person directly or indirectly refers such business to that provider or affirmatively influences the selection of that provider...

ADDITIONAL GUIDANCE REGARDING THE CBA

The following illustrations provide additional guidance on the meaning and coverage of the controlled business arrangement provisions of RESPA. Other provisions of Federal or State law may also be applicable to the practices and payments discussed in the following illustrations.

1. *Facts:* A, a provider of settlement services, provides settlement services at abnormally low rates or at no charge at all to B, a builder, in connection with a subdivision being developed by B. B agrees to refer purchasers of the completed homes in the subdivision to A for the purchase of settlement services in connection with the sale of individual lots by B.

Comments: The rendering of services by A to B at little or no charge constitutes a thing of value given by A to B in return for the referral of settlement services business and both A and B are in violation of Section 8 of RESPA.

2. *Facts:* B, a lender, encourages persons who receive federally-related mortgage loans from it to employ A, an attorney, to perform title services and related settlement services in connection with their transaction. B and A have an understanding that, in return for the referral of this business, A provides legal services to B or B's officers or employees at abnormally low rates or for no charge.

Comments: Both A and B are in violation of Section 8 of RESPA. Similarly, if an attorney gives a portion of his or her fees to another attorney, a lender, a real estate broker or any other provider of settlement services who had referred prospective clients to the attorney, Section 8 would be violated by both persons.

3. *Facts:* A, a real estate broker, obtains all necessary licenses under state law to act as a title insurance agent. A refers individuals who are purchasing homes in transactions in which A participates as a broker to B, an unaffiliated title company, for the purchase of title insurance services. A performs minimal, if any, title services in connection with the issuance of the title insurance policy (such as placing an application with the title company). B pays A a commission (or A retains a portion of the title insurance premium) for the transactions or, alternatively, B receives a portion of the premium paid directly from the purchaser.

Comments: The payment of a commission or portion of the title insurance premium by B to A, or receipt of a portion of the payment for title insurance under circumstances where no substantial services are being performed by A, is a violation of Section 8 of RESPA. It makes no difference if the payment comes from B or the purchaser. The amount of the payment must bear a reasonable relationship to the services rendered. Here A really is being compensated for a referral of business to B.

4. *Facts:* A, a "mortgage originator" receives loan applications, funds the loans with its own money or with a wholesale line of credit for which A is liable, and closes the loans in A's own name. Subsequently, B, a mortgage lender, purchases the loans and compensates A for the value of the loans, as well as for any mortgage servicing rights.

Comments: Compensation for the sale of a mortgage loan and servicing rights constitutes a secondary market transaction, rather than a referral fee, and is beyond the scope of Section 8 of RESPA. For purposes of Section 8, in determining whether a *bona fide* transfer of the loan obligation has taken place, HUD examines the real source of funding, and the real interest of the named settlement lender.

5. *Facts:* A, a credit reporting company, places a facsimile transmission machine (FAX) in the office of B, a mortgage lender, so that B can easily transmit requests for credit reports and A can respond. A supplies the FAX machine at no cost or at a reduced rental rate based on the number of credit reports ordered.

Comments: Either situation violates Section 8 of RESPA. The FAX machine is a thing of value that A provides in exchange for the referral of business from B. Computing machines, computer terminals, printers or other like items which have general use to the recipient and which are given in exchange for referrals of business also violate RESPA.

Whenever a lender has a controlled business arrangement with a service provider, RESPA requires that the buyer or seller (as applicable) be fully informed as to this arrangement.

Additional Mortgage Loan Disclosures

Appendix D of RESPA sets forth the Disclosure Statement format:

APPENDIX D TO PART 3500 -
CONTROLLED BUSINESS ARRANGEMENT DISCLOSURE
STATEMENT FORMAT
Notice

To: Buyer or Seller   Property:

_____   _____
From: [Entity Making Statement]   Date:_____

This is to give you notice that ___[referring party]___ has a business relationship with _____[provider]_____. [Describe the nature of the relationship between the referring party and the provider, including ownership and financial interests.]

Set forth below is the estimated charge or range of charges by _____[provider]___
_____

for the following settlement services:

_____ $ _____
_____ $ _____
_____ $ _____

You are not required to use _____[provider]_____ as a condition for [settlement of your loan on] [or] [purchase or sale of] the subject property. You may be able to get these services at a lower rate by shopping with other settlement service providers. [sup]

A lender is allowed to require the use of an attorney, credit reporting agency or real estate appraiser chosen to represent the lender's interest.

Where the lender is requiring an attorney, credit reporting agency or real estate appraiser to represent its interests, this paragraph should be omitted.
[As amended April 1, 1993, 58 F.R. 17[66]

IMPOUND ACCOUNTS

If a loan includes an impound account for taxes and insurance, RESPA prohibits unreasonably large accounts.

> *Lenders love impound accounts because the lender has the use of funds for loan purposes and pays either no interest or very low interest for the use of such funds.*

At loan origination, RESPA prohibits impound accounts that exceed a prorated estimate for taxes and insurance plus an estimated two months of impound costs. Each monthly payment may be required to include an amount equal to 1/12th of the annual estimated taxes and insurance.

COMPUTERIZED LOAN ORIGINATION

There are several automated mortgage loan underwriting systems (computerized loan origination).

Freddie Mac's Loan Prospector program is very sophisticated. It is limited to Freddie Mac approved seller services. An applicant's information can be processed in just a few minutes and a "go" for purchase can be achieved. The use of the system has a $100 per loan fee in addition to the purchase of necessary software.

Freddie Mac provides training for lender personnel in the use of the software. The speed of service greatly reduce lender processing costs.

While the lender uses the regular Uniform Residential Loan Application (Freddie Mac Form 65) the lender still has the responsibility to verify employment, income and assets. When verified the material is fed into the computer and analyzed. Sixty percent of all applications can be approved within four minutes. If the loan-to-value ratio is greater than 80 percent, the application is forwarded to a private mortgage insurer that the lender selects. All of the major mortgage insurers are in the computer system.

Loans are "accepted" or labeled "refer" or "caution." Those classified as "refer" are sent to the Lender's underwriting department with reasons for the "refer" ranking. A "caution" classification means that serious problems need to be resolved before the loan can be purchased.

The lender can chose among eight credit reporting companies for credit reports. Credit reports merge information from at least two of the three databases (Equifax Mortgage Information Services, TRW Redi Property Data and Trans Union Corporation).

The loan prospector can also access credit card databases to determine total credit available and the percentage being used.

Fannie Mae's program is the desktop underwriter.

HUD has given approval to automated underwriting systems but do not approve specific software programs.

> *Computerized loan origination is a real service to buyers in that it not only saves a great deal of time in loan applications but it also provides buyers with access to information on a wide variety of loans available as well as multiple lenders.*

A fee is often charged the prospective borrower for this service.

Appendix E to the Real Estate Settlement Procedures Act provides for a **fee disclosure to the borrower whenever any fee is paid by the borrower for access to computerized loan origination services**. It is included as Figure 9-11.

OPEN-END LINE OF CREDIT

When a consumer is to receive an open-end line of credit secured by his or her residence (loan that allows future advances up to an agreed limit), the consumer must be given a copy of the booklet *When Your Home Is On The Line: What You Should Know About Home Equity Lines of Credit*.

COST OF COMPLIANCE

> *"No charge or fee" can be charged to the consumer for any disclosures mandated by RESPA.*

Adjustable Rate Mortgage Loans

Civil Code 1921(b) requires any lender offering an adjustable rate loan to a borrower to provide that prospective borrower with a copy of the most recent Federal Reserve Board publication entitled *Consumer Handbook On Adjustable Rate Mortgages*. The publication shall be given upon the borrowers request or at the same time the lender first provides written information concerning an adjustable rate loan. Failure to comply could subject the lender to actual damages, court costs and attorney's fees.

Figure 9-11 The Real Estate Settlement Procedures Act Appendix E

APPENDIX E TO PART 3500—CLO FEE DISCLOSURE

Instructions: Whenever it is anticipated that a fee will be paid by the borrower for CLO access and related services, a disclosure form must be fully completed and delivered to the borrower itemizing the services provided and the specified fee to be charged as well as the other information set forth below, the form must provide a place for the purchaser to acknowledge its receipt. The disclosure format set forth below is satisfactory to the Secretary.

CLO FEE DISCLOSURE

To: [Potential Borrower]   From: [Person Making Disclosure]

NOTICE: I am proposing to charge you a fee in the amount of $ _____ for the following services:
[ ] Displaying a variety of mortgage loans and rates which may be available to you.
[ ] Counseling you regarding the different types of loans available and the relative rates in a fair and equitable manner.
[ ] Counseling you regarding the different types of loans available and the relative rates in a fair and equitable manner.
[ ] Relating your personal housing needs with available loan programs; and assisting you in deciding which, if any, loan meets your needs.
[ ] Entering information regarding you into the Computer Loan Origination System (CLO).
[ ]Other _____

THIS IS TO INFORM YOU THAT YOU ARE PAYING THIS FEE DIRECTLY TO [*Person or Company Making Disclosure*].

YOU ARE ADVISED THAT YOU MAY AVOID THIS FEE ENTIRELY IF YOU APPROACH A LENDER OR MORTGAGE BROKER DIRECTLY. ADDITIONALLY, LOWER MORTGAGE RATES OR OTHER LOWER FEES MAY BE AVAILABLE FROM OTHER MORTGAGE LENDERS WHO ARE NOT LISTED ON THIS COMPUTER SYSTEM.
I hereby pay [commit to pay] a CLO Fee in the amount of $ _____

_____
Borrower

Received by _____

Additional Mortgage Loan Disclosures

Civil Code 1921(c) allows the lender to make the adjustable rate mortgage disclosures at the same time the lender makes the adjustable rate disclosure pursuant to either Part 29 of Chapter 1 or Part 563 of Chapter 5 (Title 12 of the Code of Federal Regulations). Adjustable rate loans are more difficult for consumers to compare than are fixed rate loans.

In addition to points and loan costs, adjustable rate loans vary as to:

1. *INDICES OR INDEXES are a basis for which charges are measured.* They are tied to such as a Federal Reserve Interbank Rate or the LIBOR rate.

2. *MARGINS, which are the amount over the indice rate that the interest is payable at.* As an example, if the indice rate is at 5 1/2 percent and the borrower is to pay 2.8 percent over the indice rate than the interest rate would be 8.3 percent.

3. *CAPs, which are the most that loans will rise.* There may be CAPs for periodic adjustments as well as CAPs over the life of the loan. If the loan margin and indice indicate a rate above the CAP rate, the CAP rate is all that can be charged. However, some loans CAP the payments but not the interest assessed. Such loans can result in negative amortization where the borrower owes an increasing amount of the loan principal each month. Many adjustable rate loans, however, do not allow negative amortization.

4. *ADJUSTMENT PERIOD is the period within which an adjustment is calculated.* Loans will have different adjustment periods. When the interest rates are falling, the lender benefits by a longer adjustment period. When interest rates are rising, the borrower would benefit by a longer period.

5. Initial rate. The *INITIAL RATE* or *"TEASER RATE" is usually less than the indice rate and the margin.* Often this initial rate will be guaranteed for a six-month period or even one year. Loans often have a longer adjustment period for the first adjustment. A low initial rate will often result in borrowers who would otherwise not qualify for a fixed rate loan, meet qualifications for an adjustable rate loan.

1921. Definitions; providing prospective borrowers with publications on adjustable-rate mortgages; failure of lender to comply; liability for damages

(a). As used in this section:

(1) *ADJUSTABLE-RATE RESIDENTIAL MORTGAGE LOAN means any loan or credit sale which is primarily for personal, family or household*

purposes which bears interest at a rate subject to change during the term of the loan, whether predetermined or otherwise, and which is made upon the security of real property containing not less than one nor more than four dwelling units.

*(2) **LENDER** means any person, association, corporation, partnership, limited partnership or other business entity making, in any 12-month period, more than 10 loans or credit sales upon the security of residential real property containing not less than one nor more than four dwelling units.*

(b). Any lender offering adjustable-rate residential mortgage loans shall provide to prospective borrowers a copy of the most recent available publication of the Federal Reserve Board that is designed to provide the public with descriptive information concerning adjustable-rate mortgages (currently entitled *Consumer Handbook on Adjustable Rate Mortgages*), either upon the prospective borrower's request or at the same time the lender first provides written information, other than direct-mail advertising, concerning any adjustable-rate residential mortgage loan or credit sale to the prospective borrower, whichever is earlier. Any lender who fails to comply with the requirements of this section may be enjoined by any court of competent jurisdiction and shall be liable for actual damages, the costs of the action, and reasonable attorney's fees as determined by the court. The court may make those orders as may be necessary to prevent future violations of this section.

(c). A lender that makes adjustable-rate mortgage loan disclosures pursuant to either Part 29 of Chapter I of, or Part 563 of Chapter V of, Title 12 of the Code of Federal Regulations, may comply with this section by providing the descriptive information required by subdivision (b) at the same time and under the same circumstances that it makes disclosures in accordance with those federal regulations. Such a lender shall also display and make the descriptive information available to the public in an area of the lender's office that is open to the public.

The Consumer Handbook On Adjustable Rate Mortgages, prepared by the Federal Reserve Board, explains to the consumer, in simple terms, what an adjustable rate mortgage is. Information also explained includes:

1. Adjustment Period
2. Index
3. Margin
4. Initial Discount Rates

The booklet warns of payment shock at the first adjustment period when the initial rate ends.

The consumer is made aware of how the CAPS on payment increases work and how the loan might increase.

The consumer is warned about the possibility of negative amortization.

The consumer is told to ask about prepayment and conversion possibilities as well as assumability of the loan.

A Mortgage Checklist is included for the borrower to compare loans. (Figure 9-12.) Figure 9-13 is an Adjustable Rate Mortgage (ARM) Disclosure Worksheet.

Seller Carryback Requirements

When a seller is to carry back any part of the financing in a sale of 1-to 4-residential units, both the buyer and seller must be provided with a disclosure statement (Civil Code 2956).

This disclosure statement, while not a contract, is often an attachment to the purchase contract.

The disclosures made includes:

1. Identification of the real property
2. The credit documents used (includes lease option where parties intend title to pass)
3. Credit terms, including interest, payment requirements, balloon payments, late charges, prepayment penalties, due-on-sale clause, etc.
4. Information on any loans that will be senior to the seller's encumbrance
5. Warning that when a balloon payment is due that refinancing could be difficult
6. Any deferred interest
7. If an all-inclusive deed of trust or land contract is to be used as well as responsibilities of the parties if the senior encumbrance must be paid and the advisability of using a collection agent
8. Creditworthiness of the buyer
9. Provision for loss-payable clause on insurance policy
10. Request for Notice of Default
11. Title insurance
12. Tax service
13. Recording of documents
14. Proceeds to buyer
15. Notice of delinquency

Figure 9-12

MORTGAGE CHECKLIST
Ask your lender to help fill out this checklist.

	Mortgage A	Mortgage B
Mortgage amount	$	$

Basic Features for Comparison

Fixed-rate annual percentage rate
(the cost of your credit as a yearly rate which
includes both interest and other charges)

ARM annual percentage rate

   Adjustment period

   Index used and current rate

   Margin

   Initial payment without discount

   Initial payment with discount (if any)

   How long will discount last?

   Interest rate caps: periodic

                    overall

   Payment caps

   Negative amortization

   Convertibility or prepayment privilege

   Initial fees and charges

Monthly Payment Amounts

What will my monthly payment be
after twelve months if the index rate:

stays the same

goes up 2%

goes down 2%

What will my monthly payments be after
three years if the index rate:

stays the same

goes up 2% per year

goes down 2% per year

Take into account any caps on your mortgage
and remember it may run 30 years.

Figure 9-13

ADJUSTABLE RATE MORTGAGE (ARM) DISCLOSURE WORKSHEET

DATE:_____, 19 _____, at _____, CA

FACTS:

This ARM worksheet discloses the terms of a loan plan entitled: _____

from _____ (lender) by _____ (loan rep.)

for property referred to as _____

INTEREST RATES

1. Note Rate: (index + margin = note rate)
   1.1 Index name _____
   1.2 Index rate (current) . . . . (+)_____ %
   1.3 Margin (constant) . . . . (+)_____ %
   1.4 Note Rate (current) . . . . (=)_____ %
2. Note rate is adjusted every _____ months beginning _____/_____/_____.
   2.1 Each note rate adjustment is capped to increase no more than _____ % or decrease no more than _____ %.
   2.2 During the life of the loan, the interest rate will not exceed _____% and will not be less than _____ %.
3. Initial interest rate . . . . _____ %
   3.1 The initial interest rate is in effect for a period of _____ months.
   3.2 Note rate adjustment cap ☐ does, or ☐ does not, apply to the first adjustment at the end of the initial interest rate period.
4. Annual percentage rate — A.P.R. (Reg. Z requirement) . . . . _____ %
   NOTE: The A.P.R. is not based on the Current Note Rate. The A.P.R. is based on the qualifying rate prior to adjustment to the note rate.

PAYMENT SCHEDULES

5. The payment due monthly during the initial rate period is $ _____ .
6. The monthly payment is adjusted every _____ months beginning _____/_____/_____.
7. The payment adjustments are capped to increase no more than _____ % every _____ months.
8. The life-of-loan monthly payment parameters: Maximum payment increase is _____ % up to a total payment of $_____; Maximum payment decrease is _____ % down to a total payment of $_____.
9. The payment cap ☐ does, or ☐ does not, apply to the first payment adjustment.
10. This loan ☐ is, or ☐ is not, fully amortized at all times.
    10.1 The maximum amortization period is _____ years.

NEGATIVE AMORTIZATION:

11. Is negative amortization possible? ☐ Yes ☐ No
12. If Yes:
    12.1 During what loan period?
    _____
    12.2 The maximum build-up of principal is _____ %.

RECAST FEATURES

13. ☐ The loan will not be recast and reamortized.
14. ☐ The loan will be recast and reamortized every _____ years beginning _____/_____/_____.
    14.1 At the time of recast:
    ☐ The interest cap is given a new rate.
    ☐ The payment cap is given a new payment base.
    ☐ The life-of-loan interest rate cap is given a new note rate.

IS THE LOAN ASSUMABLE?

15. ☐ A due-on-sale clause exists.
16. Conditions of assumption: _____
    _____
    _____

IS THERE A PREPAYMENT PENALTY?

17. ☐ Yes ☐ No
18. If Yes, for what period? _____

IS THE LOAN CONVERTIBLE TO A FIXED RATE?

19. ☐ Yes ☐ No
20. If Yes, during what period? _____
    20.1 What rate index is used?
    _____ (name)
    20.2 What is the margin?_____ %
    20.3 What other charges?
    _____ (pts.) plus $_____ (fees)

Buyer's Broker: _____

By: _____

Phone: (_____) _____

Loan Rep.'s Signature: _____

Phone: (_____) _____

Broker's Approval: _____ Date: __/__/__

I have received a copy of this disclosure worksheet and understand the terms of this loan.

Date: _____, 19 _____

Buyer's Name: _____

Address: _____

_____

Phone: (_____) _____

Buyer:_____

Buyer:_____

FORM 320   09-96   ©1996 first tuesday, P.O. BOX 20069, RIVERSIDE, CA 92516 (909) 781-7300

The disclosure provides protection to both buyer and seller and should be carefully reviewed. Figure 9-15 is a Seller Carryback Disclosure Statement.

Lead Paint Disclosure

"Watch Out for Lead Based Paint" notices must be provided to buyers if all of the following conditions are met:

1. 1-to 4-residential units
2. Property was built prior to 1978
3. Purchase contract is based on an FHA loan

Credit Card Disclosure

A **SECURED CREDIT CARD** *is a card issued under an agreement which pledges, hypothecates, or places a lien on real property or money or other personal property to secure the cardholder's obligations to the cardholder.* It is really much like a secured, open line of credit extended by the lender to the consumer.

In advertising a secured credit card, the solicitation must expressly identify the credit instrument to secure the card (Civil Code 1747.94).

The cardholder may request, once a year, that the card issuer provide the amount of total finance charges assessed for the prior year (Civil Code Section 1748.5).

Section 1748.11 of the Civil Code sets forth disclosures required to be given with credit card applications other than cards secured by real property.

Housing and Community Development

PURPOSE

The Housing and Community Development Act 42 U.S.C. 5301 et. seq. is based on the premise that every American is entitled to decent housing.

One of the declaration of findings in the purpose of the act was "...inadequate public and private investment and reinvestment in housing and other physical facilities and

Figure 9-14

SELLER CARRYBACK DISCLOSURE STATEMENT

DATE:_____,19____, at _____, CA
and an attachment to the following contract:

☐ Purchase agreement

☐ Counteroffer

☐ Exchange agreement

☐ Option to purchase (with or without lease)

Dated_____, 19_____
Entered into by_____

> This statement is required by California Civil Code Section 2956 when the seller carries back a note executed by the buyer as part of the sales price for property containing four or less family units.
>
> This statement is prepared and presented by the broker or agent, to the party who offers or counteroffers to buy, sell, exchange or option as part of the offer or counteroffer received by the broker or agent.
>
> A copy of the statement shall also be delivered to the party accepting the offer or counteroffer. The statement is signed by the broker or agent who prepares it. Both buyer and seller sign it acknowledging they have read and received a copy.

DISCLOSURES:

1. General information concerning note to be executed by Buyer to Seller:

1.1 Note to be executed by Buyer in the original amount of $_____, payable in constant monthly installments of $_____ to include _____ percent per annum interest, ☐ until paid ☐ all due and payable with a final/balloon payment on _____, 19____ in the approximate amount of $_____.

1.2 The note will be secured by a trust deed on the property._____

1.3 If this note contains a FINAL/BALLOON PAYMENT, the debt is not fully amortized. When this remaining balance is due and payable, there can be no assurance that refinancing, modification or extension of the balloon payment will be available to the Buyer.

1.4 Unless stated and explained in an attached addendum, the note contains a fixed rate of interest with no variable or adjustable interest rates which would increase payments or result in a negative amortization of the debt: _____.

1.5 Unless stated, the original amount of the note will be adjusted by endorsement at close of escrow to reflect differences in the then remaining balance of any underlying trust deed obligation(s) being assumed or obtained.

1.6 If an All-Inclusive Note and Trust Deed are carried back by Seller, they will contain provisions passing through to the Buyer any prepayment penalties, late charges, due-on sale or further encumbrance acceleration and future advances.

2. Special provisions & disclosures concerning the carryback note & trust deed:

2.1 If an all-inclusive note and trust deed are carried back by the Seller, they will contain provisions that the Seller will place the note on contract collection with any institutional lender, escrow officer or real estate broker, other than the Seller, and that the collection agent is instructed to first disburse funds on payments due senior encumbrances.

2.2 A joint protection CLTA policy of title insurance will be delivered to Buyer and Seller insuring their interests in title on the close of escrow.

2.3 The trust deeds and grant deeds or land sale contracts will be executed will be recorded with the county recorded at close of escrow.

2.4 The Seller will be named, through escrow, as a loss payee under the hazard and fire insurance assigned to or obtained by the Buyer.

2.5 No tax reporting service shall be obtained for the Seller and Seller will assure himself that real estate taxes have been paid while he holds the note._____

2.6 Requests for Notice of Default and Notice of Delinquency under California Civil Code Sections 2924b and 2924e will be recorded and served on behalf of Seller on encumbrancer senior to the carryback.

2.7 Seller is aware that in the event of a default under the carryback note and trust deed, his sole source of recovery is limited to the net proceeds from foreclosure or his subsequent resale; and he is not entitled to rental value or deficiency money judgment under the note. [CCP §580b]

2.8 Unless entered, Buyer shall receive no net proceeds or cash back upon the close of escrow. Amount to be received $_____; source of funds _____; reason for receipt _____

2.9 The note shall include the following provision: "This note is subject to Section 2966 of the Civil Code, which provides that the holder of this note shall give written notice to the trustor, or his successor in interest, of prescribed information at least 90 and not more than 150 days before any balloon payment is due."

3. Encumbrances senior & prior to Seller's carryback trust deed & note:

3.1 Conditions of encumbrances, with priority over the Seller's carryback note and trust deed which will remain or be placed of record at time of closing are as follows:

	First Trust Deed	Second Trust Deed
Original balance:	$_____	$_____
Current balance:	$_____	$_____
Interest rate:	_____% ☐ VIR	_____% ☐ VIR
Type:	Type:_____	Type:_____
Monthly payments:	$_____	$_____
Due date:	_____, 19__	_____, 19__
Balloon payment:	$_____	$_____
Current defaults:	$_____	$_____

3.2 If any of the senior encumbrances contain a due date, it may be difficult or impossible to refinance, modify or extend the balloon payment in the conventional mortgage marketplace.

4. Buyer credit information (supplied by Buyer):

Buyer to hand Seller a completed credit application on acceptance. Seller may terminate the agreement within _____ days of acceptance by delivering to Buyer, Buyer's broker or escrow written Notice of Cancellation based on disapproval of Buyer's credit.

5. Broker disclosures:

5.1 Credit data is supplied by Buyer. Broker knows of no falsity or omission concerning the Buyer's credit information.

5.2 This statement and its contents being statutorily required disclosures do not limit the broker's duties to disclose other facts material to the Buyer or Seller.

5.3 The Buyer and Seller are not to sign this statement until they have read and understood all of the information in it. All parts of the form must be completed before signature.

5.5 ☐ See attached addendum for additional disclosures which are made a part hereof.

5.6 This statement was prepared by:_____.

6. Other provisions:_____

_____
_____
_____
_____
_____
_____
_____
_____
_____
_____

Buyer's Broker: _____

Address:_____

_____ Phone (____) _____

By: _____

I have read and received a copy of this statement.

Date: _____ 19 _____

Buyer: _____

Buyer: _____

Broker's approval: _____ __/__/__

Seller's Broker: _____

Address:_____

_____ Phone (____) _____

By: _____

I have read and received a copy of this statement.

Date: _____ 19 _____

Seller: _____

Seller: _____

Broker's approval: _____ __/__/__

related public and social services, resulting in the growth and persistence of urban slums and blight and the marked deterioration of the quality of urban environment..."

The goal of the act was a decent home and suitable living environment for every American family. Primary benefits were directed toward low and moderate income families.

IMPLEMENTATION

The Housing and Community Development Act consolidated a number of programs into a consistent system of aid. The act creates grants for communities for low cost housing. It provides for citizen participation in the plan. Communities receiving grants may not substitute grants for their own funds. The grants are to supplement and not to replace existing local programs. In the case of *Blackshear Residents Organization v. Austin* (1981) 659 F 2d 36, the court held that under the Housing and Community Development Act, communities may not use federal funds provided to replace local funds. It was the intent of Congress that the levels of local financial support be maintained. Local support was not to be substantially reduced.

COUNSELING

The Housing and Community Development Act of 1987 makes counseling available to low and moderate income prospective purchasers of residential property.

> *Counseling makes persons aware of the financial requirements, purchase programs available as well as benefits associated with home ownership.*

First-time buyer defaults are often blamed on the fact that low and moderate income buyers often fail to understand the extent of their obligations and lack the planning skills to meet them.

41 U.S.C.S. 5318 states:

> **(d). Social Services.** The demonstration program "shall provide for appropriate social and supportive services to be made available to residents under the demonstration program and to other residents of new town demonstration areas which may include rental and ownership counseling child care, job placement, educational programs, recreational and health care facilities and programs and other supportive services."

> 42 U.S.C.S. 5305 specifically provides that education is an activity eligible for assistance.

> **Case Example**
>
> **NAACP - Santa Rosa - Sonoma County Branch v. Hills (1976)**
>
> HUD approved a grant where nearly one-third of the funds were to acquire land for a shopping center site. The plaintiffs claimed that this was improper use of funds granted under the Housing and Community Development Act.
>
> The Court held that even though the city might have allocated more funds to activities aimed at increasing housing for low and moderate income families, the approval by HUD of the project was not arbitrary, capricious, abuse of discretion or contrary to law. The shopping center project would aid in the elimination of blight and expenditures for housing-related programs such as this were not plainly inappropriate.

CONSUMER EDUCATION CLASSES

In 1989, Fannie Mae made a commitment to make home ownership available to low and moderate income renters. Fannie Mae teamed up with a number of mortgage companies to provide consumer education classes (usually 4-8 hours). As part of the program, lenders became more flexible in underwriting guidelines offering five percent down or less to borrowers who have taken the consumer education course.

More information on this program is available by calling Fannie Mae's HomePath hotline (800) 732-6643.

Home Mortgage Disclosure Act

This federal act which requires lender disclosure of loan applications received and loans made in designated census areas has the purpose of eliminating redlining. It is included in Chapter 10 on Fair Lending Practices.

SUMMARY

The Real Estate Settlement Procedures Act is a federal act to provide consumers with an understanding of settlement costs. There are actually four purposes of this act:

1. The disclosure function mentioned above
2. The elimination of kickbacks
3. The elimination of unnecessarily large impound accounts
4. Reformation of title recordkeeping

RESPA only applies to loans meeting the following criteria:

1. Federally related
2. 1-to 4-residential units
3. Purchase loans
4. First trust deeds or mortgages

Exemptions from RESPA include:

1. Parcels of 25 or more acres
2. Home improvement loans
3. Refinancing
4. Vacant property (unless the loan includes construction)
5. Sales where there is a loan assumption
6. Construction financing (unless it is agreed to be converted to permanent financing)
7. Nonresidential property
8. Five or more units
9. Financing for construction when the land is already owned by the borrower
10. Purchase for purpose of resale
11. Land contract purchases (since title does not change hands)

Settlement is the formal process by which ownership of real property passes from the seller to the buyer. The borrower must be provided a good faith estimate of settlement costs and a settlement costs booklet within 3 days of loan application. The borrower has a right to see the Uniform Settlement Statement on the business day prior to the day of settlement. If a lender requires a particular service provider, the borrower must be told of any relationship that exists between the lender and service provider.

The lender must disclose to the borrower whether the loan can be assigned and that the right to service the loan may be transferred.

Additional Mortgage Loan Disclosures

When a loan is assigned, sold or servicing rights are transferred, the borrower must be given written notice within 15 days of the transfer.

Referral fees which were formerly prohibited by RESPA are now allowed providing they are paid by an employer or affiliate of the employer. The fee, however, cannot be related to the dollar volume or profit from the referral. However, the California Attorney General has taken the position that such referral fees will still violate California law.

Controlled business arrangements are arrangements where there is cross ownership between brokers and service providers. Owners are allowed to obtain their share of the profits of the provider, therefore indirectly benefitting from services referred. To be a *bona fide* CBA:

1. The venture must be realistically capitalized.
2. It must have its own employees.
3. It must have an office and pay fair market rent.
4. It must provide the functions of a business of its type.
5. It must bear similar risks as would similar businesses.
6. It must not subcontract services it should do itself.
7. It sends businesses exclusively to one venturer.
8. It competes for business from other than one venturer.

Buyers and sellers must be informed (disclosure) when a lender has a controlled business arrangement with a service provider.

Impound accounts are limited by RESPA to no more than prorated taxes and insurance (at closing) plus a reserve for two additional months of taxes and insurance. Monthly payments may include one-twelfth of the annual tax and insurance estimate.

A fee disclosure must be provided to a borrower whenever any borrower-paid fee is for access to computerized loan origination.

RESPA prohibits any fees to be charged by a lender for RESPA compliance requirements.

Adjustable Rate Mortgage disclosure is required. The consumer must receive a copy of the Consumer Handbook On Adjustable Rate Mortgages.

Whenever a seller carries back any portion of the financing in the sale of 1-to-4 residential units, the seller and buyer must be provided with a Seller Financing Disclosure Statement.

The "Watch Out For Lead Paint" notice must be provided to buyers of 1-to-4 residential units built prior to 1978 where there is to be an FHA loan.

Credit cards secured by a lien on real property require disclosures of the credit instrument used to secure the card.

The Housing and Community Development Act provides for counseling services for low and moderate income prospective purchasers. Fannie Mae has also made a commitment to make home ownership counseling available to low and moderate income renters.

CLASS DISCUSSION TOPICS

1. An escrow company reimburses salespersons working for the company for each escrow brought in. Do you think that real estate salespeople should be entitled to a fee for bringing in an escrow for a broker-controlled escrow company?

2. Should other referral fees be allowed? Why?

3. Why should controlled business arrangements be allowed but other kickbacks prohibited?

4. What are dangers in allowing controlled business arrangements?

5. When would a mortgage broker be involved in seller carryback financing?

6. Do you agree with the necessity of the disclosure requirements mandated for borrower and lender/purchasers?

CHAPTER 9 QUIZ

1. RESPA provides for: (p. 226)
    A. disclosure of settlement costs
    B. limitations of impound accounts
    C. limitations on kickbacks
    D. all of the above

2. Which of the following is LEAST LIKELY to be a federally related lender? (p. 227)
    A. A savings and loan
    B. A mortgage broker
    C. A lender whose deposits carry FDIC insurance
    D. A lender who only makes FHA loans

3. RESPA applies to all EXCEPT: (pp. 228-229)

    A. federally related loans

    B. 1-to 4-residential units

    C. a mobile home

    D. home improvement loans

4. Exemptions from RESPA include all of the following EXCEPT: (p. 228)

    A. refinancing

    B. vacant property

    C. loan assumptions

    D. first trust deeds and mortgages

5. A Good Faith Estimate of Settlement Costs must be given the borrower: (p. 229)

    A. on the day prior to closing

    B. upon closing

    C. within 3 days of closing

    D. within 3 days of the loan application

6. According to the California Attorney General, which of the following actions would violate California law? (p. 243)

    A. A broker who conducts her own escrows on her own loan transactions

    B. A broker who handles her own escrows rebating a portion of the escrow fee to a salesperson working for the broker who referred the escrow

    C. A broker who splits a commission with another broker who contributed toward finalizing a transaction

    D. A broker who conducts her own escrow operation within the same premises that the brokerage business occupies

7. The real estate related term "one-stop shopping" deals with: (p. 244)

    A. controlled business arrangements

    B. general brokerage handling different types of property

    C. multiple listing services

    D. all service providers located within close proximity

8. In order to be considered a *bona fide* Controlled Business Arrangement, which of the following are required? (p. 244)

    A. It must be realistically capitalized

    B. It must have an office and pay realistic rent

    C. It must compete for business from other than one venturer

    D. All of the above

9. In setting up impound accounts for a new loan, lenders may require: (p. 248)

A. two months advance tax and insurance payments

B. an amount to prorate taxes and insurance to date of closing

C. both A and B

D. neither A nor B

10. A broker who uses computerized loan origination must: (p. 249)

A. use a computer program approved by HUD

B. offer a choice of at least ten lenders

C. not charge borrowers any costs relating to access to the service

D. provide the borrower a disclosure whenever access fees are paid by the borrower

11. Lenders who incur costs in complying with RESPA can charge borrowers: (p. 249)

A. one-half of the costs with one-half to be the lender's responsibility

B. only actual costs incurred

C. actual costs plus no more than 10 percent for office overhead

D. nothing

12. Seller carryback disclosures include: (p. 253)

A. property identification

B. information on any senior loans

C. buyer's credit worthiness

D. all of the above

Answers: *1. D; 2. B; 3. D; 4. D; 5. D; 6. B; 7. A; 8. D; 9. C; 10. D; 11. D; 12. D*

Additional Mortgage Loan Disclosures

Fair Lending Practices

LEARNING OBJECTIVES

FAIR LENDING *means equal lending opportunity. It is lending in the absence of discrimination of any kind.*

To ensure the absence of discrimination we have state laws, federal laws and even professional codes of conduct. While some of these laws do not specifically mention lending, it is implicit in any legislation banning housing discrimination that it also bans lending discrimination. Allowing lending discrimination would render fair housing an impossible goal.

In this chapter you will gain an insight into the history of fair housing and learn how the various federal and state laws intermesh with some duplication of coverage.

You should understand the necessity for fair housing legislation and the value it provides to all of us.

By understanding the ramifications of fair housing laws, you will be better prepared to meet client needs in full compliance with the law.

Federal Fair Housing Laws

THE CIVIL RIGHTS ACT OF 1866

Passed by a reconstruction congress shortly after the end of the Civil War, the Civil Rights Act of 1866 stated:

> "...all citizens of the United States shall have the same rights in every state and territory as is enjoyed by white citizens thereof to inherit, purchase, lease, sell, hold and convey real and personal property."

> *This was our first Civil Rights Act and its purpose was to provide equal property rights for blacks. It provided for equal housing opportunity.*

The Civil Rights Act of 1866:

1. applies to race only.

2. applies to all types of property transactions (inherit, purchase, lease, sell, hold and convey).

3. applies to both real property and personal property. (Unlike later acts which applied to residential property only, this act was not limited to residential property.)

4. no exceptions were made to this act. (Note that the Civil Rights Act of 1968 included exceptions.)

The Civil Rights Act of 1866 could be enforced with a civil lawsuit brought by a party who has been discriminated against. Remedies included an *INJUNCTION* (an order to cease and desist), *COMPENSATORY DAMAGES* (to compensate for loss suffered), as well as *PUNITIVE DAMAGES* (to punish the wrongdoer).

The Civil Rights Act of 1866 was reenacted in 1870 to make certain that the subsequent 14th Amendment did not preempt it. However, narrow court decisions put this act into limbo until 1968 when the U.S. Supreme Court held that the act was enforceable against a private individual and that the 1866 act prohibited all racial discrimination by anyone as to the sale or lease of real and personal property. (*Jones v. Mayer* [1968] 392 U.S. 409.)

> *As previously stated, it can be implied that lending is implicit to purchasing real property and that lending discrimination, if allowed, would effectively nullify the clear intent of Congress.*

While this line of reasoning has considerable merit, other statutes and executive orders more specifically deal with lending discrimination.

EXECUTIVE ORDER 11063 (ISSUED NOVEMBER 21, 1962)

President John F. Kennedy issued this order that prohibited discrimination in residential housing where there were FHA or VA loans as well as projects involving Federal Funds.

> "...the executive branch of the government, in faithfully executing the laws of the United States which authorize federal financial assistance, directly or indirectly for the provision, rehabilitation, and operation of housing and related facilities, is charged with an obligation and duty to assure that the laws are fairly administered and that benefits thereunder are made available to all Americans without regard to their race, color, creed, or national origin."

> *This order made it clear that FHA, VA or other government related loans for residential purposes were not to be denied based upon race, color, creed or national origin.*

CIVIL RIGHTS ACT OF 1964

This act made Executive Order 11063 law. It was the first modern Civil Rights Act. However, the application of the act was restricted to cases where there was government assistance. Later laws cover this act and a great deal more.

TITLE VIII OF THE CIVIL RIGHTS ACT OF 1968
(THE FEDERAL FAIR HOUSING ACT)

Key points of the Civil Rights Act of 1968 are:

1. Housing only. (It does not apply to nonresidential property);
2. Discrimination application. This applies to national origin, color, religion, race, sex (1974), familial status (1988) and handicapped (1988).

Enforcement

> **The Department of Housing and Urban Development is responsible for enforcement of the Federal Fair Housing Act.**

Private individuals can file discrimination complaints with HUD (not limited to the person discriminated against.)

Besides administrative remedies, an aggrieved party can file a civil action in state or federal district court within two years after the occurrence or the termination of the alleged discriminatory action.

Legal remedies include:

1. injunction;
2. actual damages;
3. punitive damages (unlimited amount);
4. attorney fees and court costs.

Administrative law judges are limited to penalties up to $10,000 for the first offense, $25,000 if there was a prior offense within five years and $50,000 if there were two previous offenses within the prior seven years.

> **As it relates to loan brokerage and lending activities, the Civil Rights Act specifically prohibits redlining activities.**

REDLINING *is the refusal to lend within a designated area, restricting the number of loans within an area or restricting the size and type of loans within a designated area.*

The Civil Rights Act would seem to prohibit any discrimination in lending as lending is an integral part of housing. Lending discrimination would be housing discrimination.

Equal Housing Opportunity Poster

Should a person claim that a loan broker or lender discriminated against them under the Federal Fair Housing Law (redlining), the burden of proof could be shifted to the lender or loan broker if an *Equal Housing Opportunity Poster* is not displayed. What this means is that a loan broker who does not display the poster might have the onerous duty to prove that he or she did not discriminate when a complaint is made. Normally, the plaintiff would have the duty to prove discrimination and this is still the case if the broker displays the poster (Figure 10-1).

> *While loan brokers would display the Equal Housing Opportunity Poster, mortgage bankers and other direct lenders would display an almost identical poster labeled "Equal Housing Lender."*

COMMUNITY REINVESTMENT ACT (12 U.S.C. 2901 ET. SEQ.)

The **COMMUNITY REINVESTMENT ACT** *is based upon the finding that financial institutions are required by law to demonstrate that their deposit facilities serve the needs and conveniences of the communities in which they do business.* The purpose of the act is to require federal supervisory agencies to use their authority to make certain such institutions meet the credit needs of their local communities.

Examination of Institutions

The appropriate federal supervisory agency shall assess the record of each institution meeting the credit needs of its entire community, including low and moderate-income neighborhoods, consistent with safe and sound operations of such institutions.

The supervisory agency shall take this assessment into account in evaluating the applications of the deposit facilities.

Anti-Redlining

Although not specifically stated, it is clear that the purpose of the Community Reinvestment Act is to apply a club over financial institutions to make certain that they fairly meet credit needs in low income areas. It is really an anti-redlining act.

HOME MORTGAGE DISCLOSURE ACT

> *The main purpose of the Home Mortgage Disclosure Act of 1975 (12 U.S.C.S. 2801 et. seq.) is to expose incidents of redlining.*

Figure 10-1

U.S. Department of Housing and Urban Development

**EQUAL HOUSING
OPPORTUNITY**

We Do Business in Accordance With the Federal Fair Housing Law

(The Fair Housing Amendments Act of 1988)

> # It is Illegal to Discriminate Against Any Person Because of Race, Color, Religion, Sex, Handicap, Familial Status, or National Origin

- ■ In the sale or rental of housing or residential lots

- ■ In advertising the sale or rental of housing

- ■ In the financing of housing

- ■ In the provision of real estate brokerage services

- ■ In the appraisal of housing

- ■ Blockbusting is also illegal

Anyone who feels he or she has been discriminated against my file a complaint of housing discrimination:
 1-800-669-9777 (Toll Free)
 1-800-927-9275 (TDD)

**U.S. Department of Housing and Urban Development
Assistant Secretary for Fair Housing and Equal Opportunity
Washington, D.C. 20410**

Previous editions are obsoete

- 02184 -

form **HUD-928.1** (8/93)

Congress found that some depository institutions have sometimes contributed to the decline of certain geographic areas by their failure to provide adequate home financing to qualified applicants on reasonable terms and conditions.

This act is to provide citizens as well as public officials with information to enable them to determine whether depository institutions are filling their obligations to serve the housing needs of the communities and neighborhoods in which they are located as well as to assist public officials in their determination of public sector investments in a manner that will improve the environment of the private sector.

Duty of Depository Institutions

Every depository institution (banks, savings banks and credit unions which make federally related mortgage loans) which is located within a standard metropolitan statistical area (normally a city and its suburbs as determined by the Department of Commerce) must compile and make available to the public for their inspection the following information:

1. The number and total dollar amounts of mortgage loans that were originated or purchased by that institution during each fiscal year. The material must be itemized to clearly disclose the number and dollar amount of loans by census tract (when the county has a population of more than 30,000) within the standard metropolitan statistical area. Otherwise the breakdown is to be by county;

2. For loans made outside their standard metropolitan statistical area, lending institutions shall show their loans by county;

3. Loans shall be further itemized by loans insured under Title II of the National Housing Act or under Title V of the Housing Act of 1949 or loans guaranteed under 38 U.S.C.S. 1801 et. seq. (refers to FHA and VA loans);

4. The number and dollar amounts of loans must be separately itemized when the mortgagee does not intend to occupy the premises;

5. The number and dollar amounts of home improvement loans must be itemized;

6. Lenders must maintain and make these records available for five years;

7. Data must be set forth in a prescribed format.

Central Records

The federal **FINANCIAL INSTITUTIONS EXAMINATION COUNCIL** *is charged with consultation with the Secretary of Housing and Urban Development to implement a central depository system for data within each standard metropolitan area.* Such data shall be available to the public for examination and to copy.

12 U.S.C. 2809 requires that the Federal Financial Institutions Examination Council produce tables for each primary metropolitan statistical area showing aggregate lending patterns for various categories of census tracts according to location, age, age of housing stock, income level and racial characteristics.

This data is extremely valuable in both pointing out situations where needs are not being met as well as the basis for legal action against lenders for redlining practices.

The **FEDERAL FINANCIAL INSTITUTIONS EXAMINATION COUNCIL (FFIC)** *is a coordinating body for five government agencies.* It has released Home Mortgage Disclosure Act (HMDA) data annually since 1990. The 1996 data covered 14.8 million mortgage applications at 9,300 lending institutions. HMDA data is available on the Internet from the right-to-know network.

 www.rtk.net (Right-To-Know Network)

The data revealed since 1990 shows that minority applicants are generally turned down at a higher rate than white applicants. The 1996 data reveals that 48.8 percent of African-American applicants were denied loans and over one-third of Hispanic applicants were also rejected.

The September 1997 issue of the National Fair Housing Advocate indicated that a spokesperson for the American Bankers Association attributes the figures to the fact that lenders are "working harder to solicit applications from minority applicants."

A spokesperson for the Center For Community Change in Washington, D.C., indicated that while some lenders are improving their lending programs to serve minority applicants, others are making no progress at all. "Some individual lenders are carrying the industry as a whole on their backs and the industry as a whole isn't showing the type of gains it should."

The office of the **COMPTROLLER OF THE CURRENCY (OCC)** *which regulates nationally chartered banks,* feels that the 1996 data offers more good news in that the number of loans to low income households is increasing faster than loans to higher income households. The office also notes that lending to African-Americans and Hispanics has risen more than 50 percent in the past four years.

EQUAL CREDIT OPPORTUNITY ACT (15 U.S.C.S. 1691 ET. SEQ.)

The purpose of this act is "to require that consumer reporting agencies adopt reasonable procedures for meeting the needs of commerce for consumer credit, personnel, insurance and other information in a manner which is fair and equitable to the consumer, with regard to confidentiality accuracy, relevancy and proper utilization of such information...".

 www.law.cornell.edu/uscode (United States Code)

Discrimination

A creditor may not discriminate against any applicant for credit as to any aspect of a credit transaction:

1. on the basis of race, color, religion, national origin, sex, marital status or age (providing the applicant has the legal age for capacity to contract);

2. because all or part of an applicant's income derives from any assistance program. (The creditor must disregard the source of the income as to welfare income, aid to dependent children income, etc.); or

3. because the applicant has in good faith exercised any legal right under the Consumer Protection Act (such as legal action brought for a Truth-In-Lending violation).

Not Discriminatory

The following actions by a creditor shall not be regarded as discriminatory:

1. Making inquiry as to marital status when the purpose is not to discriminate but to ascertain the creditors rights and remedies as to a credit transaction;

2. Making inquiry as to an applicant's age or if income is derive from any public assistance program when the purpose is to determine the probable continuance of the income level, amount of income, credit history or other pertinent elements of credit worthiness;

Many persons who now receive welfare payments are scheduled to be terminated from their programs within a known period of time.

3. To use any empirically derived credit system which considers age if such system is demonstrably and statistically sound in accordance with regulations of the Board, except that in the operation of such system the age of an elderly applicant may not be assigned a negative factor or value; or

4. To make an inquiry or to consider the age of an elderly applicant when the age of such applicant is to be used by the creditor in the extension of credit in favor of such applicant.

Adverse Action

Consumers have rights when a credit application results in a refusal to loan.

1691(d). Reason for adverse action; procedure applicable; "adverse action" defined.

(1) Within thirty days (or such longer reasonable time as specified in regulations of the Board for any class of credit transaction) after receipt of a completed application for credit, a creditor shall notify the applicant of its action on the application.
(2) Each applicant against whom adverse action is taken shall be entitled to a statement of reasons for such action from the creditor...

Appraisals

Many loans are turned down because of appraisals.

Consumers are entitled to receive a copy of an appraisal report that is used in conjunction with a loan application.

(e). Appraisals; copies of reports to applicants; costs.

Each creditor shall promptly furnish an applicant, upon written request by the applicant made within a reasonable period of time of the application, a copy of the appraisal report used in connection with the applicant's application for a loan that is or would have been secured by a lien on residential real property. The creditor may require the applicant to reimburse the creditor for the cost of the appraisal.

Remedies

A creditor who fails to comply with the Equal Credit Opportunity Act shall be civilly liable:

1. for actual damages suffered by a credit applicant;

2. for punitive damages up to $10,000 (individual applicant);

3. for punitive damages up to $500,000 or one percent of the net worth of the creditor, whichever is less, in the event of a class action lawsuit.

The following is from the National Fair Housing Advocate (October 1996):

Long Beach Mortgage Company has agreed to pay $4 million to settle claims that they discriminated against borrowers on the basis of race, national origin, sex and age. They agreed to a $3 million fund to compensate more than 1,200 borrowers alleged to have been victims of discrimination and to contribute $1 million to consumer education programs in conjunction with civil rights groups. The Department of Justice claimed that the finance company allowed both its employees and brokers to charge fees and premiums to borrowers which were not based on the borrowers credit worthiness. It was claiming the pricing system was based on applicant race, national origin, sex or age as well as their credit risk level.

It was charged that African Americans, Hispanics, women and senior citizens were charged higher prices and fees for loans than other borrowers with equal credit risk and who did not have minority characteristics.

It was claimed by the government that the lender directed marketing toward minorities because officials believed minority borrowers would not discover the higher prices on their loans. The loan company emphasized monthly payments rather than their loan fees or interest.

The settlement seems to recognize the validity of risk-based pricing, providing such a system is based on objective risk related criteria.

Case Example

Miller v. American Express Co. (1982) 668 F. 2d. 1235

A credit card company had a policy of automatically canceling accounts of supplemental cardholders upon the death of the basic cardholder. Upon the death of her husband, a widow's card was canceled without any prior notice. While she was issued another card upon reapplication, she nevertheless brought an action against the card issuer. (cont'd.)

> There was no evidence in this case of either the plaintiff's inability or unwillingness to pay. The court held that automatic card cancellation was discriminatory in this case under the Equal Credit Opportunity Act.

The following is from the National Fair Housing Advocate (March 1997):

Last year, Fleet Financial Group paid $4 million to settle Justice Department claims as to lending discrimination. This year, they will pay an additional $133,000 plus attorney fees. Mortgage testing was conducted against Showmut Bank and Showmut Mortgage Corporation (Fleet subsidiaries). An African American tester and a white tester with similar income, savings and debts applied for loans. The black tester, in one instance, was kept waiting for an hour even though he had an appointment. Even then his questions as to his loan qualifications were not answered. Higher closing costs were given to the black tester and longer processing was quoted. Another loan office gave the white tester complete loan application and informational material which was not given to the black tester. He was only given a business card and told to call if he had any questions.

In another instance, the white tester was told she qualified for a loan despite a small credit problem while the black tester was told it would take three to four weeks to approve her application.

Case Example

United States v. American Future Systems, Inc. (1984) 743 F. 2d. 169

A housewares company targeted young, single white women. There credit program was designed to meet the needs of these women (18-21 years old). White single women were given better credit terms than married persons and males. The court held that the special program offered by the company was discriminatory and violated the Equal Credit Opportunity Act.

From the National Fair Housing Advocate (September 1997):

The Department of Justice filed suit against Albank, a New York based thrift, alleging that Albank had engaged in the practice of redlining in violation of the Fair Housing Act and the Equal Credit Opportunity Act. Albank had refused to make loans in certain areas in New York and Connecticut (minority areas). It was alleged that Albank gave instructions to brokers not to write loans in specified areas. Although Albank had no offices of its own in these areas, they did make loans in surrounding areas through independent mortgage brokers and their agents.

While the Department of Justice indicated that banks had the right to make decisions as to areas they would serve, they must make their decisions without regard to race or national origin.

Albank's own records indicated that they only accepted 16 applicants from minority borrowers over a four-year period. According to Janet Reno, Albank did make loans in their excluded areas but almost exclusively to whites.

To settle the suit, Albank agreed to provide $55 million in discounted mortgage loans to minority applicants and also contribute $700,000 to a homeownership counseling program and to advertise their lending in minority areas. The total cost to Albank is estimated at $9 million.

From the National Fair Housing Advocate (September 1997):

An Ohio landlord agreed to apologize to a family and pay $400,000 for not allowing them to move into an "adult building" because they had children.

The rental applicants saw a "now leasing" sign and inquired as to vacancies. They were told the adult buildings in the complex had some vacancies but the buildings for families with children were full. They were told that they could not move into an adult building because they had a two-year old daughter and five-month old son.

The couple's attorney, who also represented the Urban League, told a reporter that the landlord's preconceived notions are that children cause trouble.

According to Delbert Lancaster, the Director of the Urban League, the league has been attempting to educate landlords about fair housing laws for many years. The Federal Fair Housing Act (as to familial status) went into effect more than eight year ago.

FAIR CREDIT REPORTING ACT (15 U.S.C. 1681 ET. SEQ.)

The purpose of the **FAIR CREDIT REPORTING ACT** is to give consumers rights as to who has access to their credit files as well as to know what is in their files and the right to correct inaccurate credit information.

Permissible Issuance of Reports

A consumer reporting agency is limited as to who it may provide a credit report.

Without this limitation reports would be obtained by persons who have no legitimate need to know. Credit information is regarded by most people as personal and access to it should be privileged.

1681b. Permissible purposes of consumer reports

A consumer reporting agency may furnish a consumer report under the following circumstances and no other:

(1) In response to the order of a court having jurisdiction to issue such an order, or a subpoena issued in connection with proceedings before a Federal grand jury.

(2) In accordance with the written instructions of the consumer to whom it relates.

(3) To a person which it has reason to believe:

(A) intends to use the information in connection with a credit transaction involving the consumer on whom the information is to be furnished and involving the extension of credit to, or review or collection of an account of, the consumer; or

(B) intends to use the information for employment purposes: or

(C) intends to use the information in connection with the underwriting of insurance involving the consumer; or

(D) intends to use the information in connection with a determination of the consumer's eligibility for a license or other benefit granted by a governmental instrumentality required by law to consider an applicant's financial responsibility or status; or

(E) otherwise has a legitimate business need for the information in connection with a business transaction involving the consumer.

Case Example

Yohay v. Alexandria Employees Credit Union Inc. (1987) 827 F. 2d. 967

An attorney was retained by a credit union for legal services. She used her credit connection to obtain a credit report on her ex-husband. This report was not related to any of her legal duties with the credit union and she failed to show any legitimate purpose in obtaining the report. However, there was sufficient evidence to determine that the manager of the credit union, who was the person who ordered the report, knew of the attorney's impermissible purpose. The court held that obtaining credit reports for an impermissible purpose violated 15 U.S.C.S. 1681(n) and held both the attorney and the credit union civilly liable.

Right to Know

Upon the consumers request, a credit reporting agency shall disclose:

1. nature and substance of all information in its file at the time of the request (this does not mean that the consumer can look at his or her actual file);
2. the source of information;
3. the names of recipients of consumer report information:
   a. for employment purposes—for two years prior to the request;
   b. for other purposes—six months prior to the request.

Credit reporting agencies can reasonably charge consumers for this disclosure.

Case Example

Millstone v. O'Hanlon Reports, Inc. (1976) 528 F. 2d. 829

Millstone had applied for automobile insurance while living in Washington D.C. A credit report prepared for Fireman's Fund, the insurance company, indicated that Millstone was a "hippie" type person who wore a beard and participated in demonstrations in the capital carrying demonstrators from his home, which was a basement room, back and forth in his bus to the demonstrations. (cont'd.)

The report indicated that it was strongly suspected that Millstone was a drug user and it was rumored that he had been evicted.

Upon receiving the report, Fireman's Fund directed the agent handling the insurance to cancel the policy. The agent advised Fireman's Fund that Millstone was a highly respected assistant managing editor of the St. Louis Post Dispatch who used the Washington office when he was covering the White House (Millstone had interviewed several Presidents). Upon learning these facts, Fireman's' Fund withdrew the cancellation.

When the insurance agent informed Millstone about the credit report, Millstone was very disturbed. He requested a copy of the credit report that was furnished the insurance company. The credit reporting company refused, but after some delay did provide an oral synopsis of the report. Millstone denied the allegations. The defendant credit agency rechecked its sources and found no substance to the negative allegations in the report (the original investigation consisted of what a single woman had told the investigator).

The credit agency still refused to furnish Millstone with either a copy of the report or of the contents of the report.

At trial, the District Court ordered a judgment against O'Hanlon (the credit agency) for $2,500 actual damages, $25,000 punitive damages and $12,500 attorney's fees.

On appeal, O'Hanlon claimed he was protected by the First Amendment, but the Court of Appeals held that consumer credit reports are "commercial speech" and are outside the protection of the First Amendment.

The Court noted that "the report was rife with innuendo, misstatement and slander," and was based on a biased informant.

The Court found that O'Hanlon sought at every step to block Millstone in his attempt to secure the rights given him under the Fair Credit Reporting Act.

The Court found that O'Hanlon had willfully violated both the spirit and the letter of the Fair Credit Reporting Act and held the trial court award to be proper.

> **Case Example**
>
> **Austin v. Bank America Service Corp. (1974) 419 F. Sup. 730**
>
> A consumer credit reporting agency stated that the consumer had been a defendant in a lawsuit. The credit report failed to indicate that the lawsuit involved the consumer in his capacity as a deputy marshall and not as an individual. The defendant felt that as presented it gave a wrong impression.
>
> While 15 U.S.C.1681(e) requires agencies to follow reasonable procedures to assure maximum accuracy the court felt that the facts, while not necessarily complete, were accurate so that the defendant could not be held liable.

Errors

15 U.S.C.S.1681(e) requires credit agencies to follow reasonable procedures to assure maximum accuracy.

Because a credit report contains errors does not mean that the credit reporting agency has any liability. Errors are common in credit reports. The Federal Trade Commission determines if a credit reporting agency violated 15 U.S.C.S1681(e). The credit reporting agency has liability if the policies of the agency posed an unreasonable risk of producing error. (*Equifax, Inc. v. Federal Trade Com.* (1982) 678 F. 2d 1047).

Reinvestigation

In case a consumer disputes the accuracy of a credit report, the agency shall reinvestigate unless there are reasonable grounds to believe that the consumer's dispute is frivolous or irrelevant.

If the disputed material cannot be verified, it shall be removed.

If the dispute cannot be resolved, the consumer may file a brief statement setting forth the nature of the dispute (the Credit Reporting Agency can limit the statement to 100 words). The credit reporting company will notify future recipients that information is disputed and provide the consumer's statement or a summary thereof.

When inaccurate data is removed at the request of the consumer, the credit reporting agency shall notify persons who received information up to 2 years prior to removal for employment purposes and 6 months for other purposes.

Obsolete Information

Obsolete information must be removed from the consumer's credit file. Obsolete material includes:

1. bankruptcy over 10 years prior;

2. suits and judgments over 10 years old or until the governing statute of limitations has expired (whichever is longer);

3. paid tax liens where payment predates the report by more than 7 years;

4. accounts placed for collection or charged to profit or loss which predate the report by more than 7 years;

5. records of arrest, indictment or conviction of crime from date of disposition, release or parole that predate the report by more than 7 years;

6. any other adverse item of information which predates the report by more than 7 years;

7. the above provisions are not applicable to:

    a. credit transactions which can be expected to involve a principal amount of $50,000 or more;

    b. underwriting life insurance having a face value of $50,000 or more;

    c. employment where annual salary may be expected to equal $20,000 (at time of enactment this was a significant salary).

INVESTIGATIVE CONSUMER REPORTS

INVESTIGATIVE CONSUMER REPORTS *involve actual investigation rather than what has been reported by other creditors.* Such a report cannot be ordered unless it is disclosed to the consumer that the report shall be made. The consumer can request the nature and scope of the requested investigation.

Creditor's Duty

When credit is denied or charges increased because of an adverse report, the user of the report shall so advise the consumer and supply the name and address of the consumer reporting agency making the report.

California Fair Housing Laws

THE UNRUH ACT

"All persons within the jurisdiction of this state are free and equal, and no matter what the race, color, religion, ancestry or national origin, are entitled to full and equal accommodations, facilities of services of every kind whatsoever."

The **UNRUH ACT** *prohibits discrimination by a business.*

Mortgage brokers and lenders are businesses and are therefore covered by the Unruh Act.

The act has been interpreted liberally and the courts have held that it includes age discrimination.

Unruh Civil Rights Act - Equal Rights

51. This section shall be known, and may be cited, as the Unruh Civil Rights Act.

All persons within the jurisdiction of this state are free and equal, and no matter what their **sex, race, color, religion, ancestry, national origin, or disability** are entitled to the full and equal accommodations, advantages, **facilities, privileges or services in all business establishments of every kind whatever.**

This section shall not be construed to confer any right or privilege on a person which is conditioned or limited by law or which is applicable alike to persons of every sex, color, race, religion, ancestry, national origin or disability.

Nothing in this section shall be construed to require any construction, alteration, repair, structural or otherwise or modification of any sort whatsoever to any new or existing establishment, facility, building, improvement or any other structure, or to augment, restrict or alter in any way the authority of the State Architect to require construction, alteration, repair or modifications the at the State Architect otherwise possesses pursuant to other provisions of the law.

A violation of the right of any individual under the Americans with Disabilities Act of 1990 (Public Law 101-336) shall also constitute a violation of this section.

While other statutes clearly prohibit discrimination by lenders, you should be aware that the Unruh Act also makes such discrimination an Unruh Act violation.

The Unruh Act can be enforced by a civil action brought by the person who alleges they were discriminated against. The act provides that any person discriminated against is entitled to actual damages plus $250 for each discriminatory offense. If a lender used intimidation, such as threatening bodily harm, the possible civil penalty increases to $25,000.

RUMFORD ACT

Applicability to Mortgage Brokers and Lenders

The Rumford Act (California Fair Employment and Housing Act - Government Code 12900 et. seq.) is normally not thought of as an act dealing with mortgage brokers and lenders. However, it is clear that lender and loan broker discriminatory practices are prohibited by this act. (Note the bold type in reproducing the act.) The discrimination as defined in the act applies to sex, color, race, religion, ancestry, national origin, marital status, familial status or disability.

www.leginfo.ca.gov/cgi-bin/calawquery?codesection=
gov&codebody=&hits=20 (Government Code)

The Act

General Provisions

12900. This part may be known and referred to as the "California Fair Employment and Housing Act."

12901. There is in the state government, in the State and Consumer Services Agency, the Department of Fair Employment and Housing. The department is under the direction of an executive office known as the Director of Fair Employment and Housing....

Definitions

12927. As used in this part in connection with housing accommodations, unless a different meaning clearly appears from the context:

(a). *AFFIRMATIVE ACTIONS means any activity for the purpose of eliminating discrimination in housing accommodations because of race, color, religion, sex, marital status, national origin, ancestry, familial status or disability.*

(b). *CONCILIATION COUNCIL means a nonprofit organization, or a city or county human relations commission, which provides education, fact-finding, and mediation or conciliation services in resolution of complaints of housing discrimination.*

(c). (1) *DISCRIMINATION includes refusal to sell, rent or lease housing accommodations; includes refusal to negotiate for the sale, rental or lease of housing accommodations; includes representation that a housing accommodation is not available for inspection, sale or rental when that housing accommodation is in fact so available...*

(2) "**Discrimination**" **does not include** either of the following:

(A) Refusal to rent or lease a portion of an owner-occupied single-family house to a person as a roomer or boarder living within the household, provided that no more than one roomer or boarder is to live within the household, and the owner complies with subdivision (c) of Section 12955, which prohibits discriminatory notices, statements, and advertisements.
(B) Where the sharing of living areas in a single dwelling unit is involved, the use of words stating or tending to imply that the housing being advertised is available only to persons of one sex.

(d). *HOUSING ACCOMMODATION means any building, structure or portion thereof that is occupied as, or intended for occupancy as, a residence by one or more families and any vacant land that is offered for sale or lease for the construction thereon of any building, structure or portion thereof intended to be so occupied.*

(e). *OWNER includes the lessee, sublessee, assignee, managing agent, real estate broker or salesperson, or any person having any legal or equitable right of ownership or possession or the right to rent or lease housing accommodations, and includes the state and any of its political subdivisions and any agency thereof.*

(f). *PERSON includes all individuals and entities that are described in Section 3602(d) of Title 42 of the United States Code, and in the definition of "owner" in subdivision (e) of this section, and all institutional third parties, including the Federal Home Loan Mortgage Corporation.*

(g). *AGGRIEVED PERSON* includes any person who claims to have been injured by a discriminatory housing practice or believes that the person will be injured by a discriminatory housing practice that is about to occur.

(h). *REAL ESTATE-RELATED TRANSACTIONS* include any of the following:

(1) The making or purchasing of loans or providing other financial assistance that is for the purpose of purchasing, constructing, improving, repairing or maintaining a dwelling, or that is secured by residential real estate.

(2) The selling, brokering or appraising of residential real property.

(3) The use of territorial underwriting requirements, for the purpose of requiring a borrower in a specific geographic area to obtain earthquake insurance, required by an institutional third party on a loan secured by residential real property.

Prohibitions

12955. It shall be unlawful:

(a). For the owner of any housing accommodation to discriminate against any person because of the race, color, religion, sex, marital status, national origin, ancestry, familial status or disability of that person**...**

Commission's Actions - Penalties

12987(a). If the commission, after hearing, finds that a respondent has engaged in any unlawful practice as defined in this part, the commission shall state its findings of fact and shall issue and cause to be served on the respondent an order requiring the respondent to cease and desist from the practice and to take such actions, as, in the judgment of the commission, will effectuate the purpose of this part**...**

Enforcement

The California Fair Employment and Practices Commission has enforcement powers under the Rumford Act.

After a hearing, they can issue a cease and desist order to prohibit a discriminatory practice. They can require the payment of damages to a party discriminated against as well as civil penalties not to exceed $10,000. However, if the lender or broker committed the act intentionally and have prior violations, penalties up to $50,000 are possible.

HOUSING FINANCIAL DISCRIMINATION ACT (HOLDEN ACT)

The **HOLDEN ACT**, which was effective as of 1978, prohibits discriminatory practices by financial institutions. (Health and Safety Code 35800 et. seq.)

www.leginfo.ca.gov/cgi-bin/calawquery?codesection=
hsc&codebody=&hits=20(Health and Safety Code)

The purpose of this act is to prevent consideration of race, color religion, sex, marital status, national origin or ancestry as a reason for making loans on 1-to 4-residential units when the property is intended to be used as a residence by the owner.

The act also applies to owners seeking home improvement loans. The property need not be owner-occupied to get a home improvement loan.

Lenders, mortgage loan brokers and public agencies are prohibited from discrimination in making construction, improvement, purchase or refinance loans because of race, color, national origin, ancestry, sex, religion or marital status.

Discrimination would include different loan terms as well as loan refusals. The lender may not use loan criteria other than the credit of the applicant and the value of the property.

Discrimination As to Information

Lenders may not discriminate in informing persons as to the availability of financing.

Appraisals

The act prohibits lender appraisals using neighborhood trends based on changes in race, color, religion, sex, marital status, national origin or ancestry.

Redlining

The Holden Act prohibits redlining (also prohibited by the Civil Rights Act of 1968). A lender cannot refuse to loan within a particular designated area because of racial or ethnic composition.

Enforcement

> *The Secretary of the Business and Transportation Agency is empowered to issue rules, regulations and guidelines for enforcement of the Holden Act.*

They may investigate lending practices, attempt conciliation as to complaints or require compliance as well as payment of $1,000 to a person discriminated against.

35805. Definitions. As used in this part:

(a). AGENCY *means the Business, Transportation and Housing Agency.*

(b). FAIR MARKET VALUE *means the most probable price which a property should bring in a competitive and open market under all conditions requisite to a fair sale, the buyer and seller each acting prudently and knowledgeably, and assuming the price is not affected by undue stimulus.* The use of this definition of fair market value by a financial institution in an appraisal made at any time on or after July 1, 1986, does not violate the provisions of this part.

(c). FINANCIAL INSTITUTION *includes any bank, savings bank association or other institution in this state, including a public agency, that regularly makes, arranges or purchases loans for the purchase, construction, rehabilitation, improvement or refinancing of housing accommodations.*

(d). HOUSING ACCOMMODATION *includes any improved or unimproved real property, or portion thereof, that (1) is used or is intended to be used as a residence, and (2) is or will be occupied by the owner, and (3) contains not more than four dwelling units.* "Housing accommodation" shall also include any residential dwelling containing not more than four dwelling units where the owner thereof, whether or not the owner will occupy the property, applies or has applied for a secured home improvement loan from a financial institution, the proceeds of which loan will be used to improve the security property.

(e). SECRETARY *means the Secretary of the Business, Transportation and Housing Agency.*

CONSUMER CREDIT REPORTING AGENCIES ACT

Civil Code Section 1785.5 requires that any person who for fees, dues or on a cooperative nonprofit basis regularly assembles, evaluates or disseminates information on the checking account experiences of customers of banks or other financial institutions shall be held to the same laws that cover consumer credit reporting agencies.

The rights of consumers under state law are similar to the rights granted under the Federal Fair Credit Reporting Act.

CALIFORNIA BUSINESS AND PROFESSIONS CODE

Real estate brokers are also prohibited from discriminatory lending and loan brokerage activities by the California real estate law. The Business and Professions Code provides for disciplinary action for discriminatory acts.

Business and Professions Code 125.6

125.6. Every person who holds a license under the provisions of this code is subject to disciplinary action under the disciplinary provisions of this code applicable to such person if, because of the applicant's race, color, sex, religion, ancestry, disability, marital status or national origin, he or she refuses to perform the licensed activity or aids or incites the refusal to perform such licensed activity by another licensee, or if, because of the applicant's race, color, sex, religion, ancestry, disability, marital status or national origin, he or she makes any discrimination, or restriction in the performance of the licensed activity**...**

Definitions. as used in this section.

LICENSE, as used in this section, includes "certificate," "permit," "authority," and "registration" or any other indicia giving authorization to engage in a business or profession regulated by this code.

APPLICANT, as used in this section means a person applying for licensed services provided by a person licensed under this code.

DISABILITY means any of the following with respect to an individual:

(a). A physical or mental impairment that substantially limits one or more of the major life activities of the individual.

(b). A record of such an impairment.

(c). Being regarded as having such an impairment.

COMMISSIONER'S REGULATION 2780

These regulations describe prohibited discriminatory conducted by a real estate licensee. Loan brokerage and other financing activities are covered by these regulations.

 www.dre.cahwnet.gov/1regs97.htm (Commissioner's Regulations)

The regulations make clear that discrimination does not include refusal to finance a person who has a physical handicap because of the presence of hazardous conditions or architectural barriers.

The Commissioner has also made clear that discriminatory conduct is not limited to those activities described in the Regulation.

2780. Discriminatory Conduct as the Basis for Disciplinary Action

Prohibited discriminatory conduct by a real estate licensee based upon race, color, sex, religion, ancestry, physical handicap, marital status or national origin includes, but is not limited to, the following:

(a). Refusing to negotiate for the sale, rental or financing of the purchase of real property or otherwise making unavailable or denying real property to any person because of such person's race, color, sex, religion, ancestry, physical handicap, marital status or national origin.

(b). Refusing or failing to show, rent, sell or finance the purchase of real property to any person or refusing or failing to provide or volunteer information to any person about real property, or channeling or steering any person away from real property, because of that person's race, color, sex, religion, ancestry, physical handicap, marital status or national origin or because of the racial, religious or ethnic composition of any occupants of the area in which the real property is located...

Other sections of the act prohibit discrimination by processing applications slower or obstructing financing, etc.

Note: A single act could violate numerous laws. (See Figure 10-2.)

Figure 10-2

VIOLATIONS

FEDERAL

Civil Rights Act of 1866

Civil Rights Act of 1964

Civil Rights Act of 1968

Home Mortgage Disclosure Act

Fair Credit Reporting Act

Equal Credit Opportunity Act

CALIFORNIA

California Fair Employment and Housing Act (Rumford Act)

Housing Financial Discrimination Act (Holden Act)

Unruh Civil Rights Act

Commissioner's Regulation 2780

Consumer Credit Reporting Agencies Act

The Real Estate Industry and Fair Lending

REALTORS CODE OF ETHICS AND STANDARDS OF PRACTICE

www.dabr.com/ethics.htm (NAR Code of Ethics)

Article 10 of The Code of Ethics of the National Association of Realtors® states:

"Realtors® shall not deny equal professional services to any person for reasons of race, color, religion, sex, handicap, familial status or national origin. Realtors® shall not be parties to any plan or agreement to discriminate against a person or persons on the basis of race, color, religion, sex, handicap, familial status or national origin."

VOLUNTARY AFFIRMATIVE MARKETING AGREEMENT - VAMA

The National Association of Realtors® agreed to a Voluntary Affirmative Marketing Agreement with the U.S. Department of Housing and Urban Development. This program, which has been in place since 1975, has 4 basic objectives:

1. By signing voluntarily, Realtors are able to pledge their support of fair housing.

2. Community involvement is encouraged in determining their fair-housing problems within the community.

3. VAMA provides a method for Realtors to implement their commitment to fair housing. Methods include education as to responsibilities, developing a fair-housing plan for the firm, cooperation with community groups to promote fair housing, as well as providing equal employment opportunities within the firm.

4. Brokers are encouraged to share their commitment with the communications industry, civic organizations, as well as other groups concerned with the realization of fair housing so that fair housing can become a reality.

SUMMARY

There are both federal and state laws against housing discrimination. While these laws implicitly apply to lending discrimination, there are specific lending references in several laws as well as laws specifically dealing with lending.

Federal laws include:

1. Civil Rights Act of 1866 which gave every citizen the same rights as white citizens to lease, sell and hold property.

2. Executive Order 11063 (1962) outlawed discrimination in housing where there was any government assistance (loan guarantees, insurance or federal agency involvement).

3. Civil Rights Act of 1964 made Executive Order 11063 law.

4. Civil Rights Act of 1968. As amended, this act applies to housing only and discrimination as to national origin, color, religion, race, sex, familial status and handicapped. It specifically prohibits redlining (refusal to lend within designated areas).
   Unless a broker displays the Equal Housing Opportunity Poster, the burden of proof as to discrimination would be shifted from the person alleging discrimination to the broker. There is also an Equal Housing Lender Poster.

5. Community Reinvestment Act. This act requires that federal supervisory agencies make certain that financial institutions meet the credit needs of local communities. It's purpose is to make certain redlining type activities are not engaged in.

6. Home Mortgage Disclosure Act. By requiring financial data on loans by area, the act makes lenders point out situations that could be redlining.

7. Equal Credit Opportunity Act. This act requires that consumer reporting agencies adopt reasonable procedures for credit information. Creditors may not discriminate as to any aspect of the credit process.

8. Fair Credit Reporting Act. This act gives consumers access to know what is in their credit file and the right to have incorrect credit information as well as obsolete information removed.

California fair housing laws include:

1. Unruh Act. This act applies to discrimination by all businesses (including lenders). It has been interpreted to prevent all types of discrimination.

2. Rumford Act. This is California's fair housing act. It clearly categorizes the making and purchasing of loans as a real estate related activity that is covered by the act.

3. Holden Act. This act is directly applicable to lenders. It is California's anti-redlining law.

4. Consumer Credit Reporting Agencies Act. This state law gives consumers similar rights as are granted under the Federal Fair Credit Reporting Act.

5. California Business and Professions Code provides for disciplinary action against licensees who engage in discriminatory practices.

6. Commissioner's Regulation 2780 provides a list of activities that are considered discriminatory. Financing is clearly set forth as an area where discrimination will not be tolerated.

Besides state and federal laws, (an act can be a violation of more than one law as well as both state and federal law) the Realtors® Code of Ethics provides that licensees shall not deny equal professional services in any discriminatory manner.

The Voluntary Affirmative Marketing Agreement (VAMA) has as its purpose the voluntary support of realtors in educating others and become involved with community groups to promote fair housing.

CLASS DISCUSSION TOPICS

1. A mortgage loan company had a policy where the loan agents received, as additional compensation, one-half of any additional points agents could get borrowers to pay above the required points.

In analyzing the results of this policy, it is determined that 76 percent of people who paid additional points had Spanish surnames. It was also discovered that borrowers with Spanish surnames constituted 17 percent of the loans made by firms during this time period.

Is there a violation of law(s)? Which law(s)? Why?

2. A prospective private lender indicated that they only wanted to make a loan on property in a stable neighborhood with at least 90 percent caucasian residents. Did the loan broker violate the Federal Fair Housing laws by only bringing to the lender's attention those lending possibilities which met the lenders criteria for neighborhood racial composition?

3. For a person to be liable for wrongful discrimination, must the discrimination be intentional?

4. Why are discrimination charges more likely today then they were 10 years ago?

5. Do you agree with the courts decision in the case of *Austin v. Bank America Service Corp.*? Why?

CHAPTER 10 QUIZ

1. Which civil rights law made an executive order a law? (p. 269)
    A. Civil Rights Act of 1866
    B. Civil Rights Act of 1964
    C. Civil Rights Act of 1968
    D. Civil Rights Act of 1988

2. Which Civil Rights Act specifically prohibits redlining? (p. 270)
    A. Civil Rights Act of 1866
    B. Civil Rights Act of 1870
    C. Civil Rights Act of 1964
    D. Civil Rights Act of 1968

3. Refusing to loan within a designated geographical area of high crime and great unemployment would be: (p. 270)
    A. redlining
    B. steering
    C. blockbusting
    D. proper business practice

4. Failure of a mortgage broker to properly display the Equal Housing Opportunity Poster, could result in: (p. 271)
    A. a $10,000 fine
    B. up to six months in jail
    C. the shifting of the burden of proof of a discriminatory claim to the broker
    D. all of the above

5. Federal financial supervisory agencies are required to make certain that regulated financial institutions meet the credit needs of their local communities under which act? (p. 271)
    A. Civil Rights Act of 1964
    B. Civil Rights Act of 1968
    C. Community Reinvestment Act
    D. Real Estate Settlement Procedures Act

6. Incidents of redlining would be exposed by financial institutions' reports filed under which act? (p. 271)

    A. RESPA

    B. Home Mortgage Disclosure Act

    C. Civil Rights Act of 1964

    D. Civil Rights Amendment Act of 1988

7. The act which prohibits a lender from discriminating against income of a loan applicant because it comes from welfare payments is the: (p. 275)

    A. Equal Credit Opportunity Act

    B. Home Improvement Act of 1974

    C. Welfare Reform Act

    D. Home Mortgage Disclosure Act

8. Which federal act gives consumers the right to know the nature and substance of information in their credit file? (p. 280)

    A. Fair Credit Reporting Act

    B. Holden Act

    C. Civil Rights Act of 1968

    D. All of the above

9. The Fair Credit Reporting Act provides that: (p. 284)

    A. when credit is denied because of a report, the consumer will be notified and given the name of the consumer reporting agency

    B. the consumer will be advised when an investigative consumer report is in process

    C. adverse information more than seven years old shall be removed from the report

    D. all of the above

10. Which California act specifically prohibits discrimination by a business? (p. 285)

    A. Holden Act

    B. Rumford Act

    C. Unruh Act

    D. VAMA

11. California's Fair Employment and Housing Act prohibits discrimination based on sex, color, race, religion, ancestry, national origin, marital status, familial status or disability. The act is commonly known as: (p. 286)

    A. Section VIII

    B. Regulation Z

    C. The Unruh Act

    D. The Rumford Act

12. Commissioner's Regulation 2780 considers which of the following to be discriminatory conduct? (p. 292)

    A. Refusing to negotiate the sale, rental or financing of the purchase of real estate because of the person's race.

    B. Processing a financial application more slowly because of an applicant's race

    C. Making an effort to obstruct financing of real property because of a person's race

    D. All of the above

Answers: 1. B; 2. D; 3. A; 4. C; 5. C; 6. B; 7. A; 8. A; 9. D; 10. C; 11. D; 12. D

Trust Fund Handling

KEY WORDS AND TERMS

Advance Fees
Beneficiary Ledger
Broker Funds
Broker-Maintained Impound Account
Cash Ledger
Columnar Record
Commingling
Conflicting Claims
Daily Balance
Escrow
Fiscal Year Report
Good Funds
Interest-bearing Trust Account
Interpleader Action

Journal
Loan Brokerage Deposits
Multi-Lender Rule
Offset of Trust Funds
Pass-Through Funds
Payoffs
Reconciliation of Trust Account
Retention of Records
Threshold Amount
Threshold Notification
Trust Account
Trust Account Records
Trust Funds

LEARNING OBJECTIVES

In this chapter you will not only learn what trust funds are and how they are maintained in a trust account, you will also learn the "why" of trust fund handling.

Trust Funds

Mortgage brokerage as well as lending activities involves the acceptance of funds of others for funding loans, loan costs, services to be supplied by the broker or others as well as in servicing loans.

Funds of others coming into the broker's possession might include loan payments, impound account funds for taxes and insurance, funds to fund loans, funds for appraisals, credit reports, title insurance, etc.

*Money which is not broker funds or not yet broker funds is held by the broker for some purpose or future disbursement. Such funds are considered **TRUST FUNDS**.*

Section 10231 of the Business and Professions Code prohibits a broker from accepting funds to purchase a loan unless such funds are for a specific loan secured by real property on which the broker has a bona fide authorization to negotiate a loan. In other words, a broker cannot accept money in advance to purchase or fund a loan unless the broker has authorization to negotiate or sell the specific loan.

Trust funds do not have to be cash. As an example, the trust funds could be a personal note, or a note secured by a trust deed or even a pink slip to a car given as a deposit. (These would be trust assets.)

Funds received on behalf of a principal or others would be trust funds. Non-trust funds would be broker-owned funds.

Trust Account

DEFINITION

A **TRUST ACCOUNT** *is an account set up by a broker in a depository in which funds entrusted to the broker for the benefit of another or for some special disbursement are kept.* (Business and Professions Code 2830).

DESIGNATION OF ACCOUNT

A trust fund must clearly indicate that the account contains money held in trust for the benefit of others and is not the personal funds of the broker. "Trust Account" after the broker's name is sufficient for this purpose. If a trust account was not designated as such, creditors of the broker could seize or tie up the funds so they would not be available when required. Death, disability or bankruptcy of the broker could also lead to claims on the funds and lengthy proceedings.

> *Trust money for multiple beneficiaries can be kept in a broker's general non-interest-bearing trust account.*

MULTI-LENDER RULE

Commissioner of Corporations Regulations 260.105.30 deals with multiple lenders in a single transaction, with a series of notes secured by the same real property or the sale of undivided interests in the same note secured by real estate which is equivalent to a series transaction.

> *Effective January 1, 1998, the Department of Real Estate has acquired the responsibility of "multi-lender" transactions from the Department of Corporations.*

The real property securing the notes has to be in California and interests cannot be sold to more than 10 persons if the notes are sold by a real estate broker and proper notice and reporting is compiled with the transactions would be exempt from qualifying as a security.

In servicing a multi-lender note or notes, the payments are required to be immediately deposited in a trust account maintained with the provision of law and rule for trust accounts of licensed real estate brokers.

> *Such payments shall not be commingled with the assets of the servicing agent or used for any transaction other than for which the funds are received.*

> *Payments received on the note or notes must be transmitted to the purchasers or lenders, prorated according to their respective interests, within 25 days after receipt by the agent.*

If the source for the payment is not the maker of the note, the agent must inform the purchasers or lenders of the source for payments. A broker or servicing agent who transmits to the purchasers or lenders such broker's and/or servicing agents own funds to cover payments due from the borrower but unpaid may recover the amount of such advances from the trust fund when the past due payment is received. But the commissioner's regulation does not authorize the broker or servicing agent to guarantee or to engage in the practice of advancing funds on behalf of the borrower.

DEPOSITS RECEIVED BY THE BROKER

When a broker receives funds from others in the course of a loan transaction that are either to be used for funding or paying costs and fees associated with the loan, the broker can deliver the funds to (**Commissioner's Regulation 2832**):

1. **Escrow.** The funds can be placed in a neutral escrow depository.

2. **Trust Account.** The funds can be deposited in a trust account in the name of the broker as trustee in a bank or other financial institution.

3. **Service Provider.** The broker may pay the service provider if authorized to do so.

4. **Principal.** Deposit the money with the principal. This is not recommended. There is a danger that the transaction will not be completed and the principal may not have the funds available that should be returned to the person who deposited the funds.

DEPOSITS RECEIVED BY SALESPERSONS

A real estate salesperson who accepts funds from others on behalf of the broker must immediately deliver the funds to the broker, or if directed by the broker, shall place the funds:

1. **With Principal.** Into the hands of the broker's principal (not recommended);
2. **Into Escrow.** Into a neutral escrow depository;
3. **In a Trust Account.** Into the broker's trust account.

INTEREST-BEARING ACCOUNTS

Accounts generally shall not be interest-bearing accounts for which a notice is required prior to withdrawal.

Trust funds can be placed in an interest-bearing account at the request of the owner of the funds from whom the funds were received.

The broker can then place the funds in an interest-bearing account in a bank, savings bank, credit union or industrial loan company providing the account is insured by the Federal Deposit Insurance Corporation. Because loan brokerage and lending involves large sums of money, the interest accruing in such funds can be considerable. Therefore, loan brokering and lending often involves funds being kept in interest-bearing accounts.

In order to deposit funds in an interest-bearing account, the following criteria must be met for the account:

1. **Name of Broker.** The account must be in the name of the broker as trustee.

2. **Insurance.** All of the funds must be covered by insurance. (Deposits over the FDIC insurance limit might have to be placed in several accounts.)

3. **Separation.** The account must not only be separate from any broker funds, it must also be kept separate from trust funds held for others (this requires a separate trust fund for each such account).

4. **Disclosure.** The broker must disclose to the person from whom the funds were received and the beneficiary of the funds:
   a. the nature of the account;
   b. how interest will be calculated and paid;
   c. whether service charges will be paid to the depository and by whom;
   d. possible notice requirements or penalties for withdrawal.

5. **Broker May Not Benefit.** Interest earned on funds may not benefit the broker or any person licensed to the broker (directly or indirectly).

6. **Who Gets The Interest?** The parties to the loan transaction must have specified in the contract which person the interest is to be paid or credited.

EXAMINATION OF RECORDS

The broker must furnish the Real Estate Commissioner, upon request, an authorization to examine the financial records of interest-bearing trust accounts.

FINANCIAL INSTITUTIONS REQUIRED TO PAY INTEREST

When a financial institution makes a loan secured by one-to-four residential units and collects money in advance (with the monthly payments) for taxes, insurance, assessments or other purposes, they are required by law to pay interest on these monies of **at least 2 percent** which must be credit to the borrower. (Civil Code Section 2954.8).

Business and Professions Code Section 10145 covers interest bearing trust accounts.

www.leginfo.ca.gov/.html/bpc_table_of_contents.html
(California Business and Professions Code)

Broker Maintained Impound Accounts

A broker who is acting as an agent of a financial institution or a beneficiary of a loan who collects advance payments for taxes, assessments, insurance, etc., relating to a one-to-four family residence, may deposit such funds in an interest-bearing account in a bank or savings bank association in order to earn interest for the obligor. However, the following conditions must be met (**Commissioner's Regulations 2830.1**):

1. **In Broker's Name.** The account must be in the name of the broker as trustee.

2. **Insurance.** The account must be covered by insurance provided by an agency of the federal government.

3. **No Commingling.** All of the funds in the account are funds held in trust by the broker for others.

4. **Disclosure of Interest Calculations.** The broker discloses to the obligor how interest will be calculated and paid.

5. **No Benefit to Broker.** No interest earned on the funds shall inure directly or indirectly to the benefit of the broker nor to any person licensed to the broker.

Note: The statutes do not require trust funds for impound accounts be kept in separate accounts for each obligor. This differs from the requirement that deposits which apply to sale, lease or loan transactions be kept in separate accounts and not be mixed with funds of other obligors.

A broker handling impound funds using a single account should, where possible, seek a financial institution to calculate interest separately for each beneficiary.

Advance Fees

An **ADVANCE FEE** *is a fee paid for a service not yet rendered.* Loan brokers often receive funds in advance of their services. Section 10026 of the Business and Professions Code defines "Advance Fee."

"Advance Fee"

10026. The term "advance fee" as used in this part is a fee claimed, demanded, charged, received, collected or contracted from a principal for a listing, advertisement or offer to sell or lease property, other than in a newspaper of general circulation, issued primarily for the purpose of promoting the sale or lease of business opportunities or real estate or for referral to real estate brokers or salesmen, or soliciting borrowers or lenders for, **or to negotiate loans on, business opportunities or real estate...**

HANDLING ADVANCE FEES

Any licensee who collects an advance fee from any person must deposit said fee in a trust account with a bank or other recognized depository when collected.

An advance fee is considered to be trust funds and not the funds of the broker. An amount may only be withdrawn from the trust account for the benefit of the agent when it is actually expended for the benefit of the principal.

To preclude inappropriate use of advance fees, a broker can only collect advance fees if the contract or agreement to be used was first submitted and approved for use by the Department of Real Estate. The agreement must specifically inform the borrower how the advance fee is to be used. The broker may not profit from the advance fee in that actual costs that are less than collected must be refunded to the borrower.

The commissioner may issue rules regulating advance fee accounting. However, each principal must be furnished a verified copy of such accounting at the end of each calendar quarter and when the contract has been completely performed. The Real Estate Commissioner shall, upon demand, be furnished a verified copy of any or all accounts.

When advance fees are not handled in accordance with the above procedures, it shall be assumed that the agent has violated the Penal Code.

The principal may recover treble damages for amounts misapplied and is entitled to reasonable attorney fees required to recover the damages.

While the Department of Real Estate does not consider fees collected in advance for appraisal and credit reports as being advance fees if the broker collects an amount as near as possible to actual costs, the funds still must be deposited in the broker's trust account until expended.

Commissioner's Regulation 2972 provides for a verified accounting to the principal as required by Business and Professions Code Section 10146.

2972. Accounting Content

Each verified accounting to a principal or to the commissioner as required by Section 10146 of the Code shall include at least the following information:

(a). The name of the agent.

(b). The name of the principal.

(c). Description of the services rendered or to be rendered.

(d). Identification of the trust fund account into which the advance fee has been deposited.

(e). The amount of the advance fee collected.

(f). The amount allocated or disbursed from the advance fee for each of the following:

(1) In providing each of the services enumerated under (c) above.
(2) Commissions paid to field agents and representatives.
(3) Overhead costs and profit.

(g). In cases in which disbursements have been made for advertising, a copy of the advertisement, the name of the publication, the number of the advertisements actually published and the dates that they were carried.

(h). In the case of an advance fee for the arrangement of a loan secured by a real property or a business opportunity, a list of the names and addresses of the persons to whom information pertaining to the principal's loan requirements were submitted and the dates of the submittal.

ADVANCE FEE ADVERTISING

Business and Professions Code Section 10085 provides that the commissioner may require 10 days notice prior to use of material in advance fee solicitation.

Advance Fee Agreements and Materials

10085. The commissioner may require that any or all materials used in contract forms, letters or cards used to solicit prospective sellers, and radio and television advertising be submitted to him or her at least 10 calendar days before they are used. Should the commissioner determine that any such matter, when used alone or with any other matter, would tend to mislead he or she may, within 10 calendar days of the date he or she receives same, order that it not be used, disseminated nor published...

Any violation of any of the provisions of this part or of the rules, regulations, orders or requirements of the commissioner thereunder shall constitute grounds for disciplinary action against a licensee, or for proceedings under Section 10081 of this code, or both. These sanctions are in addition to the criminal proceedings hereinbefore provided.

Commissioner's Regulation 2970 covers criteria that would result in disapproval of advance fee advertising material.

2970. Advance Fee Materials

(a). A person who proposes to collect an advance fee as defined in Section 10026 in the Code shall submit to the Commissioner not less than ten calendar days before publication or other use, all materials to be used in advertising, promoting, soliciting and negotiating an agreement calling for the payment of an advance fee including the form of advance fee agreement proposed for use...

(c). Not less than 10-point type shall be used in advance fee agreements.

ADVANCE FEE PROHIBITIONS

Business and Professions Code Section 10085.5(a) prohibits the collection of advance fees for loan brokerage activities unless the person is a licensed real estate broker and has submitted advance fee advertising material which has been properly submitted to the commissioner and of which use has not been denied.

Loan Brokerage Deposits

Funds received for the purchase of a loan or making a loan shall be maintained by the broker in an escrow depository or trust fund account.

The money is only to be disbursed upon express written instructions of the person making the deposit.

Unless there is a written agreement to the contrary, the broker shall transmit to the owner, within 60 days of receipt, all funds in the broker's custody for which a written instruction for disbursement was not received.

 **www.leginfo.ca.gov/.html/bpc_table_of_contents.html
(Business and Professions Code 10232.4:
Disclosure Statement - Delivery - Exception - Funds Handling)**

Broker as Principal

A real estate broker who acts as a principal in selling mortgages or real property securities must place all funds received from others for the purchase of real property sales contracts or promissory notes secured by liens on real property in a neutral depository unless delivery of the contract or note is made simultaneously with the receipt of purchase funds.

A broker acting as a principal in the sale (or lease) of his or her own property, other than mortgages and real property, is not required to place funds received as purchase or lease deposits in a trust fund.

The broker is treated as any other principal in these situations.

Escrows

A broker is exempt from the licensing provisions of the escrow law when handling a transaction for which a real estate license is required. This would include loan brokerage activities [Financial Code 17006 (4)]. Nevertheless, the broker is responsible for the following:

1. **Records.** Maintaining books, records and accounts in accordance with accepted principles of accounting and good business practice.

2. **Available for Inspection.** Making the office, books records, accounts, safes, files and papers relating to escrows freely accessible and available for audit, inspection and examination by the commissioner.

3. **Deposit in Escrow.** Depositing all monies received as an escrow agent, as part of an escrow transaction, in a bank, trust account on or before the close of the next full working day after receipt thereof.

The extension to 3 days does not apply to escrow funds.

4. **Withdrawal of Funds.** Withdrawing or paying out any money deposited in the escrow account only with the written instructions of the party paying the money into escrow.

5. **Disclosure of Interest in Transaction.** Advising all parties in writing if the broker has knowledge that any licensee acting in the transaction (including him or herself) has any interest as a stockholder, officer, partner or owner of the agency holding the escrow.

6. **Accounting to Principal.** Providing each principal in the transaction with a written statement of all receipts and disbursements together with the name of the person to whom such disbursement was made.

7. **Delivery and Recording.** Only delivering or recording an instrument transferring a person's interest or title after first obtaining that persons written consent to the delivery or recording (could be in the escrow instructions).

Broker Funds in Trust Account

A broker can keep up to $200 of his or her own fund in the trust account (formerly $100).

The reason for allowing the broker to keep some of his or her own money in the account is to avoid a situation where bank charges would create a shortage in the account. (As an alternative, some brokers have the bank charges for their trust accounts charged against their general account.)

A broker may also keep earned commissions or fees in his or her trust account for a period of up to 30 days.

Commingling

COMMINGLING *involves the prohibited practice of mixing broker or general account funds with trust funds.* Commingling could also be holding cash or checks uncashed without approval of the parties involved.

> *Commingling is grounds for suspension or revocation of a real estate license (Commissioner's Regulations 10176).*

Article 8 of the Realtors® Code of Ethics states:

> "Realtors shall keep in a special account in an appropriate financial institution, separated from their own funds, monies coming into their possession in trust for other persons, such as escrows, trust funds, client monies and other like items."

> *It is considered commingling for a broker to fail to deposit designated trust funds into his or her trust account within 3 business days following receipt (formerly next business day).*

Funds belonging partly to a broker and partly to a broker's principal can be deposited into a trust account when it is not reasonably practical to separate such funds, provided that part of the funds belonging to the broker are disbursed not later than twenty-five (25) days after they are deposited and there is no dispute between the parties as to the broker's share of the funds. When the broker's share is disputed by the other party, the disputed portion shall not be withdrawn until finally settled.

> *Brokers meeting the criteria set forth in Section 10232 of the Business and Professions Code may keep broker funds in their trust account for no more than 25 days. The funds must be properly identified as broker funds.*

Commissioner's Regulations

2835. Commingling

"Commingling" as used in Section 10176(e) of the Code is prohibited except as specified in this section. For purposes of Section 10176(e), the following shall not constitute "commingling":

(a). The deposit into a trust account of reasonably sufficient funds, not to exceed $100, (now $200) to pay service charges or fees levied or assessed against the account by the bank or financial institution where the account is maintained...

While commingling is the confusion of trust funds and broker funds, **CONVERSION** *is the actual theft of trust funds.*

A common conversion takes place when a broker withdraws what he or she considers to be the commission from the trust account prior to a closing.

It makes no difference what the broker's intention was, the act is considered theft as the broker was not entitled to the money until closing. This type of conversion is likely to be discovered when a loan fails to close.

Conversion of trust funds can result in loss of license, receivership appointed, civil liability to injured parties, criminal sanctions and even federal and state income tax liability if converted funds were not declared as income.

Trust Funds Returned

If a loan cannot be completed for any reason, funds received for funding the loan as well as unexpended funds received for services must be returned to the person(s) making the deposit.

A shortage in the trust account could result if a deposit is returned before the check has cleared and the check fails to clear. This problem can be avoided by a contract which clearly indicates that any check deposited must clear before any funds will be returned.

Another solution is to have the seller instruct the broker that the earnest-money-deposit check is not to be deposited until the offer is accepted. One problem with this solution is that you will not know until after acceptance if the buyer's check is good or the buyer might stop payment on it. The property could be tied up with a contract without any earnest money unless the contract provides for nullification if the buyer's deposit fails to clear his or her bank.

*Once a deposit has cleared a bank, it is considered **GOOD FUNDS**.* Good funds also include cashier checks. A broker should not return a deposit or write a check to a service provider such as an escrow unless the check is written on "good funds."

When a trust-fund account holds funds of more than one beneficiary, any disbursement of funds that will reduce the balance of funds in the trust account to an amount less than the total existing trust fund liability of the broker to all beneficiaries of the fund requires the prior written consent of every principal who is an owner of funds in the account. In other words, a broker cannot return a deposit or pay a expenditure from funds that have not cleared without getting written approval of all other parties having interest in funds in the account. It is unlikely that the parties would agree to this.

Trust Fund Withdrawals and Disbursements

WITHDRAWALS

> *Withdrawals can be made from trust funds by a broker or by a salesperson or broker (under a written contract with the designated broker) who have been specifically authorized in writing to make withdrawals (California Code of Regulations 2834).*

An unlicensed employee of a broker can also be authorized to make withdrawals, however, the unlicensed employee must be covered by a fidelity bond that is at least equal to the amount of trust funds that employee would have access to at any time.

DISBURSEMENT OF LOAN FUNDS

Unless a lender has given a broker written authorization to disburse loan funds, the broker may not disburse funds until the trust deed securing the note has been recorded.

PAYOFFS

The broker cannot apply payoffs received to other loans or invest the receipts in other loans without the specific approval of the beneficiary of the funds received.

The broker cannot retain payments received for more than 60 days, when servicing a loan, except with the specific written agreement of the loan purchaser or lender. (Section 10231.1)

Case Example

Milner v. Fox (1980) 102 C.A. 3d 567

A real estate broker was engaged in loan brokerage as well as the servicing of the loans he arranged. The broker accepted loan payoffs and issued unsecured demand notes from his corporate affiliate.

The broker acknowledged that the Real Estate Brokers Act required that the initial investment of client funds had to be secured by a lien on real property. In this case the broker was using payoff funds which were not specifically covered by the act.

The court held that Business and Professions Code 10231 prohibits a mortgage broker from placing any funds from any source unless secured by a loan on real estate.

They also pointed out that Business and Professions Code 10231.1 requires that investors received their return promptly. The section does not permit a mortgage broker to issue unsecured notes.

Conflicting Claims on Trust Funds

Should a loan fail to be consummated and both lender and borrower make claim to funds held by the broker, the broker should not turn the disputed funds over to either party.

If the broker turned over funds to one party without approval of the other party and a court later determined that the party receiving the funds was not entitled to them, the broker could be liable if the party receiving the funds were unwilling or unable to return those funds.

If the parties are unable to reach an agreement as to the disposition of trust funds, the broker could commence an **INTERPLEADER ACTION**, *which is a legal proceeding where the stakeholder (broker) deposits the funds with the court and ask the court to distribute the monies to the rightful claimant.*

An interpleader action forces the parties to plead their case in court, which can be an expensive process for both parties.

Frequently the legal expense is not justified by the dollars involved. The broker should recommend that the parties reach an agreement or compromise. Some contracts call for mandatory arbitration of disputes involving entitlement to trust funds.

Offset of Trust Funds

Trust money held by a broker cannot be used to offset claims that the broker may have against the party depositing the funds or the broker's principal.

As an example, suppose a lender places funds with a broker and the loan is never made. Even if that lender owes the broker money from another transaction, the broker must return the funds in full to the lender and may not use it to offset the debt.

A salesperson with access to trust monies cannot take trust funds out of the account because the broker, lender or borrower owes the salesperson a debt. The money remains trust money until the funds are disbursed upon conclusion of the transaction or returned to the buyer.

If a debt is owed to the broker or salesperson the remedy would be a legal one through the courts and cannot be solved by the unilateral action of withdrawal of monies held in trust.

Trust Fund Status Reports

WHO MUST FILE?

These reports must be filed if real estate brokers intend or reasonably expect in the succeeding 12-month period to do any of the following:

Negotiations - Combination of 20

Negotiate a combination of 20 or more of the following private money transactions in an aggregate amount of more than 2 million dollars in any 12 month period:

1. Loans secured directly or collaterally by liens on real property or business opportunities as an agent;

2. Sale or exchange of real property sales contracts or promissory notes secured directly or collaterally by liens on real property or business opportunities as an agent;

3. Sales or exchanges of real property sales contracts or promissory notes secured directly or collaterally by liens on real property as the owner of those notes or contracts.

Collections

On Behalf of Owners. Makes collections of payments in a total amount of five hundred thousand dollars ($500,000) or more on behalf of owners on promissory notes secured directly or collaterally by liens on real property owners of real property, owners of real property sales contracts or both (representing creditors).

On Behalf of Obligors. Makes collections of payments in a total amount of five hundred thousand dollars ($500,000) or more on behalf of obligors of promissory notes secured directly or collaterally by liens on real property, lenders of real property sales contracts or both (representing debtors).

Note: The Trust Fund Status Report requirements only apply to the brokers involved in the activities set forth in Business and Professions Code 10232. These activities also include certain negotiations of new loans.

Business and Professions Code Section 10232 (c) (1) (c) exempts loans sold to pension funds having a net worth of $15,000,000 or more from counting when determining if the broker's level of activity requires a status report.

Pension funds having the higher net worth are treated like banks, savings banks and other licensed lenders which do not count toward the 20 transactions.

Within 30 days after meeting the threshold requirements a broker is required to submit a Threshold Notification (10232) RE 853 to the Department of Real Estate. The Department will then send the broker the information and necessary documents for the required quarterly and annual reporting.

Threshold Notification Form is included as Figures 11-1 and 11-2.

Figure 11-1

STATE OF CALIFORNIA

THRESHOLD NOTIFICATION (§10232)

RE 853 (Rev. 4/93)

DEPARTMENT OF REAL ESTATE
MORTGAGE LENDING

REPORT EFFECTIVE DATE

GENERAL INFORMATION

❖ This form is to notify the Department of Real Estate (DRE) when a broker or corporation either:

  a) meets or expects to meet the "threshold" criteria of Section 10232 *(see page 3 for complete text of §10232)*,

  b) has reported in the past under the "threshold" criteria of Section 10232 but no longer meets the criteria, or

  c) presently reports as meeting the "threshold" criteria but is changing the fiscal year reporting month or the name of the broker/corporation.

❖ Monetary penalties shall be assessed against any real estate broker failing to notify the DRE in writing of meeting the criteria of Section 10232 *(see page 3 for complete text of §10236.2).* Disciplinary action may also result from non-compliance with the provisions of these sections.

❖ Complete the appropriate sections of this form then mail to: Department of Real Estate, Mortgage Loan Section, P. O. Box 187000, Sacramento, CA 95818-7000.

PART A   LICENSE INFORMATION

1. NAME OF BROKER OR CORPORATION

2. LICENSE ID NUMBER

3. DESIGNATED OFFICER *(IF CORPORATION)*

4. LIST THE MONTH THE FISCAL YEAR ENDS

5. CURRENT BUSINESS ADDRESS *(STREET ADDRESS, CITY, STATE, AND ZIP CODE)*

6. DBA'S *(IF ANY)*

7. BRANCH OFFICE ADDRESS(ES) *(ATTACH A LIST IF NECESSARY)*

8. CHECK "NO MAILINGS" BOX IF YOU DO NOT WANT YOUR NAME AND ADDRESS TO BE INCLUDED ON MAILING LISTS SOLD TO THE PUBLIC. .... ☐ NO MAILINGS

PART B   TYPE OF REPORT — *Check appropriate box(es)*

☐ **1. Initial Notification** — Broker meets or expects to meet "threshold" criteria .... *Complete Parts C and F.*
[After receipt of this "initial notification, DRE will forward additional information and forms regarding the requirements imposed on a broker meeting the criteria of §10232.]

☐ **2. No Longer Meets Criteria** — Broker has reported as "threshold" in the past but no longer meets or expects to meet the criteria. .... *Complete Parts E and F.*

☐ **3. Change Of Fiscal Year Reporting Month** — Broker must be currently reporting as "threshold". .... *Complete Parts D and F.*

☐ **4. Change of Licensed (Company) Name** — Broker must be currently reporting as "threshold". .... *Complete Parts D and F.*

PART C   INITIAL NOTIFICATION TO DRE

If #1 in Part B is checked, mark all boxes that apply to your volume of business.

☐ In the past three months, the broker/corporation negotiated any combination of five or more loans and sales contracts of an aggregate amount of more than $500,000.

☐ In the past six months, the broker/corporation negotiated any combination of 10 or more loans and sales or exchanges of notes and real property sales contracts of an aggregate amount of more than $1,000,000.

☐ In the past 12 months, the broker/corporation negotiated any combination of 20 or more loans and sales or exchanges of notes and real property sales contracts of an aggregate amount of more than $2,000,000.

☐ In the past 12 months, the broker/corporation collected loan payments in an aggregate amount of $500,000 or more.

Figure 11-2

PART D   CHANGE OF FISCAL YEAR OR LICENSED (COMPANY) NAME

IF #3 IN PART B IS CHECKED, LIST THE PREVIOUS REPORTING MONTH AND DAY.	IF #4 IN PART B IS CHECKED, LIST THE FORMER LICENSED NAME.

PART E   NO LONGER MEETS CRITERIA

If item #2 in Part B is checked the information requested in this section is to be completed. If the criteria of Section 10232 is met in the future an initial notification must again be submitted.

During the immediate preceding periods shown below, the volume of business was approximately:

	Past 12 Months	Past 6 Months	Past 3 Months
Number of negotiated loans and/or sales			
Their dollar volume	$	$	$
Total collections on loans serviced	$	$	$

PART F   CERTIFICATION

I certify under penalty of perjury that the foregoing information is true and correct to the best of my knowledge and belief.

SIGNATURE OF BROKER OR DESIGNATED OFFICER (IF CORPORATION)	DATE
➤	
PRINTED NAME OF BROKER OR DESIGNATED OFFICER	BUSINESS TELEPHONE NUMBER

This form is also used to notify the DRE when the broker no longer meets the threshold requirements or is changing reporting periods.

Failure to notify the DRE of meeting threshold requirements can be the basis of disciplinary action against the broker.

WHEN FILED WITH DRE

Within 30 days of the end of each of the first 3 fiscal quarters covering the period of the fiscal quarter (unless an extension is granted) of the end of the broker's fiscal year (unless an extension is granted).

CONTENTS OF REPORT

Compliance With Regulations

A representation that the form and contents of the trust-account records of the broker are in compliance with the regulations of the commissioner. The Trust Fund Status Report (RE855) is shown in Figures 11-3 and 11-4.

Maintenance of Trust Account

A representation that the broker's trust-fund bank account is maintained in compliance with the regulations of the commissioner.

Aggregate Accountability

A statement of the broker's aggregate accountability for trust funds.

Funds In Custody

A report of trust funds in the broker's custody consisting of the trust account bank statements as of the bank's accounting date immediately preceding the end of the fiscal quarter and a schedule of withdrawals and deposits adjusting the account to its true balance as of the end of the fiscal quarter.

Differences As To Accountability and Balance

A statement explaining any difference in amount between the broker's total accountability (Paragraph 3 above) and the adjusted trust account bank balance (Paragraph 4 above).

Figure 11-3

STATE OF CALIFORNIA

TRUST FUND STATUS REPORT

DEPARTMENT OF REAL ESTATE
MORTGAGE LENDING

RE 855 (Rev. 4/96)

GENERAL INFORMATION

✔ This report is required from all real estate brokers who engage in mortgage loan activities as specified in §10131(d) and (e) of the B&P Code. If the threshold criteria of §10232 is met, a copy of this report is to be mailed to DRE, otherwise the report is to be retained in file in the broker's office per §10232.25(e).

✔ If completed per §10232 *(threshold criteria is met)* mail to: Department of Real Estate, Mortgage Loan Unit, P. O. Box 187000, Sacramento, CA 95818-7000

✔ If completed per §10232.25(e), retain in file subject to DRE inspection. Refer to full text of §10232.25 on reverse side.

✔ Only one report is needed even if you have two or more bank accounts.

✔ Attach the following to this report: *(whether mailing or retaining)*
  • Trust Fund Bank Account Reconciliation (RE 856) and
  • a copy of the bank statement for *each* trust fund bank account.

REPORT INFORMATION

NAME OF BROKER	LICENSE TYPE	REAL ESTATE ID#
	☐ INDIVIDUAL BROKER ☐ CORPORATION	

FICTITIOUS BUSINESS NAME(S) (IF ANY)

MAIN OFFICE ADDRESS (STREET, CITY, STATE, ZIP CODE)	TELEPHONE NUMBER
	( )

REPORT PERIOD (CHECK ONE) ☐ 1ST QUAR. ☐ 2ND QUAR. ☐ 3RD QUAR. ☐ 4TH QUARTER — NON-THRESHOLD BROKERS ONLY	DATE QUARTER ENDED (M/D/Y)	START OF FISCAL YEAR (M/D/Y)	END OF FISCAL YEAR (M/D/Y)

1. As of the end of the report quarter, the broker's aggregate trust fund accountability was: $ _____

    Did this amount *agree* with the total of all positive balances as reflected on the separate beneficiary records as of end of report quarter? .... ☐ Yes   ☐ No
    If NO, explain on reverse side.

2. The total of trust funds on deposit in the broker's trust fund bank account(s), as of the end of the report quarter, was: .... $ _____

    The number of trust fund bank accounts where the funds were on deposit: .... _____
    Attach RE 856 and bank statement for each of these accounts.

3. Explain on the reverse side any difference between the total accountability (line #1) and the total adjusted bank account(s) balance(s):

REPORT PREPARED BY	POSITION OR CAPACITY WITH BROKER

BUSINESS ADDRESS

Declaration

I/We declare that: a) the form and content of the trust account records of the above-named real estate broker were in conformance with Sections 2831 and 2831.1 of the Real Estate Commissioner's Regulations, and b) all trust fund bank account(s) of the above-named broker were maintained in compliance with Sections 2830, 2832.1 and 2834 of the Real Estate Commissioner's Regulations.

I/We declare under penalty of perjury that the information in this report is true and correct to the best of my/our knowledge and belief.

SIGNATURE OF BROKER OR BROKER-OFFICER OF CORPORATION	DATE
➤	

PRINTED NAME OF SIGNER

SIGNATURE OF CORPORATE C.E.O. *(LEAVE BLANK IF C.E.O. IS THE BROKER OFFICER)*	DATE
➤	

Figure 11-4

EXPLANATION OF DIFFERENCES

- The difference between the accountability (line #1) and the total of all positive balances as reflected on the separate beneficiary records which total was $ _____, is attributable to:

- The difference between the total accountability (line #1) and the total adjusted bank account(s) balance(s) (line #2) is attributable to:

Section 10232.25. Business and Professions Code

(a) A real estate broker who meets the criteria of subdivision (a) of Section 10232 shall, within 30 days after the end of each of the first three fiscal quarters of the broker's fiscal year, or within such additional time as the Real Estate Commissioner may allow for good cause, file with the commissioner a trust funds status report as of the last day of the fiscal quarter which shall include the following:

  (1) A representation that the form and content of the trust account records of the broker are in compliance with the regulations of the Real Estate Commissioner.

  (2) A representation that the broker's trust fund bank account is maintained in compliance with the regulations of the Real Estate Commissioner.

  (3) A statement of the broker's aggregate accountability for trust funds.

  (4) A report of trust funds in the broker's custody consisting of the trust account bank statements as of the bank's accounting date immediately preceding the end of the fiscal quarter and a schedule of withdrawals and deposits adjusting the account to its true balance as of the end of the fiscal quarter.

  (5) A statement explaining any difference in amount between the broker's total accountability under paragraph (3) above and the adjusted trust account bank balance under paragraph (4) above.

(b) Each report made pursuant to subdivision (a) shall include the following:

  (1) The name, address, and position or capacity of the person who prepared the report.

  (2) A declaration under penalty of perjury by the broker that the information and representations in the report are true, complete, and correct to the best of the broker's knowledge and belief. The declaration in a report submitted on behalf of a corporate broker shall be signed by a broker-officer through whom the corporation is licensed as a real estate broker and by the chief executive officer of the corporation if he or she is not the signing broker-officer.

(c) If a broker fails to file a report required under subdivision (a) within the time permitted the commissioner may cause an examination and report to be made and may charge the broker one and one-half time the cost of making the examination and report.

(d) A broker who meets the criteria of Section 10232, but who, in carrying on the activities described in subdivisions (d) and (e) of Section 10131, did not during a fiscal quarter, accept for the benefit of a person to whom the broker is trustee, any payment or remittance in a form convertible to cash by the broker, need not comply with the provisions of subdivision (a). In lieu thereof, the broker shall submit to the commissioner within 30 days after the end of the fiscal quarter or within such additional time as the commissioner may allow for good cause, a statement under penalty of perjury on a form provided by the department attesting to the fact that the broker did not receive any trust funds in cash or convertible to cash during the fiscal quarter.

(e) Any real estate broker who engages in any of the activities specified in subdivision (d) or (e) of Section 10131, but who is not required by this section to file trust funds status reports with the commissioner and who is not exempt therefrom under subdivision (d), shall complete trust funds status reports in accordance with the requirements of subdivisions (a) and (b) applicable to trust funds status reports filed with the commissioner. The broker shall retain all trust funds status reports prepared under that subdivision on file at the broker's offices, where they shall be subject to inspection by representatives of the commissioner upon 24 hours' notice.

Additional Information

Each report shall also include:

1. Name, address, position or capacity of the person who prepared the report.
2. A declaration under penalty of perjury that the information and representations in the report are true, complete and correct to the best of the broker's knowledge and belief.

FAILURE TO FILE

If a broker fails to file a status report, the commissioner may require an examination and report and may charge the broker 1 1/2 times the cost of making the examination and report.

A broker who did not accept funds as trustee during a fiscal quarter need not submit a status report, but shall submit a statement attesting to that fact within 30 days after the end of the fiscal quarter.

RETENTION OF REPORTS

The broker shall retain all trust-fund status reports at the broker's office subject to commissioner inspections upon 24-hour notice.

COMMISSIONER'S STATUS REPORT

The commissioner, using an official form, publishes the content of trust fund status reports. The report is available to interested parties.

Fiscal Year Report

WHO FILES?

A real estate broker who meets the criteria set forth in XIV, shall file an annual report 90 days after the end of the broker's fiscal year (or within such additional time allowed by the commissioner). (**Business and Professions Code 10232.2**)

> *Like the Quarterly Status Report, this report is only required for brokers involved in loan brokerage, lending and loan servicing activities.*

The report includes a review by a California licensed public accountant of trust fund financial statements conducted in accordance with accepted accounting practices.

The independent public accountant shall confirm that:

1. the broker maintains required records and reconciles such records in accordance with the statutes;

2. each trust bank account is maintained by the broker in compliance with the statutes;

3. the accountant has reviewed the accompanying balance sheet of trust funds held by the broker as of the end of the fiscal year and accompanying statement of receipts and disbursements of trust funds and changes in cash for the fiscal year, in accordance with standards established by the American Institute of Certified Public Accountants;

4. the accountant is not aware of any material modifications that should be made to the trust fund financial statements in order for them to be in conformity with generally accepted accounting principles;

5. the adjusted balances of the bank trust account(s) maintained by the broker were on deposit as of the date of the financial statement;

6. the trust-fund account balance(s) and receipts and disbursements shown on the financial statements agreed with the amounts reflected on the cash records;

7. the trust-fund liability balance for each open account (as itemized in the financial statements) agreed with the amount reflected in the separate beneficiary records;

8. the receipt and disposition of all funds of others to be applied to the making of loans and the purchasing of promissory notes or real property sales contracts. (Making and selling real estate loans);

9. the receipt and disposition of all funds of others in connection with the servicing by the broker of the accounts of owners of promissory notes and real property sales contracts including installment payments and loan or contract payoffs by obligors (Loan Servicing);

10. an itemized trust fund accounting of the broker and confirmation that the funds are on deposit in an account or accounts maintained by the broker in a financial institution.

A broker who qualifies for filing an annual report but has not accepted any payment in a form that the broker could convert to cash need not file the report described above. Instead the broker shall submit a notarized statement under penalty of perjury attesting to the fact. This statement shall be submitted to the commissioner within 30 days after the end of the broker's fiscal year (or within any extension period granted by the commissioner).

A second report is also required that shall include:

1. and aggregate dollar amount of loan, trust-deed sales and real-property sales contract transactions negotiated;

2. number and aggregate dollar amount of promissory notes and contracts serviced by the broker or an affiliate of the broker;

3. number and aggregate dollar amount of late payment charges, prepayment penalties and other fees or charges collected and retained by the broker under servicing agreements with beneficiaries and obligees;

4. default and foreclosure experience in connection with promissory notes and contracts subject to servicing agreements between the broker and beneficiaries or obligees;

5. commissions received by the broker for services performed as agent in negotiating loans and sales of promissory notes and real property sales contracts;

6. aggregate costs and expenses (in making loans paid by borrowers to the broker).

If the broker fails to file either of these reports within the time permitted, the commissioner can cause an investigation and report and charge the broker 1 1/2 times the cost of making the examination and report.

Figure 11-5 is the Fiscal Year Report. If a broker meets the threshold reporting requirements but does not receive trust funds during the reporting period, the broker may file RE Form 854, which is a non-accountability report.

Figure 11-5

State of California

Department of Real Estate
Mortgage Loans

Trust Fund
Non-Accountability Report

RE 854 (Rev. 6/89) *Formerly RE 585*

General Information

- This report may be submitted by a mortgage broker who meets the threshold criteria of Business and Professions (B&P) Code §10232 in lieu of the:

    - Quarterly Trust Fund Status Report (B&P §10232.25), or
    - Annual Report of a Review of Trust Fund Financial Statements (B&P §10232.2),

    if the broker did not accept trust funds during the report quarter or fiscal year, respectively.

- If this report is being submitted in lieu of the annual report of a review of Trust Fund Financial Statements, it *must be notarized.*

- Refer to B&P §10232.2(b) and 10232.25(d) for more information.

- Forward completed form to:
    Department of Real Estate
    Mortgage Loan Unit
    P. O. Box 187000
    Sacramento, CA 95818-7000

Report Information

Name of Broker	License Type	Real Estate ID#
	☐ Individual Broker	
	☐ Corporation	

Fictitious Business Name(s) (if any)

Main Office Address (Street, City, State, Zip Code)	Telephone Number ( )

This report is submitted in lieu of the: (check one)	Report Period (1st, 2nd, 3rd)	Date Quarter Ended (m/d/y)
☐ Quarterly Trust Fund Status Report → → →	Quarter	
	Start of Fiscal Year (m/d/y)	End of Fiscal Year (m/d/y)
☐ Annual Report of a Review of Trust Fund Financial Statements *(must be notarized)* → → →		

Declaration

In engaging in acts for which a real estate license is required under subdivisions (d) and (e) of Section 10131 during the reporting period stated above, the broker did not accept as trustee for the benefit of any other person, any payment or remittance (trust funds) in cash or in a form convertible to cash by the broker or by an employee or affiliate or any other persons subject to the control of the broker.

I declare under penalty of perjury that the information in this report is true and correct to the best of my knowledge and belief.

Signature of Broker or Broker-Officer of Corporation	Date
➤	

Trust Account Records

FUNDS RECEIVED AND DISBURSED

Brokers must keep a record of all trust funds received including uncashed checks held.

This record (including computer records) must set forth in chronological order the following information in columnar form (**Commissioner's Regulation 2831**):

1. **Date.** Date the trust funds are received.

2. **Source.** Source from whom trust funds were received.

3. **Amount.** The amount received.

4. **Date Deposited.** With respect to funds deposited in an account, date of said deposit.

5. **Disbursement Data.** With respect to trust funds previously deposited to an account, check number and date of related disbursement.

6. **Pass Through Funds.** With respect to trust funds not deposited in an account, identify other depository and the date that the funds were forwarded. (If the funds pass through the broker's hands, even though the check or note is made out to another party, they are still considered to be trust funds.)

7. **Daily Balance.** Daily balance of said account. (Trust accounts must be balanced daily and reconciled with bank account at least once a month.)

A separate record must be kept for each beneficiary or transaction that sets forth information sufficient to identify the transaction and the parties to the transaction, and also includes the information required above.

While computer records may be kept rather than using forms, a backup disk is a safety factor that should be considered. There are a number of excellent software programs available for trust account record keeping.

A broker is not required to keep records of checks made payable to service providers, including but not limited to escrow, credit and appraisal services when the total amount of each checks does not exceed $1,000. (Refers to checks written by other than the broker.)

However, upon request of the Department of Real Estate or the maker of such checks, a broker shall account for the receipt and distribution of such checks. A broker shall retain copies of receipts issued or obtained in connection with receipt and distribution of such checks for three years.

The Department of Real Estate does not require that records be kept on particular forms, although we have included the following forms which have been prepared by the California Association of Realtors (CAR).

Figure 11-6

Columnar Record of All Trust Funds Received and Paid Out CAR TF11-1

Figure 11-7

Record of All Trust Funds Received - Not Placed In Broker's Trust Account CAR TF11-2

2831.1 Separate Record for each Beneficiary or Transaction

(a). A broker shall keep a separate record for each beneficiary or transaction, accounting for all funds which have been deposited to the broker's trust bank account and interest, if any, earned on the funds on deposit...

RECONCILIATION OF TRUST ACCOUNT

> *(Commissioner's Regulation 2831.2) The trust account must be reconciled at least once a month with the record of all trust funds received and disbursed (this applies to separate beneficiary records).*

An exception is made for those months in which the bank account did not have any activity (no deposits or withdrawals).

A trust fund bank account reconciliation must also accompany each status report (RE855 - Figure 11-8).

A record of the reconciliation must be maintained. This record must identify the:

1. **Identification of Account.** Bank account name and number;
2. **Date.** Date of the reconciliation;
3. **Beneficiaries.** Account number or name of the principals or beneficiaries or transactions;

Figure 11-6

COLUMNAR RECORD OF ALL TRUST FUNDS RECEIVED AND PAID OUT

CALIFORNIA ASSOCIATION OF REALTORS® (CAR) STANDARD FORM

TRUST FUND BANK ACCOUNT

| Date Received | From Whom Received Or To Whom Paid | Description | Received | | | | | Paid Out | | | | | Daily Balance of Trust Account |
			Amount Received	Cross Ref.	Date of Deposit	xx		Amount Paid Out	Check No.	Date of Check	xx	

TF-11-1

Figure 11-7

RECORD OF ALL TRUST FUNDS RECEIVED — NOT PLACED IN BROKERS TRUST ACCOUNT

CALIFORNIA ASSOCIATION OF REALTORS® (CAR) STANDARD FORM

Date Received	Form of Receipt (Cash, Note, etc.)	TRUST FUNDS Including Uncashed Checks Received — Received From	Amount	Description Property or Identification	Disposition of Uncashed Checks or Other Funds Forwarded to Escrow or Principal	Date Forwarded

TF-11-2

Figure 11-8

STATE OF CALIFORNIA

DEPARTMENT OF REAL ESTATE
MORTGAGE LENDING

TRUST FUND BANK ACCOUNT RECONCILIATION

RE 856 (Rev. 2/90)

REPORT DATE *(DATE QUARTER ENDED)*

GENERAL INFORMATION

- Complete *one* form for *each* trust fund bank account.
- Attach this form and copy of the corresponding bank statement to Trust Fund Status Report (RE 855).
- Refer to mailing instructions on RE 855.

NAME OF BROKER

REAL ESTATE ID#

NAME OF BANK

ACCOUNT NAME

ACCOUNT NUMBER

BANK BUSINESS ADDRESS (STREET, CITY, STATE, ZIP CODE)

REPORT PERIOD

DATE QUARTER ENDED (MM/DD/YY)

❏ FIRST QUARTER   ❏ SECOND QUARTER   ❏ THIRD QUARTER

BANK ACCOUNT RECONCILIATION

1. Account Balance as of _____ *(per appended bank statement).* .... $ _____

   Plus: Deposits in transit (deposits made through end of fiscal quarter not reflected in bank statement). .... + _____

   Number of deposits in transit: .... _____

   Less: Outstanding (uncleared) checks (checks issued through end of fiscal quarter not reflected in bank statement)......... .... – _____

   Number of outstanding checks: .... _____

2. *SubTotal:* .... _____

3. *Other Adjustments (describe)*

   _____

   _____

   _____   _____

4. *Adjusted Trust Fund Bank Account Balance (as of end of the report quarter)* .... $ _____

5. The balance on line #4 ❏ *agreed* ❏ *did not agree* with the balance reflected in the broker's records. Aattach explanation if different.

4. **Broker Liability.** The trust fund liability of the broker to each of the principals, beneficiaries or transactions.

RETENTION OF TRUST RECORDS

A real estate broker must maintain trust records (as well as other records relating to a transaction for three years. (Business and Professions Code 10148)

The retention period shall run from the date of closing of the transaction.

After notice, the records shall be made available for examination, inspection and copying by the commissioner (or representative) during regular business hours and, upon the appearance of sufficient cause, be subject to audit without further notice, however, the audit shall not be harassing in nature.

DRE TRUST FUND PAMPHLET

The following sections covering accounting records, other accounting systems and records, recording process, reconciliation of accounting records and documentation requirements has been taken from a pamphlet entitled *Trust Funds* (dated November 1995), which was published by the California Department of Real Estate.

The material is included because it does an excellent job of clarifying and amplifying material we have included in this chapter.

Accounting Records

General Requirements

An important aspect of the broker's fiduciary responsibility to the client is the maintenance of adequate records to account for trust funds received and disbursed. This is true whether the funds are deposited to the trust fund bank account, sent to escrow, held uncashed as authorized under Commissioner's Regulation 2832, or released to the owner(s) of the funds. These records:

1. provide a basis upon which the broker can prepare an accurate accounting for clients.

2. state the amount of money the broker owes the account beneficiaries at any one time. (This is especially important when there are a large number of transactions.)

3. prove whether or not there is an imbalance in the trust account. Some brokers audited by DRE have disagreed that their trust accounts had a shortage or an overage in the amount disclosed by the audit, but could not provide documentation to support their position.

4. guarantee that beneficiary funds deposited in the trust account will be insured up to the maximum FDIC insurance coverage.

There are two types of accounting records that may be used for trust funds: columnar records in the formats prescribed by Commissioner's Regulations 2831 and 2831.1; and records other than columnar that are in accordance with generally accepted accounting practices. Regardless of the type of records used, they must include the following information:

1. All trust fund receipts and disbursements, with pertinent details, presented in chronological sequence;

2. The balance of the trust fund account, based on recorded transactions;

3. All receipts and disbursements affecting each beneficiary's balance, presented in chronological sequence; and

4. The balance owing to each beneficiary or for each transaction.

Either manually produced or computerized accounting records are acceptable.

The type and form of records appropriate to a particular real estate operation as well as the means of processing transactions will depend on factors such as the nature of the business, the number of clients, the volume of transactions and the types of reports needed. For example, manual recording on columnar records might be satisfactory for a broker handling a small number of transactions, while a computerized system might be more appropriate and practical for a large property management operation.

Columnar Records

A broker may decide to use the columnar records prescribed by Commissioner's Regulations 2831 and 2831.1. The records required will depend on whether the trust funds received are deposited to the trust account or are forwarded to an escrow depository or to the owner of the funds. These records are:

1. Columnar Record of All Trust Funds Received and Paid Out - Trust Fund Bank Account (DRE form ARE 4522).

2. Separate Record for Each Beneficiary or Transaction (DRE form ARE 4523).

3. Record of All Trust Funds Received - Not Placed in Broker's Trust Account (DRE form RE 4524).

The first two records are required when trust funds are received and deposited to the trust fund bank account.

The third record is required when trust funds received are not deposited to the trust account, but are instead forwarded to the authorized person(s).

If the trust fund account involves clients' funds from rental properties managed by the broker, the Separate Record for Each Property managed (DRE form RE 4525) may be used in lieu of the Separate Record for Each Beneficiary or Transaction.

A broker who has an escrow division pursuant to Financial Code Section 17006(a)(4) must keep the above mentioned records for escrow funds. (Commissioner's Regulation 2951)

Record of All Trust Funds Received and Paid Out - Trust Fund Bank Account

This record is used to journalize all trust funds deposited to and disbursed from the trust fund bank account. At a minimum, it must show the following information in columnar form: date funds were received; name of payee or payor; amount received; date of deposit; amount paid out; check number and date; and the daily balance of the trust account.

All transactions affecting the trust account are entered in chronological order on this record regardless of payee, payor or beneficiary. If there is more than one trust fund bank account, a different columnar record must be maintained for each account, pursuant to Commissioner's Regulation 2831.

Separate Record for Each Beneficiary or Transaction

This record is maintained to account for funds received from or for the account of each beneficiary, or for each transaction, and deposited to the trust account. With this record, the broker can ascertain the funds owed to each beneficiary or for each transaction. The record must show the following in chronological order: date of deposit; amount of deposit; name of payee or payor; check number; date and amount; and balance of the individual account after posting transactions on any date.

A separate record must be maintained for each beneficiary or transaction from whom the broker received funds that were deposited to the trust fund bank account.

If the broker has more than one trust account, each account must have its own set of beneficiary records so that they can be reconciled with the individual trust fund bank account record required by Commissioner's Regulation 2831.2.

Record of All Trust Funds Received - Not placed in Broker's Trust Account

This record is used to keep track of funds received and not deposited to a trust fund bank account. In this situation, the broker is handling the funds and must keep records of same. Examples are:

1. Earnest money deposits forwarded to escrow;

2. Rents forwarded to landlords;

3. Borrowers' payments forwarded to lenders; and

4. Credit and appraisal fees forwarded to credit reporting companies and appraisers.

This record must show the date funds were received, the form of payment (check, note, etc.), amount received, description of property, identity of the person to whom funds were forwarded and date of disposition. Trust fund receipts are recorded in chronological sequence, while their disposition is recorded in the same line where the corresponding receipt is recorded.

Transaction folders usually maintained by a broker for each real estate sales transaction showing the receipt and disposition of non-deposited checks are not acceptable alternatives to the Record of Trust Funds Received But Not Deposited to the Trust Fund Bank Account.

Separate Record for Each Property Managed

This record is similar to, and serves the same purpose as, the Separate Record for Each Beneficiary or Transaction. It does not have to be maintained if a separate record is already used for a property owner's account. The Separate Record for Each Property Managed is useful when the broker wants to show some detailed information about a specific property being managed.

Chapter 11

Other Accounting Systems and Records

A broker may use trust fund records not in the columnar form as prescribed by Commissioner's Regulations 2831 and 2831.1. Such records must be in accordance with generally accepted accounting principles. Whether prepared manually or by computer, they must include at least the following:

1. A journal to record in chronological sequence the details of all trust fund transactions.

2. A cash ledger to show the bank balance as affected by the transactions recorded in the journal. The ledger is posted in the form of debits and credits. (In some cases the cash ledger may be combined with the journal.)

3. A beneficiary ledger for each of the beneficiary accounts to show in chronological sequence the transactions affecting each beneficiary's account, as well as the balance of the account.

To comply with generally accepted accounting principles, there must be one set of journal, cash ledger and beneficiary ledger for each trust fund bank account.

Journal

A *JOURNAL is a daily chronological record of trust fund receipts and disbursements.* A single journal may be used to record both the receipts and the disbursements, or a separate journal may be used for each. To meet minimum record keeping requirements, a journal must:

1. Record all trust fund transactions in chronological sequence.

2. Contain sufficient information to identify the transaction such as the date, amount received or disbursed, name of or reference to payee or payor, check number or reference to another source document of the transaction and identification of the beneficiary account affected by the transaction.

3. Correlate with the ledgers. For example, it should show the same figures that are posted, individually or in total, in the cash ledger and in the beneficiary ledgers. The details in the journal must be the basis for posting transactions in the ledgers and arriving at the account balances.

4. Show the total receipts and total disbursements regularly, at least once a month.

Cash Ledger

The **CASH LEDGER** *shows, usually in summary form, the periodic increases and decreases (debits and credits) in the trust fund bank account and the resulting account balance.* It can be incorporated into the journal or it can be a separate record, for example a general ledger account. If a separate record is used, the postings must be based on the transactions recorded in the journal.

> *The amounts posted on the ledger must be those shown in the journal.*

Beneficiary Ledger

A separate beneficiary ledger must be maintained for each beneficiary or transaction or series of transactions. This **BENEFICIARY LEDGER** *shows, in chronological sequence, the details of all receipts and disbursements related to the beneficiary's account, and the resulting account balance.* It reflects the broker's liability to a particular beneficiary. Entries in all these ledgers must be based on entries recorded in the journal.

Recording Process

> *Keeping complete and accurate trust fund records is easier when specific procedures are regularly followed.*

The following procedures may be useful in developing a record keeping routine:

1. Record transactions daily in the trust fund bank account and in the separate beneficiary records.

2. Use consistently the same specific source documents as a basis for recording trust fund receipts and disbursements. (For example, receipts pertaining to real estate resales will be recorded based on the Real Estate Contract and Receipt for Deposit form, and disbursements will always be recorded based on the checks issued from the trust account or debit notices from the bank.)

3. Calculate the account balances on all applicable records at the time entries are made.

4. Reconcile the records monthly to ascertain that transactions are properly recorded in the bank account record and the applicable subsidiary records.

5. If more than one trust fund bank account is maintained, keep a different set of properly labeled columnar records (cash record and beneficiary record) for each account.

Reconciliation of Accounting Records

Purpose

> *The trust fund bank account record, the separate beneficiary or transaction record and the bank statement are all interrelated.*

Any entry made on the bank account record must have a corresponding entry on a separate beneficiary record. By the same token, any entry or transaction shown on the bank statement must be reflected on the bank account record. This applies to columnar as well as to other types of records.

The accuracy of the records is verified by reconciling them at least once a month. **RECONCILIATION** *is the process of comparing two or more sets of records to determine whether their balances agree*. It will disclose whether the records are completed accurately.

For trust fund record keeping purposes, two reconciliations must be made at the end of each month:

1. Reconciliation of the bank account record (RE 4522) with the bank statement; and,

2. Reconciliation of the bank account record (RE 4522) with the separate beneficiary or transaction records (RE 4523).

Reconciling the Bank Account Record With the Bank Statement

> *The reconciliation of the bank account record with the bank statement will disclose any recording errors by the broker or by the bank.*

If the balance on the bank account record agrees with the bank statement balance as adjusted for outstanding checks, deposits in transit and other transactions not yet included in the bank statement, there is more assurance that the balance on the bank account record is correct. Although this reconciliation is not required by the Real Estate Law or the Commissioner's Regulations, it is an essential part of any good accounting system.

Reconciling the Bank Account Record With the Separate Beneficiary or Transaction Records

This reconciliation, which is required by Commissioner's Regulation 2831.2, will substantiate that all transactions entered on the bank account record were posted on the separate beneficiary or transaction records.

The balance on the bank account record should equal the total of all beneficiary record balances.

Any difference should be located and the records corrected to reflect the correct bank and liabilities balances. Commissioner's Regulation 2831.2 requires that this reconciliation process be performed monthly except in those months when there is no activity in the trust fund bank account, and that a record of each reconciliation be maintained. This record should identify the bank account name and number, the date of the reconciliation, the account number or name of the principals or beneficiaries or transactions and the trust fund liabilities of the broker to each of the principals, beneficiaries or transactions.

Suggestions for Reconciling Records

The following is a general discussion on how to perform the trust account reconciliations.

1. Before performing the reconciliations, record all transactions up to the cut-off date in both the bank account record and the separate beneficiary or transaction records.

2. Use balances as of the same cut-off date for the two records and the bank statement.

3. For the bank account reconciliation, calculate the adjusted bank balance from the bank statement and from the bank account record. (Brokers commonly err by calculating the adjusted bank balance based solely on the bank statement, ignoring the bank account record. While they may know the correct account balances, they may not realize their records are incomplete or erroneous.)

4. Keep a record of the two reconciliations performed at the end of each month, along with the supporting schedules.

5. Locate any difference between the three sets of accounting records. A difference can be caused by:

a. not recording a transaction

b. recording an incorrect figure

c. erroneous calculation of entries used to arrive at account balances

d. missing beneficiary records

e. banks errors.

Documentation Requirements

Activities and Related Documents

In addition to accounting records, the Department of Real Estate requires that the broker maintain all documents prepared or obtained in connection with any real estate transaction handled.

Here is a list of typical activities and the corresponding documentation.

Activity	Documentation
1. Receiving trust funds in the form of: Purchase deposits from buyers	• Real estate purchase contract receipt for deposit, signed by the buyer
Rents and security deposits from tenants	• Collection receipts
Other receipts	• Collection receipts
2. Depositing trust funds	• Bank deposit slips
3. Forwarding buyers' checks to escrow	• Receipt from title company and copy of check
4. Returning buyers' checks	• Copy of buyer's check signed and buyer's receipt of check
5. Disbursing trust funds	• Checks issued
	• Supporting papers for the

checks, such as invoices, escrow statements, billings, receipts, etc.

6. Receiving offers and counter offers from buyers and sellers

- Real estate purchase contract and receipt for deposit, signed by respective parties

- Agency disclosure statement
- Transfer disclosure statement

7. Collecting management fees from the trust fund bank account

- Property management agreements between broker and property owners. (**Note:** If only one trust fund check is issued for management fees charged to various property owners, there should be a schedule or listing on file showing each property and amount charged, and the total amount, which should agree with the check amount.)

8. Reconciling bank account record with separate beneficiary records

- Record of reconciliation

DRE Audits

The California Department of Real Estate views a shortage in a trust account and an unauthorized use of funds as very serious violations of the law.

Because of the importance of safeguarding funds of others, the commissioner has a continuous program of examination of broker's records. Audits may result in disciplinary action if the trust fund is not in balance or if dangerous handling procedures are discovered. Criminal violations may be referred to the appropriate district attorney for possible criminal prosecution.

Upon notice from the commissioner, a licensee must make books, accounts and records available for copying and examination.

Availability shall be during regular business hours. If examination warrants an audit, that audit may be performed without further notice. Audits shall not be harassing in nature.

SUMMARY

Trust funds are funds which come into the broker's possession which are not broker funds or not yet broker funds.

A trust account is an account set up in a depository naming the broker as trustee of such funds.

Multi-lender funds received must be disbursed pro rata within 25 days of receipt of the funds.

When a broker receives trust funds, the broker can:

1. Deposit funds directly into an escrow.
2. Deposit funds into a trust account.
3. Make an authorized payment to a service provider.
4. Give the funds to the broker's principal.

Accounts are generally to be non-interest bearing but may be interest bearing at the request of the fund owner. The broker may not benefit from the interest accrued. Separate interest-bearing trust accounts must be maintained for each beneficiary with the exception of impound accounts for taxes and insurance. Accounts must be insured by FDIC.

Financial institutions must pay at least two percent interest on impound accounts for loans on 1 to-4-residential units.

Advance fees are fees received for a service not yet rendered. They are regarded as trust funds. Marketing material for advance fee brokerage must be submitted to the commissioner 10 days prior to use.

When the broker has not received written instructions from the owner of how funds are to be disbursed, they must be returned to the owner within 60 days of receipt of the funds.

Even when the broker is a principal selling mortgages or trust deeds, the funds received from others must be placed in a neutral depository unless there is a simultaneous delivery of the contract or note.

Brokers may act as escrows of their own transactions, but the broker must still comply with accounting and record-keeping procedural laws for the transaction.

Brokers can keep up to $200 of their own funds in a trust account and may also keep earned commissions and fees in the account for up to 30 days.

Commingling, mixing personal and trust funds, is grounds for disciplinary action.

Misappropriation of trust funds is conversion which carries with it criminal penalties and civil liability as well as administrative disciplinary action.

Before trust monies are to be returned to an owner they should be "good funds."

Withdrawals from trust accounts may only be made by the broker, an authorized licensee in the broker's office or an authorized, unlicensed employee of the broker who is covered by a fidelity bond at least equal to the amount of the trust funds likely to be in the account.

Loan funds may not be disbursed without a written authorization and the recording of the trust deed.

Payoffs of loans may not be invested by the broker without specific approval of the beneficiary. In servicing loans, payments received must be disbursed within 60 days in the absence of written instructions to the contrary.

When there are conflicting claims about trust funds the broker should commence an interpleader action.

A broker may not use trust money to offset any claim the broker may have against the depositor of the funds.

Quarterly trust fund status reports must be filed by brokers who have a threshold number of transactions of specific types (20) or who make collections of $500,000 or more in a 12-month period.

A fiscal year report is also required by brokers who meet the reporting threshold.

Trust account records must be kept. Separate records are required for each beneficiary or transaction. Records may be stored on computer disks.

The trust account must be reconciled at least once a month and records maintained for three years.

Trust accounts must be available for examination by the commissioner within regular business hours and the commissioner may copy records and/or conduct an audit.

CLASS DISCUSSION TOPICS

1. A large California brokerage firm took approximately $10 million dollars out of their trust account and placed it in a money market account. If no one was injured by this action, why should the broker's license have been revoked?

2. Why should brokers be precluded from having investor funds on hand to take advantage of loan opportunities which may arise?

3. How could a non-cash deposit be used to fund a loan?

4. When would an investor want his or her funds in an interest bearing account?

5. How does your office keep records of accounts? (Discuss paper and computer software programs that are used).

6. Why do you suppose most conversion of trust funds to personal use occur?

CHAPTER 11 QUIZ

1. Which of the following funds coming into the possession of a broker who is acting for another would be regarded as trust funds? (p. 302)

    A. Loan payments
    B. Impound account funds
    C. Money to fund loans
    D. All of the above

2. A broker's trust account: (pp. 302-303)

    A. must be an interest bearing account

    B. can be the broker's general business account

    C. must be designated as a trust account

    D. can be cash kept in the broker's safe

3. In servicing multi-lender loans, payments received must be transmitted pro rata to the purchaser or lender within: (p. 303)

    A. 8 hours of receipt

    B. 24 hours of receipt

    C. 25 days of receipt

    D. 90 days of receipt

4. A broker who receives funds from others in the course of a transaction, unless otherwise directed, could legally deposit the funds: (p. 304)

    A. in his or her trust account

    B. in an escrow depository

    C. with the principal

    D. any of the above

5. The broker can deposit funds in an interest bearing account if: (p. 304)

    A. the broker is the only one who benefits from interest earned

    B. directed to do so by the owner of the funds

    C. the broker determines it is in the best interest of the parties involved

    D. the interest is split evenly between both principals to the transaction

6. Financial institutions must pay interest on funds kept as impound accounts for 1- to 4-residential units in an account of at least: (p. 305)

    A. 2 percent

    B. 6 percent

    C. 10 percent

    D. the prime rate

7. How long before its use must advance fee advertising be submitted to the commissioner? (p. 309)

    A. 24 hours

    B. 10 days

    C. 30 days

    D. 90 days

8. How much of a broker's own funds may be kept in a trust account? (p. 311)

    A. None

    B. $1.00

    C. $200.00

    D. $2,000.00

9. Conversion of trust funds could result in: (p. 313)

    A. disciplinary action against the licensee

    B. civil liability for losses sustained

    C. criminal liability

    D. all of the above

10. Trust funds may be withdrawn from the trust account: (p. 314)

    A. only by the broker

    B. by any licensee in the broker's office

    C. by a bonded unlicensed employee of the broker who is authorized to do so

    D. by the owner of the funds

11. A threshold requirement for filing status and fiscal reports is a combination of transactions within 12 months. The combination must amount to: (p. 316)

    A. 6 or more

    B. 10 or more

    C. 20 or more

    D. 100 or more

12. For how long a period must a real estate broker retain trust records? (p. 332)

    A. 60 days

    B. 1 year

    C. 3 years

    D. 20 years

Answers: 1. D; 2. C; 3. C; 4. D; 5. B; 6. A; 7. B; 8. C; 9. D; 10. C; 11. C; 12. C

Chapter 12

Hard Money Makers and Arrangers

KEY WORDS AND TERMS

Annual Report
(Real Property Securities)
Article 5
Article 6
Article 7
Asset Based Loans
Broker Controlled Funds
Equity Based Loans
Hard Money Arranger
Hard Money Loan
Hard Money Maker
Good Funds
Holding Costs

Marketing Costs
Mortgage Broker's Loan Statement
Mortgage Lender/Investor
Disclosure Statement
125 Percent Mortgage
Pension Funds
Permit (Real Property Securities)
Premiums
Promotional Note
Real Property Securities
Servicing Agreement
Sheltered Loans
Soft Money Loans

LEARNING OBJECTIVES

In this chapter you will learn how hard money loans differ from other loans as well as who makes these loans and why. Included in this chapter will be a credit criteria which differs from that used by institutional lenders. The documentation of the loan file will be explained. You will also understand the basis and requirements of Article 5, 6 and 7 of the real estate law.

Definitions

HARD MONEY

HARD MONEY *refers to cash.* In a hard money loan cash actually changes hands, although generally in the form of checks.

> *The term "hard money loan" has come to mean more than just a cash loan. It is a loan made by an individual rather than institutional lender.*

SOFT MONEY LOAN

A **SOFT MONEY LOAN** *is a loan where credit is extended but cash does not change hands, such as a purchase money loan where the seller finances the buyer.* The buyer would give the seller a trust deed secured by the property purchased for the seller's equity rather than pay cash by using savings or a loan from a third party lender.

HARD MONEY MAKER

A **HARD MONEY MAKER** *would be a lender who uses lender funds to make the loan.* While the funds used may be borrowed, the lender is at risk (we do not generally regard institutional lenders as hard money makers. We consider private lenders to be hard money makers).

HARD MONEY ARRANGER

A **HARD MONEY ARRANGER** *is neither the borrower nor the lender. The arranger is the person who brings the parties together such, as a real estate loan broker.* The arranger finds a person willing to put up cash secured by a lien on real property and a person willing to place a lien on real property in exchange for cash.

> *When we speak of hard money arrangers, we are normally speaking of arrangers between private investors, rather than institutional investors and borrowers.*

Sources of Funds

PRIVATE INDIVIDUALS

Most loan funds are from personal or business savings.

Some loan arrangers have sought investors owning homes who had very low debt-to-equity ratios as well as those having debt free residences. By refinancing, they are often able to borrow at a much lower interest rate than they can loan their money at. They are thus able to make money on this interest differential by trading on their equity. Even if their loans are well secured, the investor in such a situation is placed at risk. Should the lien that they hold go into default, they may not have the funds to make their own mortgage payments, which would place their home at risk of foreclosure.

PENSION FUNDS

Pension funds are not taxed on earnings so theoretically they should be able to make investments with lesser yields. In practice, pension funds are being pushed to perform well.

Pension funds have discovered real property secured loans as an acceptable balance between risk and yield. Both private individuals and private pension funds can avoid the usury limitations and receive higher rates of interest by using brokers as arrangers of their loans. (If they made the loans direct, the usury law would apply.) Public pension plans are exempt from usury limitations as are other licensed lenders (Civil Code 1916.2).

Disclosure statements as to the particulars of a loan being offered that is secured by real estate is required by Section 10232.4 of the Business and Professions Code.

Disclosures need not be given to trustees of pension, profit sharing or welfare funds having assets of $15 million or more. Pension funds with less than $15 million in assets are treated as other non-institutional lenders. These pension funds receive the protection of required disclosures. (Business and Professions Code 10232.4[g] [4] [c].)

Persons who are borrowers on these hard money loans are generally willing to pay interest charges greater than they would have to pay from institutional lenders because, for a variety of reasons, they are unable to obtain financing from banks or savings bank institutions.

Loan Characteristics and Requirements

ASSET BASED

Loans are secured by real property.

The value of the real property is the paramount criteria for making the loan.

The lender, while generally preferring performance from the borrower, wants to know that in a worse case scenario (foreclosure) he or she is protected. The following factors are of far lesser importance.

Poor Credit

A history which indicates problems in the past will deter most conventional lenders. Since hard money makers are primarily interested in the security, many will make loans in cases where the borrower appears risky and even likely to default if the property value warrants the loan. Some hard money lenders are also dealers in real property. These lenders will make loans in situations where they would be delighted if the borrower defaulted and they ended up owning the property.

Credit Disclosure

Even though a loan may be based on asset value, the arranger of hard money loans has a duty to protect and fully inform lenders and borrowers. Credit of a borrower must be checked out. Assuming that a borrower has financial strength based on his or her possessions and lifestyle could result in loan broker liability. The normal procedure is to obtain a TRW-type credit report from a credit reporting agency. If the report is insufficient, such as no reported credit history, the loan arranger should request an investigative report.

The credit information must be disclosed to the lender.

Income

INCOME *indicates a borrower's capacity to make loan payments.* The income figures should be obtained from the borrower and verified where possible. Verification might be from the borrower's pay check stubs or even copies of prior income tax returns. Information of the income and what verification was made must be given to the lender.

Reported income on tax returns for owners of small businesses may be less significant to a lender than would wage income.

In cases of under reporting of income to defraud the government, small business owners frequently jeopardize their position when conventional lenders will not grant them purchase or equity loans because the small business owners lack the capacity (on paper) to repay the loan.

LOAN TYPES

Purchase Money Loans

PURCHASE MONEY LOANS *are loans to purchase real property*. It is an equity based purchase loan.

Most purchase money loans are made by institutional lenders who offer significantly lower loan costs and interest rates.

Some of the reasons hard money arrangers get involved in purchase money loans include:

1. **Property Type**. Most institutional lenders are not interested in loans on raw land or lots. It is often difficult to obtain loans on special purpose buildings or properties which are considered distressed for a variety of reasons.

2. **Capacity.** Due to outstanding debt or low income, a person might not meet the proper ratio requirements of income to debt service costs (see Chapter 1). In reality, people can often afford what they want. In Orange County, many people pay over 50 percent of their income to be able to live in a desirable area.

   Ratios are more likely to be used as a guide by hard money lenders rather than as a rule that has been cast in stone.

3. **Credit.** Prior credit problems because of personal problems or just neglect disqualify many buyers from conventional loans. Hard money lenders are less likely to be concerned with minor credit problems and sometimes they are not terribly concerned with major problems.

Equity Based Loans

EQUITY LOANS are loans that cover a property owner's equity. *EQUITY* is the difference between all of the liens and obligations against a property and the fair market value of the property.

The majority of hard money loans are equity-based loans.

For reasons covered under purchase loans, borrowers frequently cannot obtain equity loans from conventional lending institutions. In addition, appraisals by lending institutions have changed. At one time, appraisals were very much on the optimistic side when lenders wanted to increase loans at the expense of greater risk. The savings and loan industry suffered from loose lending with foreclosures and eventual government bailouts to protect depositors.

Today, many lenders have gone the other way and prefer to use very conservative appraisers. Some lender appraisals may vary significantly from appraisals commissioned by a loan broker.

Loans in Excess of Equity (125 Percent Mortgages)

According to an article by Fred R. Bleakley in the November 17, 1997, issue of the *Wall Street Journal*, credit card debt has increased from $174 billion in 1988 to $526 billion in 1997. A great many consumers are heavily in debt because of the ease in obtaining and using credit cards. Many consumers have maximum charges on multiple cards.

Relief has been in the form of a dangerous product, the 125 percent second mortgage.

These are second mortgages that exceed the home value by 25 percent. It is estimated that $10 billion in these loans were made in 1997. They are considered by some mortgage arrangers as a very hot product. While many of the larger mortgage companies will not touch these products, many mortgage brokers, including some of the larger ones, are actively seeking borrowers and lenders. In some cases, they are using boiler room techniques employing dozens of telemarketers.

Consumers are able to use proceeds to pay off relatively short term, high interest credit card debt at interest rates of up to 21 percent and substitute a second mortgage at 13 to 14 percent interest. This creates lower monthly payments for the borrower. In addition, the interest on the second mortgage will probably be deductible for income tax purposes while paid credit card interest is not deductible. The net effect is that the effective rate of interest for the borrower is lowered significantly.

These loans are risky to the purchaser in that borrowers who fail to cut up their credit cards are likely to get into trouble again. If foreclosure becomes necessary, the lender will have no security for funds lent in excess of the homeowner's equity.

According to Mr. Bleakley, a tell tale sign that the expansion is nearing an end is the willingness of lenders to make riskier loans. There is a fear that these loans could result in disaster similar to the savings and loan crisis. However, in this case there will be no government bail out. Small lenders could be hurt.

A few mortgage companies are making these loans and packaging them in large bundles. They are then sold on the secondary mortgage market. The large number of loans is believed to reduce the risk.

> *Although legal, the authors believe that these loans are dangerous.*

Investors should be made fully aware of the fact that loan funds in excess of borrowers' equity is in reality unsecured loans. These loans are likely being made to persons who, in the past, have spent themselves into debt which they could not handle.

LOAN TERMS

Higher Interest Rates

> *Loans made by hard money lenders bear interest rates higher than rates charged by institutional lenders.*

Risk is related to rate. No one will invest money in a higher risk investment unless the greater risk was compensated for in return. As an example, the most risk free long-term investment is government bonds which also provides the lowest rate of return of any long-term investment.

Shorter Terms

Loans made by hard money lenders are more likely to have a shorter repayment term than are loans made by institutional lenders.

Non-amortized

Loans made by hard money lenders are more likely to have a balloon payment than loans made by institutional lenders.

Fixed Rate

> *Relatively few hard money loans have adjustable rates.*

The reason being that the interest rates are quite high to begin with, and hard money lenders who have a few loans do not want to be bothered with the accounting required to handle adjustable rate loans. (The loan could be serviced by a firm set up to handle adjustable rate loans.)

Investor Protection

As previously stated, the most important lending criteria for hard money lenders is the value of the property securing the loan.

RULE OF THUMB

> *As a rule of thumb, the loan-to-value ratio should not exceed 70 percent.*

With a 70 percent ratio, the lender should not suffer a loss if the borrower defaults on his or her loan payments. The 30 percent equity should be sufficient to cover the following.

Interest Lost

Payments not made means lost interest.

Foreclosure Costs

Besides the direct costs of foreclosure, there is the time factor to consider. The time value of money (interest) must be considered.

Senior Liens

If the investor's junior lien is in default, chances are the senior liens are also in default.

Marketing Costs

Marketing costs to recoup the loss involve a number of expenses.

1. **Commissions.** Costs paid to a sales agent.
2. **Escrow and Closing Costs.** These are normal costs involved in any sale transaction.
3. **Maintenance Costs.** The property will probably have maintenance costs during the marketing period. In addition, owners in foreclosure often neglect regular maintenance and in some case are actually destructive, which could result in considerable expense.
4. **Holding Costs.** Depending on the type of property, it could take six months for a sale after foreclosure. To not suffer any loss, the sale proceeds should be enough to cover the taxes and insurance during this time period as well as the interest lost on the money the lender has invested. The interest will compound without the payments being made and with additional cash expenditures. Therefore, the actual lender investment has risen significantly.

   Of course, there is always the risk that values will decline and/or the loan appraisal was not realistic. This could result in the lender taking a significant loss as to sale price versus loan balance in addition to the other costs listed above.

   The 70 percent ratio is close to a break-even ratio based upon a sale at appraisal value. If greater security is desired by a lender, the loan can either be reduced or additional assets can be added to the security. (Note that 125 percent loans violate the 70 percent rule).

ABILITY TO SERVICE DEBT

If a hard money equity lender lacks the financial ability to make the payments (service the senior loans) and maintain the property upon which the borrowers default, then that lender should not have been a lender.

Investors must consider the "What Ifs" of an investment. Investors are taking a huge risk if default would leave them owning on a property having loan obligations beyond their payment ability.

If a hard money lender would find it very difficult financially to be in a position of ownership, then the loan should not be made.

Loan File -
Minimum Documentation

At a very minimum, a hard money arranger should cover the following in his or her loan file.

LOAN APPLICATION

The application should include credit information. While these are not federally related loans, the Uniform Residential Loan Application is an excellent form to use. (See Chapter 14).

CREDIT REPORT

A copy of the credit report should be maintained in the file as well as a signed receipt from the lender that they received the credit information prior to funding the loan.

VERIFICATION OF MORTGAGES

Verification should be obtained as to balances on all senior encumbrances as well as on the status of senior loans.

PRELIMINARY TITLE REPORT

A Preliminary Title Report should be obtained and a copy retained in the loan file. A receipt from the lender showing receipt of the information should also be in the file.

APPRAISAL

The file should include an appraisal by a licensed or certified appraiser.

> *The broker is exposed to considerable liability if, as an arranger of the loan, he or she is also appraising the property.*

A subsequent foreclosure and resale at a significantly lower figure than the appraisal might result in a lawsuit. The lender could claim either negligence or fraud. However, if the arranger of the loan does make the appraisal, it should be well documented to stand a possible challenge by expert witnesses.

MORTGAGE LOAN DISCLOSURE STATEMENT

Copies of the Lender and Purchaser Mortgage Loan Disclosure Statement should be kept on file indicating, by the signatures of the parties, that the statements were received.

SERVICING AGREEMENT

If the arranger of credit (Mortgage Loan Broker) will not service the loan, the file should have signed documentation that the lender was so informed.

> *Most arrangers of mortgages do not service loans that they arrange.*

A few do so. These are usually multi-office loan brokers who have a significant volume and are able to treat loan servicing as a separate profit base.

If the hard money arranger will be servicing the loan, then the file should include a copy of the loan servicing agreement.

Case Example

Howard Tamkin & Co. v. Carpeteria Investment Co. (1968) 265 C.A. 2d 617

A prospective borrower entered into a written contract with a broker, where the broker was to obtain a $950,000 loan for the permanent financing of a shopping center.

The plaintiff broker obtained a loan commitment for the loan. However, the commitment introduced a condition not contemplated by the loan procurement agreement. As a condition of the loan, the lender required the limited partners to sign personally on the note and trust deed. This would override their exemption from liability which was one of the purposes of being a limited partner.

The loan was refused on these conditions and the broker sued for a commission since a loan had been found.

The trial court held that the plaintiff had not performed as the offered loan had a condition that was reasonably unacceptable. The trial court was affirmed by the Court of Appeals.

ARTICLE 5

The purpose of Article 5 is to curb broker abuses in arranging loans.

Article 5 is set forth in Business and Professions Code 10230 et seq. It is applicable to real estate licensees engaged in the business of brokering mortgage loans or acting as agents in the sale, purchase or exchange of existing loans.

www.leginfo.ca.gov/.html/bpc_table_of_contents.html
(Califorina Business and Professions Code)

> **Note: Every mortgage loan solicitation by a real estate broker shall include the broker's license number as well as a special Department of Real Estate consumer telephone number. This requirement (effective July 1, 1998) also applies to investor solicitations and whenever a borrower or investor signs any documentation related to a loan negotiated by a broker. THERE ARE NO EXCEPTIONS.**

EXEMPTIONS FROM COVERAGE

The provisions of Article 5 do not apply to the following.

Broker Transactions in Connection With Sales

The provisions of Article 5 do not apply to negotiation of a loan by or for a real estate broker in connection with a sale or exchange of real property where the real estate broker acted as an agent.

Nor do the provisions of Article 5 apply to the sale or exchange by or for the broker of a promissory note created to finance the sale or exchange where the broker acted as an agent for one of the parties. This exemption applies regardless of the relationship between the time of the sale or exchange of the promissory note and the time of the sale or exchange of the property.

Broker Direct Benefit

The above exemptions do not apply to negotiations of loans and sales or exchanges of promissory notes in connection with the financing of a real property sale or exchange transaction in which the broker, as a party, had a direct or indirect financial interest.

Note: Section 10230(a) covers the exemption in connection with a broker sale or exchange but paragraph (b) of Section 10230 removes transactions from the exemption where the broker had a financial interest (was a principal rather than an agent).

RESTRICTIONS ON RETENTION OF LOAN FUNDS

A person engaged in any of the activities listed below, either as an agent or a principal, shall not retain funds payable under the terms of a real property secured promissory note for more than 60 days, except with a written agreement with the purchaser or lender. (**Business and Professions Code 10231.1**) The following are activities covered by this restriction.

Soliciting/Servicing

Soliciting borrowers or lenders for loans or negotiating loans or collecting payments or performing services for borrowers, lenders or note owners in connection with loans secured by (directly or collaterally) by liens on real property or business opportunities.

Selling/Buying

Selling, offering to sell, buying, offering to buy, exchanging or offering to exchange a lien secured by real property or a business opportunity and performing services for the holders thereof.

Acting As A Principal

Acting as a principal in the business of buying from, selling to, or exchanging with the public, real property sales contracts or promissory notes secured directly or collaterally by liens or real estate or making agreements with the public for the collection of payments of for the performance of services in connection with sales contracts or promissory notes secured by real property.

BROKER BENEFITS

Submission to the DRE When Broker Benefits

When a real estate broker, who acts within the scope of the above, proposes or causes the solicitation and acceptance of funds to be applied to the purchase of a loan transaction where the broker will directly benefit (other than commission and costs), the broker must first submit a statement to the Department of Real Estate.

The statement shall include:

1. a copy of the statement given to the person solicited,
2. that it is being submitted pursuant to Business and Professions Code 10231.2.

Statement to Person Solicited When Broker Benefits

When the broker benefits from a loan transaction, the broker will deliver, or cause to be delivered, a completed statement not less than 24 hours before (whichever is earlier) either the acceptance of any funds or the execution of an agreement to obligate the person to make the loan or purchase. The statement must be signed by the prospective lender or purchaser and by the broker (or a salesperson on the broker's behalf). The broker must keep a copy of the statement for four years. The contents of the statement shall include, but is not limited to:

1. address or identification of the property securing the borrower's obligation.

2. estimated fair market value. If the broker relies on an appraisal, the date of the appraisal and who made it for whom.

3. age, size, type of construction and a description of the improvements if contained in the appraisal or as represented by the prospective borrower.

4. identity, occupation, employment, income and credit data of prospective borrower(s) as represented to the broker by the borrower(s).

5. the terms by the promissory note to be given to the lender.

6. information concerning all encumbrances that are liens against the securing property as known by the broker and pertinent information about other loans the borrower expects will result in being recorded against the property.

7. any provisions for servicing the loan including disposition of late charges and prepayment penalty fees.

8. information concerning any arrangement under which the prospective lender along with persons associated with him or her will be joint beneficiaries or obligees.

9. if the solicitation is subject to the provisions of Section 10231.2, which involves collection of advance fees, there must be a detailed statement of the intended use and disposition of funds solicited including any direct or indirect benefits to the broker.

If the broker is selling existing obligations secured by real estate as either a principal or as an agent, the following must be included:

10. ability of the trustor or vendee to make his or her payments including the trustors or vendees payment history

11. a statement as to whether or not the dealer is acting as a principal or as an agent in the transaction.

Exemption from Statements to DRE and Persons Solicited

Disclosure Statements do not apply to the offering of a security pursuant to Article 6 (covered later in this chapter) or transactions subject to the Corporate Securities Law.

Application to Corporate Brokers

The disclosures apply to funds which are intended for the direct or indirect use or benefit of any officer, director or stockholder (holding more than 10 percent interest in the corporation) when the funds were solicited by the corporate real estate broker.

Solicitation and Acceptance of Funds Other Than for Services

Specified Statement and Its Use

10231.2(a). A real estate broker who, through express or implied representations that the broker or salespersons acting on the broker's behalf are engaging in acts for which a real estate license is required by subdivision (d) or (e) of Section 10131, proposes to solicit and accept funds, or to cause the solicitation and acceptance of funds, to be applied to a purchase or loan transaction in which the broker will directly or indirectly obtain the use or benefit of the funds other than for commissions, fees and costs and expenses as provided by law for the broker's services as an agent, shall, prior to the making of any representation, solicitation or presentation of the statement described in subdivision (b), submit the following to the Department of Real Estate:

(1) A true copy of the statement described in subdivision (b) complete except for the signature of the prospective lender or purchaser.
(2) A statement that the submittal is being made to the department pursuant to Section 10231.2...

ADVERTISING BY LOAN BROKERS

A real estate broker who meets the threshold requirements for submission of quarterly and fiscal reports (Chapter 11) must obtain prior approval of advertising in connection with activities requiring these reports.

Advertising - Definition

ADVERTISING *includes newspapers, circular form letters, brochures or similar publications, signs, displays, radio broadcast or telecasts which concern:*

1. Use of terms, rates, conditions or the amount of any loan or sale.
2. The security, solvency or stability of any person carrying on the activities of the loan brokerage activities.

Not Considered Advertising

1. Information distributed to other brokers and persons who the broker had previously acted for as an agent.
2. Information restricted to the identification and description of terms of loans, mortgages, deeds of trust and land contracts offered for funding or purchase through the loan broker.
3. Advertising a real property security (Article 6 of the real estate law).

Premiums

A broker may not advertise a premium or gift to induce a borrower, lender or purchaser.

Different Yield

A broker may not advertise a yield different than the rate on the note unless the advertisement states the rate on the note and the discount from face value for which the loan can be purchased.

Submission of Advertising

The submission of advertising for approval to the Department of Real Estate was formerly mandatory. **Business and Professions Code Section 10232.1** has changed "shall " to "may" which makes the submission voluntary.

When submitted, a true copy shall be accompanied by a fee not to exceed $40. The approval is for five years. If advertising submitted for approval is not given within 15 calendar days, the proposed advertising shall be considered approved.

Advertising Identification

The Department of Real Estate assigns an identifying number to each advertisement submitted for approval. Brokers who use visual advertisements will include the number in their advertisements.

Advertising Criteria

The commissioner may prevent or halt the publication of false, misleading or deceptive advertising. Commissioner's Regulation 2848 of the Commissioner's Regulations sets forth examples of false, misleading and deceptive advertising.

BROKER ADVANCING OTHER THAN OBLIGOR'S FUNDS

If, in servicing a real property secured loan, the broker pays funds to the lender other than the funds of the obligor, the broker must give written notice to the lender or owner of the note of this fact. The notice must be given within 10 days of making any such payment and include the date and amount of payment, the name of the person to whom payment was made, the source of funds and the reason for making the payment. (**Business and Professions Code 10233.1**)

> **Note:** Prior to this requirement some mortgage brokers would hide the fact that a borrower was in default from the lender while trying to get the borrower current. They felt it could be bad for business, to get additional lenders, when a borrower was constantly late with his or her payment.

MORTGAGE LENDER/INVESTOR DISCLOSURE STATEMENT

In addition to the borrower disclosure statements, which are required in loan transactions other than federally related loans, there is a lender/investor disclosure statement. This statement is limited to:

1. private lenders,
2. small pension funds (less than $15,000,000 in assets),
3. credit unions.

The disclosure statement is known as LPDS.

Every real estate broker who solicits and negotiates with a private investor for a loan secured by real property or for the purchase of a real property sales contract or a note secured by a deed of trust is required to deliver to the investor the applicable completed statement as early as practical, but before the investor is obligated to purchase or make the loan.

The statement must be signed by the prospective lender and by the broker (or a licensed salesperson authorized to act on behalf of the broker). An exact copy must be given to the investor or purchaser. Depending upon the type of transaction, the form used can be one of three versions. These versions are for:

1. loan origination.
2. sale of an existing note.
3. a collateralized note.

This form is included in Chapter 15.

MORTGAGE BROKERS LOAN STATEMENT/BORROWER

This statement is covered in Chapter 15.

RECORDING OF TRUST DEEDS

If a real estate broker negotiates a loan secured by a trust deed on real estate, the broker must record the trust deed (naming the lender as beneficiary) prior to the release of any funds (unless the lender provides a written authorization for a prior release of funds.)

If the funds are released on the written authorization of the lender prior to recording, the broker shall either record the trust deed within 10 days of release of funds or deliver the trust deed to the lender with a written recommendation that it be immediately recorded.

RECORDING OF ASSIGNMENTS

When a real estate broker sells or otherwise arranges a transfer of an existing trust deed or sales contract secured by real estate, the broker shall record the assignment naming the assignee as purchaser.

Recording must be within 10 working days after the seller receives funds from escrow or the buyer for the assignment. As an alternative the broker may deliver the real property sales contract or trust deed to the purchaser with a written recommendation that it be immediately recorded. (**Business and Professions Code 10234**)

Article 6

Article 6 of the Real Estate Law (beginning with Business and Professions Code Section 10237) has been repealed as of January 1, 1998. The Department of Corporations has taken over responsibility for issuance of security permits. The Department of Corporations now has jurisdiction over all securities transactions.

Article 7

Article 7 sets forth disclosure requirements as well as limits on loan costs and fees that can be charged by a mortgage loan broker.

SHELTERED LOANS

The provisions of Article 7 (exclusive of the statement requirements) shall not apply to first trust deeds (senior loans) of $30,000 or more and second trust deeds (junior loans) of $20,000 or more.

The limitations as to loan costs and broker's commission only apply to smaller loans. The parties can agree to commissions and costs without limitation on the larger loans.

INSURANCE LIMITATIONS

The broker may not require as a condition of the loan, that the borrower purchase credit life insurance or credit disability insurance. (Business and Professions Code 10241.1)

This insurance pays off the loan if the insured dies and makes the payments if the insured become disabled.

If the borrower elects to purchase such insurance coverage it must be in a form approved by the insurance commissioner and may not be in an amount in excess of what is required to pay off the loan. The licensee can only collect one premium on the loan even when there are multiple borrowers (only one borrower may be insured unless another borrower's wages are necessary to make the payments).

The licensee can collect the cost of fire and hazard insurance if the policy is payable to the borrower and it is sold at a standard rate through a licensed agent.

If insurance premiums are to be paid from the proceeds of this loan, the premium amount cannot be used to determine if the loan is exempt from limitations on cost and fees.

BROKER CONTROLLED FUNDS

If a broker makes or arranges loans secured by real property and uses any broker controlled funds, the broker must advise the borrower of this fact not later than the business day following this decision but, in any event, prior to close of escrow. (**Business and Professions Code 10241.2**)

BROKER CONTROLLED FUNDS *are funds owned by the broker, a spouse, child, parent, grandparent, brother, sister, in-law or any entity in which the broker alone or with one of the above has a 10 percent or greater interest.*

APPRAISAL REPORT (COPY)

If the borrower pays for an appraisal of real property, a copy of the appraisal report must be given to both the borrower and lender at or before closing the loan transaction. (**Business and Professsions Code 10241.3**)

MAXIMUM ALLOWABLE CHARGES

Cost and Charges

> *The costs and expenses of a loan include appraisal fees, escrow fees, title charges, notary fees, recording fees and credit investigation fees.*

Maximum costs for first trust deed under $30,000 and second trust deeds under $20,000 cannot exceed 5 percent of the loan or $390, whichever is greater, but never more than $700. (Costs and expenses can never exceed actuals or reasonably earned costs and fees.) (**Business and Professions Code 10242**)

What the above paragraph means is that the minimum costs and fees will be $390 and the maximum will be $700 with the five percent applicable to numbers in between. As examples:

$5,000 Loan

> 5% = $250
> But fees can be 5% or
> $390 whichever is greater
> <u>$390</u> is greater than $250

$9,000 Loan

> 5% = $450
> But fees can be 5% or
> $390 whichever is greater
> <u>$450</u> is greater than $390

$19,000 Loan

> 5% = $950
> But fees can be 5% to a maximum of
> $700 so, the fee cannot exceed
> <u>$700</u>

Broker's Commission

The brokers commission is regulated for first trust deeds under $30,000 and second trust deeds under $20,000. Maximum commissions for applicable loans are as follows:

1st Trust Deeds

> Less than 3 year term - 5%
> 3 year or more term -10%

2nd Trust Deeds

> Less than 2 year term - 5%
> 2 years but less than 3 years -10%
> 3 years or more -15%

There is of course no limit as to the commission that can be charged for first trust deeds of $30,000 or more and second trust deeds of $20,000 or more.

Case Example

Pacific Plan v. Fox (1979) 84 C.A. 2d 215

A loan broker (Pacific Plan) charged the maximum escrow fees without accounting for expenses individually for every transaction. The broker maintained that this was proper since costs were reasonable and they sustained a loss on their escrow operations.

The Court of Appeals upheld the trial court in holding that Business and Professions Code 10242 (a) specifically required individual accounting to insure that the borrower is not charged the statutory fee when the actual costs are less than the maximum. The court held that the fact that costs were reasonable was irrelevant. A writ of mandamus was upheld that ordered Pacific Plan to refrain from charging escrow fees in disregard of actual costs.

> **Note:** This case followed *Pacific Plan of California v. Kinder* (1978) 84 C.A. 3d 215, where the court assessed damages against Pacific Plan for charging maximum allowable costs on loans rather than actuals. The court in that case held that individual accounting was necessary and that the statute did not allow costs to be averaged.

Case Example

Realty Projects Inc. v. Smith (1973) 32 C.A. 3d 204

A mortgage borrower requested a loan in an amount that would have been within the limits of broker compensation and loan charges. The loan broker suggested that the borrower seek a larger loan. The loan broker did not inform the borrower that the larger loan exceeded the dollar amount under which brokers' compensation and costs were limited.

The court determined that the increase was suggested for the purpose of placing the loan outside the statutory limitations so that commissions substantially higher than those on regulated loans could be charged.

The Department of Real Estate had ordered the plaintiff's license revoked and the court refused to set aside the DRE order. **Note:** The broker clearly breached a fiduciary duty of disclosure to the borrower.

EQUAL PAYMENTS

Loans Under Three Years

Loans secured by a lien on real property (other than a note given back to the seller by the buyer) which provide for installment payments over a term less than three years shall require equal payments over the loan period with the final payment not payable until the maturity date. (**Business and Professions Code 10244**)

> *No installment, including the final payment, shall be greater than twice the amount of the smallest payment.*

The above paragraph really says that there can be no balloon payments on broker arranged loans for less than three years.

Loans Under 6 Years - Owner-occupied

When the loan is for an owner-occupied dwelling, payments must be equal for loans under six years. No balloon payments for loans under six years. (**Business and Professions Code 10244.1**)

MORTGAGE LOAN DISCLOSURE STATEMENT

This statement will be covered in detail in Chapter 15. It is a disclosure statement set forth in Business and Professions Code 10244 and 10244.1 to provide the borrower with complete information prior to obligation.

LATE CHARGES

A late charge can be imposed for late payments on loans secured by real estate that are made or arranged by real estate brokers. The following relate to late charges.

Grace Period

A late charge cannot be imposed if an installment is paid or offered in full within 10 days after due date.

Pyramiding Prohibited

Only one charge can be made for a late payment. (If an earlier payment was not paid in full the lender cannot consider all future payments late because of the balance due off the partial or missed payment.)

Maximum and Minimum Charges

Late charges may not exceed 10 percent of the installment due. A minimum charge of $5 can be assessed when the amount due is less than $50.

PREPAYMENT PENALTIES

> *Prepayment penalties are not allowed on loans for owner-occupied dwellings after 7 years (a penalty can be charged within 7 years). (Business and Professions Code 10242.6)*

Twenty percent of the unpaid balance can be prepaid in any 12 month period without being subject to a prepayment penalty. This means that the prepayment penalty would ordinarily only apply to 80 percent of the loan when it is prepaid.

The prepayment penalty cannot exceed six months advance interest on the amount prepaid (after the 20 percent exemption).

Trust Fund Handling

Trust fund handling is covered in Chapter 11. You will note that much of the material covers "hard money" lending applications. They include:

1. Trust Deed Investor Funds
2. Credit Report and Appraisal Fees
3. Impound Accounts
4. Loan Servicing
5. Loan Payoffs

Required Disclosures

STATE REQUIREMENTS

1. **Mortgage Loan Disclosure Statement.** (See Chapter 15.)
2. **Fair Housing.** (See Chapter 10.)
3. **Lender Purchaser Disclosure Statement.** (See Chapter 15.)
4. **Home Mortgage Disclosure Act Reporting.** (See Chapter 9.)
5. **Seller Carryback Requirements.** (See Chapter 15.)

Case Example

Keystone Mortgage Co. v. MacDonald (1967) 254 C.A. 2d 808

Defendant signed a written agreement employing the plaintiff to secure a trust deed of $700,000 for 20 years with interest that was not to exceed 6 1/4 percent and monthly payments of $5,117 or less including principal and interest.

Keystone found a lender willing to loan $700,000 for 19 years at 6 1/4 percent and monthly payments of $5,253.30 plus taxes and insurance. There were also 14 conditions to the loan including a standby fee and non-cancellable 15-year lease with a specified tenant.

The defendant (MacDonald) paid the standby fee of $14,000 but the lease was disapproved by the lender and the defendant was unable to negotiate it to meet the lenders objections.

MacDonald also attempted to meet the other provisions of the loan as to other leases but was not successful. Keystone claimed that they were entitled to a commission as soon as MacDonald accepted the condition of the loan commitment.

The court held that the loan broker must place a client in touch with a lender who is ready, willing and able to make the loan or have carried out negotiations to such a point as to reach an unqualified agreement to make the loan upon the terms proposed.

Since the lenders loan offer was not unconditional, the broker's commission is not earned if the conditions are unable to be met.

The court compared this case to a purchase offer accepted conditioned upon financing. If the financing cannot be obtained, there is no earned commission. A condition precedent that cannot be performed does not constitute performance.

FEDERAL REQUIREMENTS

1. **Truth In Lending.** (See Chapter 8.)
2. **Real Estate Settlement Procedures Act.** (See Chapter 9.)
3. **Equal Credit Opportunity Act.** (See Chapter 10.)
4. **Transfer Disclosure.** (See Chapter 9.)
5. **Written Authorization to Run Credit Report.** (See Chapter 10.)

> **Case Example**
>
> **Never v. King (1969) 276 C.A. 2d 461**
>
> This case involved an action by a loan broker for a commission. A medical group had contacted the loan broker for help in financing. They wanted 100 percent financing for a building that was to be built. The plaintiff secured a loan offer of $110,000 which the doctors rejected. The agreement entered into called for a 15-year loan of $150,000 (or such amount as is mutually agreed upon) at 6 3/4 percent interest.
>
> The plaintiff then found a $130,000 loan that the defendants would not accept. The plaintiff claimed that $130,000 would be enough to build the building and stated that a $150,000 loan was not possible.
>
> The defendants told the plaintiff that if they couldn't get a $150,000 loan, they had someone who would build the building and lease it to them. This was 16 days before the contract was to expire. The plaintiff indicated that they could get a separate $39,000 unsecured loan to cover the cost of the land so that $39,000 plus $130,000 would give them $169,000 which was more than the $150,000 the defendants had asked for.
>
> The court held that there is a difference between a $150,000 mortgage and a $130,000 mortgage plus being personally obligated for $39,000. The court determined that the broker knew the defendants' terms and could not require the defendants to vary them so that the broker could earn a commission.
>
> While the court did not decide if the plaintiff had repudiated the agreement by saying a $150,000 loan was not possible or if the defendants had breached the contract by deciding to rent prior to expiration of the contract, the court held that, in the absence of proof that the plaintiff could have earned a commission in the absence of any breach by the defendants, the verdict of the trial court in favor of the defendants was proper.

RE FORM 833

RE 883 includes the Good Faith Estimate required by RESPA as well as additional California required disclosures. This form is shown in Figures 12-1 and 12-2.

Figure 12-1

Mortgage Loan Disclosure Statement/Good Faith Estimate

RE 883 (New 12/93)

Borrower's Name(s): _____

Real Property Collateral: The intended security for this proposed loan will be a Deed of Trust on (street address or legal description) _____

This joint Mortgage Loan Disclosure Statement/Good Faith Estimate is being provided by _____, a real estate broker acting as a mortgage broker, pursuant to the Federal Real Estate Settlement Procedures Act (RESPA) and similar California law. In a transaction subject to RESPA, a lender will provide you with an additional Good Faith Estimate within three business days of the receipt of your loan application. You will also be informed of material changes before settlement/close of escrow. The name of the intended lender to whom your loan application will be delivered is:

☐ Unknown   ☐ _____ (Name of lender, if known)

GOOD FAITH ESTIMATE OF CLOSING COSTS

The information provided below reflects estimates of the charges you are likely to incur at the settlement of your loan. The fees, commissions, costs and expenses listed are estimates; the actual charges may be more or less. Your transaction may not involve a charge for every item listed and any additional items charged will be listed. The numbers listed beside the estimate generally correspond to the numbered lines contained in the HUD-1 Settlement Statement which you will receive at settlement if this transaction is subject to RESPA. The HUD-1 Settlement Statement contains the actual costs for the items paid at settlement. When this transaction is subject to RESPA, by signing page two of this form you are also acknowledging receipt of the HUD Guide to Settlement Costs.

HUD-1	Item	Paid to Others	Paid to Broker
800	*Items Payable in Connection with Loan*		
801	Lender's Loan Origination Fee	$ _____	$ _____
802	Lender's Loan Discount Fee	$ _____	$ _____
803	Appraisal Fee	$ _____	$ _____
804	Credit Report	$ _____	$ _____
805	Lender's Inspection Fee	$ _____	$ _____
808	Mortgage Broker Commission/Fee	$ _____	$ _____
809	Tax Service Fee	$ _____	$ _____
810	Processing Fee	$ _____	$ _____
811	Underwriting Fee	$ _____	$ _____
812	Wire Transfer Fee	$ _____	$ _____
		$ _____	$ _____
900	*Items Required by Lender to be Paid in Advance*		
901	Interest for ____ days at $_____ per day	$ _____	$ _____
902	Mortgage Insurance Premiums	$ _____	$ _____
903	Hazard Insurance Premiums	$ _____	$ _____
904	County Property Taxes	$ _____	$ _____
905	VA Funding Fee	$ _____	$ _____
		$ _____	$ _____
1000	*Reserves Deposited with Lender*		
1001	Hazard Insurance: ____ months at $_____ /mo.	$ _____	$ _____
1002	Mortgage Insurance: ____ months at $_____ /mo.	$ _____	$ _____
1004	Co. Property Taxes: ____ months at $_____ /mo.	$ _____	$ _____
		$ _____	$ _____
1100	*Title Charges*		
1101	Settlement or Closing/Escrow Fee	$ _____	$ _____
1105	Document Preparation Fee	$ _____	$ _____
1106	Notary Fee	$ _____	$ _____
1108	Title Insurance	$ _____	$ _____
		$ _____	$ _____
1200	*Government Recording and Transfer Charges*		
1201	Recording Fees	$ _____	$ _____
1202	City/County Tax/Stamps	$ _____	$ _____
		$ _____	$ _____
1300	*Additional Settlement Charges*		
1302	Pest Inspection	$ _____	$ _____
		$ _____	$ _____

Subtotals of Initial Fees, Commissions, Costs and Expenses $ _____ $ _____

Total of Initial Fees, Commissions, Costs and Expenses $ _____

Compensation to Broker (Not Paid Out of Loan Proceeds):

Mortgage Broker Commission/Fee $ _____

Any Additional Compensation from Lender   ☐ No ☐ Yes $ _____ (if known)

Page 1 of 2

Figure 12-2

ADDITIONAL REQUIRED CALIFORNIA DISCLOSURES

I. Proposed Loan Amount: $ _____

    Initial Commissions, Fees, Costs and
      Expenses Summarized on Page 1: $ _____

    Payment of Other Obligations (List):
      Credit Life and/or Disability Insurance (see VI below) $ _____

    _____ $ _____

    _____ $ _____

Subtotal of All Deductions: $ _____

Estimated Cash at Closing ☐ **To You** ☐ **That you must pay** $ _____

II. Proposed Interest Rate: _____%   ☐ Fixed Rate ☐ Initial Variable Rate

III. Proposed Loan Term: _____   ☐ Years   ☐ Months

IV. Proposed Loan Payments: Payments of $_____ will be made ☐ Monthly ☐ Quarterly ☐ Annually for _____ (number of months, quarters or years). If proposed loan is a variable interest rate loan, this payment will vary (see loan documents for details).

The loan is subject to a balloon payment: ☐ No ☐ Yes. If Yes, the following paragraph applies and a final balloon payment of $_____ will be due on __/__/__ *[estimated date (day/month/year)]*.

NOTICE TO BORROWER: IF YOU DO NOT HAVE THE FUNDS TO PAY THE BALLOON PAYMENT WHEN IT COMES DUE, YOU MAY HAVE TO OBTAIN A NEW LOAN AGAINST YOUR PROPERTY TO MAKE THE BALLOON PAYMENT. IN THAT CASE, YOU MAY AGAIN HAVE TO PAY COMMISSIONS, FEES, AND EXPENSES FOR THE ARRANGING OF THE NEW LOAN. IN ADDITION, IF YOU ARE UNABLE TO MAKE THE MONTHLY PAYMENTS OR THE BALLOON PAYMENT, YOU MAY LOSE THE PROPERTY AND ALL OF YOUR EQUITY THROUGH FORECLOSURE. KEEP THIS IN MIND IN DECIDING UPON THE AMOUNT AND TERMS OF THIS LOAN.

V. Prepayments: The proposed loan has the following prepayment provisions.
    ☐ No prepayment penalty.
    ☐ Other (see loan documents for details).
    ☐ Any payment of principal in any calendar year in excess of 20% of the ☐ original balance ☐ unpaid balance will include a penalty not to exceed _____ months advance interest at the note rate, but not more than the interest that would be charged if the loan were paid to maturity (see loan documents for details).

VI. Credit Life and/or Disability Insurance: The purchase of credit life and/or disability insurance by a borrower is NOT required as a condition of making this proposed loan.

VII. Other Liens: Are there liens currently on this property for which the borrower is obligated? ☐ No ☐ Yes
If Yes, describe below:

Lienholder's Name	*Amount Owing*	*Priority*
_____	_____	_____
_____	_____	_____
_____	_____	_____

Liens that will remain or are anticipated on this property after the proposed loan for which you are applying is made or arranged (including the proposed loan for which you are applying):

Lienholder's Name	*Amount Owing*	*Priority*
_____	_____	_____
_____	_____	_____
_____	_____	_____

NOTICE TO BORROWER: Be sure that you state the amount of all liens as accurately as possible. If you contract with the broker to arrange this loan, but it cannot be arranged because you did not state these liens correctly, you may be liable to pay commissions, costs, fees, and expenses even though you do not obtain the loan.

VIII. Article 7 Compliance: If this proposed loan is secured by a first deed of trust in a principal amount of less than $30,000 or secured by a junior lien in a principal amount of less than $20,000, the undersigned licensee certifies that the loan will be made in compliance with Article 7 of Chapter 3 of the Real Estate Law.

A. This loan ☐ may ☐ will ☐ will not be made wholly or in part from broker controlled funds as defined in Section 10241(j) of the Business and Professions Code.

B. If the broker indicates in the above statement that the loan "may" be made out of broker-controlled funds, the broker must inform the borrower prior to the close of escrow if the funds to be received by the borrower are in fact broker-controlled funds.

Name of Broker	*License #*	*Broker's Representative*	*License #*
_____	_____	_____	_____

Broker's Address _____

Signature of Broker	*Date*	OR	*Signature of Representative*	*Date*
_____	_____		_____	_____

IX. NOTICE TO BORROWER: THIS IS NOT A LOAN COMMITMENT. Do not sign this statement until you have read and understood all of the information in it. All parts of this form must be completed before you sign. Borrower hereby acknowledges the receipt of a copy of this statement.

Borrower	*Date*	*Borrower*	*Date*
_____	_____	_____	_____

Review completed on _____ by _____

    Date   *Broker or Designated Representative*   *Dept. of Real Estate License #*

RE 883 — Page 2 of 2

SUMMARY

Hard money loans are regarded as cash loans made by other than institutional lenders. Most hard money loans are made by individual investors but some are made by pension plans.

Hard money loans are primarily based on the value of the security (asset based) although credit is generally checked and income verified.

Reasons why some purchase money loans are made by loan arrangers rather than institutional lenders include:

1. Property type. Raw land, vacant commercial property and problem properties are some of the properties institutional lenders hesitate to lend on.

2. Capacity. A borrower does not fulfill the capacity requirement of the lender (front-end and back-end ratios).

3. Credit. A credit history showing significant problems will disqualify a borrower from institutional lender loans.

Most hard money loans are not purchase loans, they are equity-based loans on the borrower's property.

Characteristics of hard money loans generally are:

1. Higher interest rates than institutional made loans.

2. Shorter terms (often a balloon payment) than loans by institutional lenders.

3. Non-amortized versus amortized loans by institutional lenders.

4. Fixed Rate Loans. Because of higher interest and shorter term, few lenders want to be bothered with adjustable rate loans.

Lender risk in the event of foreclosure includes:

1. Foreclosure costs.

2. Senior Lien Deficiency. If a loan is in default, the chances are the senior lien is also in default and will have to be made current.

3. Marketing costs that can include commission, escrow and closing costs, maintenance costs during holding period and lost interest and use of money during the holding period.

4. Danger that the appraisal was not realistic and/or values will decline resulting in a sale below the amount owed.

Hard money lenders could service the loans which they sell but most do not do so.

The minimum documentation for the loan file should be:

1. Loan application.

2. Credit report.

3. Verification of mortgages (and other liens)

4. Preliminary title report.

5. Appraisal.

6. Mortgage loan disclosures (lender and borrower).

7. Servicing agreement (or signed statement by lender acknowledged the fact that broker will not service the loan).

Article 5 of the real estate law covers loan brokerage activities. Exempt from the requirements are loans made in connection with a sale or where the broker is a principal to the loan.

Article 5 includes the following:

1. Restriction on retaining funds for more than 60 days except with written authorization.

2. When a broker benefits from a loan (other than fees or commission), he or she must submit a statement to the Department of Real Estate.

3. Threshold brokers (See Chapter 11) should obtain prior approval of advertising.

4. Brokers may not offer a premium or gift to induce a lender or borrower.

5. False, misleading or deceitful advertising can result in disciplinary action.

6. If a broker advances other than obligor's funds in servicing a loan, the lender or owner of the note must be notified within 10 days.

7. Mortgage lender/investor disclosure must be provided to the investor before the investor is obligated to the loan.

8. A Mortgage Broker's Loan Statement similarly must be provided to the borrower.

9. Brokers who negotiate loans must record the trust deed prior to the release of funds. If funds are authorized for prior release, the broker shall either record

the trust deed within 10 days of release of funds or deliver it to the lender with a written recommendation that it is to be recorded.

10. When a real estate broker sells an existing loan, the broker shall record the assignment within 10 days of the seller receiving funds from escrow.

Article 6 of the real estate law has been repealed as of January 1, 1998. The Department of Corporations has taken over responsibility for issuance of secuirty permits.

Article 7 of the Real Estate Law governs maximum loan costs and fees. It only applies to first trust deeds under $30,000 and second trust deeds under $20,000. Loans which exceed these amounts are not limited to commissions or costs.

The broker is precluded from requiring, as a condition of a loan, that the borrower purchase credit life or disability insurance.

The broker must advise the borrower if any broker-controlled funds are used to fund the loan.

If the borrower is paying for an appraisal, a copy of the appraisal must be given to the borrower and lender.

For regulated loans, loan costs are as follows:

5% of the loan or $390 whichever is greater but never more than $700.

Loan commissions for regulated loans (first trust deeds less than $30,000 and second trust deeds less than $20,000) have the following maximum charges:

First Trust Deeds:

Less than 3 years - 5%
3 years or more -10%

Second Trust Deeds:

Less than 2 years - 5%
2 years but less than 3 years -10%
3 Years or more-15%

Loans under three years shall have equal payments. (No balloon payments.)

For loans under six years on owner-occupied dwellings, there can be no balloon payments.

CLASS DISCUSSION TOPICS

1. Are the $20,000 and $30,000 limits on Article 7 protection realistic? What do you think they should be?

2. Do you know any brokers who have any significant number of Article 5 transactions?

3. Do you know any investors who deal with hard money lending? Describe basic characteristics as to sophistication, understanding of risk and financial depth.

4. Do you know any active mortgage loan broker that is also active in real estate listings and sales?

5. Is there a danger that a broker will seek appraisals from appraisers who tend to take an optimistic approach to value?

6. Why should only "threshold brokers" be required to gain prior approval on advertising?

7. Do you feel abuses would be more likely by a broker arranging many loans or by a broker who arranges just a few loans?

8. Do you agree with the Keystone decision? Why?

CHAPTER 12 QUIZ

1. Which of the following would be a hard money loan? (p. 350)
   A. A purchase money loan made by an institutional lender
   B. Seller carryback financing
   C. Assuming existing loans with no balance
   D. A loan arranged by a mortgage loan broker

2. The most important criteria used by lenders of hard money loans would be the borrowers: (p. 352)
   A. equity
   B. credit history
   C. job
   D. history

3. Reasons why institutional lenders turn down loan applications could deal with: (p. 353)

    A. borrowers capacity to make payments

    B. borrower's credit history

    C. the type of property the loan is sought on

    D. all of the above

4. Characteristics of hard money loans, as compared with loans made by institutional lenders, are: (pp. 355-356)

    A. shorter terms

    B. higher rate of interest

    C. non-amortized

    D. all of the above

5. Hard money lending is not without risk. Risks include: (pp. 356-357)

    A. foreclosure costs

    B. costs associated with delinquent senior liens

    C. marketing costs after foreclosure

    D. all of the above

6. Article 5 of the real estate law does NOT apply to: (p. 360)

    A. licensed real estate brokers

    B. broker loans arranged as part of a sale

    C. brokers who make fewer than 20 loans per year

    D. all of the above

7.A mortgage loan broker, without authorization to the contrary, cannot retain funds received for a loan payment for more than: (p. 361)

    A. 24 hours

    B. 7 days

    C. 30 days

    D. 60 days

8. A broker may not advertise a yield different than the rate of the note: (p. 364)

    A. under any circumstances

    B. unless a permit was issued by the DRE

    C. unless the rate of the note and discount are stated

    D. unless the broker has put up a $10,000 bond

9. In servicing a loan, a broker used her own funds to remit a note to an owner when a purchaser was late on a payment. The broker: (p. 365)

A. has placed her license in jeopardy

B. must be licensed by the Department of Corporations to advance funds

C. must give written notice to the lender within 10 days of making the payment

D. has 7 days to notify the Department of Corporations

10. A broker released funds prior to close of a loan transaction and recording the deed. The broker should deliver the deed to the lender with the recommendation of recording or record it within: (p. 366)

A. 24 hours of release of funds

B. 3 days of release of funds

C. 10 days of release of funds

D. 60 days of release of funds

11. Which of the following loans would a broker NOT be limited as to commission or loan costs? (p. 367)

A. A first trust deed for $10,000

B. A second trust deed for $20,000

C. Both A and B

D. Neither A nor B

12. The maximum loan costs that can be charged for a $10,000 second trust deed would be: (p. 368)

A. 15 percent of the loan

B. $390

C. $500

D. $700

Answers: 1. D; 2. A; 3. D; 4. D; 5. D; 6. B; 7. D; 8. C; 9. C; 10. C; 11. B; 12. B

Chapter 13

Securities In The Lending Industry

KEY WORDS AND TERMS

CMOs

Intrastate

Interstate

Investment Contract

10 Strips

Issuer

Joint Venture

Limited Partnership

Mortgage Backed Securities

Mortgage Pool

Multi-Lender Rule

Note

Offer to Sell

Pooling of Funds

P.O. Strips

Private Offering

Public Offering

Qualification

REITs

REMICs

Risk Capital

Securities

Tranche

Unqualified Offer

LEARNING OBJECTIVES

This chapter will introduce you to security transactions. You will learn what constitutes a security as well as requirements for qualifying and selling a security. You will also learn about the exemptions to the California Corporate Securities Act.

Corporate Security Act of 1968

The Corporate Security Act of 1968 prohibits an offer of, or sale of, a security in California unless the security is qualified or exempt from qualification. (Corporations Code 25110.)

www.leginfo.ca.gov/.html/corp_table_of_contents.html
(California Corporations Code)

25110. Qualification required

... The offer or sale of such a security in a manner that varies or differs from, exceeds the scope of or fails to conform with either a material term or material condition of qualification of the offering as set forth in the permit or qualification order, or a material representation as to the manner of offering which is set forth in the application for qualification, shall be an unqualified offer or sale.

Corporation Code Section 25120 and 25130 reiterates this requirement unless the security is subject to an exemption.

25120. Necessity of qualification of security or exemption of security or transaction

It is unlawful for any person to offer or sell in this state any security in an issuer transaction.... unless the security is qualified for sale under this chapter... or unless such security or transaction is exempted under Chapter 1 (commencing with Section 25100) of this part.

25130. Necessity of qualification of security or exemption of security or transaction

It is unlawful for any person to offer or sell any security in this state in any nonissuer transaction unless it is qualified for such sale under this chapter or under Section 25111 or 25113 of Chapter 2... or unless such security or transaction is exempted under Chapter 1 (commencing with Section 25100) of this part.

SECURITY DEFINED

SECURITIES *include interests in businesses, associations or property whereby the holder of such interest has no rights of management or control.* Holders of interests are, however, entitled to information and an accounting.

> *While a security is often viewed as stock of a corporation, it can include profit sharing agreements such as limited partnerships.*

A condominium purchase, where the owner is not allowed occupancy and is subject to a rental management agreement, would likely be regarded as a security.

> *Corporation Code Section 25019 defines securities.*

"Security" does not include: (1) any beneficial interest in any voluntary inter vivos trust which is not created for the purpose of carrying on any business or solely for the purpose of voting, or (2) any beneficial interest in any testamentary trust, or (3) any insurance or endowment policy or annuity contract under which an insurance company admitted in this state promises to pay a sum of money (whether or not based upon the investment performance of a segregated fund) either in a lump sum or periodically for life or some other specified period, or (4) any franchise subject to registration under the Franchise Investment Law, or exempted from such registration by Section 31100 or 31101 of that law.

As defined by Section 25019, the following would be securities:

1. **Notes.**
2. **Pooling of Funds.** Pooling of funds for lending purposes, regardless of form, creates a security.
3. **Investment Contracts.** An investment contract is a transaction or scheme whereby a person invests money in a common enterprise and is led to believe that profits will be made solely from the efforts of the promoter or a third party.
4. **Limited Partnership.** A limited partnership may be a security under the appropriate circumstances.

Case Example

People v. Coster (1984) 151C.A. 3d 1188

A defendant issued installment notes bearing interest which provided for a percentage of the defendant's gross business. His advertisements stated "20 percent interest and one percent of the gross."

An investment contract is a transaction where the investor invests in a common enterprise with the expectation of deriving a profit from the efforts of another. The purpose of the law is to protect the public against spurious schemes.

The court held that the transaction came within the purpose of the corporate securities law.

Case Example

People v. Park (1978)87 C.A. 3d 550

Defendant obtained money from an unsophisticated woman for the purpose of acquiring lots on which a 16-unit condominium was to be built. The defendant was to handle all aspects of the investment and the investor would realize profit. The defendant did not purchase the lots but instead appropriated the money to his own use.

The Court of Appeals held that this was an investment contract. The investor had no control over the enterprise. It was clearly not a joint venture or partnership which would have exempted the transaction from the Corporation Code.

Note: This was a criminal proceeding for violation of the securities law.

Case Example

People v. Leach (1930)106 C.A. 442

A series of promissory notes were issued, each secured by a separate lot in a tract. The proceeds were to be used for improvement of the tract.

The notes were considered by the court to be securities.

The defendants had failed to obtain a permit for the offering from the Corporation Commissioner.

Note: This was a criminal proceeding for violation of the securities law.

Case Example

Hamilton Jewelers v. Department of Corporations (1974) 37 C.A. 3d 330

A jeweler advertised unmounted diamonds with a guarantee of return of purchase price with interest within 3 years of purchase.

The Department of Corporations claimed that this was an offer of a security.

The court held it was not a security since there was no risk capital. The stones were sold below the general retail price so it was not a security as defined by Corporation Code 25019.

California follows the risk capital approach in ascertaining if a transaction is a security. The court in this case held this was not an unsecured or under secured promissory note.

MORTGAGE BACKED SECURITIES (MBS)

MORTGAGE BACKED SECURITIES *are pools of residential mortgages that back securities.* The mortgages in the pools have been insured against loss due to borrower default by Fannie Mae, Freddie Mac and/or private mortgage insurers. The insurance feature turns the loans into MBS.

> *Investors therefore have little if any risk based on lender default.*

CMOs

CMOs *are securities issued which are backed by mortgages. They are a series of bonds each of which is called a* **TRANCHE**. They have varying maturities and coupons. Tranches that have earlier due dates bear less investor risk based on changing interest rates. The last tranche to be paid is called the CMO residual. It bears the greatest risk to an investor since higher interest rates are more likely over a longer period of time. The yield in twenty years may be much less than investors would be satisfied with at that time. Therefore, the yield toward the end of the life of the CMO is greater than tranches due in just a few years.

IO AND PO STRIPS

IO (INTEREST ONLY PAYMENTS) and PO (PRINCIPAL ONLY PAYMENTS) strips are securities. They take the mortgage interest from a pool of loans and break it down into IOs and POs . These can be sold separately.

> *CMOs, IOs and POs are only for sophisticated investors.*

Many Wall Street investment firms handle these products as well as options on them which can be very risky. Several California Community Pension Funds suffered serious losses dealing in these securities.

REMICs

REMICs are very similar to CMOs. The difference is primarily one of accounting. When a CMO is created no gain or loss is realized. The assets and liabilities remain on the mortgage owner's balance sheet. When a *REMIC is created, it is treated as a sale and the loans are removed from the balance sheet of the REMIC creator.*

MORTGAGE REITs

> *A REIT is a real estate investment trust.*

Shares in the REIT are securities and are traded publicly. Many REITS are listed on the New York Stock Exchange. A number of limited partnerships have become REITS. Advantages a REIT has over a limited partnership are that there is a ready market for shares and additional capital can be obtained by additional public offerings of stock.

> *REITs avoid the double taxation of corporations. However, their dividends are taxed to the stockholders.*

REITs must distribute 95 percent of their income to the shareholders. REITs can be real estate equity REITs investing in real property, mortgage REITs, or Hybrid REITs investing in both real property and mortgages.

Case Example

People v. Graham (1985) 163 C.A. 3d 1159

The defendant sold limited partnerships in a machine which purportedly was capable of detoxifying chemical waste. The defendant asked investors to promote the investment to their friends.

The Court of Appeals affirmed the trial court conviction of the defendant for violating the Corporate Securities Act (Corporation Code 25000 et. seq.) by making a public offering of an unqualified security. The court held that a limited partnership constitutes a security unless it qualifies as an exemption. The term security has a broad scope and even though the statute does not mention limited partnerships, it is a security when investor's capital is at risk in the promoter's enterprise.

The court held that asking investors to promote the sales to their friends made it a public offering.

Case Example

People v. Woodson (1947) 78 C.A. 2d 132

This case involved limited partnerships. The court held that certificates in limited partnerships of an interest in a lease or in a profit sharing agreement are securities and their sale without a permit is a violation of securities law.

INTRASTATE DEFINED

INTRASTATE *means within a state.*

> *Securities issued or sold within the state of California are subject to the jurisdiction of the Department of Corporations.*

Corporations Code 25008 states that an offer is made in California when an offer to sell is made in California, or an offer to buy is accepted in California or if both seller and purchaser are residents of California and the security is delivered to the purchaser in California.

SALE OR SELL DEFINED

According to California Corporation Code 25017, **SALE** or **SELL** *includes any disposition of a security or interest in a security for value.* This includes exchanges.

OFFER TO SELL DEFINED

An **OFFER TO SELL** *includes every attempt to dispose of a security interest for value* (Corporation Code 25008 and 25017).

25017. Sale; sell; offer or offer to sell

(a). "Sale" or "sell" includes every contract of sale of, contract to sell or disposition of, a security or interest in a security for value.

(b). "Offer" or "offer to sell" includes every attempt or offer to dispose of, or solicitation of an offer to buy, a security or interest in a security for value.

(c). Any security given or delivered with, or as a bonus on account of, any purchase of securities or any other thing constitutes a part of the subject of the purchase and is considered to have been offered and sold for value.

(d). A purported gift of assessable stock involves an offer and sale.

(e). Every sale or offer of a warrant or right to purchase or subscribe to another security of the same or another issuer, as well as every sale or offer of a security which gives the holder a present or future right or privilege to convert the security into another security of the same or another issuer, includes an offer and sale of the other security only at the time of the offer or sale of the warrant or right or convertible security; but neither the exercise of the right to purchase or subscribe or to convert nor the issuance of securities pursuant thereto is an offer or sale.

(f). The terms defined in this Section do not include: (1) any bona fide secured transaction in or loan of outstanding securities; (2) any stock dividend payable with respect to common stock of a corporation (except for any cash or scrip paid for fractional shares)**...** or (3) any act incident to a judicially approved arrangement or reorganization in which securities are issued and exchanged for one or more outstanding securities, claims or property interests or partly in such exchange and partly for cash.

> ### Case Example
>
> ### Hall v. Superior Court (1983) 15 C.A. 3d 411
>
> A general partner wanted the limited partners to exchange their limited partnership interest for shares of common stock. The general partner conveyed the offers telephonically to the limited partners from the corporate office of the general partner, which was in California.
>
> The court held that the offer was made in California since it was spoken into the telephone in California. Therefore, an offer to sell or buy (exchange) was made in California and pursuant to California Corporate securities law, the parties could not evade or waive by private agreement, the requirements of the law.
>
> **Note:** A great many real estate limited-partnership owners have agreed to exchange their interests for shares in Real Estate Investment Trusts (REITs). An advantage of such a trade is that obtaining corporate shares in a public corporation gives the investor a liquid asset which has a readily ascertainable value and can be easily sold or pledged. Because limited partnerships have a relatively thin market, it is often difficult to sell the interests and a sale often involves a steep discount from the value the interest would have if it were in the form of corporate shares.

Exceptions to Department of Corporation Jurisdiction

INTERSTATE SECURITY SALES

Securities issued interstate are subject to the federal jurisdiction of the Securities and Exchange Commission.

REAL PROPERTY SECURITIES PERMITS

Securities issued pursuant to real property securities permits (formerly Article VI of the Real Estate Law) are under the jurisdiction of the Department of Corporations.

Application to Real Estate Brokers

BROKER AS ISSUER

According to Corporation Commissioner Regulation 260.115, *a real estate broker who offers and sells notes secured by real property of various makers where an undivided interest is sold, would be an **ISSUER**.* (Issuer is defined in **Corporation Code Section 25010**.)

> *Corporation Code 25011 exempts a party from issuer status if the transaction does not directly or indirectly benefit the issuer.*

Nonissuer transaction

> **NONISSUER TRANSACTION** *means any transaction not directly or indirectly for the benefit of the issuer.* (**Corporations Code 25011**)

QUALIFICATION REQUIREMENTS

It is unlawful to offer or sell any security unless such sale has been qualified or the transaction is exempt. (**Corporation Code 25110**)

> *Qualification involves obtaining a permit or qualification order allowing the sale.*

While the California securities laws are modeled after federal securities laws, they are not the same. However, if a registration statement has previously been filed in connection with the same offer under the Securities Act of 1933, then qualification for the sale of the security under California law would be by Coordination (Corporation Code 25111). Prior federal registration allows simplified California approval by coordination.

LICENSING

It is unlawful for a real estate broker to sell a security unless the broker is certified as a "broker-dealer" in accordance with Corporation Code Section 25004 unless:

1. **No Public Offering.** The transaction is exempt from licensing where there is no public offering [Corporation Code 25102(e)].

2. **Multiple Criteria Exemptions.** Licensing is not required if all of the following criteria are met [Corporation Code 25102(f)].
   a. Sale to not more than 35 persons.
   b. All purchasers have a preexisting personal or business relationship.
   c. Purchasers are buying for their own account.
   d. No advertising is published.

3. **Real Estate Commissioner Authorization.** Section 25100(e) of the Corporation Code exempts securities (other than subdivided parcel sales) if they are subject to Department of Real Estate regulation.

See **Corporation Code 25102** for a full explanation of transactions exempt from the provisions of Section 25110.

SANCTIONS

Violation of Corporate Securities Act can result in:

Civil Liability

> *A person would be liable for losses caused by their misrepresentation to induce the purchase or sale of a security or to manipulate the price of the security.*

Damages would be the difference between the price for the transaction and the market value at the time of the transaction. Punitive damages might also be assessed based on outrageous conduct.

Criminal Penalties

A person who wilfully violates any provision of the Corporate Securities Act can be fined up to $1,000,000 and/or be imprisoned for up to one year. No person shall be imprisoned if that person can prove that he or she had no knowledge of the rule or order. (Corporations Code 25540[a])

A person who wilfully violates Section 25400, 25401 or 25402 of the Corporations Code (misrepresentation, or unlawful acts to induce a purchase or sale, use of false statements or omissions to induce a purchase or sale or using insider information), can be fined not more than $1,000,000 and/or be imprisoned for two, three or five years.

Administrative Actions

Actions brought by the Department of Corporations can include asking the court for an injunction to cease an action, the investigation and seizure of books, orders to desist or refrain, restrictions on transfer and discovered evidence referred to the district attorney for criminal action.

> *Administrative action also includes action to revoke any license issued by the Corporation Commissioner.*
>
> *These sanctions are similar to sanctions possible by the Department of Real Estate as to real estate licensees.*

Exemptions from California Securities Law for Loan Transactions

NOTE SOLD TO ONE PERSON

A note secured by a lien on real estate in which the beneficial interest is sold to only one person.

Corporation Code, Section 25013, defines "person" to mean an individual, corporation, partnership, joint venture, joint stock company, trust, unincorporated organization as well as a political subdivision of government.

Section 25100(p) of the Corporations Code describes this exemption as:

> **(p).** A promissory note secured by a lien on real property, which is neither one of a series of notes of equal priority secured by interests in the same property nor a note in which beneficial interests are sold to more than one person or entity.

NOTE PURSUANT TO REAL PROPERTY SECURITIES PERMIT

A note secured by a lien on real property which was made pursuant to a real properties securities permit issued under the jurisdiction of the Department of Corporations.

Section 10237 of the Business and Professions Code defines a real property securities dealer.

Real Property Securities Dealer Defined

10237. A real property securities dealer within the meaning of this article is any person, acting as principal or agent, who engages in the business of:

(a). Selling real property securities as defined by subdivision (a) or (b) of Section 10237.1, to the public, or

(b). Offering to accept or accepting funds for continual reinvestment in real property securities, or for placement in an account, plan or program whereby the dealer implies that a return will be derived from a specific real property sales contract or promissory note secured directly or collaterally by a lien on real property which is not specifically stated to be based upon the contractual payments thereon.

Section 10237.1 defines real property security.

Real Property Security Defined

10237.1. The term real property security as used in this article means:

(a). An agreement made in connection with the arranging of a loan evidenced by a promissory note secured directly or collaterally by a lien on real property or made in connection with the sale of a promissory note secured directly or collaterally by a lien on real property or a real property sales contract where in the real property securities dealer or his principal expressly or impliedly agrees to do any of the following:

    1) Guarantee the note or contract against loss at any time, or
    2) Guarantee that payments of principal or interest will be paid in conformity with the terms of the note or contract, or
    3) Assume any payments necessary to protect the security of the note or contract, or
    4) Accept, from time to time, partial payments for funding the loan or purchasing the note or contract, or
    5) Guarantees a specific yield or return on the note or contract, or
    6) Pay with his or her own funds any interest or premium for a period prior to actual purchase and delivery of the note or contract, or
    7) Repurchase the note or contract...

See **Business and Professions Code Section 10237** for a more detailed definition of real property security.

MULTI-LENDER RULE LOANS

Loans made or arranged pursuant to Corporation Code of Regulations 260.105 are exempt. The multi-lender rule requires:

1. **10 or Fewer Investors.** No more than 10 investors or purchasers are defined by Corporations Code of Regulations 260.105.30.

2. **Notification.** The broker/issuer must notify the Department of Corporations within 30 days of the transaction.

3. **Service the Loan.** The broker/issuer must service the loan and have a specific written contract to that effect.

4. **Reports.** Quarterly and annual reports regarding trust funds as well as proper accounting is required. (See Chapter 11.)

5. **Loan to Value Restrictions.** The Corporation Code of Regulations imposes loan-to-value ratio restrictions. [260.105.30 (g)].

6. **Financial Standing of Investors.** There are restrictions on the economic standing of lenders/investors.

7. **Lender Disclosures.** Disclosure to lenders must include loan-to-value information, appraisal value of secured property, property description, etc.

8. **Nature of Loan.** The value of the loan is regulated:
   a. Collateralization is not allowed.
   b. Limitations are placed on self dealing.
   c. By its terms, the loan cannot be subordinated to a subsequent deed of trust.
   d. It cannot be a promotional note (Business and Professions Code 10237.1).

9. **Designated Funds.** Funds provided to the broker must be designated to a specific loan or rate.

10. **Identical Interests.** The interests of the purchaser must be identical in their underlying value.

260.105.30. Real Estate Loans: Multiple Lender Transactions

There is hereby exempted from the provisions of Section 25110 of the Code as not being comprehended within the purposes of the Corporate Securities Law and the qualification of which is not necessary or appropriate in the public interest or for the protection of investors, any transaction which is the sale of a series of notes secured by an interest in the same real property, or the sale of undivided interests in a note secured by real property equivalent to a series transaction, if each of the following conditions are met:

(a). The Notice. A notice in the following form and containing the following information is filed with the Commissioner within 30 days after the first transaction pursuant to this exemption and within 30 days of any material change in the information required therein. The failure to file this notice shall not affect the use of this exemption by the broker unless such failure persists during any four-month period during which more than one such transaction is conducted.

To: Commissioner of Corporations
    980 9th Street, 5th Floor
    Sacramento, CA 95814-2725

This notice is filed pursuant to Rule 260.105.30, Title 10, California Code of Regulations.

() Original Notice ( ) Amended Notice
1. Name of Broker conducting transaction under Rule 260.105.30:

_____

2. Firm name, if different than "1":

_____

3. Street Address (main location):

_____
and Street   City   State   Zip

4. Mailing address (if different than "3"):

_____

5. Type of License held by Broker (check applicable boxes):

() California Real Estate
    Brokers License   License No._____
() California Industrial Loan
    Company License   File No. _____
() California Personal Property
    Brokers License   File No. _____
() Consumer Finance Lender License   File No. _____

() California Bank or Savings
   and Loan Association
() National Bank or Savings and Loan Association

6. Servicing Agent: Identify the person or persons who will act as the servicing agent in transactions pursuant to Rule 260.105.30 (including the undersigned Broker if such is the case):

7. Inspection of trust account (before answering this question, review the provisions of subsection (j) (3) of Rule 260.105.30).

CHECK ONLY ONE OF THE FOLLOWING:

() The undersigned Broker is (or expects to be) required to file reports of inspection of its trust account(s) with the Commissioner of Corporations pursuant to Rule 260.105.30(j)(3).

() The undersigned Broker is NOT (or does NOT expect to be) required to file reports of inspection of its trust account(s) with the Commissioner of Corporations pursuant to Rule 260.105.30(j)(3).

8. Signature. The contents of this notice are true and correct.

_____	_____
Date	Type Name of Broker
	_____
	Signature of Broker or of Officer or Partner of Broker
	_____
	Type name of person signing this notice, if signed by officer or partner of Broker

NOTE AN AMENDED NOTICE MUST BE FILED BY THE BROKER WITHIN 30 DAYS OF ANY MATERIAL CHANGE IN THE INFORMATION REQUIRED TO BE SET FORTH HEREIN.

(See Corporations Code of Regulations 260.105 for more details.)

Securities in the Lending Industry

State of California

Department of Corporations

REPORT OF TRANSACTIONS UNDER RULE 260.105.30

Broker _____ Fiscal year ended _____

A.   Volume data
1.   Number of transactions under rule.................... _____
2.   Face amount of notes......................................$_____
3.   Number of purchasers/lenders............................ _____

B.   Servicing arrangements
1.   By broker or affiliate of broker.............................. _____
2.   Other servicing agent.. _____

C.   Loan experience (during the fiscal year on all
       Rule 260.105.30 transactions)
1.   Notices of default filed.. _____
2.   Loans in default refinanced under Rule 260.105.30..... _____
3.   Loans in default upon which foreclosure occurred,
      or the property was sold by the borrower and the
      loan paid off.. _____

Date of report_____

_____
Signature

_____
Name and title of signator

(See Corporations Code of Regulations 260.105 for more details.)

ISSUED OR GUARANTEED BY A BANK OR SAVINGS AND LOAN

Any security issued by a bank or savings and loan is exempt [Corporations Code 25100(c) and (d)].

ISSUED OR GUARANTEED BY A CREDIT UNION

Securities issued or guarantees by a credit union are exempt [Corporations Code 25100(h)].

INVESTMENT CERTIFICATE IN LOAN COMPANY

The issuance or sale of an investment certificate in an individual loan company would be exempt (Financial Code Section 18026). Section 18424 of the Financial Code covers sales qualifications dealing with investment certificates.

MORTGAGE POOL

A security in a pool of mortgage loans, when loans are originated or purchased by a bank or savings and loan are exempt [Corporations Code 25100(s)].

SOLD TO A FINANCIAL INSTITUTION

A security offered or sold to a bank, savings and loan trust company, insurance company, investment company (registered under the Investment Securities Act of 1940), pension or profit sharing trust (excluding that of the issuer or self employed individual plans) or to a corporation with outstanding securities (Section 12 of the Securities and Exchange Act of 1934), are exempt. However, the purchaser must buy the security for its own account and not for resale [Section 25102(i) of Corporations Code].

PRIVATE OFFERING

A private sale or offering of evidence of indebtedness is exempt. A private offering described by the **Regulations of the Corporation Commissioner 260.102.2**, would be:

1. **No More Than 25 Persons.** The offering is to a limited number of investors.

2. **Sales to No More Than 10 Persons.** Sales are not consummated to more than 10 of the offerees.

> *A "person" does not include a bank, savings bank, trust company, insurance company, investment company or other institutional type investors.*

3. **Preexisting Business or Personal Relationship.** An existing relationship or the capacity to protect his or her own interests.

Case Example

Sherman v. Lloyd (1986) 181 C.A. 3d 693

Sherman was approached by a general partner to invest in a limited partnership that was to invest in real property.

Sherman did not know any other partners other than the general partner, and the partners did not even meet for the signing of the partnership agreement. There was no common relationship between the investors.

Because of the lack of any relationship between investors, the court held that the investment was a security and was not an exempt transaction.

Note: A private offering exemption requires a preexisting business or personal relationship

---

PRIVATE OFFERINGS OF OTHER SECURITIES

A private offering of securities other than evidence of indebtedness (trust deeds and mortgages) has a different definition from that listed above. (Regulation of the Corporation Commissioner 260.102.1).

1. **35 or Fewer Investors.** (Not the 25 and 10 requirement for evidence of indebtedness.)

2. **Preexisting Relationship.** Either a preexisting business or personal relationship or the capacity to protect their own interests.

3. **For Investors Own Account.** Investment purchase cannot be for resale.

4. **No Advertising.** Publication of solicitation is forbidden.

Prior to a private offering, obtain the advise of an attorney. A disclosure statement and business plan are generally required. There is also a limitation on the number of such offerings and other restrictions on the exemptions.

For the purposes of Section 260.102.1, a husband and wife (together with any custodian or trustee acting for the account of their minor children) are counted as one person and a partnership, corporation or other organization which was not specifically formed for the purpose of purchasing the security offered in reliance upon this exemption is counted as one person.

This section does not create any presumption that a public offering is involved in offers made to more than 35 persons and the determination of whether or not a transaction not covered by this section involves a public offering shall be made without reference to this section.

PRIVATE OFFERINGS OF SECURITIES TO SPECIFIED INSTITUTIONAL INVESTORS

Generally, offerings to institutional investors are exempt (Corporation Commissioners Regulations 25102(i)).

REAL ESTATE BROKER TRANSACTIONS

Commissioner of **Corporations Regulation 260.204.1** exempts transactions of real estate brokers where securities are an *integral part of the sale*, such as securities of a business.

Shares in the business (corporation) transfer with the business when it is sold.

Section 25100 sets forth exemptions. It is reproduced here in its entirety:

> **25100. Securities exempt from provisions of sections 25110, 25120, 25130**
>
> *Text of section operative July 1, 1997.*
>
> The following securities are exempted from Sections 25110, 25120 and 25130:
>
> **(a).** Any security (including a revenue obligation) issued or guaranteed by the United States, any state, any city, county, city and county, public district, public authority, public corporation, public entity or political subdivision of a state or any agency or corporate or other instrumentality of any one or more of the foregoing; or any certificate of deposit for any of the foregoing.

(b). Any security issued or guaranteed by the Dominion of Canada, any Canadian province, any political subdivision or municipality of that province or by any other foreign government with which the United States currently maintains diplomatic relations, if the security is recognized as a valid obligation by the issuer or guarantor; or any certificate of deposit of any of the foregoing.

(c). Any security issued or guaranteed by and representing an interest in or a direct obligation of a national bank or a bank or trust company incorporated under the laws of this state, and any security issued by a bank to one or more other banks and representing an interest in an asset of the issuing bank.

(d). Any security issued or guaranteed by a federal savings... association or federal savings bank or federal land bank or joint land bank or national farm loan association or by any savings association, as defined in subdivision (a) of Section 5102 of the Financial Code, which is subject to the supervision and regulation of the... Commissioner of Financial Institutions of this state.

(e). Any security (other than an interest in all or portions of a parcel or parcels of real property which are subdivided land or a subdivision or in a real estate development), the issuance of which is subject to authorization by the Insurance Commissioner, the Public Utilities Commission or the Real Estate Commissioner of this state.

(f). Any security consisting of any interest in all or portions of a parcel or parcels of real property which are subdivided lands or a subdivision or in a real estate development; provided that the exemption in this subdivision shall not be applicable to any investment contract sold or offered for sale with, or as part of, any such interest, or to any person engaged in the business of selling, distributing, or supplying water for irrigation purposes or domestic use which is not a public utility.

(g). Any mutual capital certificates or savings accounts, as defined in the Savings Association Law, issued by a savings association, as defined by subdivision (a) of Section 5102 of the Financial Code, and holding a license or certificate of authority then in force from the...Commissioner of Financial Institutions of this state.

(h). Any security issued or guaranteed by any federal credit union, or by any credit union organized and supervised, or regulated, under the Credit Union Law.

(i). Any security issued or guaranteed by any railroad, other common carrier, public utility or public utility holding company which is (1) subject to the jurisdiction of the Interstate Commerce Commission or (2) a holding company registered with the Securities and Exchange Commission under the Public Utility Holding Company Act of 1935, or a subsidiary of that company within the meaning of the act or (3) regulated in respect of the issuance or guarantee of the security by a governmental authority of the United States, of any state, of Canada or of any Canadian province; and the security is subject to registration with or authorization of issuance by that authority.

(j). Any security (except evidences of indebtedness, whether interest bearing or not) of an issuer (1) organized exclusively for educational, benevolent, fraternal, religious, charitable, social or reformatory purposes and not for pecuniary profit, if not part of the net earnings of the issuer inures to the benefit of any private shareholder or individual, or (2) organized as a chamber of commerce or trade or professional association. The fact that amounts received from memberships or dues or both will or may be used to construct or otherwise acquire facilities for use by members of the nonprofit organization does not disqualify the organization for this exemption. This exemption does not apply to the securities of any nonprofit organization if any promoter thereof expects or intends to make a profit directly or indirectly from any business or activity associated with the organization or operation of that nonprofit organization or from remuneration received from that nonprofit organization.

(k). Any agreement, commonly known as a "life income contract," of an issuer (1) organized exclusively for educational, benevolent, fraternal, religious, charitable, social or reformatory purposes and not for pecuniary profit and (2) which the commissioner designates by rule or order, with a donor in consideration of a donation of property to that issuer and providing for the payment to the donor or persons designated by him or her of income or specified periodic payments from the donated property or other property for the life of the donor or those other persons.

(l). Any note, draft, bill of exchange or banker's acceptance which is freely transferable and of prime quality, arises out of a current transaction or the proceeds of which have been or are to be used for current transactions, and which evidences an obligation to pay cash within nine months of the date of issuance, exclusive of days of grace, or any renewal of that paper which is likewise limited, or any guarantee of that paper or of any such renewal, provided that the paper is not offered to the public in amounts of less than twenty-five thousand dollars ($25,000) in the aggregate to any one purchaser. In addition, the commissioner may, by rule or order, exempt ;any issuer of any notes, drafts, bills of exchange or banker's acceptances from qualification of those securities when the commissioner finds that the qualification is not necessary or appropriate in the public interest or for the protection of investors.

(m). Any security issued by a corporation organized and existing under the provisions of Chapter 1 (commencing with Section 54001) of Division 20 of the Food and Agricultural Code.

(n). Any beneficial interest in an employees' pension, profit-sharing, stock bonus or similar benefit plan which meets the requirements for qualification under Section 401 of the federal Internal Revenue Code or any statute amendatory thereof or supplementary thereto. A determination letter from the Internal Revenue Service stating that an employees' pension, profit-sharing, stock bonus or similar benefit plan meets those requirements shall be conclusive evidence that the plan is an employees' pension, profit-sharing, stock bonus or similar plan within the meaning of the first sentence of this subdivision until the date the determination letter is revoked in writing by the Internal Revenue Service, regardless of whether or not the revocation is retroactive.

(o). Any security listed or approved for listing upon notice of issuance on a national securities exchange or designated or approved for designation upon notice of issuance as a national market system security on an interdealer quotation system by the National Association of Securities Dealers, Inc., if the exchange or interdealer quotation system has been certified by rule or order of the commissioner and any warrant or right to purchase or subscribe to the security. The exemption afforded by this subdivision does not apply to securities listed or designated, or approved for listing or designation upon notice of issuance, in a rollup transaction unless the rollup transaction is an eligible rollup transaction as defined in Section 25014.7.

That certification of any exchange or system shall be made by the commissioner upon the written request of the exchange or system if the commissioner finds that the exchange or system: (i) in acting on applications for listing of common stock substantially applies the minimum standards set forth in either alternative (A) or (B) of paragraph (1), and (ii) in considering suspension or removal from listing or designation, substantially applies each of the criteria set forth in paragraph (2).

(1) Listing standards:

(A)(i) Shareholders' equity of at least four million dollars ($4,000,000).
(ii) Pretax income of at least seven hundred fifty thousand dollars

($750,000) in the issuer's last fiscal year or in two of its last three fiscal years.

(iii) Minimum public distribution of 500,000 shares (exclusive of the holdings of officers, directors, controlling shareholders and other concentrated or family holdings), together with a minimum of 800 public holders or minimum public distribution of 1,000,000 shares together with a minimum of 400 public holders. The exchange or system may also consider the listing or designation of a company's securities if the company has a minimum of 500,000 shares publicly held, a minimum of 400 shareholders and daily trading volume in the issue has been approximately 2,000 shares or more for the six months preceding the date of application. In evaluating the suitability of an issue for listing or designation under this trading provision, the exchange or system shall review the nature and frequency of that activity and any other factors as it may determine to be relevant in ascertaining whether the issue is suitable for trading. A security which trades infrequently shall not be considered for listing or designation under this paragraph even though average daily volume amounts to 2,000 shares per day or more.

Companies whose securities are concentrated in a limited geographical area, or whose securities are largely held in block by institutional investors, normally may not be considered eligible for listing or designation unless the public distribution appreciably exceeds 500,000 shares.

(iv) Minimum price of three dollars ($3) per share for a reasonable period of time prior to the filing of a listing or designation application; provided, however, in certain instances an exchange or system may favorably consider listing an issue selling for less than three dollars ($3) per share after considering all pertinent factors, including market conditions in general, whether historically the issue has sold above three dollars ($3) per share, the applicant's capitalization, and the number of outstanding and publicly held shares of the issue.

(v) An aggregate market value for publicly held shares of at least three million dollars ($3,000,000).

(B)(i) Shareholders' equity of at least four million dollars ($4,000,000).
(ii) Minimum public distribution set forth in clause (iii) of subparagraph (A) of paragraph (1).

(iii) Operating history of at least three years.

(iv) An aggregate market value for publicly held shares of at least fifteen million dollars ($15,000,000).

(2) Criteria for consideration of suspension or removal from listing:

(i) If a company which (A) has shareholders' equity of less than one million dollars ($1,000,000) has sustained net losses in each of its two most recent fiscal years, or (B) has net tangible assets of less than three million dollars ($3,000,000) and has sustained net losses in three of its four most recent fiscal years.

(ii) If the number of shares publicly held (excluding the holdings of officers, directors, controlling shareholders and other concentrated or family holdings) is less than 150,000.

(iii) If the total number of shareholders is less than 400 or if the number of shareholders of lots of 100 shares or more is less than 300.

(iv) If the aggregate market value of shares publicly held is less than seven hundred fifty thousand dollars ($750,000).

(v) If shares of common stock sell at a price of less than three dollars ($3) per share for a substantial period of time and the issuer shall fail to effectuate a reverse stock split of the shares within a reasonable period of time after being requested by the exchange to take that action.

A national securities exchange or interdealer quotation system of the National Association of Securities Dealers, Inc. certified by rule or order of the commissioner under this subdivision shall file annual reports when requested to do so by the commissioner. The annual reports shall contain, by issuer: the variances granted to an exchange's listing standards or interdealer quotation system's designation criteria, including variances from corporate governance and voting rights' standards, for any security of that issuer, the reasons for the variances; a discussion of the review procedure instituted by the exchange or interdealer quotation system to determine the effect of the variances on investors and whether the variances should be continued; and any other information that the commissioner deems relevant. The purpose of these reports is to assist the commissioner in determining whether the quantitative and qualitative requirements of this subdivision are substantially being met by the exchange or system in general or with regard to any particular security.

The commissioner, after appropriate notice and opportunity for hearing in accordance with the provisions of the Administrative Procedure Act, Chapter 5 (commencing with Section 11500) of Part 1 of Division 3 of Title 2 of the Government Code, may, in his or her discretion, by rule or order, decertify any exchange or interdealer quotation system previously certified which ceases substantially to apply the minimum standards or criteria as set forth in paragraph (1) and (2).

A rule or order of certification shall conclusively establish that any security listed or approved for listing upon notice of issuance on any exchange, or designated or approved for designation upon insurance as a national market system security on any interdealer quotation system, named in a rule or order of certification, and any warrant or right to purchase or subscribe to any such security, is exempt under this subdivision until the adoption by the commissioner of any rule or order decertifying the exchange or interdealer quotation system.

(p). A promissory note secured by a lien on real property, which is neither one of a series of notes of equal priority secured by interests in the same real property nor a note in which beneficial interests are sold to more than one person or entity.

(q). Any unincorporated interindemnity or reciprocal or inter-insurance contract, which qualifies under the provisions of Section 1280.7 of the Insurance Code, between members of a cooperative corporation, organized and operating under Part 2 (commencing with Section 12200) of Division 3 of Title 1, and whose members consist only of physicians and surgeons licensed in California, which contracts indemnify solely in respect to medical malpractice claims against the members, and which do not collect in advance of loss any moneys other than contributions by each member to a collective reserve trust fund or for necessary expenses of administration.

(1) Whenever it appears to the commissioner that any person has engaged or is about to engage in any act or practice constituting a violation of any provision of Section 1280.7 of the Insurance Code, the commissioner may in the commissioner's discretion bring an action in the name of the people of the State of California in the superior court to enjoin the acts or practices or to enforce compliance with Section 1280.7 of the Insurance Code. Upon a proper showing a permanent or preliminary injunction, restraining order or writ of mandate shall be granted and a receiver or conservator may be appointed for the defendant or the defendant's assets.

(2) The commissioner may, in the commissioner's discretion, (A) make such public or private investigations within or outside of this state as the commissioner deems necessary to determine whether any person has violated or is about to violate any provision of Section 1280.7 of the Insurance Code or to aid in the enforcement of Section 1280.7, and (B) publish information concerning the violation of Section 1280.7.

(3) For the purpose of any investigation or proceeding under this section, the commissioner or any officer designated by the commissioner may administer oaths and affirmations, subpoena witnesses, compel their attendance, take evidence and require the production of any books, papers, correspondence, memoranda, agreements or other documents or records which the commissioner deems relevant or material to the inquiry.

(4) In case of contumacy by, or refusal to obey a subpoena issued to, any person, the superior court, upon application by the commissioner, may issue to the person an order requiring the person to appear before the commissioner, or the officer designated by the commissioner, there to produce documentary evidence, if so ordered, or to give evidence touching the matter under investigation or in question. Failure to obey the order of the court may be punished by the court as a contempt.

(5) No person is excused from attending or testifying or from producing any document or record before the commissioner or in obedience to the subpoena of the commissioner or any officer designated by the commissioner, or in any proceeding instituted by the commissioner, on the ground that the testimony or evidence (documentary or otherwise), required of the person may tend to incriminate the person or subject the person to a penalty or forfeiture, but no individual may be prosecuted or subjected to any penalty or forfeiture for or on account of any transaction, matter, or thing concerning which the person is compelled, after validly claiming the privilege against self-incrimination, to testify or produce evidence (documentary or otherwise), except that the individual testifying is not exempt from prosecution and punishment for perjury or contempt committed in testifying.

(6) The cost of any review, examination, audit or investigation made by the commissioner under Section 1280.7 of the Insurance Code shall be paid to the commissioner by the person subject to the review, examination, audit or investigation, and the commissioner may maintain an action for the recovery of these costs in any court of competent jurisdiction. In determining the cost, the commissioner may use the actual amount of the salary or other compensation paid to the persons making the review, examination, audit or investigation plus the actual amount of expenses including overhead reasonably incurred in the performance of this work.

The recoverable cost of each review, examination, audit or investigation made by the commissioner under Section 1280.7 of the Insurance Code shall not exceed twenty-five thousand dollars ($25,000), except that costs exceeding twenty-five thousand dollars ($25,000) shall be recoverable if the costs necessary to prevent a violation of any provision of Section 1280.7 of the Insurance Code.

(r). Any shares or memberships issued by an corporation organized and existing pursuant to the provisions of Part 2 (commencing with Section 12200) of Division 3 of Title 1, provided the aggregate investment of any shareholder or member in shares or memberships sold pursuant to this subdivision does not exceed three hundred dollars ($300). This exemption does not apply to the shares or memberships of any such corporation if any promoter thereof expects or intends to make a profit directly or indirectly from any business or activity associated with the corporation or the operation of the corporation or from remuneration, other than reasonable salary, received from the corporation. This exemption does not apply to non-voting shares or memberships of any such corporation issued to any person who does not possess, and who will not acquire in connection with the issuance of non-voting shares or memberships, voting power (Section 12253) in the corporation. This exemption also does not apply to shares or memberships issued by a nonprofit cooperative corporation organized to facilitate the creation of an unincorporated interindemnity arrangement that provides indemnification for medical malpractice to its physician and surgeon members as set forth in subdivision (q).

(s). Any security consisting of or representing an interest in a pool of mortgage loans which meets each of the following requirements:

(1) The pool consists of whole mortgage loans or participation interests in those loans, which loans were originated or acquired in the ordinary course of business by a national bank or federal savings...association or federal savings bank having its principal office in this state, by a bank incorporated under the laws of this state or by a savings association as defined in subdivision (a) of Section 5102 of the Financial Code and which is subject to the supervision and regulation of the ...Commissioner of Financial Institutions, and each of which loans at the time of transfer to the pool is an authorized investment for such originating or acquiring institution.

(2) The pool of mortgage loans is held in trust by a trustee which is a financial institution specified in paragraph (1) as trustee or otherwise.

(3) The loans are serviced by a financial institution specified in paragraph (1).

(4) The security is not offered in amounts of less than twenty-five thousand dollars ($25,000) in the aggregate to any one purchaser.

(5) The security is offered pursuant to a registration under the Securities Act of 1933, or pursuant to an examination under Regulation A under that act, or in the opinion of counsel for the issuer, is offered pursuant to an exemption under Section 4(2) of that act.

(t). (1) Any security issued or guaranteed by and representing an interest in or a direct obligation under the laws of a state of the United States other than this state, that is insured by the Federal Deposit Insurance Corporation, and that maintains a branch office in this state.

(u). Any security issued by an issuer registered as an open-end management company or unit investment trust under the Investment Company Act of 1940, provided that all of the following requirements are met:

(1) The registration statement for the securities is currently effective under the Securities Act of 1933.

(2) Prior to any offer or sale in this state of securities claimed to be exempt under this subdivision, there is filed with or paid to the commissioner each of the following:

(A) A notice of intention to sell that has been executed by the issuer and that includes the name and address of the issuer and the name of the securities to be offered and sold under this subdivision.

(B) A copy of the current prospectus to be used in the offer and sale of the security.

(C) The fee provided in subdivision (f) of Section 25608.

If any offer or sale is made pursuant to this exemption more than 12 months after the date the notice was filed under this subdivision, the issuer shall file another notice of intention to sell, a copy of the prospectus the issuer is currently utilizing for the purpose of making that offer and the fee specified in subparagraph (C) of paragraph (2).

> **Case Example**
>
> **People v. Wahlberg (1968) 263 C.A. 2d 286**
>
> Promissory notes were issued by a nonprofit missionary corporation. The loans were solicited from the public at large. Solicitation was from the church pulpit and suggested this was "a wonderful, Christian opportunity." The defendant also used his daily radio broadcast to get investors to put their money to a Christian use.
>
> The purpose of the note sales was to refurbish a hotel owned by the corporation. The hotel was operated as a commercial business.
>
> The court held that the Corporation Code exemptions did not apply. This was not a private offering, it was made to the public. The trial court order granting probation to the defendant was affirmed.

SUMMARY

The Corporate Securities Act of 1968 provides for Department of Corporations regulation of security transactions unless they are exempt or are subject to federal regulations (interstate transactions).

Before a security can be offered for sale, the issuer must receive a permit or a qualification order (unless the security falls into one of the exemption categories). An offer is considered an unqualified sale if it exceeds the scope or does not conform to the terms of qualification. A sale that is not qualified (or exempt) violates the law.

Securities are interest where the holder of the interest has no management rights. Securities could be:

1. Shares of stock in a corporation.
2. Notes.
3. Certificates of interest or participation.
4. Investment contracts.
5. Pooling of funds for lending purposes.
6. Limited partnerships.

Mortgage backed securities are securities backed by pools of insured residential mortgages.

CMOs are securities backed by mortgages. They are bonds, and each bond known as a tranche has a different maturity date.

REMICs are similar to CMOs . The difference is in accounting.

REITs are Real Estate Investment Trusts. Shares in the trust are securities and may be publicly traded. They invest in real property, mortgages or both. They avoid corporate double taxation if 95 percent of funds from the operation are distributed to the stockholders.

Intrastate means within a state. Intrastate security transactions are regulated by the Department of Corporations.

Interstate transactions are subject to federal jurisdiction (Securities and Exchange Commission).

Securities for which a permit was issued by the Department of Real Estate (Article VI) are exempt from Department of Corporation regulation.

A real estate broker may also sell securities (besides real property securities) without being licensed by the Department of Corporations, if there is no public offering or the following criteria is met:

1. Sale to no more than 35 persons.
2. Purchasers have a preexisting personal or business relationship.
3. Purchasers are buying for their own account (not resale).
4. No published advertising.

Violation of the securities law could result in:

1. Civil liability.
2. Criminal penalties.
3. Administrative action.

Loan transactions exempt from California Securities law include:

1. Notes sold to a single person (no undivided interests).
2. Notes sold with a Real Property Securities permit.
3. Multi-lender loans where:

    a. 10 or fewer investors.
    b. Department of Corporations is notified within 30 days.

c. The broker will service the loan.

d. Trust fund reports will be filed.

e. The loan meets loan-to-value restrictions set by Corporation Commissioner.

f. Investors meet restrictions as to economic worth.

g. Lenders receive disclosure as to loan-to-value, appraisal value and property particulars.

h. The loan meets regulatory rules.

i. Funds received by the broker are for a specified loan.

j. The interests of the purchasers/lenders must be identical.

4. Securities issued or guaranteed by a bank or savings and loan.

5. Securities issued or guaranteed by a credit union.

6. Investment certificate in a loan company.

7. A security interest in a mortgage pool where loans are originated or purchased by a bank or savings and loan.

8. Securities sold to a financial institution.

9. Private offerings:

a. No more than 25 persons.

b. Sales to no more than 10 persons.

c. Preexisting business or personal relationships between issuers and investors.

10. Private offering of other securities not involving debts secured by real estate have different requirements for exemption.

11. Private offerings to institutional investors.

12. Real estate broker transactions in connection with a sale such as shares in a mutual water company that transfer with real estate.

CLASS DISCUSSION TOPICS

1. What transactions are you familiar with that have involved securities?

2. What role do securities play in our mortgage market?

3. How can commercial and industrial brokers use mortgage REITs?

4. In setting up a limited partnership to purchase a property, what can you do to reduce the likelihood of it being regarded later as a security?

5. Why would a loan broker fractionalize a mortgage by selling undivided interests?

CHAPTER 13 QUIZ

1. The Corporate Securities Act of 1968 requires that before a security can be sold: (p. 386)
    A. the seller must have a federal securities dealer license
    B. it must be qualified or exempt from qualification
    C. it must be appraised by a certified appraiser
    D. all of the above are required

2. Securities include all of the following EXCEPT: (p. 387)
    A. a condominium sale where the buyer must allow the property to be rented and managed by a management company
    B. stock of a corporation
    C. property owned by an investor which is used as security for a loan
    D. investment contracts

3. Which security would have the LOWEST RISK of losing the investment? (p. 389)
    A. Corporate Stock
    B. Limited Partnerships
    C. Mortgage-backed securities
    D. The last tranche

4. A former limited partnership investment in apartment buildings now has a different form of ownership. It is traded on the New York Stock Exchange as a: (p. 390)
    A. tranche
    B. REIT
    C. IO strip
    D. PO strip

5. A California issuer of securities sold only to California residents. These transactions are: (p. 391)
    A. interstate
    B. intrastate
    C. subject to the jurisdiction of the Department of Corporation
    D. both B and C

6. A real estate broker who offers and sells an undivided interest in notes secured by real property, would be a(n): (p. 394)
    A. issuer
    B. tranche
    C. IO
    D. CMO

7. A real estate broker in selling securities may be exempt from certification as a "broker-dealer" if: (p. 395)

    A. there is no public offer

    B. sales are to no more than 100 investors

    C. purchasers are buying for resale

    D. the sales are published

8. Transactions that may be exempt from qualification include: (p. 395)

    A. sales not involving a public offering

    B. sales where purchasers represent that they are buying for their own account

    C. both A and B

    D. neither A nor B

9. A person who violates the securities law may be: (pp. 395-396)

    A. subject to civil liability

    B. subject to criminal penalties

    C. subject to administrative action

    D. any or all of the above

10. Loan transactions exempt from California securities law include: (pp. 398-401)

    A. a note secured by real property sold to a single person

    B. a note secured by real property for which a permit was received from the Department of Corporations

    C. securities issued or guaranteed by a bank

    D. all of the above

11. Security transactions exempt from the California securities law include: (pp. 401-404)

    A. securities guaranteed by a credit union

    B. a security in a pool of mortgages originated or purchased by a bank

    C. securities sold to licensed financial institutions

    D. all of the above

12. Transactions exempt from qualification and permits include: (pp. 404-413)

    A. securities that are an integral part of a real estate broker transaction

    B. securities issued by a savings and loan

    C. real property securities

    D. all of the above

Securities in the Lending Industry

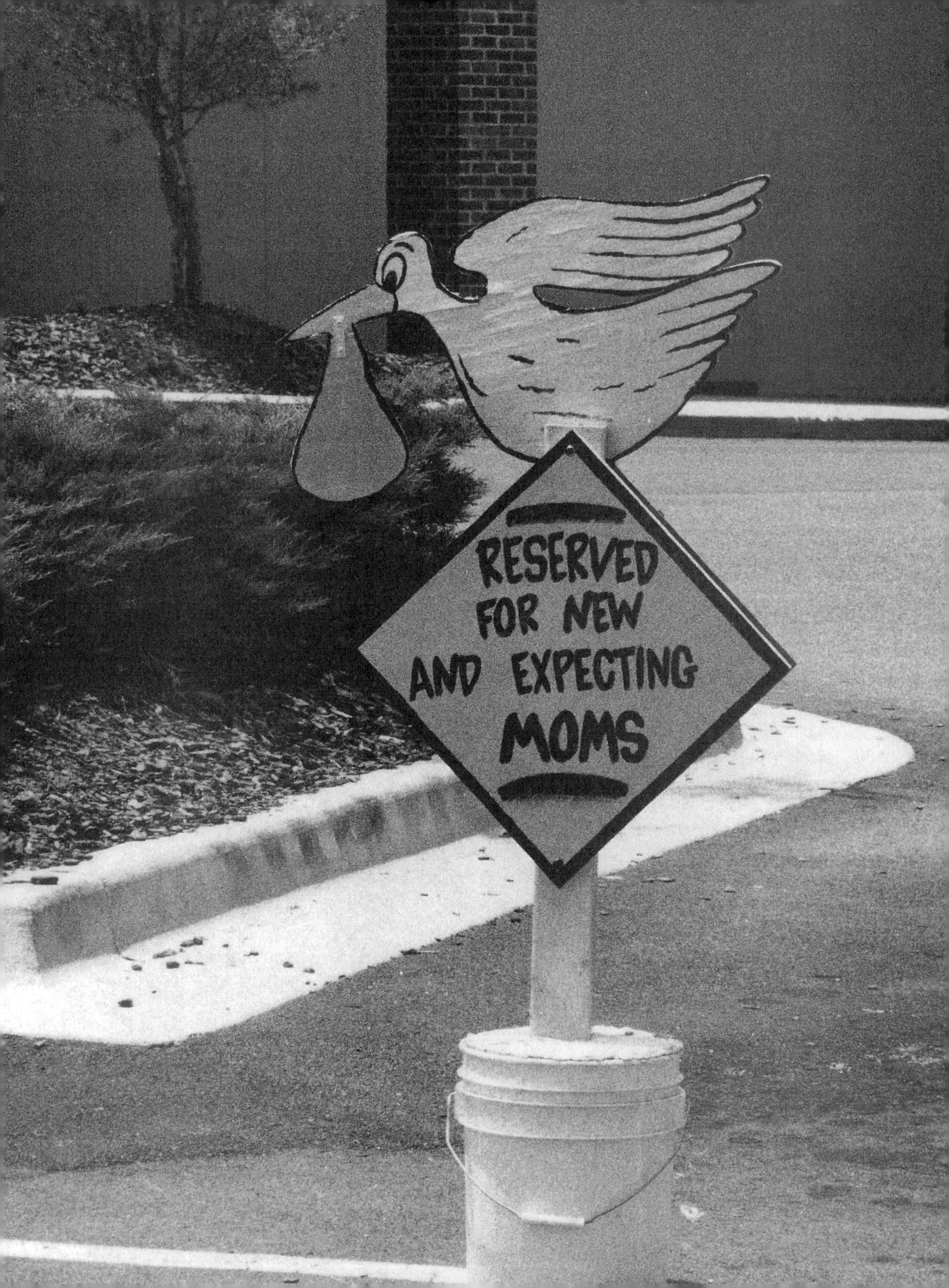
RESERVED
FOR NEW
AND EXPECTING
MOMS

Third Party Originators

KEY WORDS AND TERMS

Bait-and-Switch
Confirmation Letter
Cover Letter
Finder
Lock-in Form
Mortgage/Landlord Rating
Out of State Funding
Payoff Demand
Preliminary Title Report
Quality Control

Seller Carryback Financing
Stocking Order
Submission Sheets
Table Funding
Transmittal Form
Underwriter
Uniform Residential Loan Application
Verifications
Wholesale Agreements

LEARNING OBJECTIVES

This chapter will introduce you to third party originators who take loan applications and package them for submission to lenders. You will learn the role they play in mortgage lending and their duties in the conduct of their business. You will also be introduced to the loan package which is submitted to lenders for funding.

Definition - Third Party Orginator

Third party originators are parties who originate loans but are neither the lender nor the borrower.

They solicit borrowers and obtain loan applications. These loans are to be secured by real estate. They then submit a complete loan package to lenders who if they approve the loan will fund it.

Should the originator fund the loan with his or her own funds, then the broker would likely be regarded as a principal rather than a third party originator, even if the originator intended to immediately sell the loan to a lender. In fact, this would be a mortgage banking activity which is covered in Chapter 15.

On some larger loans, mortgage bankers will act as third party originators because of the amount of funds involved. More often, mortgage bankers act as principals in funding the loan for resale.

While third party originators prepare the loan for funding and take a significant paperwork function away from the lender, they do not close the transaction. They merely submit the loan for approval.

Why Third Party Originators?

While most California lending institutions are prepared to take loan applications and fund their own applications, many out-of-state lenders loan in California. California historically has been an importer of capital for funding real property loans. Out of state lenders who wish to have California loans have a choice of two methods to do so:

1. Out-of-state lenders can buy existing loans which have been funded by mortgage bankers (mortgage companies).
2. They can also be the original lender by utilizing the services of third party originators.

In addition, third party originators prepare loan packages for lenders not prepared to solicit loan applications, such as pension funds and trusts.

Some mortgage bankers use affiliated brokers to locate prospective borrowers and prepare loan packages to the mortgage banker's specifications. The mortgage banker will then fund the loan which they will later sell. The affiliate brokers are third party originators although they are doing so for just one lender, the mortgage company.

An advantage to the mortgage bankers is a significant expansion of operation without hiring additional employees (other than underwriters to check the loan packages for funding). The third party originators (affiliates) are independent contractors rather than employees and get paid by their loan production.

Licensing

A third party originator of loans secured by liens on real property must be licensed by the Department of Real Estate as a broker.

Section 10131(d) of the Business and Professions Code requires persons who "solicit borrowers," or "performs services for borrowers," to be licensed as real estate brokers.

Third party originators do both of these functions. After soliciting borrowers, they perform services for borrowers by preparing loan packages to be submitted to lenders. The borrower would pay service providers for services such as credit reports, appraisals, etc. In some cases third party originators perform some of the service functions.

As explained in Chapter 6, salespersons of the broker, the third party originator, must be supervised by the broker. Business and Profession Code 10177(h) provides that failure to exercise reasonable supervision of the activities of salespersons is grounds for disciplinary action against the broker. This applies to the officer designated by a corporate broker licensed as well as non-corporate brokers.

Salesperson of third party originators who solicit borrowers must be licensed as either a real estate salesperson or broker.

An employee whose activities were purely clerical in preparing loan application packages and did not solicit or sell borrowers on the services offered need not be licensed. Business and Professions Code 10133.2 is the clerical exemption from licensing.

Finders

A **_LOAN FINDER_** _is a person who, for a fee, will locate a lender for a borrower._ Finders look for prospective borrowers and try to match them with parties or lenders willing to make a required loan. In times of tight money, finders will charge substantial fees for their efforts. In some areas of the county, finders were known as "ten percenters" since it was common for finders who located lenders for difficult loans to charge 10% of the loan proceeds as their fee. Some "loan consultants" are really just finders.

Section 10131(d), in the definition of a broker, reads:

> **(d).** Solicits borrowers or lenders for or negotiates loans or collects payments or performs services for borrowers or lenders or note owners in connection with loans secured directly or collaterally by liens on real property or on a business opportunity.

> _While the language of the statute seems to be clear, the interpretation of the courts seems to disregard the clear intent of the legislature._

Finders do "solicit borrowers." However, the courts have determined that more than solicitation is needed to require licensing as a real estate broker. As long as the finder confines his or her activities to introducing the borrower to the lender, a broker's license is not required.

If the finder engages in any loan negotiation, then the finder would be engaging in an activity requiring a broker's license. If the finder was not licensed, and did negotiate with the lender, then the finder could not enforce his or her agreement for a finder's fee.

> _If a finder collects an advance fee then the finder must have a broker's license._

Business and Professions Code 10131.2 states:

> "A real estate broker is also a person who engages in the business of claiming, demanding, changing, collecting or contracting for the collection of an advance fee in connection with the sale or lease of real property or to obtain a loan or loans thereon."

An unlicensed finder who prepared a loan package for a borrower would apparently also be in violation of the law as this would constitute the performance of services for a borrowers.

Finders can engage in activities very similar to those of third party originators, with the exception of preparing the loan package, and avoid both licensing and regulation by the Department of Real Estate.

Finders therefore do not have to meet any educational or other minimum standards.

While not necessarily in the best interest of consumers, this is the current law.

Case Example

Tenzer v. Superscope, Inc. (1978) 39 C.A. 3d 18

A director of a corporation was asked by the corporate president to locate a buyer for corporate owned property. The president verbally agreed to pay the director a finders fee of 10 percent of the purchase price. The director (Tenzer) found a buyer who purchased the property for $16 million dollars. The corporation (Superscope) refused to pay Tenzer his $1.6 million finder's fee.

The court held that the statute of frauds did not apply (verbal agreements) because Tenzer revealed the name of the purchaser based on the verbal promise. Superscope was estopped from raising this as a defense.

The California Supreme Court indicated that their primary concern was if Tenzer was a "finder" or if he participated in negotiations, if he participated in the sale negotiations, then Tenzer would have had to be licensed to be entitled to a finder's fee.

The California Supreme Court sent the case back to the trial court to determine if Tenzer was a "finder" or a participant in negotiating the sale.

Case Example

Sullivan v. Hopkins (1970) 435 F.. 2d 1128

Kellogg wished to sell her ranch near Santa Barbara. She agreed orally to pay Sullivan, a friend, a commission of 5 percent of the purchase price if he could locate a buyer. Sullivan, who was not a real estate broker, contacted an attorney whom he knew in Denver. The attorney in turn interested several of his clients (Stegall and Hopkins) in the ranch. They all came to Santa Barbara where Sullivan introduced them to Kellogg and her attorney. The parties all assumed that Sullivan was a licensed real estate broker although there was no evidence that he claimed to be one. The parties entered into negotiations. While Sullivan did not participate in the negotiations, he supplied information requested by the parties. Such information was available to the public.

The parties entered into a written agreement for a sale price of $1,700,000.

As part of the agreement, the buyers agreed to pay the 5 percent commission to Sullivan ($85,000). The buyers later refused the payment because Sullivan was not a licensed real estate broker. Sullivan admitted this but claimed he was a finder.

The Court of Appeals pointed out that a finder receives a fee for bringing the parties together, however, the finder cannot be involved in negotiating the price or terms of the sale. All Sullivan was obligated to do was introduce the parties, which he did. He did not participate in negotiations. Negotiations were between the buyers and seller and their attorneys. The requested information which was supplied was simply in the spirit of helpfulness and did not effect the sale or Sullivan's status as a finder. Therefore, Sullivan was entitled to the finder's fee.

Agency

Third party originators can easily become dual agents (of borrower and lender) even if they did not intend such an agency. By aiding the prospective borrowers and working close with them, borrowers can easily be led to believe that the broker is representing them in obtaining financing. In many cases third party originators will counsel loan applicants not to make any significant credit purchases, such as new furniture or a car, until their loan has been funded. A court could very well determine that prospective borrowers were reasonable in believing that the broker represented them.

Of course in some cases the broker will intend to represent the borrower or even be a dual agent of both borrower and lender.

> *Third party originators should make their agency relationships clear before any funds are received for services required.*

A good time to do so would be contemporaneously with filling out the loan application. The borrowers should sign a statement provided by the agent showing that they understand and consent to the agent's declared agency.

Many third party originators deal with only one lender. It is clear that in such a case the third party originator would have agency duties to that lender. The agent could be a lender's agent or a dual agent.

When the agent intends to "shop around" a loan application, the agent is more likely to be a borrower's agent than a lender's agent, although dual agency is possible.

The importance of agency deals with the fiduciary duties is explained in Chapter 7. When problems arise, the parties tend to use 20/20 hindsight and sue, claiming the agent had a duty to protect them against the other party or to disclose some fact that at the time might not have seemed of great importance.

> *Business and Professions Code 10176(d) provides that acting for more than one party in a transaction (dual agency) without the knowledge or consent of all parties is grounds for disciplinary action against the licensee.*

Advertising

NAME

Like all real estate licensee advertising, third party originators, in advertising their services, must indicate that they are a real estate licensee (Business and Professions Code 10140.6).

Disclosure of Licensed Status in Advertising

10140.6. A real estate licensee shall not publish, circulate, distribute nor cause to be published, circulated or distributed in any newspaper or periodical, or by mail, any matter pertaining to any activity for which a real estate license is required which does not contain a designation disclosing that he or she is performing acts for which a real estate license is required.

The provisions of this section shall not apply to classified rental advertisements reciting the telephone number at the premises of the property offered for rent or the address of the property offered for rent.

Commissioners Regulations 2770.1 allows license designation to be an abbreviation such as "bro." or "agt."

Use of the terms and abbreviations set forth above do not satisfy the requirements of Sections 10235.5 and 17539.4 of the Code.

This abbreviation, while allowed in normal brokerage, is not enough by itself for an arranger of loans.

Business and Professions Code 10235.5 requires that a licensee's advertisement include the broker's license number under which the loan would be made or arranged.

THRESHOLD REQUIREMENT

Prior to recent changes in the real estate law (Business and Professions Code 10232.1 and 10232), real estate brokers who met threshold requirements were required to submit advertising to the real estate commissioner for approval. The thresholds requiring submission to the commissioner for a 12-month period were:

1. Negotiate a combination of 20 transactions in an aggregate amount of more than $2 million from the following:

   a. Loans secured by liens on real property or business opportunities.

   b. Sales or exchange of real property sales contracts or notes secured by real property (Trust Deeds).

   c. Sales or exchange (as the owner) of sales contracts or notes secured by real property.

2. Make collections of $500,000 or more on behalf of owners on promissory notes secured by real property (servicing trust deeds).

3. Make collections of $500,000 or more on behalf of obligors of trust deeds.

Even prior to the changes making submission of advertising voluntary rather than mandatory, most third party originators were exempt from submission of advertising under Business and Professions Code 10232(d) which is now 10232(c). Exempt in determining threshold numbers are banks, savings banks, pension funds having a net worth of $15 million or more, licensed brokers, etc. These are the lenders to whom most third party originators submit loan packages.

> *Persons under common management, direction or control in conducting the activities enumerated above shall be considered as one person for the purpose of applying the above criteria.*

Because Business and Professions Code 10232.1 now reads "may submit" rather than the prior "shall," no prior submission of advertising for approval is required. However, if such approval is sought, failure of the DRE to notify the broker within 15 calendar days from receipt of the request shall constitute approval by the DRE.

Proposed Advertising - Submission - Fee - Regulations - Duration of Approval

10232.1(a). A real estate broker, prior to the use of any proposed advertisement in connection with the conduct of activities described in subdivisions (d) and (d) of Section 10131 and Section 10131.1, may submit a true copy thereof to the Department of Real Estate for approval...

To be on the "safe side," many third party originators do submit advertising to the commissioner. It removes any danger that the DRE might later decide the advertising is misleading or otherwise violates statutes or regulations.

BAIT-AND-SWITCH

Bait-and-switch advertising is an illegal activity policed by the Federal Trade Commission (FTC).

A *BAIT-AND-SWITCH advertisement is one which advertises a product or service and/or price that will not be available to the consumer.* Instead, the consumer is led to something other than what he or she contacted the broker about which is usually at a different price.

Making disparaging remarks about an advertised loan in order to promote another loan would also be regarded by the FTC as bait-and-switch advertising.

Another example of bait-and-switch advertising would be advertising no-point loans when the advertiser realizes that such loans are unlikely to be obtained at the APR advertised. The third party originator would then prepare the loan package and submit it to the lender who would agree to fund the loan with designated points. Because the borrower has been anticipating a loan, and the fact that going to another lender for a loan at the interest rate quoted would involve points, the borrower is likely to acquiesce to the points.

The above scenario, while fictitious, would not only be reprehensible conduct from a moral standpoint, it would also be illegal bait-and-switch advertising.

Still another variety of bait-and-switch is a tactic that was formerly prevalent with small direct lenders. They would quote competitive rates and tell the borrower that the loan was certain to be approved by their loan committee. They would delay approval and finally tell the borrower that because of some reason or other the points had to be increased or interest raised. The borrower often was forced to accept the new terms because there was not sufficient time to find another loan.

The prohibition against bait-and-switch advertising applies to all lenders and arrangers of credit.

The FTC may ask the attorney general to bring charges against an advertiser which can result in six months imprisonment and/or a fine.

Trust Fund Handling

Third party originators of loans secured by real property are required to be real estate brokers [Business and Professions Code 10131(d)]. Therefore, the trust fund handling procedures and regulations of Chapter 11 apply to third party originators. Thus, the third party orginator must make certain that the following procedures are followed.

DESIGNATION OF ACCOUNT

The trust fund account must be designated as a trust account.

DEPOSITS RECEIVED BY BROKER

Deposits received by the broker can be deposited with:

1. Escrow
2. Trust account
3. Service provider
4. Principal

INTEREST BEARING

Trust accounts generally cannot be interest bearing accounts for which a prior withdrawal notice is required. However, funds may be placed in an interest bearing account at the request of the person depositing such funds. While it is not likely that third party originators will have interest bearing accounts, if they do the following criteria is required to be met:

1. **Name of Broker.** The account must be in the broker's name as a trustee.
2. **FDIC Insurance.** Deposits must be covered by insurance.
3. **Separate Accounts.** Commingling of interest bearing funds with other beneficiaries is not allowed for interest bearing trust funds for a loan transaction.
4. **Disclosure.** The broker must disclose to person depositing funds:

    a. the nature of the account.

    b. how interest will be calculated and paid.

    c. who will pay the service charges for the account.

    d. any notice of withdrawal requirements and penalties.

5. **Broker Not to Benefit.** Interest earned may not benefit the broker or any person licensed under the broker either directly or indirectly.
6. **Who Gets the Interest.** The loan application must have specified who gets the interest.
7. **Examination of Records.** The broker, upon request, must furnish the Real Estate Commissioner authorization to examine the financial records of interest bearing accounts.

ADVANCE FEES

Advertising

Solicitation material for advance fee transactions require 10 days notice to the commissioner prior to use.

BROKER FUNDS IN TRUST ACCOUNT

A broker can keep no more than $200 of his or her own funds in the trust account.

COMMINGLING

A broker may not mix trust funds and personal funds although funds of multiple beneficiaries may be maintained in the same noninterest-bearing trust account.

WITHDRAWALS

Withdrawals from the trust account may be made by:

1. **The Broker**
2. **A Licensed Employee**. A licensed employee can withdraw funds with broker authorization.
3. **Non-licensed Employees.** An employee can withdrawal funds from the trust account if bonded and authorized to do so.

CONFLICTING CLAIMS

If more than one party makes a claim to funds held in trust, the broker should commence with an interpleader action where the court will decide as to rights of the parties to the funds.

OFFSET OF TRUST FUNDS

The broker may not use trust-fund deposits to offset any claim the broker might have against persons with an interest in the funds.

TRUST ACCOUNT RECORDS

Records must include:

1. **Date.** When the funds were received.
2. **Source.** Name of person depositing funds.
3. **Amount.** Amount received.

4. **Date Deposited.** When funds were placed in the trust account.

5. **Disbursement Data.** Check numbers and payee information.

6. **Pass-Through Funds.** Identify to whom depository or service provider funds were remitted to.

7. **Daily Balance.** Account must be balanced daily and reconciled monthly.

8. **Service Providers.** A record need not be kept of checks of $1,000 or less that are made out directly to service providers.

Reports

The quarterly and fiscal year reports as covered in Business and Professions Code 10232.2 and 10232.25 generally need not be filed by third party arrangers since the same threshold requirement apply to these reports as apply to submission of advertising (Business and Professions Code 10232). Exempt from the threshold numbers are transactions where the lender is a bank, a subsidiary of a bank, trust company, savings bank, credit union industrial loan company, commercial finance lender, personal property broker, consumer finance lender, insurance company, public corporation, trustees of pension plans having a net worth of $15,000,000 or more, licensed residential mortgage lender and real estate brokers. Few third party originators would meet the threshold requirements for reporting unless they used small pension funds (under $15,000,000 in net worth) and private trusts to fund their loans.

The reporting requirements as to quarterly status and fiscal year reports can be found in Chapter 11.

Disclosures

TRUTH-IN-LENDING DISCLOSURE

"Arranger of credit" was deleted from the definition of creditor in the Truth-In-Lending Act. This effectively exempts third party originators from the requirements of disclosure of loan terms.

The broker would still be bound in his or her advertising to full disclosure if any trigger terms were used in the ads.

However, the disclosures must be made by the lender. Truth-in-lending advertising requirements apply to third party originators. However, the loan disclosures would be made by the lender. See Chapter 8 for disclosure requirements.

MORTGAGE LOAN DISCLOSURE STATEMENT

In making a solicitation to a person for a real property secured loan, a real estate broker must supply a disclosure statement to the person solicited (Business and Professions Code 10232.4).

The statement must be given to the borrower as early as practicable and before receiving any funds from the prospective borrower (costs and fees).

Exemptions

The disclosure applies to lenders as well as purchasers. However, the disclosure to lenders does not apply if the lender is a bank, savings bank, credit union, industrial bank, industrial loan company or other licensed lender or broker as well as pension plans having a net worth of $15,000,000 or more [Business and Professions Code 10232.4(4)]. Therefore, a third party originator generally would not be required to provide lender disclosure, although disclosures must be made to borrowers.

Contents

Department of Real Estate disclosure statements are duplicated in Chapter 15. As a minimum the disclosure must include:

1. Adequate identification of the real property which will secure the loan.

2. An estimated value of the property.

3. Age, size type of construction and description of property improvements.

4. Identify of borrower (occupation, employment, income, credit, etc.,) as related by the borrower.

5. Terms of any note.

6. Information as to encumbrances.

7. Provision, if any for, servicing the loan.

8. Benefits to the broker.

Although the third party arranger is responsible for the disclosure statement because of soliciting for the loan, the disclosure statement may in fact be provided by the lender.

Some of the information required in the disclosure statement, such as loan terms, might not be available to the third party originator.

Completion

The name of the lender would normally be marked as "unknown" unless the originator deals only with one lender.

Form RE883 (Mortgage Loan Disclosure Statement/Good Faith Estimate) also meets the requirements of RESPA in providing the Good Faith Estimate of closing costs (See Chapter 15).

Proposed loan terms, payments and prepayments are to be included as well as the notice to borrower as to balloon payments.

A statement must be included that the loan does not require credit life and/or disability insurance. Current liens must be listed as well as any liens which will remain after the proposed loan is made.

Material Changes

The borrower must be informed of any material changes prior to the close of escrow.

Government Loans

A disclosure statement is not required to be given if the lender or purchaser of the loan is the Untied States, or any unit of state or federal government, the Federal National Mortgage Association, the Government National Mortgage Association, federal Home Loan Mortgage Corporation, FHA or the Department of Veterans Affairs.

FAIR HOUSING

Civil Code 1785.1 deals with credit reporting agencies. The legislature felt that there was a need to insure that consumer credit reporting agencies exercised their responsibilities with fairness, impartiality and respect for the consumer's rights to privacy.

1785.1. Legislative Findings and Declaration

The Legislature finds and declares as follows:

(a). An elaborate mechanism has been developed for investigating and evaluating the credit worthiness, credit standing, credit capacity and general reputation of consumers.

(b). Consumer credit reporting agencies have assumed a vital role in assembling and evaluating consumer credit and other information on consumers.

(c). There is a need to insure that consumer credit reporting agencies exercise their grave responsibilities with fairness, impartiality and a respect for the consumer's right to privacy.

(d). It is the purpose of this title to require that consumer credit reporting agencies adopt reasonable procedures for meeting the needs of commerce for consumer credit, personnel, insurance, hiring of a dwelling unit and other information in a manner which is fair and equitable to the consumer, with regard to the confidentiality, accuracy, relevancy and proper utilization of such information in accordance with the requirements of this title.

(e). The Legislature hereby intends to regulate consumer credit reporting agencies pursuant to this title in a manner which will best protect the interests of the people of the State of California.

(f). The extension of credit is a privilege and not a right. Nothing in this title shall preclude a creditor from denying credit to any applicant providing such denial is based on factors not inconsistent with present law.

(g). Any clauses in contracts which prohibit any action required by this title are not in the public interest and shall be considered unenforceable. This shall not invalidate the other terms of such a contract.

Civil Code 1785.1 et. seg. (The California Consumer Credit Reporting Agencies Act) is similar to the Federal Fair Credit Reporting Act (See Chapter 10) in that the consumer has the right to know what is in his or her credit file, as well as the right to have obsolete material removed.

Users of consumer credit agency material have the right to disclose the contents of the consumer credit report to the consumer. Consumers also have the right to request and receive a decoded version of their file as well as the information set forth in Civil Code 1785.15.

1785.15. Supply Files and Information; Right to Information

(a). A consumer credit reporting agency shall supply files and information required under Section 1785.10 during normal business hours and on reasonable notice**...**

(b). Files maintained on a consumer shall be disclosed promptly as follows:

> (1) In person, at the location where the consumer credit reporting agency maintains the trained personnel required by subdivision (d), if he or she appears in person and furnishes proper identification.
> (2) By mail, if the consumer makes a written request with proper identification for a copy of the file or a decoded written version of that file to be sent to the consumer at a specified address**...**

(c). "Proper identification," as used in subdivision (b), means that information generally deemed sufficient to identify a person**...**

(f). ... The written summary of rights required under this subdivision is sufficient if in substantially the following form:

"You have a right to obtain a copy of your credit file from a consumer credit reporting agency. You may be charged a reasonable fee not exceeding eight dollars ($8). There is no fee, however, if you have been turned down for credit, employment, insurance or a rental dwelling because of information in your credit report within the preceding 60 days. The consumer credit reporting agency must provide someone to help you interpret the information in your credit file.

You have a right to dispute inaccurate information by contacting the consumer credit reporting agency directly. However, neither you nor any credit repair company or credit service organization has the right to have accurate, current and verifiable information removed from your credit report. Under the Federal Fair Credit Reporting Act, the consumer credit reporting agency must remove accurate, negative information from your report only if it is over seven years old. Bankruptcy information can be reported for 10 years.

If you have notified a credit reporting agency in writing that you dispute the accuracy of information in your file, the consumer credit reporting agency must then, within 30 business days, reinvestigate and modify or remove inaccurate information. The consumer credit reporting agency may not charge a fee for this service. Any pertinent information and copies of all documents you have concerning an error should be given to the consumer credit reporting agency.

"If reinvestigation does not resolve the dispute to your satisfaction, you may send a brief statement to the consumer credit reporting agency to keep in your file, explaining why you think the record is inaccurate. The consumer credit reporting agency must include your statement about disputed information in a report it issues about you.

"You have a right to receive a record of all inquiries relating to a credit transaction initiated in six months preceding your request. This record shall include the recipients of any consumer credit report.

"You may request in writing that the information contained in your file not be provided to a third party for marketing purposes.

"You have a right to bring civil action against anyone who improperly obtains access to a file or knowingly or willfully misuses file data."

> *Fair Housing disclosures also include the Equal Housing Lender Poster (See Chapter 10).*

HOME MORTGAGE DISCLOSURE ACT

This is a federal act that requires lenders disclosure of loan applications received and loans made by area.

> *The purpose of this act is to highlight and thus eliminate lender redlining (See Chapter 10).*

The Home Mortgage Disclosure Act does not apply to third party originators but does apply to the lenders who deal with third party originators if they are depository institutions.

Information, as set forth in Chapter 10, must be compiled and be made available to the public as well as filed with HUD.

SELLER CARRYBACK FINANCING

When the seller is to carry back financing, a disclosure statement must be provided to both the seller and buyer. (See Chapter 9). This is set forth in Civil Code 2956 and 2963.

It would be extremely rare for a third party originator to be involved in seller carryback financing. Most loan applications prepared by third party originators are for home purchase (first trust deeds) or home equity loans and would generally not involve seller financing. The arranger of credit is responsible for this disclosure who would normally be the listing or selling broker.

REAL ESTATE SETTLEMENT PROCEDURES ACT

RESPA and required disclosures are set forth in Chapter 9.

12 U.S.C.S. 2603 Section 2500.5(b)(7), states that "neither the creation of a dealer loan or dealer consumer credit contract, nor the first assignment of such a loan or contract to a lender is a secondary market transaction." This would make a transfer subject to RESPA when the loan was made by a dealer and later resold.

The intention, at the time the loan was made, was resale.

EQUAL CREDIT OPPORTUNITY ACT

This act and disclosure requirements are set forth in Chapter 10.

TRANSFER DISCLOSURE

If a loan is to be for a home purchase, the seller has disclosure requirements (Civil Code 1102 et. seg.).

Violations of the Code do not invalidate the transfer.

The seller's disclosure deals with physical elements known to the seller as well as zoning problems, neighborhood problems, homeowner associations, flood problems, citations against the property, hazardous substances, etc.

The seller Transfer Disclosure Statement is often combined with the agent's disclosure based on a reasonable inspection of the property. A new disclosure form set forth in Civil Code 1102.6 became effective July 1, 1997.

Required Disclosure Form (Text of section operative July 1, 1997)

1102.6. The disclosures required by this article pertaining to the property proposed to be transferred are set forth in, and shall be made on a copy of, the following disclosure form:

REAL ESTATE TRANSFER DISCLOSURE STATEMENT

THIS DISCLOSURE STATEMENT CONCERNS THE REAL PROPERTY SITUATED IN THE CITY OF _____, COUNTY OF _____, STATE OF CALIFORNIA DESCRIBED AS _____. THIS STATEMENT IS A DISCLOSURE OF THE CONDITION OF THE ABOVE DESCRIBED PROPERTY IN COMPLIANCE WITH SECTION 1102 OF THE CIVIL CODE AS OF ___, 19___, IT IS NOT A WARRANTY OF ANY KIND BY THE SELLER(S) OF ANY AGENT(S) REPRESENTING ANY PRINCIPAL(S) IN THIS TRANSACTION, AND IS NOT A SUBSTITUTE FOR ANY INSPECTIONS OR WARRANTIES THE PRINCIPAL(S) MAY WISH TO OBTAIN.

I

COORDINATION WITH OTHER DISCLOSURE FORMS

This Real Estate Transfer Disclosure Statement is made pursuant to Section 1102 of the Civil Code. Other statutes require disclosures, depending upon the details of the particular real estate transaction (for example: special study zone and purchase-money liens on residential property).

Substituted Disclosures: The following disclosures have or will be made in connection with this real estate transfer, and are intended to satisfy the disclosure obligations on this form, where the subject matter is the same:
___ Inspection reports completed pursuant to the contract of sale or receipt for deposit.
___ Additional inspection reports or disclosures:

_____

_____

_____

II

SELLER'S INFORMATION

The Seller discloses the following information with the knowledge that even though this is not a warranty, prospective Buyers may rely on this information in deciding whether and on what terms to purchase the subject property.

Seller hereby authorizes any agent(s) representing any principal(s) in this transaction to provide a copy of this statement to any person or entity in connection with any actual or anticipated sale of the property.

THE FOLLOWING ARE REPRESENTATIONS MADE BY THE SELLER(S) AND ARE NOT THE REPRESENTATIONS OF THE AGENT(S), IF ANY. THIS INFORMATION IS A DISCLOSURE AND IS NOT INTENDED TO BE PART OF ANY CONTRACT BETWEEN THE BUYER AND SELLER.

Seller _____ is _____ is not occupying the property.

A. The subject property has the items checked below (read across):

_ Range	_ Oven	_ Microwave
_ Dishwasher	_ Trash Compactor	_ Garbage Disposal
_ Washer/Dryer Hookups		_ Rain Gutters
_ Burglar Alarms	_ Smoke Detector(s)	_ Fire Alarm
_ TV Antenna	_ Satellite Dish	_ Intercom
_ Central Heating	_ Central Air Cond.	_ Evaporative Cooler(s)
_ Wall/Window Air Cond.	_ Sprinklers	_ Public Sewer System
_ Septic Tank	_ Sump Pump	_ Water Softener
_ Patio/Decking	_ Built-in Barbecue	_ Gazebo
_ Sauna		
_ Hot Tub-Locking Safety Cover*	_ Pool-Child Resistant Barrier*	_ Spa-Locking Safety Cover*
_ Security Gate(s)	_ Automatic Garage Opener(s)*	_ Number Remote Controls
Garage:_Attached	_ Not Attached	_ Carport
Pool/Spa Heater:_Gas	_ Solar	_ Electric
Water Heater:_Gas	_ Water Heater Braced, or Strapped	_ Private Utility or Other _____
Water Supply:_City	_ Well	
Gas Supply: _Utility	_ Bottled	
_Window Screens	_ Window Security Bars	
	_ Quick Release Mechanism on Bedroom Windows*	

Exhaust Fan(s) in __ 220 Volt Wiring in __ Fireplace(s) in __
Gas Starter _____ Roof(s): Type:_____ Age:_(approx.)
Other: _____

Are there, to the best of your (Seller's) knowledge, any of the above that are not in operating condition? __Yes __ No. If yes, then describe.

(Attach, additional sheets if necessary): _____

_____

_____

_____

B. Are you (Seller) aware of any significant defects/malfunctions in any of the following? __Yes __ No. If yes, check appropriate space(s) below.
_Interior Walls _Ceilings _Floors _Exterior Walls _Insulation
_Roof(s) _Windows _Doors _Foundation _Slab(s) _Driveways
__Sidewalks __Walls/Fences __Electric Systems __Plumbing/Sewers/Septics
Other Structural Components (Describe: _____

_____

If any of the above is checked, explain. (Attach additional sheets if necessary):

_____

_____

_____

* This garage door opener or child resistant pool barrier may not be in compliance with the safety standards relating to automatic reversing devices as set forth in Chapter 12.5 (commencing with Section 19890) of Part 3 of Division 13 of, or with the pool safety standards of Article 2.5 (commencing with Section 115920) of Chapter 5 of Part 10 of Division 104 of the Health and Safety Code. The water heater may not be anchored, braced or strapped in accordance with Section 19211 of the Health and Safety Code. Window security bars may not have quick-release mechanisms in compliance with the 1995 Edition of the California Building Standards Code.

C. Are you (Seller) aware of any of the following:

1. Substances, materials or products which may be an environmental hazard such as, but not limited to, asbestos, formaldehyde, radon gas, lead-based paint, fuel or chemical storage tanks and contaminated soil or water on the subject property.._Yes _No

2. Features of the property shared in common with adjoining landowners, such as walls, fences, and driveways, whose use or responsibility for maintenance may have an effect on the subject property............._Yes _No

3. Any encroachments, easements or similar matters that may affect your interest in the subject property.._Yes _No

4. Room additions, structural modifications or other alterations or repairs made without necessary permits.._Yes _No

5. Room additions, structural modifications or other alterations or repairs not in compliance with building codes..._Yes _No

6. Fill (compacted or otherwise) on the property or any portion thereof...._Yes _No

7. Any settling from any cause, or slippage, sliding or other soil problems.._Yes _No

8. Flooding, drainage or grading problems...................................._Yes _No

9. Major damage to the property or any of the structures from fire, earthquake, floods, or landslides..._Yes _No

10. Any zoning violations, nonconforming uses, violations of "setback" requirements.. _Yes _No

11. Neighborhood noise problems or other nuisances...................._Yes _No

12. CC&R's or other deed restrictions or obligations......................._Yes _No

13. Homeowners' Association which has an authority over the subject property..._Yes _No

14. Any "common area" (facilities such as pools, tennis courts, walkways or other areas co-owned in undivided interest with others).................._Yes _No

15. Any notices of abatement or citations against the property..._Yes _No

16. Any lawsuits by or against the seller threatening to or affecting this real property, including any lawsuits alleging a defect or deficiency in this real property or "common areas" (facilities such as pools, tennis courts, walkways or other areas co-owned in undivided interest with others)............._Yes _No

If the answer to any of these is yes, explain. (Attach additional sheets if necessary)_____

_____

_____

Seller certifies that the information herein is true and correct to the best of the Seller's knowledge as of the date signed by the Seller.

Seller _____ Date _____
Seller _____ Date _____

III

AGENTS INSPECTION DISCLOSURE

(to be completed only if the Seller is represented by an agent in this transaction.)

THE UNDERSIGNED, BASED ON THE ABOVE INQUIRY OF THE SELLER(S) AS TO THE CONDITION OF THE PROPERTY AND BASED ON A REASONABLY COMPETENT AND DILIGENT VISUAL INSPECTION OF THE ACCESSIBLE AREAS OF THE PROPERTY IN CONJUNCTION WITH THAT INQUIRY, STATES THE FOLLOWING:

_Agent notes no items for disclosure.
_Agent notes the following items:

_____
_____
_____

Agent(Broker
Representing Seller)_____ By_____ Date _____
               (Please Print)   (Associate Licensee
                                 or Broker-Signature)

IV

AGENTS INSPECTION DISCLOSURE

(to be completed only if the agent who has obtained the offer is other than the agent above.)

THE UNDERSIGNED, BASED ON A REASONABLY COMPETENT AND DILIGENT VISUAL INSPECTION OF THE ACCESSIBLE AREAS OF THE PROPERTY, STATES THE FOLLOWING:

_Agent notes no items for disclosure.
_Agent notes the following items:

_____
_____
_____
_____

Agent (Broker
obtaining the Offer)_____ By_____ Date_____
        (Please Print)   (Associate Licensee
                  or Broker-Signature)

V

BUYER(S) AND SELLER(S) MAY WISH TO OBTAIN PROFESSIONAL ADVICE AND/OR INSPECTIONS OF THE PROPERTY AND TO PROVIDE FOR APPROPRIATE PROVISIONS IN A CONTRACT BETWEEN BUYER AND SELLER(S) WITH RESPECT TO ANY ADVICE/INSPECTIONS/DEFECTS.

I/WE ACKNOWLEDGE RECEIPT OF A COPY OF THIS STATEMENT

Seller_____ Date_____ Buyer_____ Date_____
Seller_____ Date_____ Buyer_____ Date_____

_Agent (Broker
Representing Seller) _____ By_____ Date_____
                           (Associate Licensee
                           or Broker-Signature)

_Agent (Broker
Obtaining the Offer) _____ By_____ Date_____
                           (Associate Licensee
                           or Broker-Signature)

SECTION 1102.3 OF THE CIVIL CODE PROVIDES A BUYER WITH THE RIGHT TO RESCIND A PURCHASE CONTRACT FOR AT LEAST THREE DAYS AFTER THE DELIVERY OF THIS DISCLOSURE IF DELIVERY OCCURS AFTER THE SIGNING OF AN OFFER TO PURCHASE. IF YOU WISH TO RESCIND THE CONTRACT, YOU MUST ACT WITHIN THE PRESCRIBED PERIOD.

A REAL ESTATE BROKER IS QUALIFIED TO ADVISE ON REAL ESTATE. IF YOU DESIRE LEGAL ADVICE, CONSULT YOUR ATTORNEY.

_____
_____
_____
_____

Agent (Broker
obtaining the Offer)_____ By_____ Date_____
(Please Print)   (Associate Licensee
                         or Broker-Signature)

WRITTEN AUTHORIZATION TO RUN A CREDIT REPORT

An investigative credit report cannot be made without full disclosure to the consumer that the report will be made and why.

When there is insufficient or no data in a prospective borrower's credit file, an investigative report would be required. The third party arranger would order the report and it would be one of the loan documents for processing that would be forwarded to the lender (See Chapter 10).

Forms and Stacking Order

If a loan may be resold on the secondary mortgage market to Fannie Mae or Freddie Mac or is to be used for the issuance of government backed securities, the lender will be extremely particular as to the loan application packet. This includes the proper forms as well as the order the forms and other documents are arranged in the packet. A proper package can be processed by a lender in an expeditious manner.

FORMS

Uniform Underwriting and Transmittal Summary

See Freddie Mac Form 1077 (Figures 14-1 and 14-2).

Loan Application

(Fannie Mae 1003). This form is known as the Uniform Residential Loan Application (See Figures 14-3 through 14-6).

It sets forth the loan applied for, property information, borrower information, employment information, income and expense information as well as the consumer's assets and liabilities.

Figure 14-1

Uniform Underwriting and Transmittal Summary

I. Borrower and Property Information

Borrower Name _____   SSN: _____

Co-Borrower Name _____   SSN: _____

Property Address _____

Property Type
- [ ] Detached Housing
- [ ] Attached Housing
- [ ] Condominimun
- [ ] PUD   [ ] CO-OP

Project Classification
- [ ] A/III Condo   [ ] E PUD   [ ] 1 CO-OP
- [ ] B/II Condo   [ ] F PUD   [ ] 2 CO-OP
- [ ] C/I Condo   [ ] III PUD

Project Name _____

Occupancy Status
- [X] Primary Residence
- [ ] Second Home
- [ ] Investment Property

Number of Units _____

Sales Price _____

Appraised Value _____

II. Mortgage Information

Loan Type
- [X] Conventional
- [ ] FHA
- [ ] VA
- [ ] FmHa

Amortization Type
- [ ] Fixed-rate--Monthly Payments
- [ ] Fixed-rate--Bi-Weekly Payments
- [ ] Balloon
- [ ] ARM (type) _____
- [ ] Other (specify)_____

Loan Purpose Type
- [X] Purchase
- [ ] Cash-Out Refinance
- [ ] No Cash-Out Refinance

Purpose of Refinance _____

Lien Position
- [X] First Mortgage
- [ ] Second Mortgage

Amount of Subordinate Financing _____

Note Information

Original Loan Amount _____

Initial P&I Payment _____

Initial Note Rate _____ **%**

Note Date _____

Term (in months) _____ **0 months**

Mortgage Originator
- [ ] Seller
- [ ] Third Party

Third Party Name: _____

Buydown
- [ ] Yes
- [ ] No

If Second Mortgage

Owner of First Mortgage
- [ ] Fannie Mae   [ ] Freddie Mac
- [ ] Seller/Other

Original Loan Amount of First Mortgage _____

III. Underwriting Information

Underwriter's Name _____   Appraiser's Name/License # _____   Appraisal Company Name _____

Stable Monthly Income

	Borrower	Co-Borrower	Total
Base Income	_____	_____	$0.00
Other Income	_____	_____	0.00
Total	$0.00	$0.00	$0.00
Positive Cash Flow (Subject Property)			_____
Total Income			$0.00

Qualifying Ratios

Primary Housing Expense/Income _____ **%**

Total Obligations/Income _____ **%**

Loan-to-Value Ratios

LTV _____ **%**

Total LTV _____ **%**

- [ ] Note Rate __0.000%__
- [ ] _____ % Above Note Rate _____
- [ ] _____ % Below Note Rate _____

- [ ] Bought Down Rate _____
- [ ] Other _____

Proposed Monthly Payments
Borrowers Primary Residence

First Mortgage P&I	$0.00
Second Mortgage P&I	_____
Hazard Insurance	_____
Taxes	_____
Mortgage Insurance	_____
Homeowners Association Fees	_____
Lease/Ground Rent	_____
Other	_____
Total Primary Housing Expenses	$0.00
Other Obligations	
Negative Cash Flow (subject property)	_____
All Other Monthly Payments	_____
Total All Monthly Payments	$0.00

Underwriter Comments (If more space is needed, use page two)_____

_____

_____

_____

_____

_____

_____

_____

_____

_____

IV. Seller, Contract, and Contact Information

Seller Name _____

Seller Address _____

Seller No. _____ Investor Loan No. _____

Seller Loan No. _____

Master Commitment No. _____

Contract Number _____

Contact Name _____

Contact Title _____

Contact's Phone Number _____

Contact's Signature _____

Date _____

Type of Commitment   [ ] Standard   [ ] Negotiated

V. Delivery Data (Completion of this section is optional; however, the data must be transmitted on the applicable Fannie Mae or Freddie Mac delivery form when the mortgage is delivered for sale.) (See FNMA 1008A/FHLMC 1077A for a list of valid codes).

Borrower Information

Number of Borrowers _____

Borrower Age _____

Co-Borrower Age _____

Are any of the occupant borrowers first time homebuyers?   [ ] Yes   [ ] No

Property Information

Number of Bedrooms

		Gross Monthly Rents		Year Built _____
Unit 1	_____	Unit 1	_____	
Unit 2	_____	Unit 2	_____	
Unit 3	_____	Unit 3	_____	
Unit 4	_____	Unit 4	_____	

Information for Government Monitoring Purposes Only

Borrower Race Code __0__   Borrower Gender Code __0__   Co-Borrower Race Code __0__   Co-Borrower Gender Code __0__

Mortgage Insurance

Mortgage Insurer (MI) Code _____

Certificate Number _____

Percentage of Coverage _____

Adjuster Coverage   [ ] Yes   [ ] No

Special Feature/Characteristics Codes

Code 1 _____   Code 3 _____   Code 5 _____

Code 2 _____   Code 4 _____   Code 6 _____

Freddie Mac Form 1077 11/92
Wasatch Document Systems
To order: 800-453-7900

Fannie Mae Form 1008 11/92

Figure 14-2

(Completion of this section is optional; however, the data must be transmitted on the applicable Fannie Mae or Freddie Mac delivery form when the mortgage is delivered for sale.) (See FNMA 1008A/FHLMC 1077A for a list of valid codes.)

A. All Mortgages

Loan Information

First P&I Payment Date _____

Current UPB _____

Fannie Mae Only

Assumable ☐ Yes ☐ No

Interest Only ☐ Yes ☐ No

Interest Only End Date _____

FHA/VA Section of Act _____

Original term (in months) _____

Amortization Term (in months) _____

Maximum Term (in months) _____

Due Date of Last Paid
Installment _____

Freddie Mac Only

Reduced Documentation ☐ Yes ☐ No

Loan Feature Code _____

Interest Paid-to-Date _____

Note Maturity Date _____

B. Adjustable Rate Mortgages (ARMs)

Loan Information

Current Interest Rate _____

Current P&I Payment _____

First Rate Change Date _____

Mortgage Margin _____

Maximum Interest Rate _____

Minimum Interest Rate _____

Fannie Mae Only

First Payment Change Date _____

Original Index Value _____

Lookback (in days) _____

Rounding Feature Code

☐ 027 (1/8%)

☐ _____ (negotiated commitment code)

Freddie Mac Only

Next Rate Adjustment Date _____

Next Payment Adjustment Date _____

Is Arm Convertible? ☐ Yes ☐ No

Net Negative Amortization _____

Periodic Interest Rate Cap ☐ Yes ☐ No

Rate Cap Percent

Payment Cap ☐ Yes ☐ No

Payment Cap ☐ Opt ☐ Man

Payment Cap Percent

Rate Rounded ☐ Yes ☐ No

Percent Rounded By _____

C. Other Mortgage Programs

Fannie Mae Only

For Growing Equity Mortgages (GEMS):
Percent of Increase _____

For Balloon Mortgages
Balloon Call Date _____

Freddie Mac Only

For Graduated-Payment Mortgages (GPMs):
Yearly Payment Increase _____

For EQUALim and Tiered-Payment Mortgages (TPMs):
Borrower's First Payment Change Date _____
Borrower's Initial P&I Payment
Yearly Payment Increase _____

For affordable Housing Initiatives Program Mortgages:

Down Payment		Closing Costs		Secondary Financing	
Source Codes	Amounts	Source Codes	Amounts	Source Codes	Amounts
_____	_____	_____	_____	_____	_____
_____	_____	_____	_____	_____	_____
_____	_____	_____	_____		

Borrower Education Counseling Codes

Administrator Codes	Format Codes
_____	_____
_____	_____

_____

_____

_____

_____

_____

_____

_____

_____

_____

_____

_____

_____

_____

Freddie Mac Form 1077 11/92
Wasatch Document Systems
To order: 800-453-7900

Fannie Mae Form 1008 11/92

Figure 14-3

Uniform Residential Loan Application

This application is designed to be completed by the applicant(s) with the lender's assistance. Applicants should complete this form as "Borrower" or "Co-Borrower", as applicable. Co-Borrower information must also be provided (and the appropriate box checked) when ☐ the income or assets of a person other than the "Borrower" (including the Borrower's spouse) will be used as a basis for loan qualification or ☐ the income or assets of the Borrower's spouse will not be used as a basis for loan qualification, but his or her liabilities must be considered because the Borrower resides in a community property state, the security property is located in a community property state, or the Borrower is relying on other property located in a community property state as a basis for repayment of the loan.

Mortgage Applied for:	☐ V.A. ☐ Conventional ☐ Other: ☐ FHA ☐ FmHA	Agency Case Number	Lender Case Number

Amount	Interest Rate	No. of Months	Amortization Type:	☐ Fixed Rate ☐ Other (explain): ☐ GPM ☐ ARM (type):
$	%			

Subject Property Address (street, city, state, ZIP)	No. of Units

Legal Description of Subject Property (attach description if necessary)	Year Built

Purpose of Loan	☐ Purchase ☐ Construction ☐ Other (explain): ☐ Refinance ☐ Construction-Permanent	Property will be: ☐ Primary Residence ☐ Secondary Residence ☐ Investment

Complete this line if construction or construction-permanent loan.

Year Lot Acquired	Original Cost	Amount Existing Liens	(a) Present Value of Lot	(b) Cost of Improvements	Total (a + b)
	$	$	$	$	$

Complete this line if this is a refinance loan.

Year Acquired	Original Cost	Amount Existing Liens	Purpose of Refinance	Describe Improvements ☐ made ☐ to be made
	$	$		Cost: $

Title will be held in what Name(s)	Manner in which Title will be held	Estate will be held in: ☐ Fee Simple ☐ Leasehold (show expiration date)

Source of Down Payment, Settlement Charges and/or Subordinate Financing (explain)

Borrower's Name (include Jr. or Sr. if applicable)	Co-Borrower's Name (include Jr. or Sr. if applicable)

Social Security Number	Home Phone (incl. area code)	Age	Yrs. School	Social Security Number	Home Phone (incl. area code)	Age	Yrs. School

☐ Married ☐ Unmarried (include single, divorced, widowed) ☐ Separated	Dependents (not listed by Co-Borrower) no. ___ ages ___	☐ Married ☐ Unmarried (include single, divorced, widowed) ☐ Separated	Dependents (not listed by Borrower) no. ___ ages ___

Present Address (street, city, state, ZIP) ☐ Own ☐ Rent ___ No. Yrs.	Present Address (street, city, state, ZIP) ☐ Own ☐ Rent ___ No. Yrs.

If residing at present address for less than two years, complete the following:

Former Address (street, city, state, ZIP) ☐ Own ☐ Rent ___ No. Yrs.	Former Address (street, city, state, ZIP) ☐ Own ☐ Rent ___ No. Yrs.

Former Address (street, city, state, ZIP) ☐ Own ☐ Rent ___ No. Yrs.	Former Address (street, city, state, ZIP) ☐ Own ☐ Rent ___ No. Yrs.

Name & Address of Employer ☐ Self Employed	Yrs. on this job	Name & Address of Employer ☐ Self Employed	Yrs. on this job
	Yrs. employed in this line of work/profession		Yrs. employed in this line of work/profession

Position/Title/Type of Business	Business Phone (incl. area code)	Position/Title/Type of Business	Business Phone (incl. area code)

If employed in current position for less than two years or if currently employed in more than one position, complete the following:

Name & Address of Employer ☐ Self Employed	Dates (from - to)	Name & Address of Employer ☐ Self Employed	Dates (from - to)
	Monthly Income $		Monthly Income $

Position/Title/Type of Business	Business Phone (incl. area code)	Position/Title/Type of Business	Business Phone (incl. area code)

Name & Address of Employer ☐ Self Employed	Dates (from - to)	Name & Address of Employer ☐ Self Employed	Dates (from - to)
	Monthly Income $		Monthly Income $

Position/Title/Type of Business	Business Phone (incl. area code)	Position/Title/Type of Business	Business Phone (incl. area code)

Freddie Mac Form 65 10/92   Fannie Mae Form 1003 10/92

VMP-21 (9210)   Page 1 of 4   Printed on Recycled Paper
VMP MORTGAGE FORMS • (800)521-7291

Figure 14-4

Gross Monthly Income	Borrower	Co-Borrower	Total	Combined Monthly Housing Expense	Present	Proposed
Base Empl. Income *	$	$	$	Rent	$	▓▓▓▓
Overtime				First Mortgage (P&I)		$
Bonuses				Other Financing (P&I)		
Commissions				Hazard Insurance		
Dividends/Interest				Real Estate Taxes		
Net Rental Income				Mortgage Insurance		
Other (before completing, see the notice in "describe other income," below)				Homeowner Assn. Dues		
				Other:		
Total	$	$	$	Total	$	$

* Self Employed Borrower(s) may be required to provide additional documentation such as tax returns and financial statements.

B/C	Describe Other Income Notice: Alimony, child support, or separate maintenance income need not be revealed if the Borrower (B) or Co-Borrower (C) does not choose to have it considered for repaying this loan.	Monthly Amount
		$

This Statement and any applicable supporting schedules may be completed jointly by both married and unmarried Co-Borrowers if their assets and liabilities are sufficiently joined so that the Statement can be meaningfully and fairly presented on a combined basis; otherwise separate Statements and Schedules are required. If the Co Borrower section was completed about a spouse, this Statement and supporting schedules must be completed about that spouse also.

Completed ☐ Jointly ☐ Not Jointly

ASSETS Description	Cash or Market Value	Liabilities and Pledged Assets. List the creditor's name, address and account number for all outstanding debts, including automobile loans, revolving charge accounts, real estate loans, alimony, child support, stock pledges, etc. Use continuation sheet, if necessary. Indicate by (*) those liabilities which will be satisfied upon sale of real estate owned or upon refinancing of the subject property.	Monthly Pmt. & Mos. Left to Pay	Unpaid Balance
Cash deposit toward purchase held by:	$	**LIABILITIES**		
		Name and address of Company	$ Pmt./Mos.	$
List checking and savings accounts below				
Name and address of Bank, S&L, or Credit Union				
		Acct. no.		
		Name and address of Company	$ Pmt./Mos.	$
Acct. no.	$			
Name and address of Bank, S&L, or Credit Union				
		Acct. no.		
		Name and address of Company	$ Pmt./Mos.	$
Acct. no.	$			
Name and address of Bank, S&L, or Credit Union				
		Acct. no.		
		Name and address of Company	$ Pmt./Mos.	$
Acct. no.	$			
Name and address of Bank, S&L, or Credit Union				
		Acct. no.		
		Name and address of Company	$ Pmt./Mos.	$
Acct. no.	$			
Stocks & Bonds (Company name/number & description)	$			
		Acct. no.		
		Name and address of Company	$ Pmt./Mos.	$
Life insurance net cash value	$			
Face amount: $				
Subtotal Liquid Assets	$			
Real estate owned (enter market value from schedule of real estate owned)	$	Acct. no.		
Vested interest in retirement fund	$	Name and address of Company	$ Pmt./Mos.	$
Net worth of business(es) owned (attach financial statement)	$			
Automobiles owned (make and year)	$			
		Acct. no.		
		Alimony/Child Support/Separate Maintenance Payments Owed to:	$	▓▓▓▓
Other Assets (itemize)	$	Job Related Expense (child care, union dues, etc.)	$	▓▓▓▓
		Total Monthly Payments	$	
Total Assets a.	$		**Total Liabilities b.**	$

Figure 14-5

Schedule of Real Estate Owned (If additional properties are owned, use continuation sheet.)

Property Address (enter S if sold, PS if pending sale or R if rental being held for income)	Type of Property	Present Market Value	Amount of Mortgages & Liens	Gross Rental Income	Mortgage Payments	Insurance, Maintenance, Taxes & Misc.	Net Rental Income
		$	$	$	$	$	$
Totals		$	$	$	$	$	$

List any additional names under which credit has previously been received and Indicate appropriate creditor name(s) and account number(s):

Alternate Name	Creditor Name	Account Number

	If you answer "Yes" to any questions a through i, please use continuation sheet for explanation.	Borrower Yes	Borrower No	Co-Borrower Yes	Co-Borrower No
a. Purchase price $	a. Are there any outstanding judgments against you?	☐	☐	☐	☐
b. Alterations, improvements, repairs	b. Have you been declared bankrupt within the past 7 years?	☐	☐	☐	☐
c. Land (if acquired separately)	c. Have you had property foreclosed upon or given title or deed in lieu thereof in the last 7 years?	☐	☐	☐	☐
d. Refinance (incl. debts to be paid off)	d. Are you a party to a lawsuit?	☐	☐	☐	☐
e. Estimated prepaid items	e. Have you directly or indirectly been obligated on any loan which resulted in foreclosure, transfer of title in lieu of foreclosure, or judgment? (This would include such loans as home mortgage loans, SBA loans, home improvement loans, educational loans, manufactured (mobile) home loans, any mortgage, financial obligation, bond, or loan guarantee. If "Yes," provide details, including date, name and address of Lender, FHA or V.A. case number, if any, and reasons for the action.)	☐	☐	☐	☐
f. Estimated closing costs					
g. PMI, MIP, Funding Fee					
h. Discount (if Borrower will pay)					
i. Total Costs (add items a through h)	f. Are you presently delinquent or in default on any Federal debt or any other loan, mortgage, financial obligation, bond, or loan guarantee? If "Yes," give details as described in the preceding question.	☐	☐	☐	☐
j. Subordinate financing	g. Are you obligated to pay alimony, child support, or separate maintenance?	☐	☐	☐	☐
k. Borrower's closing costs paid by Seller	h. Is any part of the down payment borrowed?	☐	☐	☐	☐
l. Other Credits (explain)	i. Are you a co-maker or endorser on a note?	☐	☐	☐	☐
	j. Are you a U.S. citizen?	☐	☐	☐	☐
	k. Are you a permanent resident alien?	☐	☐	☐	☐
m. Loan amount (exclude PMI, MIP, Funding Fee financed)	l. Do you intend to occupy the property as your primary residence? If "Yes," complete question m below.	☐	☐	☐	☐
n. PMI, MIP, Funding Fee financed	m. Have you had an ownership interest in a property in the last three years?	☐	☐	☐	☐
o. Loan amount (add m & n)	(1) What type of property did you own—principal residence (PR), second home (SH), or investment property (IP)?				
p. Cash from/to Borrower (subtract j, k, l & o from i)	(2) How did you hold title to the home—solely by yourself (S), jointly with your spouse (SP), or jointly with another person (O)?				

The undersigned specifically acknowledge(s) and agree(s) that: (1) the loan requested by this application will be secured by a first mortgage or deed of trust on the property described herein; (2) the property will not be used for any illegal or prohibited purpose or use; (3) all statements made in this application are made for the purpose of obtaining the loan indicated herein; (4) occupation of the property will be as indicated above; (5) verification or reverification of any information contained in the application may be made at any time by the Lender, its agents, successors and assigns, either directly or through a credit reporting agency, from any source named in this application, and the original copy of this application will be retained by the Lender, even if the loan is not approved; (6) the Lender, its agents, successors and assigns will rely on the information contained in the application and I/we have a continuing obligation to amend and/or supplement the information provided in this application if any of the material facts which I/we have represented herein should change prior to closing; (7) in the event my/our payments on the loan indicated in this application become delinquent, the Lender, its agents, successors and assigns, may, in addition to all their other rights and remedies, report my/our name(s) and account information to a credit reporting agency; (8) ownership of the loan may be transferred to successor or assign of the Lender without notice to me and/or the administration of the loan account may be transferred to an agent, successor or assign of the Lender with prior notice to me; (9) the Lender, its agents, successors and assigns make no representations or warranties, express or implied, to the Borrower(s) regarding the property, the condition of the property, or the value of the property.

Certification: I/We certify that the information provided in this application is true and correct as of the date set forth opposite my/our signature(s) on this application and acknowledge my/our understanding that any intentional or negligent misrepresentation(s) of the information contained in this application may result in civil liability and/or criminal penalties including, but not limited to, fine or imprisonment or both under the provisions of Title 18, United States Code, Section 1001, et seq. and liability for monetary damages to the Lender, its agents, successors and assigns, insurers and any other person who may suffer any loss due to reliance upon any misrepresentation which I/we have made on this application.

Borrower's Signature	Date	Co-Borrower's Signature	Date
X		X	

The following information is requested by the Federal Government for certain types of loans related to a dwelling, in order to monitor the Lender's compliance with equal credit opportunity, fair housing and home mortgage disclosure laws. You are not required to furnish this information, but are encouraged to do so. The law provides that a Lender may neither discriminate on the basis of this information, nor on whether you choose to furnish it. However, if you choose not to furnish it, under Federal regulations this Lender is required to note race and sex on the basis of visual observation or surname. If you do not wish to furnish the above information, please check the box below. (Lender must review the above material to assure that the disclosures satisfy all requirements to which the Lender is subject under applicable state law for the particular type of loan applied for.)

BORROWER

Race/National Origin:
☐ I do not wish to furnish this information
☐ American Indian or Alaskan Native ☐ Asian or Pacific Islander ☐ White, not of Hispanic Origin
☐ Black, not of Hispanic origin ☐ Hispanic
☐ Other (specify) _____

Sex: ☐ Female ☐ Male

CO-BORROWER

Race/National Origin:
☐ I do not wish to furnish this information
☐ American Indian or Alaskan Native ☐ Asian or Pacific Islander ☐ White, not of Hispanic Origin
☐ Black, not of Hispanic origin ☐ Hispanic
☐ Other (specify) _____

Sex: ☐ Female ☐ Male

To be Completed by Interviewer

This application was taken by:
☐ face-to-face interview
☐ by mail
☐ by telephone

Interviewer's Name (print or type): _____

Interviewer's Signature _____ Date

Interviewer's Phone Number (incl. area code) _____

Name and Address of Interviewer's Employer

Freddie Mac Form 65 10/92   Page 3 of 4   Fannie Mae Form 1003 10/92

Figure 14-6

Continuation Sheet/Residential Loan Application

Use this continuation sheet if you need more space to complete the Residential Loan Application. Mark **B** for Borrower or **C** for Co-Borrower.	Borrower:	Agency Case Number:
	Co-Borrower:	Lender Case Number:

I/We fully understand that it is a Federal crime punishable by fine or imprisonment, or both, to knowingly make any false statements concerning any of the above facts as applicable under the provisions of Title 18, United States Code, Section 1001, et seq.

Borrower's Signature:	Date	Co-Borrower's Signature:	Date
X		X	

VERIFICATIONS

Verification Forms are sent out by the third party originator to verify:

1. **Employment.** (See Fannie Mae Form 1005 Figure 14-7).
2. **Deposit.** That the down payment is available. If it is to be supplied by another, an acknowledgment by that party that they promise the down payment as a gift is required. (See Fannie Mae Form 1006 - Not shown).
3. **Rent or Mortgage Account.** If the applicants rent payment history was satisfactory and also the amount of rent paid. If the loan applicant was a purchaser it verifies the mortgage history, payments and balance as well as that payments were satisfactory (See VMP Form 24R 9303 - Not shown).
4. **Loan.** This verification shows the type of loan(s) the applicant has as well as balances, payments and loan status. See VMP Form 313 293-8100 - Not shown).
5. **Credit.** This is a request for a credit report.

PAYOFF DEMAND

This form asks the lender for the total loan payoff amount as of a particular date.

SUBMISSION SHEET

This sheet sets forth documentation of the loan package as well as any special circumstances or information not revealed by other documentation that would be of interest to the loan underwriter who will approve or disapprove the loan being applied for.

If the verification forms or other documents raise questions, this is the place to answer them. If the employment verification showed one month's employment, the fact that the employer was a successor in interest to a company where the applicant had worked for eight years would be material information. Also, if a firm had a history of giving all employees a large end-of-year bonus, this would be significant if the employee's income was marginal.

Any information in a verification that appears negative should be looked at to see if it accurately reports the information. If an explanation is needed, it should be included in a straight forward and factual manner.

STACKING ORDER

The stacking order of documents will vary slightly by the lender. It varies based on the type of financing and if the loan is to be conforming or nonconforming.

Figure 14-7

FannieMae   Request for Verification of Employment

Privacy Act Notice: This information is to be used by the agency collecting it or its assignees in determining whether you qualify as a prospective mortgagor under its program. It will not be disclosed outside the agency except as required and permitted by law. You do not have to provide this information, but if you do not your application for approval as a prospective mortgagor or borrower may be delayed or rejected. The information requested in this form is authorized by Title 38, USC, Chapter 37 (if V.A.), by 12 USC, Section 1701 et. seq. (if HUD/FHA); by 42 USC, Section 1452b (if HUD/CPD), and Title 42 USC, 1471 et. seq., or 7 USC, 1921 et. seq. (if USDA/FmHA).

Instructions: Lender - Complete items 1 through 7. Have applicant complete item 8. Forward directly to employer named in item 1.
Employer - Please complete either Part II or Part III as applicable. Complete Part IV and return directly to lender named in item 2.
The form is to be transmitted directly to the lender and is not to be transmitted through the applicant or any other party.

Part I - Request

1. To (Name and address of employer)	2. From (Name and address of lender)

I certify that this verification has been sent directly to the employer and has not passed through the hands of the applicant or any other interested party.

3. Signature of Lender	4. Title	5. Date	6. Lender's No. (Optional)

I have applied for a mortgage loan and stated that I am now or was formerly employed by you. My signature below authorizes verification of this information.

7. Name and Address of Applicant (include employee or badge number)	8. Signature of Applicant
	X

Part II - Verification of Present Employment

9. Applicant's Date of Employment	10. Present Position	11. Probability of Continued Employment

12A. Current Gross Base Pay (Enter Amount and Check Period)	13. For Military Personnel Only	14. If Overtime or Bonus is Applicable, Is Its Continuance Likely?

☐ Annual ☐ Weekly ☐ Other (Specify)
☐ Monthly ☐ Hourly

$_____

Pay Grade

Type

Monthly Amount

Overtime ☐ Yes ☐ No   Bonus ☐ Yes ☐ No

12B. Gross Earnings

Type	Year To Date	Past Year 19 ___	Past Year 19 ___			
Base Pay	Thru ___ 19 ___ $	$	$	Base Pay	$	15. If paid hourly - average hours per week
Overtime	$	$	$	Rations	$	16. Date of applicant's next pay increase
Commissions	$	$	$	Flight or Hazard	$	17. Projected amount of next pay increase
Bonus	$	$	$	Clothing	$	
				Quarters	$	18. Date of applicant's last pay increase
				Pro Pay	$	
Total	$	$	$	Overseas or Combat	$	19. Amount of last pay increase
				Variable Housing Allowance	$	

20. Remarks (If employee was off work for any length of time, please indicate time period and reason)

Part III - Verification of Previous Employment

21. Date Hired	23. Salary/Wage at Termination Per (Year) (Month) (Week)
22. Date Terminated	Base ___ Overtime ___ Commissions ___ Bonus ___
24. Reason for Leaving	25. Position Held

Part IV - Authorized Signature - Federal statutes provide severe penalties for any fraud, intentional misrepresentation, or criminal connivance or conspiracy purposed to influence the issuance of any guaranty or insurance by the V.A. Secretary, the USDA, FmHA/FHA Commissioner, or the HUD/CPD Assistant Secretary.

26. Signature of Employer	27. Title (Please print or type)	28. Date

29. Print or type name signed in Item 26

30. Phone No.

Fannie Mae
Form 1005 Mar. 90

-23 (9007) .05

VMP MORTGAGE FORMS - (313)293-8100 - (800)521-7291

Generally the stacking order will be:

1. Submission Sheet.

2. Transmittal (Form 1008).

3. Cover Letter. This is a simple letter to the lender explaining the loan package.

4. Loan Application (Form 1003).

5. Credit Report. Support documentation might include copies of pink slips for automobiles, bankruptcy papers, payment coupons, etc.

6. Mortgage/Landlord Rating. Information on payments of owner/tenant. As an example, is tenant consistently a few days late in paying rent.

7. Income Verification. This could include payroll stubs, W-2 forms, explanation of employment gaps, etc. For self employed, copies of 1040's for the last few years might be included as well as bank deposits.

8. Down Payment Verification. The funds for down payment should be verified by the depository holding them. (FNMA Form 1006).

   If funds are being taken from an IRA or other pension fund, this fund must be verified as well as the ability to withdraw funds.

   If the down payment is to be a gift, then a gift letter from the donor should be included as well as verification of the donor's ability to make the gift such as a verification of deposit.

9. Contracts. The purchase contract should be included (for a purchase money loan). If the borrower is selling a residence, the contract for the sale must also be included. (If the borrower did not sell, then two trust deed payments could lead to default.)

10. Preliminary Title report. This will reveal liens that would need to be paid off (it should substantially agree with the loan application). It could also reveal problems as to title as well as interests of others.

11. Appraisal. The intended lender might have a list of appraisers to be used. Such a list would be based on experience with the appraisers. The appraiser must be licensed or certified. The Uniform Residential Appraisal Form would be used.

12. Additional Disclosures. As applicable, additional disclosures that have been made should be attached. Examples are:

1. Transfer disclosure

2. Fair housing

3. Equal Credit Opportunity Act

4. Good Faith Estimate of closing costs

13. Lock-In Forms and Confirmation Letters. If the rate has been locked in (agreement that it will not change) the lock-in form should be included as well as lenders confirmation letter agreeing to this rate.

14. Lender Appraisal Sheets. This is a sheet for the underwriter to rate the risk of the loan for their approval.

BROKER AGREEMENTS

Wholesale Agreements

Some brokers work exclusively for single lenders and have an agreement to direct their applications to these lenders, such as a banks, savings banks, pension plan or mortgage bankers.

> *This exclusive agreement is known as a "wholesale agreement."*

Out-Of-State Funding

If funding is to be on a property that is not in California, the following should be considered:

1. The lender/investor must be exempt from securities laws. (Corporations Code 25102(i) exempts institutional lenders buying for their own account).

2. Third party arrangers may be required to be licensed in state where property is located (based on state law).

TABLE FUNDING

TABLE FUNDING *refers to a settlement at which a loan is funded by a contemporaneous advance of loan funds and an assignment of the loan to the person advancing the funds.* In other words, the loan is given to the arranger of the loan who immediately transfers it to the lender. A table-funded transaction is not considered to be a secondary market transaction (secondary market transactions are exempt from RESPA). Mortgage Table Funded Loans require RESPA disclosures.

Liability

Generally, since an escrow is not involved, the liability for error would be with the party preparing the closing statement.

Assignments

If the lender intends to assign the loan to another, this must be disclosed at time of closing.

Home Mortgage Disclosure Act

The reporting requirements of the Home Mortgage Disclosure Act as set forth in Chapter 10 must be met. The purpose is to prevent redlining activities by providing information on loans by specific areas.

Trust Fund Handling

Even though an escrow might not be involved in table funding, the rules and reporting for trust funds apply as set forth in Chapter 11.

QUALITY CONTROL

QUALITY CONTROL *refers to efforts to insure against making loans which end in foreclosures.*

Pre-Funding

The third party originators must make certain that the loan application is accurate and be alert for red flags that might indicate problems. Red flags would include a sudden change in income, a number of disputed credit claims, an irregular work history, etc. Explanations should be included and further investigation conducted if indicated. The third party originator's integrity is tied to the submitted loan application. An above average default record could result in lenders refusing to deal with the originator. The originator must be willing to forgo a single loan based on future relationships.

For self employed individuals one check that can be made is based on the borrower's tax return (IRS Form 1040). By asking to see canceled checks to the IRS or verify the checks with their bank, a forged 1040 Form will be readily discovered.

Post-Funding

1. Lenders can spot funding problems by tracking the originators of loans in default to specific originators and/or specific underwriter's records. If an underwriter or originator has too many problems, it indicates a change is needed.

2. In servicing loans, late payments, bad checks and excuses should be considered and the loans tracked to originators and underwriters. An audit may be indicated as to a particular underwriter or originator.

SUMMARY

A third party originator is a broker that solicits loan applications and submits the application as part of a completed loan package to a lender for approval and funding.

Third party originators deal with out-of-state lenders and other lenders who do not have the capacity to deal directly with borrowers in preparing the loan package. They also deal with lenders wishing to expand their market presence.

Third party loan originators solicit borrowers for loans and perform services for them, so they must be licensed by the Department of Real Estate.

Loan finders need not be licensed but they cannot prepare loan packages or negotiate loans.

Third part originators are agents in that they represent borrowers, lenders or both.

The threshold requirements for submission of advertising to the DRE are no longer of great importance since the former mandatory submission is now voluntary.

Bait-and-switch advertising is an illegal activity and involves advertising a loan without the intention of getting such a loan for the consumer. Instead the consumer is switched to another loan.

Third party originators do accept funds for fees and costs associated with the loan application package so the trust fund requirements of Chapter 11 apply.

Because the quarterly and fiscal trust account reports have an exemption for institutional lenders, third party originators are unlikely to cross the threshold number of transactions requiring the reports.

Truth-in-Lending disclosures apply to broker advertising as well trust deeds and notes.

The broker must supply the prospective borrower with a mortgage loan disclosure statement as early as practical. Disclosures need not be made to lenders if they are institutional lenders or pension plans having $15,000,000 or more in assets. Material changes from the disclosure statement must be communicated prior to close of escrow.

Consumers have the right to know what is in their credit report.

Lenders must comply with the Home Mortgage Disclosure Act and report mortgages by area (to police against redlining).

Seller carryback financing disclosure is required, if applicable, as are RESPA disclosures and Equal Credit Opportunity Act disclosures set forth in Chapter 10.

The seller must supply a transfer disclosure statement and the broker has a responsibility to report the result of his or her diligent inspection of the premises.

A written authorization is required to conduct an investigative credit report.

Normal stacking order of documents in a loan package to be submitted to a lender, would be:

1. Submission Sheet
2. Transmittal Form
3. Cover letter
4. Loan application
5. Credit report
6. Mortgage/Landlord Rating
7. Income verification
8. Down payment verification
9. Contract
10. Preliminary Title Report
11. Appraisal
12. Any additional disclosure
13. Lock-In Form and Confirmation Letter
14. Lender Approval Sheet

Third party originators might have a wholesale agreement where they deal with just one lender.

In dealing with property located outside California, the third party originator might need to be licensed in the state where the property is located. The lender must be exempt from securities law.

Simultaneous loans and assignments are know as table funding.

Quality control deals with the broker's efforts to make loans to borrowers who will honor their commitments and lenders efforts to evaluate loans that are funded to discover problems in underwriting and/or loan origination.

CLASS DISCUSSION TOPICS

1. Do you know of any local firms which act as third party originators? If so, how do they solicit borrowers and how are they compensated?

2. Are there any unlicensed finders active in your area? If so, discuss their activities.

3. What are the advantages of a broker being a third party originator rather than a loan broker or mortgage banker?

4. What would be the personal attributes of a successful third party originator?

5. Discuss possible conflict of interest facing the third party originator in preparing a loan package.

CHAPTER 14 QUIZ

1. A third party originator would NOT: (p. 422)

    A. send the loan package to an institutional lender

    B. fund the loan with his or her own funds

    C. solicit borrowers for loans secured by real property

    D. work for only one lender

2. Which agency would license a third party originator? (p. 423)

    A. Department of Real Estate

    B. Department of Commerce

    C. Finance Department

    D. Securities and Exchange Commission

3. A third party originator in advertising loans MUST: (p. 428)

    A. use the abbreviations "bro" or "agt"

    B. indicate the license under which the loan will be arranged

    C. offer a choice of at least two lenders

    D. none of the above

4. A third party originator who meets the threshold requirements: (p. 429)

    A. must submit advertising for prior approval

    B. may submit advertising for prior approval

    C. can only use advertising which has been prepared by the DRE

    D. may not advertise that they can help meet borrowing needs

5. A third party originator made disparaging remarks about an advertised loan type which a consumer inquired about. Instead, the broker suggested another type of loan. This MOST LIKELY would be: (pp. 429-430)

    A. a violation of truth-in-lending

    B. a table loan

    C. bait and switch advertising

    D. a tacking violation

6. A broker's trust fund must: (p. 430)

    A. be designated as a trust account

    B. be interest-bearing

    C. contain at least $200 of broker funds

    D. not contain funds of more than a single beneficiary

7. The mortgage loan disclosures statement would NOT require: (p. 435)

    A. any lender disclosure

    B. term life and/or disability insurance as a condition of the loan

    C. notice as to balloon payments

    D. a listing of liens

8. Verification forms included in the loan package would verify: (p. 453)

    A. employment

    B. minority status of applicant

    C. physical or mental disabilities

    D. all of the above

9. Which of the following forms is LIKELY to be first in the stacking order? (p. 455)

    A. Transmittal

    B. Lock-In

    C. Verification of employment

    D. Verification of deposit

10. Which of the following is LIKELY to be last in the stacking order? (p. 456)

    A. Lock-In
    B. Lender Appraisal Sheets
    C. Preliminary Title Report
    D. Purchase Contract

11. Which of the following is true as to table funding? (p. 456)

    A. It is a secondary market transaction
    B. Assignment is contemporaneous with funding
    C. It is for personal property only
    D. The lender must be a licensed broker

12. How would a third party originator verify a self employed person's tax return income? (p. 457)

    A. Obtain a notarized statement from the borrower that it is a true copy
    B. Ask to see cancelled checks corresponding to claimed amounts paid to the IRS
    C. Include a statement that material was supplied by borrower and broker has not independent knowledge to the contrary
    D. Use the rule of thumb by multiplying tax paid by eight to arrive at the income

Answers: *1. B; 2. A; 3. B; 4. B; 5. C; 6. A; 7. B; 8. A; 9. A; 10. B; 11. B; 12. B*

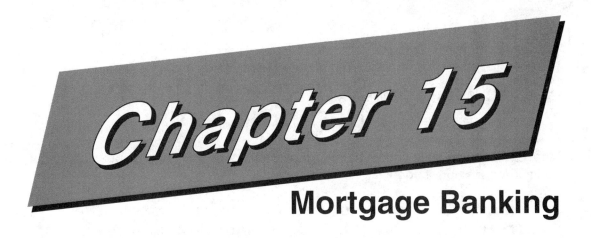

Mortgage Banking

KEY WORDS AND TERMS

Arbitrage
Collaterally Secured
CMOs
Conduits
Discount Rate
Fannie Mae
Federal Home Loan Mortgage
Corporation (FHLMC)
Federally Charter Savings
and Loans
Federal National Mortgage
Association (FNMA)
Federal Reserve
Firm Commitment
Freddie Mac
Garn - St. Germain Depository
Institutions Act of 1982

Ginnie Mae
Government National Mortgage
Association (GNMA)
Guarantor Program
Loan Correspondent
Mortgage Backed Securities
Mortgage Warehousing
National Banks
Open Market Operations
Participation Certificate
Pass Through Certificate
Reserve Requirements
Swap Program
Tandem Plan
Unsecured Line of Credit

LEARNING OBJECTIVES

This, our last, chapter will provide you with an in-depth understanding of mortgage banking. It will bring together material you have previously learned so you will understand it as a whole. You will understand the significant role played by mortgage bankers in our economy.

Definition, Scope and History of Mortgage Banking

Mortgage banking (also known as mortgage bankers or mortgage companies) is not traditional banking with depositors.

> *Mortgage bankers utilize their own funds rather than funds of others. They personally bear any risk involved in their operations.*

The **MORTGAGE BANKER** *is a firm or individual engaged in the business of originating loans secured by real property and then selling these loans to others.* Unlike mortgage brokers, mortgage bankers generally service the loans they originate.

Servicing includes collection of payments and disbursement to the investor who has been assigned the loan (purchaser of the loan). Servicing also includes maintaining any impound account, making certain taxes are being paid (since they are a priority lien), that insurance policies are current with a loss payable clause to the trust deed holder, that nothing is being done to jeopardize the lien holder (committing waste) and handling any collection problems including foreclosures, if necessary.

SOURCE OF FUNDS

Because of the dollar amount involved in real estate loans, a mortgage banker requires credit and the ability to borrow funds. The source of funds for mortgage bankers is generally commercial banks, although some Real Estate Investment Trusts will make secured loans. Money may also be borrowed on unsecured lines of credit or by using mortgages in inventory as security for loans.

Unsecured Line of Credit

Large mortgage companies with audited financial statements are able to obtain substantial lines of unsecured credit. This allows borrowing for short terms. The interest on unsecured lines of credit would generally be higher than for secured loans. The advantage of unsecured lines of credit over secured loans is the short time factor in obtaining funds for loan purposes.

Mortgage Warehousing

When a mortgage company wants to hold or to assemble a large dollar quantity of mortgages (or trust deeds), they will generally borrow using their inventory of loans as security. *This is known as* **MORTGAGE WAREHOUSING**. Because the loans are secured, the interest rate would generally be lower than if the loan were unsecured as it reduces the risk to the commercial bank.

Assume a mortgage company had a buyer for a $100 million package of loans. The buyer might desire the package to collateralize it by selling mortgage backed securities. In such a case, the mortgage company would have to borrow on their inventory as it accumulated so that they could assemble such a package of loans.

In other cases, a mortgage company might decide to take a risk and bet that interest rates will drop. If they are able to hang on to a large inventory of loans bearing a higher rate of interest, they could realize significant profits in reselling such loans at a premium after interest rates drop.

On the other hand, if the mortgage company feels that interest rates will rise, they would not want to hold on to a significant quantity of mortgages. When interest rates rise, existing loans at lower than current rates would have to be offered at a discount if they are to be sold.

To understand mortgage warehousing, assume a mortgage banker has $10,000,000 in mortgages. The mortgage banker might obtain a line of credit of $9,500,000 on these mortgages. If the mortgage banker then makes $9,500,000 in new mortgages, then 95% of this amount may be borrowed, or $9,025,000, which can then be used to make loans and in turn can then be borrowed against, etc., etc. A liquid net worth of $10,000,000 could likely be turned into over $100,000,000 of mortgages subject to loans.

DISPOSITION OF LOANS

Loans are made by mortgage companies to large investors which may include banks, savings banks, thrifts, credit unions, insurance companies and pension plans. The growth of mortgage REITs (Real Estate Investment Trusts) has resulted in significant funds for large commercial and industrial loans secured by real property. Because large REITs are publicly traded, they are able to obtain funds by issuing stock.

Mortgage companies might act as loan correspondents for just a single lender or several lenders. A **LOAN CORRESPONDENT** *makes loans which meet the purchase requirements of the lender(s)/purchaser(s).* The mortgage company knows that when they make the loan they will sell the loan to a particular lender based on an agreement with that lender.

Mortgage companies are the largest originators of home loans.

They are also the largest originator of loans sold to Fannie Mae and Freddie Mac (covered later in this chapter).

THIRD PARTY TO LOANS

Mortgage bankers seldom act as loan brokers (See Chapter 12) or third party originators (See Chapter 14). However, there may be circumstances when the mortgage banker does not act as the initial funding source for the loan.

The investor might want the loan to be made direct. In which case the investor would likely service the loan. Or the sheer size of the loan might result in a situation where the lender would prefer to be an arranger of the loan rather than a lender, as this reduces any risks due to problems arising which could delay the transfer of the loan. An actual example of such a loan was a $700,000,000 commercial loan where the insurance company investor funded the loan that the mortgage banker arranged.

HISTORY OF MORTGAGE BANKING

While we generally speak of a national economy, we have local and regional economies that vary significantly. As an example one area of the country might have a boom in demand and construction and a shortage of available local mortgage funds. Other areas of the country might have a demand for mortgage funds that fall far short of the funds that are available. Because savings banks and some thrifts were formerly limited to mortgage loans, they had to get their cash earning interest. This led to the growth of the mortgage banking business with money flowing across the country to areas of high demand for capital. Until the mid-1980s, California had greater demand for mortgage funds than local money could meet. California was a net importer of capital for mortgage purposes.

In addition to lenders from out of the area who required the services of mortgage companies for loan origination and servicing, some investors are not prepared to originate large quantities of loans. Such investors include pension plans, trusts and insurance companies. They are able to obtain relatively high secured yields by purchasing loans originated by mortgage companies.

Deregulation of the savings and loans in 1982 led to disaster for many of them.

The Garn-St. Germain Depository Institutions Act of 1982 provided for deregulation designed to allow lending institutions to make a broader range of choices. One purpose of this act was to make more mortgage money available through the private sector. The industry had been clamoring for greater freedom and this act provided it.

Much of the deregulation under this act was prompted by inflation in the late 1970s. Lending institutions were limited as to where they could invest depositors funds while money market accounts at stock brokerage houses offered interest rates in excess of 18 percent compounded on a daily basis. Lenders suffered **DISINTERMEDIATION**, *which is a sudden withdrawal from savings accounts.* Savings and loans were particularly hard hit with most of their deposits in certificates of deposit which paid their depositors higher rates of interest than the savings and loans were receiving on their mortgage portfolios. Many savings and loans were hemorrhaging funds. One major California savings and loan (now defunct) was losing $400,000 per week. The Garn-St. Germain Act was to make certain this situation did not happen again. The act had a significant effect on the restrictions applying to national banks and federally chartered savings and loan institutions.

National Banks

The act gave nationally chartered banks great freedom in that statutory restrictions on real estate loans were removed. The comptroller of currency governs national bank lending activities and in carrying out the Garn-St. Germain Depository Institutions Act of 1982, they eliminated:

1. **Loan-to-Value Ratio Restrictions.** Federal banks could now make loans for any percentage of appraised value.
2. **Schedule of Payments.** Loans no longer had to be amortized.
3. **Length of Loans.** The length of a loan is now subject to negotiation between the borrower and lender.
4. **Removal of Limits.** National banks could now lend any percentage of their capital on real estate and make loans without dollar limits.
5. **Leases as Security.** Restrictions on leases to qualify for a leasehold security for a loan were removed.

National banks did not abuse the power given them by deregulation to the extent the savings and loan institutions did. National banks are really not a major player in mortgage lending when compared to mortgage companies.

Federally Chartered Savings and Loan Institutions

The Garn-St. Germain Depository Institutions Act of 1982 gave free rein to activities of federally chartered savings and loans.

1. They were able to offer interest-bearing checking accounts.
2. Interest ceilings were removed as to what could be paid to savings accounts.
3. They were allowed to make commercial loans.
4. They were allowed to make equity loans secured by real estate (second trust deeds).
5. They were allowed to engage in leasing activities.
6. They were allowed to offer commercial lines of credit, both secured and unsecured.
7. They were allowed to make real estate loans for other than housing.
8. They were allowed to invest up to 30 percent of association assets in unsecured consumer loans (this included credit card lending).
9. They were allowed to make loans up to 100 percent of appraisal.
10. They were allowed to refinance property.

The result of the Garn-St. Germain Depository Institutions Act of 1982, was that many savings and loans were lured to make large investments in office structures, shopping centers and other major developments because of higher interest rates. In many cases, they were lured by "a piece of the action." **PARTICIPATION LOANS** *made them both limited partners who could share in the profits as well as lenders entitled to interest and the return of principal.*

> *Developers in some well publicized cases gained control of savings and loans to their personal advantage.*

One major California developer, who controlled a savings and loan in another state, offered high certificate of deposit interest (insured by FSLIC). The savings and loan was able to bring in a tremendous amount of depository funds. Their pockets were kept wide open to the developer who was like a kid in a candy store. This "partnership" started developing many golf course related projects and purchased others.

A change in the economy led to recession where buyers were reluctant to buy and firms were reluctant to expand. Many savings and loans found themselves with a significant portion of their loans delinquent. Subsequent foreclosures left savings and loans with many "see-through buildings" (glass towers without tenants). They had an inventory of overbuilt and overpriced products. Sales would have resulted in their balance sheets suffering a devastating loss.

The problem became so severe that the Resolution Trust Corporation took over the assets and liquidated many savings and loans. The Federal Savings and Loan Insurance Corporation (FSLIC) was unable to cover losses and thus was merged with the FDIC (Federal Deposit Insurance Corporation).

> *This was not enough: The deregulation ended up costing taxpayers over $400 billion.*

The "good times" of deregulation led many state regulated savings and loans to change to federally chartered savings and loans and they enjoyed the wild party for a few years.

> *Today, savings and loans (savings banks) are more subdued and conservative in their policies. They do not want to prompt federal regulatory scrutiny.*

They still make a wide variety of loans and are now practically identical to banks in everything but name.

The home loans that savings banks produce are usually sold rather than held as inventory. Savings banks have now patterned their lending activities after those of mortgage companies. They loan and sell the loans avoiding risk.

The problems of the savings and loans left a void in home loans for a period of time. It allowed mortgage companies to come in and fill that void. Mortgage companies were able to surpass the once dominant savings and loans in the home mortgage field.

MORTGAGE BANKING PROFIT

Mortgage bankers make money from a number of sources.

Loan Points

Loan origination generally involves points. Each **POINT** *is one percent of the loan.* If an originator of a $200,000 loan charges two points, it comes to $4,000. In some cases the originator will have to share the points with the investor who will be purchasing the loan but generally it serves as a fee for the loan originator.

Fees and Costs

When fees are charged for services to be performed by the originator of the loan, there could be some profit factor in these fees. When the mortage originator has in-house escrow service, the escrow costs contribute to the originator's profit.

Controlled Business Arrangements (discussed in Chapter 9) might eventually serve as another source of profit for loan originators.

Interest Earned

Interest accrues between closing of the loan transaction and selling the loan.

Impound Accounts

The control of impound funds can provide financial benefit to the originator.

Service Fees

For servicing loans they originate, mortgage companies may charge between one-quarter percent and one-half percent of the loan balance. For a $100,000 loan balance, the service fee would probably be between $250 to $500 per year or between $20.83 and $41.66 per month. In addition there may be fees for other services such as foreclosures.

Arbitrage

There may be a positive difference between the sale price of a trust deed and its face amount at origination.

Where there are no or low loan points, which is often the case for certain adjustable rate loans, the investor will generally be paying a premium over the loan face amount which makes up for the points.

The Assumability Problem

In the 1970s, a number of state courts determined that loans with due-on-sale clauses were in fact assumable loans unless the lender could show that an assumption would damage his or her security interest.

People began assuming loans and loan brokers and mortgage bankers arranged secondary financing to pay off sellers. The reason for this great interest in loan assumptions was that many loans made during the 1960s and early 1970s bore interest of between six and seven and one-half percent while interest rates in the late 1970s were soaring to over 12 percent.

The California Supreme Court ruled in the case of *Wellenkamp v. Bank of America*, 1978, 21 C. 3d 943, that institutional lenders could not automatically invoke the due-on-sale clause unless a change in owners would increase the risk of default or otherwise impair the security for the loan.

Brokers were telling borrowers as well as lenders that, based on the above decision, all loans could be assumed and a great many loans were so assumed.

The U.S. Supreme Court, in *Fidelity Federal Savings and Loan v. de la Questa*, 1982, 486 U.S. 141, ruled that due-on-sale clauses were enforceable by federally licensed lenders. The reasoning was that the parties made a contract and the court indicated that they had no right to modify the contract.

The result of this case was that a great many state chartered savings and loan associations sought federal charters in order to be able to enforce their due-on-sale clauses.

Then Congress passed the Garn-St. Germain Depository Institutions Act (Garn Act). The Garn Act stated that all due-on-sale clauses would be enforceable, but the act left a three-year window of opportunity. If, when the loan was made or assumed, state law allowed loan assumptions (Ct cases), then the loans would be assumable by anyone until October 15, 1985. Since that date, due-on-sale clauses mean what they say; the loan must be paid when a property is transferred.

In lieu of enforcing a due-on-sale clause, some lenders will agree to an assumption with a boost in interest rates.

When there are advantages in existing loans, people will try to avoid the due-on-sale clause. There are a number of schemes to do so which include:

1. Use of an unrecorded deed or contract of sale.
2. Use of lease options that are actually sales because so very little is paid at the end of the lease for title.
3. Keeping the insurance in the name of the seller and buyers buying their own property insurance (lenders are alerted to a transfer when they get their copy of insurance containing a loss payable clause which lists a change in ownership).

These schemes must be avoided; not only are these schemes a fraud involving a federally insured lender, they are also a fraud against the city and county. Property is assessed for tax purposes upon sale. If however, the sale is not recorded the taxes are not reassessed which generally means a much lower tax.

Conduits

A **CONDUIT** purchases mortgages from the mortgage originator (such as a mortgage company) and then resells the loans to either investors or a Real Estate Investment Trust (REIT).

Conduits do not make loans nor do they service loans they sell.

Their primary income is from the arbitrage of yield differentials. When interest rates are falling conduits buy loans for a short holding period which they hope can be resold at a premium because of the higher yield. Conduits change tactics with changing situations.

In an improving economy, investors are more willing to take greater risks. In a contracting economy, there is less interest in higher risk situations. In an improving economy, conduits might buy sub-prime mortgages which have a higher yield for resale to investors. To profit, the conduit must receive a price differential.

With the help of computers, conduits search for opportunities in different market areas and may buy mortgages in one area of the country and resell them in another because of an area interest and price differential.

Government Involvement in Lending

The government plays a significant role in lending. The establishment of Fannie Mae, Freddie Mac and Ginnie Mae plays a significant role in our secondary mortgage market. In addition, numerous government programs serve to make loans available to consumers who otherwise would not qualify for credit.

The Federal Reserve really controls the money supply of the nation and tightens or relaxes the money supply which effects the cost of money thus bearing a direct relationship to mortgage activity.

FANNIE MAE (FNMA)

Federal National Mortgage Association (FNMA) or Fannie Mae was establish as a federal agency in 1938. Its purpose was to encourage lenders to make FHA loans.

This was accomplished by providing a secondary mortgage market to purchase FHA loans from the loan originators. Banks, which still had a depression mentality, now had an economic reason to originate low down payment loans with long amortization periods. The function of the agency was expanded in 1944 when VA loans were added.

In 1968, the Federal National Mortgage Association was divided into two organizations. One was Ginnie Mae which was placed under the auspices of HUD and the other kept the name Federal National Mortgage Association.

FNMA was privatized. FNMA was able to issue stock under a federal charter and operates as a private profit-making corporation. FNMA is still-quasi governmental in nature in that the President names five of the 18 directors and the agency was given a substantial federal line of credit.

Activities of Fannie Mae

Fannie Mae now purchases and sells conventional loans, second trust deeds, mortgages and FHA and VA loans. Fannie Mae deals with a variety of loan types such as adjustable rate mortgages tied to different indexes.

Fannie Mae will give lenders such as mortgage brokers firm commitments that they will purchase loans made which meet their requirements. Those commitments are made for up to 60 days. The mortgage company knows when they make a loan under a Fannie Mae commitment that they can sell that loan and know what they will receive. They thus eliminate risk and lock in their profit upon making the loan.

Mortgage Backed Securities (MBS)

Fannie Mae formerly used the sale of bonds to finance much of their activity, but now they convert mortgages and trust deeds into securities which are publicly traded. They put together large blocks of mortgages and sell the securities which are really a participation share in the block of mortgages. The interest and loan payments pass through to the security holder. FNMA charges a fee for this pass-through service.

Fannie Mae Requirements

Loans purchased by the Federal National Mortgage Association must meet underwriting requirements set by Fannie Mae.

1. Loans must be conforming loans. **CONFORMING** *means that the loans meet underwriting standards of FNMA.* A conforming loan for a single-family dwelling cannot exceed $227,150. (Note: this number is subject to change). *Loans over $227,150 are known as* **JUMBO LOANS** and they will not be purchased by FNMA. Therefore, jumbo loans generally bear a higher rate of interest.

2. Loan origination must be on forms specified by FNMA.

3. Loans must be secured by one to-four residential units.

4. Homebuyers must meet qualification standards set by FNMA.

 www.fanniemae.com (Federal National Mortgage Association)

GINNIE MAE (GNMA)

> *The Government National Mortgage Association (GNMA) has remained a government corporation. It is a division of HUD.*

Ginnie Mae has increase the liquidity of mortgages and has also increased sources of financing for residential loans. It was Ginnie Mae that initiated the use of Mortgage Backed Securities (MBS).

Mortgage Backed Securities (MBS)

> *Ginnie Mae does not purchase mortgages.*

They simply guarantee mortgage backed securities issued by approved (private) lenders. The *securities issued are said to be* **COLLATERALLY SECURED** *by real estate (borrowing on the mortgages—not the real estate).*

The securities are secured by pools of mortgages (generally $1,000,000,000 pools). The mortgages in the pools are either government guaranteed (VA) or government insured (FHA, Federal Farm Home Administration) loans. GNMA pools are the primary financing for FHA and VA loans.

The certificates issued require an initial investor investment of $25,000. The certificates are **PASS-THROUGH CERTIFICATES** *in that interest and principal paid, including loan payoffs, passes through to the investor each month.* While the investor is certain as to the interest which will be paid, since the certificates are backed by the full faith and credit of the United States, there is an uncertainty as to when the principal will be repaid because of sales of individual property and refinancing. When interest rates drop, homebuyers tend to refinance at lower rates which means that a great many loans in the pool are paid off early.

Besides buying Ginnie Mae certificates, investors can invest in GNMA mutual funds which allow for a much smaller investment.

Because loans in the pools are amortized, pools decrease in value each month so existing GNMA securities sell for current face value plus a discount or premium based on the interest rate of the pool.

GNMA certificates attract many of the same investors who invest in government bonds. However, GNMA yields may be about one percent greater. The greater yield reflects the risk attached to early repayment of principal and the necessity to reinvest the principal received.

The principal differences between FNMA and GNMA securities are:

1. FNMA buys the mortgages; GNMA does not buy mortgages.
2. The government does not guarantee FNMA securities but they do guarantee GNMA securities.
3. FNMA mortgage pools include conventional loans; GNMA pools only include government guaranteed or insured loans.

Special Assistance Program

Under Ginnie Mae's special assistance program GNMA will purchase low interest loans made under various government programs for low income families. These loans were made by HUD approved lenders. GNMA will pay par or face value for these loans.

Under the **TANDEM PLAN**, *GNMA will sell these HUD-approved loans to Fannie Mae.* Fannie Mae buys these loans at a discount from face value reflecting their below-market interest rates. In other words Ginnie Mae suffers a loss on each sale. This is the cost of government support of low income housing programs. Without this program, lenders would not make below-market rate loans and low income families would not be able to become homeowners.

The loans that qualify for the tandem plan are limited to the budget allocation for this program.

Management and Liquidation Function

Ginnie Mae has been charged with liquidation responsibilities of selling off government owned mortgages.

FEDERAL HOME LOAN MORTGAGE CORPORATION (FHLMC)

*FHLMC (also known as **FREDDIE MAC**), now publicly owned, was orginally created as a government agency by Congress in 1970.*

> *The purpose of the creation of FHLMC was to increase mortgage opportunities which in turn would increase the number of homeowners.*

fatty.law.cornell.edu/uscode/12/ch11A.html
(Federal Home Loan Mortgage Corporation)

To accomplish this purpose, Freddie Mac was to provide a secondary mortgage market for conventional residential mortgages. Freddie Mac now has a similar status as Fannie Mae.

Purchase of Loans

Freddie Mac will buy loans, which meet its specifications, from savings bank institutions, other thrifts and from mortgage companies that originate the loans. Under its standard program, these loans are for one to-four residential units. The loans may be fixed rate or adjustable rate loans for home purchase or home improvement purposes. Most loans purchased by Freddie Mac are generally less than one year old. While Freddie Mac can buy from any HUD approved lender, most loans purchased today were originated by mortgage companies.

Participation Certificates (PCs)

Initial Freddie Mac funding comes from the sale of stock to Federal Home Loan Banks. It can now sell preferred stock to the general public. However, most of the operational funds come from the sale of **MORTGAGE PARTICIPATION CERTIFICATES**, known as **PCs**. PCs are securities.

PCs are undivided interests in a pool of mortgages. While not really guaranteed by the full faith and credit of the United Sates, PCs are guaranteed by the agency (Federal Home Loan Mortgage Corporation). The PCs issued are sold directly to investors.

CMOs

CMOs are Collateralized Mortgage Obligations (See Chapter 13). The cash flow from a pool of mortgages is broken down into four categories of bonds having various maturity dates.

Freddie Mac sells CMOs to investors.

Guarantor Program (SWAP)

Also known as the "SWAP" program. Under this program lenders can trade lower yielding loans (usually older loans) for PCs backed by these loans. What they accomplish by the swap is to obtain a very liquid security from an illiquid investment since the PCs can be readily sold for cash.

FEDERAL RESERVE

The **FEDERAL RESERVE** or "Fed" is our nation's central bank. *The Federal Reserve controls the supply of money.* The actions of the Federal Reserve effect mortgage activity. Because the Federal Reserve can control the supply of money, it can increase or decrease interest rates. As rates increase, more prospective borrowers are priced out of the mortgage market. As rates decrease the volume of mortgage lending and real estate activity tends to increase as housing becomes affordable to more families.

The Federal Reserve attempts to fine-tune the economy so that we will have stable growth without inflation.

The Federal Reserve has several methods to accomplish this.

Reserve Requirements

By raising or lowering the reserve requirements of member banks, the Federal Reserve has some control as to how much member banks are able to lend. To fight inflation, the Federal Reserve could raise the reserve requirements but to stimulate a sluggish or recessionary economy, the Federal Reserve could reduce reserve requirements.

Discount Rate

Member banks borrow funds from the Federal Reserve at what is known as the **DISCOUNT RATE**. Raising the rate causes interest rates for loans made by member banks to rise. When the Federal Reserve raises the discount rate, the effect is a general increase in interest rates. Interest rates drop when the Federal Reserve lowers the interest rate. To fight inflation, the Federal Reserve would raise the interest rate. The rate would be lowered to stimulate the economy.

Open-Market Transactions

The Federal Reserve can buy government bonds in the open market. This would place more money in circulation which would stimulate the mortgages. Freddie Mac now has a similar economy. By selling bonds, money is taken out of the economy which would tend to slow down growth and inflation.

Besides the Federal Reserve activities, the government's ability to tax has a significant effect on the real estate market and real estate lending. Reducing taxes makes more money available. This is actually inflationary and it tends to stimulate the economy.

Raising taxes is deflationary as it takes money out of circulation and negatively effects the real estate market.

Licensing Requirements

DEPARTMENT OF REAL ESTATE

Most mortgage bankers are real estate brokers licensed by the California Department of Real Estate.

Business and Professions Code Section 10131(d) allows real estate brokers to engage in mortgage activities. (See Chapter 4).

Loan officers of real estate brokers must be licensed as salespersons or brokers. (The broker supervisory requirements are set forth in Chapter 6).

DEPARTMENT OF CORPORATIONS

The new California Residential Lending Act (covered in Chapter 3) provides for licensing by the Corporation Commissioner.

The **RESIDENTIAL MORTGAGE LENDERS LICENSE** *allows persons, partnerships and corporations to make and service loans.* Theoretically, a person licensed by the Department of Corporations could act as a mortgage banker, making and selling loans.

The Residential Mortgage Lender License is completely separate from the Real Estate Broker's License but covers the same activities. A licensee must, however, make a choice. A mortgage company can only operate under one license a Commissioner of Corporations license or a real estate broker's license.

Reporting Requirements

For a discussion of advertising requirements including threshold requirements, FTC requirements, etc., see Chapter 11.

Trust Fund Handling

The trust fund requirements as set forth in Chapter 11 apply to mortgage banking.

Disclosures

The disclosure requirements, as set forth in Chapter 5, apply to mortgage banking when the broker is licensed by the Department of Real Estate.

Forms and Stacking

The forms and stacking order, set forth in Chapter 14, apply as well to mortgage banking. The recipient of the loan will cause variations in the stacking order.

There is a difference in the mortgage file because the mortgage banker performs the underwriting for the loan. The loan file is provided a loan purchaser after the fact if the purchaser requests it. For loans sold to Fannie Mae and Freddie Mac, the file using approved forms would be submitted to allow them to ascertain that the loan meets their requirements.

Quality Control

The quality control of mortgage banker loans would be in-house as well as by Fannie Mae, Freddie Mac and others who purchase the loans.

IN-HOUSE CONTROL

By checking on loans sold as to loan status, mortgage bankers can ascertain if a particular underwriter has an unusual percentage of loans in default. It might indicate a communication problem or a need for closer monitoring or better investigation. Similarly, a default ratio close to zero might indicate that underwriting requirements are too strict.

QUALITY CONTROL BY OTHERS

Persons who buy loans originated by others will relate loan problems to the originators. An unusually high percentage of problems that are not related to local economic changes would indicate an underwriting problem.

SUMMARY

Mortgage bankers originate loans using equity or borrowed capital. The loans they originate are sold, primarily to institutional type investors. Mortgage bankers generally service the loans that they sell.

Lines of credit as well as loans secured by inventories of loans (mortgage warehousing) give mortgage bankers needed capital for operations.

Mortgage bankers might make loans to the requirements of a single investor or institutional purchaser, such as Fannie Mae, or might make loans to different specifications of a number of investors or loan purchasers. Mortgage bankers, at times, might act in a loan broker capacity rather as a principal to a loan (lender).

Problems and opportunities associated with deregulation aided the growth of mortgage banking in that savings and loans were seeking more lucrative fields.

The Garn-St. Germain Depository Institutions Act of 1982 deregulated federally chartered savings and loans in that:

1. They could offer interest-bearing checking accounts.
2. Interest ceilings were removed from savings accounts.
3. They were allowed to make commercial and other real estate loans.
4. They were allowed to make second trust deed equity loans.
5. They were allowed to engage in leasing activities.
6. They could now offer commercial lines of credit.
7. They were allowed to invest in unsecured credit card loans.
8. Restrictions as to loan-to-value ratio were removed.
9. They were allowed to refinance existing loans.

Mortgage bankers profit from loan points, fees and costs, service fees and interest earned on funds and deposits held as well as by the difference in the sale price (arbitrage).

A conduit is a party who purchases loans from an originator such as a mortgage banker, for resale to others.

The federal government has a significant involvement in lending both for consumer protection and for economic reasons. A healthy lending industry plays a significant part in having a healthy economy.

Fannie Mae (FNMA), a private corporation chartered by the government, provides a secondary mortgage market for FHA, VA and conventional loans. FNMA buys mortgages which are converted to securities (MBS) for resale to investors. Fannie Mae limits the loans which it buys to one to-four residential units. Fannie Mae also has restrictions as to the size of loans that Fannie Mae will purchase. The borrowers must also meet qualifying standards.

Ginnie Mae (GNMA) does not purchase mortgages. GNMA guarantees mortgage backed securities issued by private lenders. The securities are pass-through certificates in that interest and principal, as paid, is passed through to the holder of the certificate.

Ginnie Mae purchases, at par value, loans made under various low interest government programs. Ginnie Mae will then sell these loans to Fannie Mae at the value of the loans (discounted because of lower interest). This is known as the Tandem Plan.

Freddie Mac (FHLMC) buys loans that meet its specifications. Most of Freddie Mac's funds come from the sale of Mortgage Participation Certificates (PCs) which are interests in pools of loans.

Freddie Mac is also involved in breaking down the cash flow of a pool of mortgages into a series of bonds with various maturity dates. These are known as CMOs (Collateralized Mortgage Obligations).

Under the swap program, FHLMC will take lower yield mortgages from investors and trade them for PCs which have greater liquidity.

The Federal Reserve regulates our nation's money supply and interest rates so that they are able to stimulate the economy or slow down economic growth. The Federal Reserve can accomplish this by:

1. Changing reserve requirements of member banks. By lowering the funds which must be kept as a reserve, the Federal Reserve allows more funds to be loaned and thus stimulates the economy. By raising reserve requirements, the Federal Reserve restricts the lending capability of banks.

2. Open market transactions. Buying existing government bonds will put money into the economy and act as a stimulant. On the other hand, selling bonds takes money from the economy and slows it down.

Mortgage bankers are generally licensed as real estate brokers although Department of Corporations licensing is possible.

Mortgage bankers are subject to the same trust fund requirements as any broker.

Quality control of mortgage banking operations are evaluated by problem loans and default rates. Significant variance from normal could indicate underwriting problems.

CLASS DISCUSSION TOPICS

1. Which lender(s) in your community gets the greatest number of referrals from your office? Why? Are they mortgage bankers?

2. Compare the service you receive on loans from savings banks, banks and mortgage companies in your area.

3. To your knowledge have any of your local mortgage companies been involved in brokering loans rather than funding them direct?

4. Who buys most of the loans originated by your local mortgage companies?

5. After deregulation, were any savings and loan associations in your area taken over by the government? Why?

6. Do you feel that history could repeat itself with lenders again making imprudent loans resulting in the need for another bailout? Why?

7. Do you feel that functions of Freddie Mac and Ginnie Mae should be combined?

8. Are there any benefits in allowing both the Department of Real Estate and the Department of Corporations to license mortgage company activities?

CHAPTER 15 QUIZ

1. Which of the following is true as to mortgage banking? (p. 466)
    A. Mortgage bankers fund loans
    B. Mortgage bankers sell the loans that they originate to others
    C. Mortgage bankers service loans
    D. All of the above

2. Mortgage warehousing involves: (pp. 466-467)
    A. issuing CMOs for a pool of mortgages
    B. borrowing on an inventory of loans
    C. issuing Participation Certificates guaranteed by Ginnie Mae
    D. buying a loan at one interest rate and selling it at a higher rate

3. A loan correspondent: (p. 467)
    A. handles the paperwork of a loan for the originator of the loan
    B. makes loans for sale to a particular lender(s)
    C. buys loans from mortgage bankers and sells them to other investors
    D. is a middleman who, for a fee, brings borrowers and lenders together

4. Which of the following is the largest originator of home loans? (p. 468)
    A. Mortgage companies
    B. Pension funds
    C. Commercial banks
    D. Mortgage brokers

5. The Garn-St. Germain Depository Institutions Act of 1982: (p. 469)
    A. placed tight restrictions on the lending capability of federally chartered savings and loans
    B. allowed federally chartered savings and loans to make second trust deeds
    C. allowed federally chartered savings and loans to make real estate loans for other than housing purposes
    D. both B and C

6. A conduit is:(p. 474)
    A. a loan originator who resells loans as soon as they are made
    B. a person who buys loans originated by others for resale to investors
    C. a loan originator who acts as a loan correspondent for only one lender
    D. a finder of funds who charges a fee to borrowers

7. Fannie Mae: (p. 475)

    A. purchases FHA, VA and conventional loans

    B. is a federal agency

    C. is restricted to buying loans from savings and loans

    D. may not profit from its operations

8. Fannie Mae operations include: (pp. 475-476)

    A. the conversion of mortgages and trust deeds into mortgage backed securities

    B. raising and lowering of the discount rate and reserve requirements

    C. guaranteeing pools of mortgages owned by investors

    D. offering mortgage insurance

9. "It is a division of HUD," describes: (p. 476)

    A. Fannie Mae

    B. Ginnie Mae

    C. the Federal Reserve

    D. Freddie Mac

10. Which of the following is true as to Ginnie Mae? (p. 476)

    A. GNMA guarantees mortgage backed securities issued by private investors

    B. It is the largest originator of FHA loans

    C. It is a subsidiary corporation of Fannie Mae

    D. All of the above

11. Which of the following is true as to Freddie Mac? (pp. 478-479)

    A. Freddie Mac will purchase loans from the loan originators

    B. Freddie Mac sells Participation Certificates (PCs) in pools of mortgages to investors

    C. Freddie Mac sells Collateralized Mortgage Obligations (CMOs) to investors

    D. All of the above

12. To fight inflation and slow down growth of the economy, the Federal Reserve might: (pp. 479-480)

    A. raise taxes

    B. lower the reserve requirements of member banks

    C. raise the discount rate for loans made to member banks

    D. buy government bonds on the open market

Answers: 1. D; 2. B; 3. B; 4. A; 5. D; 6. B; 7. A; 8. A; 9. B; 10. A; 11. D; 12. C

Glossary of Lending Terms

A

Accusation: The first step in a disciplinary action against a licensee.

Adjustable Rate Mortgage: A mortgage tied to an index allowing the interest rate to change based on changes in the index.

Adjustment Period: The frequency in which adjustments to an adjustable rate mortgage are possible.

Advance Commitment: Lenders agreement to provide funding upon completion of construction or purchase.

Advance Fee: A fee for advertising, promoting a sale or negotiating a loan received prior to actual expenditure or performance.

Amortized Loan: A loan that will be paid off by regular payments of the same amount.

Annual Percentage Rate (APR): The cost of credit expressed as a yearly rate considering loan related costs.

Arbitrage: Borrowing at one interest rate and investing at a higher rate.

Article 5: Provides for broker disclosure and restrictions on broker arranged mortgage loans.

Article 6: The provision of the real estate law dealing with real property securities dealers.

Article 7: The provision of the real estate law regulating broker commissions and costs for some loans.

Assumable Mortgage: A mortgage that may be assumed by a purchaser.

B

Back End Ratio: The ratio of monthly housing costs (PITI) plus long-term debt service to total monthly income.

Bait and Switch Advertising: The unlawful advertising of prices, credit terms or goods that will not be available to the consumer.

Balloon Payment: A final loan payment significantly greater than the monthly payments.

Bankruptcy Score: A scoring system to indicate risk of borrower default.

Beneficiary Ledger: A ledger maintained for each beneficiary.

Blanket Mortgage: A mortgage covering more than one property.

Blended Mortgage Rate: A rate of interest less than market interest rate but more than the old rate (refinancing).

Blue Sky Laws: Security registration requirements.

Broker Dealer: Designation of securities dealer under corporation code.

Brokerage: The business of a broker in acting as a third party agent to a transaction.

Buydown: A loan where the seller pays points to a lender in order to offer a purchaser an attractive rate of interest.

C

California Residential Mortgage Lending Act: An act administered by the Commissioner of Corporations which provides licensing authorizing mortgage lending and brokering.

CAPS: Maximum amounts that interest may be raised for a periodic adjustment and/or the life of the loan.

Carryback Financing: Financing provided by sellers of real property.

Cash Lender: A ledger showing balances in trust accounts.

Civil Rights Act of 1866: The first federal civil rights act which provided that all citizens should have the same rights as white citizens as to inheriting, purchasing, leasing, selling and holding real and personal property.

Civil Rights Act of 1964: Act which made Executive Order 10063 law (prohibited discrimination where federal funds were involved).

CMOs: Securities issued backed by mortgages. They are a series of bonds.

Collateral: Property that secures a loan.

Collaterally Secured Loans: Loans secured by other loans.

Commingling: Wrongful mixing of broker and trust monies.

Community Reinvestment Act: Requires the examination of loans to make certain that lending institutions are meeting the credit needs of their communities.

Compensating Balance: Requirement that a borrower keep a portion of the funds borrowed on deposit in the lender's institution. It increases the effective rate of interest.

Computerized Loan Origination: A loan that is applied for by computer.

Conduits: A party that purchases loans from one lender and resells the loans to investors.

Conforming Loan: A loan that meets the loan purchase requirements of Fannie Mae.

Consumer Credit Reporting Agencies Act: State act providing consumer protection similar to rights under the Federal Fair Credit Reporting Act.

Consumer Finance Lenders Law: A law that provides for Corporation Commission licensing of persons authorized to make loans secured by personal property or a combination of real and personal property.

Controlled Business Arrangement: A business arrangement where party making referral has an ownership interest in the company receiving the referral and shares in the profits of the service provider.

Corporate Securities Act of 1968: California act prohibiting sale of unqualified securities which are not exempt from the act.

D

Discounting a Loan: Selling a loan for less than face value.

Discount Rate: The rate banks pay to borrow from the Federal Reserve.

Disintermediation: The sudden withdrawal of funds from institutional lenders for investment at higher interest rates elsewhere.

Dragnet Clause: A clause in a mortgage covering future advances.

Dual Agent: An agent who has fiduciary duties to both borrower and lender.

Due On Sale Clause: A clause prohibiting loan assumption.

E

Equal Credit Opportunity Act: An act that requires consumer credit reporting agencies to meet the needs for credit in a manner that is fair to the consumer.

Equal Housing Opportunity Poster: A poster which, if not displayed, places the burden of proof on the broker if a charge of discriminatory practice is made.

Equity Loan: A loan made based on an owner's equity in property.

Escrow: A neutral depository which handles property closings and loan transactions.

Executive Order 1 1063: Order issued by President John F. Kennedy prohibiting discrimination in residential housing involving federal funds.

F

Facilitator: A person claiming to be a middle person to a transaction but not an agent of either principal.

Fair Credit Reporting Act: This act provides consumers access to information and the right to have corrected any incorrect data in their credit files.

Fannie Mae (FNMA Federal National Mortgage Association): A quasi-private corporation that creates a secondary market in FHA, VA and conventional loans.

FDIC (Federal Deposit Insurance Corporation): A federal agency that insures consumer deposits in banks and savings and loans.

Federal Block: The disclosures required by Truth in lending set forth together in an advertisement or contract.

Federally Related Loan: A loan made by a federally insured lender, that will be insured or guaranteed by a federal agency or which will be resold to Fannie Mae, Ginnie Mae or Freddie Mac.

Federal Reserve: Our nations central bank which controls our money supply.

FICO Bureau Score: A scoring system to determine likelihood of borrower default.

Fictitious Mortgage: A recorded mortgage referenced in other loans in order to incorporate boilerplate clauses by reference.

Fiduciary Duty: The duty of trust owed by an agent to his or her principal (s).

Finder: A person who locates borrowers or lenders for a fee.

Finders Fee: A fee paid to non-licensee for introducing parties or situations. A finder cannot engage in negotiations.

Fiscal Year Report: Trust fund report required by brokers who have met threshold requirements.

Foreclosure Consultants: Persons who claim to be able to aid homeowners who are in default.

Freddie Mac (FHLMC Federal Home Loan Mortgage Corporation): A federally chartered corporation to provide a secondary mortgage market for savings and loan associations.

Front-end Ratio: The ratio of monthly housing cost (PITI) to gross monthly income.

G

Garn St. Germain Depository Institutions Act: An act that deregulated lenders allowing them a wide range of operations.

Ginnie Mae (GNMA Government National Mortgage Association): A federal corporation that assists low income housing programs and guarantees securities backed by pools of mortgages.

Good Faith Estimate: An estimate of closing related costs required by RESPA.

Good Funds: Funds which have cleared the bank of the depositor.

H

Hard Money Arranger: A loan broker acting in a brokerage capacity.

Hard Money Loan: A cash loan made by a non-institutional lender.

Holden Act (Housing Financial Discrimination Act): California's act which prohibits discrimination by financial institutions.

Home Mortgage Disclosure Act: A federal act requiring lender disclosure of loan applications received and loans granted by area. The purpose is to provide data as to possible redlining.

Housing and Community Development Act: An act providing grants to communities to provide decent housing and living environment for residents.

Hypothecate: Giving property as security for a loan but retaining possession of the security property.

I-L

Impound Account: An account kept by a loan servicer for taxes and insurance costs.

Injunction: A legal order to cease an activity.

Interpleader Action: An action commenced by a broker when there are conflicting claims on trust monies.

Investment Contract: A Transaction where money is invested in a common enterprise in the hope of profit based on efforts of another party.

Junior Lien: Any lien which has a secondary position to another prior recorded lien.

Kickback: A generally illegal practice of giving a portion of a fee to the person who steered a consumer to a particular service provider.

Land Contract: A contract for a sale where seller keeps title and buyer gains possession.

Late Payment Charge: A charge imposed on a consumer for failing to pay on time or during any grace period.

Lead Paint Disclosure: A notice to buyers required for FHA loans for one to four residential units built prior to 1978.

Lender/Purchaser Disclosure Statement: A disclosure required to be provided by loan brokers to lenders.

Loan Broker: A third party who arranges loans but is not a principal to the loan.

Loan Correspondent: A person or entity that acts for a lender in arranging loans or the sale of loans.

Lock In Clause: A clause in a loan requiring interest be paid to maturity even when the loan is prepaid.

M

Margin: Amount that the loan interest is set at over the index or indice.

Margin of Security: The difference between the property value and the lender's lien.

Mortgage: A lien secured by real property that is given by a borrower to a lender. The borrower retains possession of the property.

Mortgage Backed Securities: Pools of residential mortgages that back securities.

Mortgage Banker: A mortgage lender that makes loans with their own funds and resells them on the secondary mortgage market.

Mortgage Loan Disclosure Statement: Borrower disclosure mandated by Article 7 of the Real Estate Law.

Multi-Lender Rule: Commissioner of Corporations Regulation dealing with a series of notes secured by the same parcel of real property.

Multi-Lender Rule Loans: Loans involving 10 or fewer investors regulated by the Corporation Commissioner.

N-O

Negative Amortization: Loan payments that are not sufficient to pay the interest so that the principal owed increases with each payment.

Nonconforming Loan: A loan that does not meet the purchase requirements of Freddie Mac or Fannie Mae.

One Stop Shopping: An arrangement where settlement and service providers are all available through the broker.

Open Market Transactions: The activities of the Federal Reserve in buying and selling government securities on the open market.

Or More Clause: A clause in a mortgage allowing prepayment without penalty.

P-Q

Participation Certificates (PCs): Certificates issued by Freddie Mac backed by pools of mortgages.

Participation Loan: A loan where the lender takes an equity position in addition to interest on the loan.

Pass Through Funds: Funds received which are passed on (usually to service providers) and are not cashed by the broker.

Piggyback Loan: A loan divided into two parts with one lender taking a secondary security position.

Points: Percentages of a loan charged for loan origination which raises the effective interest rate.

Portfolio Loan: A loan held by a lender for his or her own account.

Prepayment Penalty: A penalty imposed for payment of a loan before it is due.

PO Strips: Principal only strips from a pool of mortgages.

Primary Mortgage Market: The direct loan market.

Private Offering: An offering of securities to no more than 25 persons and sale to no more than 10 persons.

Promissory Note: An unconditional promise to pay a certain sum of money by a specified date or upon demand.

Promotional Note: A note considered a security to finance a subdivision prior to the first sale.

Purchase Money Loan: A loan made to finance the purchase of real property.

Quality Control: Control function to determine loan origination or underwriting problems based on loans history and red flags.

R

Real Estate Investment Trust (REIT): Publicly traded shares in corporations investing in mortgages and/or real property.

Real Estate Settlement Procedures Act (RESPA): A disclosure act to provide purchasers of residential property with settlement cost data so as to be able to make informed decisions.

Real Property Security: A guaranteed loan or a loan where the broker will assume payments.

Reconciliation of Trust Account: Trust account is reconciled with ledgers and checks.

Recovery Account: An amount in the real estate fund to reimburse members of the public for damages sustained by wrongful acts of licensees.

Red Flag: Anything that would alert a lender to a possible problem concerning a loan.

Redlining: Refusal to loan within designated areas.

Referral Fee: An unearned fee (See kickback).

Regulation Z: A designation used for the Federal Truth In Lending Act.

Release Clause: A provision in a blanket mortgage that provides for release of the lien as to a particular property upon payment of an agreed.

REMICs: Similar to CMO's but differ as to accounting.

Rescission Rights: Rights a person may have to rescind a loan or other transaction.

Restricted License: A license issued after a hearing which restricts the activities of licensees to conditions imposed by the commissioner.

Reverse Mortgage: A mortgage where the borrower receives monthly payments from the lender. It is repaid upon sale or death of the borrower.

Rumford Act: California's Fair Housing Act.

S

Second Mortgage: A loan which takes a secondary position to an existing loan.

Secondary Mortgage Market: The market involving the sale of existing loans.

Secured Credit Card: A credit card where purchases are secured by a lien against the purchaser's home.

Security: An interest where the holder has no management rights or control.

Security Interest: An interest in personal or real property given to the creditor by the consumer as security for the loan.

Service Providers: Persons or firms that provide services necessary to complete a loan (escrow, pest inspection, title insurer, etc.).

Servicing Agreement: Signed documentation as to who will service the loan.

Soft Money Loan: A loan where credit not cash is extended. Usually by the seller carrying all or part of the financing.

Stacking Order: Order of documents in a loan package.

Steering: The illegal practice of directing consumers to particular areas.

SWAP Program: A Freddie Mac program where lower yield mortgages are exchanged for Participation Certificates (PCs).

T

Table Funding: Simultaneous conveyance of purchase price and title as well as all loan papers at a closing.

Take Out Loan: Permanent financing that replaces the construction loan.

Tandem Plan: A plan where Ginnie Mae sells low interest loans to Fannie Mae at face value and makes up the difference between market and face value.

Teaser Rate: An initial rate for an adjustable rate loan that is less than the index plus margin at the time of origination.

Telemarketing: Telephone solicitation for lenders or borrowers.

Ten Strips: Interest only strips from a pool of mortgages.

Third Party Originator: A party who originates loans and prepares the loan package, but the loan is funded by others.

Threshold Advertising Requirements: A broker who meets threshold loan transaction requirements and must submit advertising prior to use.

Threshold Notification: Notification by brokers that they have met the threshold requirements for filing status and fiscal year reports on trust fund activities.

Title VIII of Civil Rights Act of 1968: The federal fair housing law.

Tranche: A series of bonds issued for a CMO.

Transfer Disclosure: Seller disclosure that is required for residential sales.

Trigger Terms: Terms in an advertisement which trigger additional disclosure of all credit terms.

Trust Account: An account in a depository designated as a trust account.

Trust Deed: A three party loan security transaction where the borrower (trustor) gives title to real property to a third party (trustee) as security for the benefit of the mortgagee.

Trust Funds: Funds of others held by a broker for some purpose or future disbursement.

Trust Fund Status Report: A quarterly report required from brokers who handle a threshold number of loans and/or collections.

Truth In Lending: Federal loan disclosure act to enable consumers to make informed comparisons between various credit sources.

U - W

Unconscionable Contract: An agreement that is so unfair and one sided that the courts will refuse to honor it.

Underwriting: Process of evaluating a loan application.

Uniform Residential Loan Application: A loan application form required by Freddie Mac and Fannie Mae.

Unruh Act: A California Civil Rights Act which prohibits discrimination by a business.

Usury: Interest over the amount allowed by law.

Verification of Deposit: Verification that a buyer has funds for down payment and loan costs.

Verification of Employment: Documentation as to loan applicants employment and income.

Verification of Loan: Information on existing loans and loan balances.

Verification of Rent or Mortgage: Information on landlord or creditor.

Voluntary Affirmative Marketing Agreement (VAMA): A realtor program to implement a program of fair housing.

Warehousing: Borrowing on mortgages.

Wholesale Agreements: An agreement of a loan originator to work exclusively with a single lender.

Index

T

U

V

W

Order Department

Sometimes our textbooks are hard to find!

If your bookstore does not carry our textbooks, send us a check or money order and we'll mail them to you with our 30-day money back guarantee.

Additional Textbooks from Educational Textbook Company:

California Real Estate Principles, 9th ed., by Huber	$50.00	_____
How To Pass The Real Estate Exam (850 Questions), by Huber	$50.00	_____
California Real Estate Law, by Huber & Pivar	$50.00	_____
Financing California Real Estate, by Huber	$50.00	_____
Real Estate Economics, by Huber & Pivar	$50.00	_____
Real Estate Appraisal, by Huber & Pivar	$50.00	_____
Mortgage Loan Brokering, by Huber & Pivar	$50.00	_____
Property Management, by Huber & Pivar	$50.00	_____
California Real Estate Practice, by Huber & Bond	$50.00	_____
Escrow I: An Introduction, by Walt Huber	$50.00	_____
California Business Law, by Huber, Owens, & Tyler	$50.00	_____
Six-Hour Survey, Continuing Education, by Huber	$15.00	_____

SUBTOTAL _____

Add shipping & handling @ $5.00 per book _____

Add California sales tax @8.25% _____

TOTAL _____

Allow 2-3 weeks for delivery

Name _____

Address: _____

City, State, Zip: _____

Phone: _____

Make check or money order payable to:
Educational Textbook Company, PO Box 3597, Covina, CA 91722, (626) 339-7733, etcbooks.com

**For cheaper prices and faster results, order by credit card direct from
Glendale College: 1-818-240-1000 ext. 3024**

™

"Hubie" the R E Internet Mouse